Kaplan Publishing are constantly fi ways to make a difference to your exciting online resources really d(different to students looking for exam

This book comes with free MyKaplan online resources so that you can study anytime, anywhere. This free online resource is not sold separately and is included in the price of the book.

Having purchased this book, you have access to the following online study materials:

CONTENT	ACCA (including FFA,FAB,FMA)		FIA (excluding FFA,FAB,FMA)	
	Text	Kit	Text	Kit
iPaper version of the book	✓	✓	✓	✓
Interactive electronic version of the book	✓			
Check Your Understanding Test with instant answers	✓			
Material updates	✓	✓	✓	✓
Latest official ACCA exam questions*		✓		
Extra question assistance using the signpost icon**		✓		
Timed questions with an online tutor debrief using clock icon*		✓		
Interim assessment including questions and answers	✓		✓	
Technical answers	✓	✓	✓	✓

* Excludes F1, F2, F3, F4, FAB, FMA and FFA; for all other papers includes a selection of questions, as released by ACCA

** For ACCA P1-P7 only

How to access your online resources

Kaplan Financial students will already have a MyKaplan account and these extra resources will be available to you online. You do not need to register again, as this process was completed when you enrolled. If you are having problems accessing online materials, please ask your course administrator.

If you are already a registered MyKaplan user go to www.MyKaplan.co.uk and log in. Select the 'add a book' feature and enter the ISBN number of this book and the unique pass key at the bottom of this card. Then click 'finished' or 'add another book'. You may add as many books as you have purchased from this screen.

If you purchased through Kaplan Flexible Learning or via the Kaplan Publishing website you will automatically receive an e-mail invitation to MyKaplan. Please register your details using this email to gain access to your content. If you do not receive the e-mail or book content, please contact Kaplan Flexible Learning.

If you are a new MyKaplan user register at www.MyKaplan.co.uk and click on the link contained in the email we sent you to activate your account. Then select the 'add a book' feature, enter the ISBN number of this book and the unique pass key at the bottom of this card. Then click 'finished' or 'add another book'.

Your Code and Information

This code can only be used once for the registration of one book online. This registration and your online content will expire when the final sittings for the examinations covered by this book have taken place. Please allow one hour from the time you submit your book details for us to process your request.

Please scratch the film to access your MyKaplan code.

Please be aware that this code is case-sensitive and you will need to include the dashes within the passcode, but not when entering the ISBN. For further technical support, please visit www.MyKaplan.co.uk

ACCA

Paper F5

Performance Management

Complete Text

British library cataloguing-in-publication data

A catalogue record for this book is available from the British Library.

Published by:
Kaplan Publishing UK
Unit 2 The Business Centre
Molly Millars Lane
Wokingham
Berkshire
RG41 2QZ

ISBN: 978-1-78415-677-0

Printed and bound in Great Britain.

Acknowledgements

We are grateful to the Association of Chartered Certified Accountants and the Chartered Institute of Management Accountants for permission to reproduce past examination questions. The answers have been prepared by Kaplan Publishing.

Contents

Paper Introduction

How to Use the Materials

These Kaplan Publishing learning materials have been carefully designed to make your learning experience as easy as possible and to give you the best chances of success in your examinations.

The product range contains a number of features to help you in the study process. They include:

(1) Detailed study guide and syllabus objectives

(2) Description of the examination

(3) Study skills and revision guidance

(4) Complete text or essential text

(5) Question practice

The sections on the study guide, the syllabus objectives, the examination and study skills should all be read before you commence your studies. They are designed to familiarise you with the nature and content of the examination and give you tips on how to best to approach your learning.

The **complete text or essential text** comprises the main learning materials and gives guidance as to the importance of topics and where other related resources can be found. Each chapter includes:

- The **learning objectives** contained in each chapter, which have been carefully mapped to the examining body's own syllabus learning objectives or outcomes. You should use these to check you have a clear understanding of all the topics on which you might be assessed in the examination.
- The **chapter diagram** provides a visual reference for the content in the chapter, giving an overview of the topics and how they link together.
- The **content** for each topic area commences with a brief explanation or definition to put the topic into context before covering the topic in detail. You should follow your studying of the content with a review of the illustrations. These are worked examples which will help you to understand better how to apply the content for the topic.

- **Test your understanding** sections provide an opportunity to assess your understanding of the key topics by applying what you have learned to short questions. Answers can be found at the back of each chapter.
- **Summary diagrams** complete each chapter to show the important links between topics and the overall content of the paper. These diagrams should be used to check that you have covered and understood the core topics before moving on.

Quality and accuracy are of the utmost importance to us so if you spot an error in any of our products, please send an email to mykaplanreporting@kaplan.com with full details, or follow the link to the feedback form in MyKaplan.

Our Quality Co-ordinator will work with our technical team to verify the error and take action to ensure it is corrected in future editions.

Icon Explanations

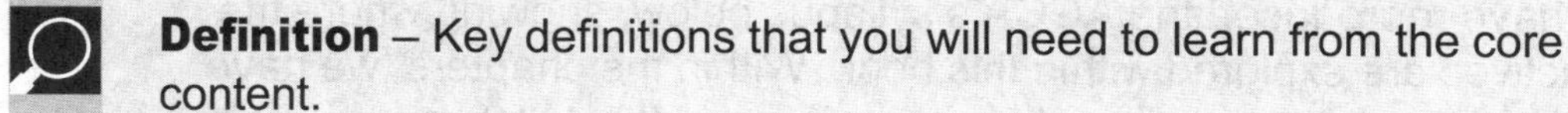

Definition – Key definitions that you will need to learn from the core content.

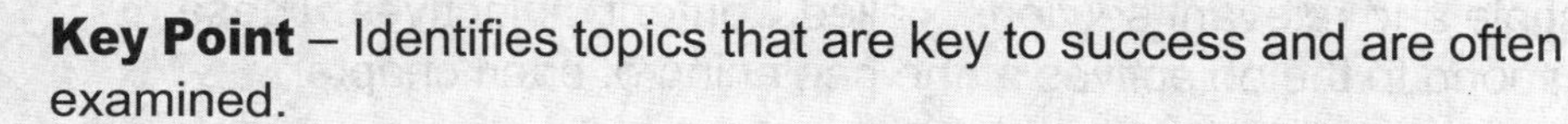

Key Point – Identifies topics that are key to success and are often examined.

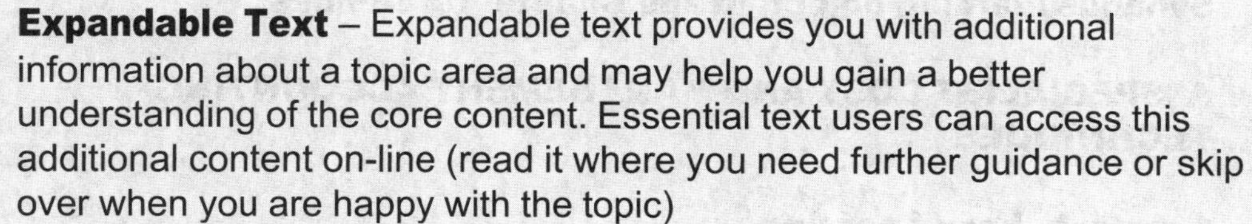

Expandable Text – Expandable text provides you with additional information about a topic area and may help you gain a better understanding of the core content. Essential text users can access this additional content on-line (read it where you need further guidance or skip over when you are happy with the topic)

Illustration – Worked examples help you understand the core content better.

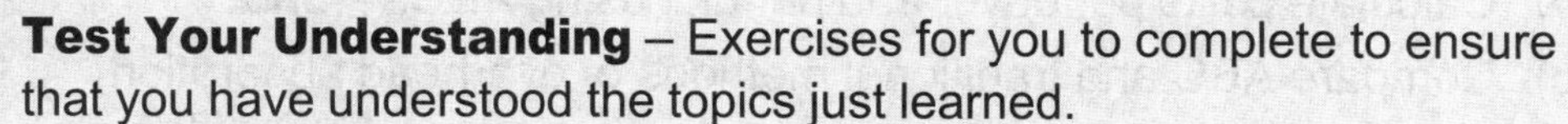

Test Your Understanding – Exercises for you to complete to ensure that you have understood the topics just learned.

Tricky topic – When reviewing these areas care should be taken and all illustrations and test your understanding exercises should be completed to ensure that the topic is understood.

On-line subscribers

Our on-line resources are designed to increase the flexibility of your learning materials and provide you with immediate feedback on how your studies are progressing.

If you are subscribed to our on-line resources you will find:

(1) On-line referenceware: reproduces your Complete or Essential Text on-line, giving you anytime, anywhere access.

(2) On-line testing: provides you with additional on-line objective testing so you can practice what you have learned further.

(3) On-line performance management: immediate access to your on-line testing results. Review your performance by key topics and chart your achievement through the course relative to your peer group.

Ask your local customer services staff if you are not already a subscriber and wish to join.

Syllabus

Syllabus objectives

We have reproduced the ACCA's syllabus below, showing where the objectives are explored within this book. Within the chapters, we have broken down the extensive information found in the syllabus into easily digestible and relevant sections, called Content Objectives. These correspond to the objectives at the beginning of each chapter.

Syllabus learning objective and Chapter references

A SPECIALIST COST AND MANAGEMENT ACCOUNTING TECHNIQUES

1 Activity-based costing

(a) Identify appropriate cost drivers under ABC.[1] **Ch.2**

(b) Calculate costs per driver and per unit using ABC.[2] **Ch.2**

(c) Compare ABC and traditional methods of overhead absorption based on production units, labour hours or machine hours.[2] **Ch.2**

2 Target costing

(a) Derive a target cost in manufacturing and service industries.[2] **Ch.2**

(b) Explain the difficulties of using target costing in service industries. [2] **Ch.2**

(c) Suggest how a target cost gap might be closed.[2] **Ch.2**

3 Life-cycle costing

(a) Identify the costs involved at different stages of the lifecycle.[2] **Ch.2**

(b) Derive a life cycle cost in manufacturing and service industries. **Ch.2**

(c) Identify the benefits of life cycle costing. **Ch.2**

4 Throughput accounting

(a) Discuss and apply the theory of constraints.

(b) Calculate and interpret a throughput accounting ratio (TPAR).[2] **Ch.2**

(c) Suggest how a TPAR could be improved.[2] **Ch.2**

(d) Apply throughput accounting to a multi-product decision making problem.[2] **Ch.2**

5 Environmental accounting

(a) Discuss the issues business face in the management of environmental costs. **Ch.2**

(b) Describe the different methods a business may use to account for its environmental costs. **Ch.2**

B DECISION-MAKING TECHNIQUES

1 Relevant cost analysis

(a) Explain the concept of relevant costing. **Ch.6**

(b) Identify and calculate relevant costs for a specific decision situations from given data. **Ch.6**

(c) Explain and apply the concept of opportunity costs. **Ch.6**

2 Cost volume profit analysis

(a) Explain the nature of CVP analysis. **Ch.3**

(b) Calculate and interpret breakeven point and margin of safety. **Ch.3**

(c) Calculate the contribution to sales ratio, in single and multi-product situations, and demonstrate an understanding of its use. **Ch.3**

(d) Calculate target profit or revenue in single and multi-product situations, and demonstrate an understanding of its use. **Ch.3**

(e) Prepare break even charts and profit volume charts and interpret the information contained within each, including multi-product situations. **Ch.3**

(f) Discuss the limitations of CVP analysis for planning and decision making. **Ch.3**

3 Limiting factors

(a) Identify limiting factors in a scarce resource situation and select an appropriate technique. **Ch.4**

(b) Determine the optimal production plan where an organisation is restricted by a single limiting factor, including within the context of "make" or "buy" decisions. **Ch.4**

(c) Formulate and solve multiple scarce resource problem both graphically and using simultaneous equations as appropriate. **Ch.4**

(d) Explain and calculate shadow prices (dual prices) and discuss their implications on decision-making and performance management. **Ch.4**

(e) Calculate slack and explain the implications of the existence of slack for decision-making and performance management.(Excluding simplex and sensitivity to changes in objective functions.) **Ch.4**

4 Pricing decisions

(a) Explain the factors that influence the pricing of a product or service. [2] **Ch.5**

(b) Explain the price elasticity of demand.[1] **Ch.5**

(c) Derive and manipulate a straight line demand equation. Derive an equation for the total cost function (including volume-based discounts).[2] **Ch.5**

(d) Calculate the optimum selling price and quantity for an organisation, equating marginal cost and marginal revenue. **Ch.5**

(e) Evaluate a decision to increase production and sales levels considering incremental costs, incremental revenues and other factors.[2] **Ch.5**

(f) Determine prices and output levels for profit maximisation using the demand based approach to pricing (both tabular and algebraic methods) **Ch.5**

(g) Explain different price strategies, including: [2] **Ch.5**

   (i) all forms of cost plus

   (ii) skimming

   (iii) penetration

   (iv) complementary product

   (v) product-line

   (vi) volume discounting

   (vii) discrimination

   (viii)relevant cost.

(h) Calculate a price from a given strategy using cost plus and relevant cost.[2] **Ch.5**

5 Make-or-buy and other short-term decisions

(a) Explain the issues surrounding make vs buy and outsourcing decisions.[2] **Ch.6**

(b) Calculate and compare 'make' costs with 'buy-in' costs.[2] **Ch.6**

(c) Compare in-house costs and outsource costs of completing tasks and consider other issues surrounding this decision.[2] **Ch.6**

(d) Apply relevant costing principles in situations involving make or buy in, shut down, one-off contracts and the further processing of joint products.[2] **Ch.6**

6 Dealing with risk and uncertainty in decision making

(a) Suggest research techniques to reduce uncertainty, e.g. focus groups, market research.[2] **Ch.7**

(b) Explain the use of simulation, expected values and sensitivity.[1] **Ch.7**

(c) Apply expected values and sensitivity to decision making problems. [2] **Ch.7**

(d) Apply the techniques of maximax, maximin, and minimax regret to decision making problems including the production of profit tables. [2] **Ch.7**

(e) Draw a decision tree and use it to solve a multi-stage decision problem. **Ch.7**

(f) Calculate the value of perfect information and the value of imperfect information. **Ch.7**

C BUDGETING AND CONTROL

1 Budgetary systems and types of budget

(a) Explain how budgetary systems fit within the performance hierarchy.[2] **Ch.8**

(b) Select and explain appropriate budgetary systems for an organisation, including top down, bottom up, rolling, zero base, activity base, incremental and feed-forward control).[2] **Ch.8**

(c) Describe the information used in budget systems and the sources of the information needed.[2] **Ch.8**

(d) Indicate the usefulness and problems with different budget types (including fixed, flexible, zero-based, activity-based incremental, rolling, top-down bottom up, master, functional).[2] **Ch.8**

(e) Prepare rolling budgets and activity based budgets.[2] **Ch.8**

(f) Explain the beyond budgeting model, including the benefits and problems that may be faced if it is adopted in an organisation.[2] **Ch.8**

(g) Discuss the issues surrounding setting the difficulty level for a budget.[2] **Ch.8**

(h) Explain the benefits and difficulties of the participation of employees in the negotiation of targets.[2] **Ch.8**

(i) Explain the difficulties of changing a budgetary system or type of budget used.[2] **Ch.8**

(j) Explain how budget systems can deal with uncertainty in the environment.[2] **Ch.8**

2 Quantitative analysis in budgeting

(a) Analyse fixed and variable cost elements from total cost data using high/low method. **Ch.9**

(b) Estimate the learning rate and learning effect.[2] **Ch.9**

(c) Apply the learning curve to a budgetary problem, including calculations on steady states.[2] **Ch.9**

(d) Discuss the reservations with the learning curve.[2] **Ch.9**

(e) Apply expected values and explain the problems and benefits.[2] **Ch.9**

(f) Explain the benefits and dangers inherent in using spreadsheets in budgeting.[1] **Ch.9**

3 Standard costing

(a) Explain the use of standard costs.[2] **Ch.1**

(b) Outline the methods used to derive standard costs and discuss the different types of costs possible.[2] **Ch.1**

(c) Explain the importance of flexing budgets in performance management.[2] **Ch.8, Ch.10**

(d) Explain and apply the principle of controllability in the performance management system.[2] **Ch.8, Ch.10**

4 Material mix and yield variances

(a) Calculate, identify the cause of and explain mix and yield variances.[2] **Ch.10**

(b) Explain the wider issues involved in changing mix e.g. cost, quality and performance measurement issues.[2] **Ch.10**

(c) Identify and explain the relationship of the material usage variance with the material and mix and yield variances.[2] **Ch.10**

(d) Suggest and justify alternative methods of controlling production processes.[2] **Ch.10**

5 Sales mix and quantity variances

(a) Calculate, identify the cause of, and explain sales mix and quantity variances. **Ch.10**

(b) Identify and explain the relationship of the sales volume variances with the sales mix and quantity variances. **Ch.10**

6 Planning and operational variances

(a) Calculate a revised budget.[2] **Ch.10**

(b) Identify and explain those factors that could and could not be allowed to revise an original budget.[2] **Ch.10**

(c) Calculate, identify the cause of and explain planning and operational variances for:

(i) sales (including market size and market share)

(ii) materials

(iii) labour, including the effect of the learning curve.[2] **Ch.10**

(d) Explain and resolve the manipulation issues in revising budgets.[2] **Ch.10**

7 Performance analysis

(a) Analyse and evaluate past performance using the results of variance analysis.[2] **Ch.10**

(b) Use variance analysis to assess how future performance of an organisation or business can be improved. **Ch.10**

(c) Identify the factors which influence behaviour. **Ch.8**

(d) Discuss the effect that variances have on staff motivation and action. **Ch.8**

(e) Describe the dysfunctional nature of some variances in the modern environment of JIT and TQM. **Ch.10**

(f) Discuss the behavioural problems resulting from using standard costs in rapidly changing environments. **Ch.8**

D PERFORMANCE MEASUREMENT AND CONTROL

1 Performance management information systems

(a) Identify the accounting information requirements and describe the different types of information systems used for strategic planning, management control and operational control and decision making. [2] **Ch.14**

(b) Define and identify the main characteristics of transaction processing systems; management information systems; executive information systems; and enterprise resource planning systems.[2] **Ch.14**

(c) Define and discuss the merits of, and potential problems with, open and closed systems with regard to the needs of performance management.[2] **Ch.14**

2 Sources of management information

(a) Identify the principal internal and external sources of management accounting information.[2] **Ch.14**

(b) Demonstrate how these principal sources of management information might be used for control purposes. [2] **Ch.14**

(c) Identify and discuss the data capture and process costs of management accounting information.

(d) Identify and discuss the indirect cost of producing information. [2] **Ch.14**

(e) Discuss the limitations of using externally generated information. [2] **Ch.14**

3 Management reports

(a) Discuss the principal controls required in generating and distributing internal information. [2] **Ch.14**

(b) Discuss the procedures that may be necessary to ensure security of highly confidential information that is not for external consumption. [2] **Ch.14**

4 Performance analysis in private sector organisations

(a) Describe and calculate and interpret financial performance indicators (FPIs) for profitability, liquidity and risk in both manufacturing and service businesses. Suggest methods to improve these measures.[2] **Ch.11**

(b) Describe, calculate and interpret non-financial performance indicators (NFPIs) and suggest methods to improve the performance indicated.[2] **Ch.11**

(c) Analyse past performance and suggest ways for improving financial and non-financial performance.[2] **Ch.11**

(d) Explain the causes and problems created by short-termism and financial manipulation of results and suggest methods to encourage a long term view.

(e) Explain and interpret the Balanced Scorecard, and the Building Block model proposed by Fitzgerald and Moon.[2] **Ch.11**

(f) Discuss the difficulties of target setting in qualitative areas.[2] **Ch.11**

5 Divisional performance and transfer pricing

(a) Explain and illustrate the basis for setting a transfer price using variable cost, full cost and the principles behind allowing for intermediate markets.[2] **Ch.12**

(b) Explain how transfer prices can distort the performance assessment of divisions and decisions made.[2] **Ch.12**

(c) Explain the meaning of, and calculate, Return on Investment (ROI) and Residual Income (RI), and discuss their shortcomings.[2] **Ch.12**

(d) Compare divisional performance and recognise the problems of doing so.[2] **Ch.12**

6 Performance analysis in not-for-profit organisations and the public sector

(a) Comment on the problems of having non-quantifiable objectives in performance management.[2] **Ch.13**

(b) Explain how performance could be measured in these sectors.[2] **Ch.13**

(c) Comment on the problems of having multiple objectives in these sectors.[2] **Ch.13**

(d) Outline Value for Money (VFM) as a public sector objective.[1] **Ch.13**

7 External considerations and behavioural aspects

(a) Explain the need to allow for external considerations in performance management. (External considerations to include stakeholders, market conditions and allowance for competitors.)[2] **Ch.11**

(b) Suggest ways in which external considerations could be allowed for in performance management.[2] **Ch.11**

(c) Interpret performance in the light of external considerations.[2] **Ch.11**

(d) Identify and explain the behaviour aspects of performance management.[2] **Ch.11**

The superscript numbers in square brackets indicate the intellectual depth at which the subject area could be assessed within the examination. Level 1 (knowledge and comprehension) broadly equates with the Knowledge module, Level 2 (application and analysis) with the Skills module and Level 3 (synthesis and evaluation) to the Professional level. However, lower level skills can continue to be assessed as you progress through each module and level.

The examination

Paper F5, Performance Management, seeks to examine candidates' understanding of how to manage the performance of a business.

The paper builds on the knowledge acquired in Paper F2, Management Accounting, and prepares those candidates who will decide to go on to study Paper P5, Advanced performance management, at the Professional level.

There will be calculation and discursive elements to the paper. Generally the paper will seek to draw questions from as many of the syllabus sections as possible.

Examination format

The syllabus is assessed by a three-hour 15 minute examination. The examination paper will contain both computational and discursive elements. All questions are compulsory.

Section A of the examination comprises 15 objective test (OT) questions of 2 marks each).

Section B of the examination comprises three objective test cases (OT cases), each of which includes five OT questions of 2 marks each.

Section C of the examination comprises two 20 mark constructed response (long) questions.

The two 20 mark questions will come from decision making techniques, budgeting and control and/or performance measurement and control areas of the syllabus. The Section A questions and the questions in Section B can cover any area of the syllabus.

Examination tips

Spend time reading the examination paper carefully. We recommend that 15 minutes should be spent reading the paper, paying particular attention to Sections B and C, where questions will be based on longer scenarios than the 2 marks OTs in Section A.

If 15 minutes are spent reading the examination paper, this leaves three hours to attempt the questions:

- **Divide the time** you spend on questions in proportion to the marks on offer.
- One suggestion **for this examination** is to allocate 1.8 minutes to each mark available (180 minutes/100 marks), so a 20-mark question should be completed in approximately 36 minutes. If you plan to spend more or less time than 15 minutes reading the paper, your time allocation per mark will be different.

F5 is divided into three different sections, requiring the application of different skills to be successful.

Section A

Stick to the timing principle of 1.8 minutes per mark. This means that the 15 OT questions in Section A (30 marks) should take 54 minutes.

Work steadily. Rushing leads to careless mistakes and the OT questions are designed to include answers which result from careless mistakes.

If you don't know the answer, eliminate those options you know are incorrect and see if the answer becomes more obvious.

Remember that there is no negative marking for an incorrect answer. After you have eliminated the options that you know to be wrong, if you are still unsure, guess.

Section B

There is likely to be a significant amount of information to read through for each case. You should begin by reading the OT questions that relate to the case, so that when you read through the information for the first time, you know what it is that you are required to do.

Each OT question is worth two marks. Therefore you have 18 minutes (1.8 minutes per mark) to answer the five OT questions relating to each case. It is likely that all of the cases will take the same length of time to answer, although some of the OT questions within a case may be quicker than other OT questions within that same case.

Once you have read through the information, you should first answer any of the OT questions that do not require workings and can be quickly answered. You should then attempt the OT questions that require workings utilising the remaining time for that case.

All of the tips for section A are equally applicable to each section B question.

Section C

The constructed response questions in section C will require a written response rather than being OT questions. Therefore, different techniques need to be used to score well.

Unless you know exactly how to answer the question, spend some time planning your answer. Stick to the question and tailor your answer to what you are asked. Pay particular attention to the verbs in the question e.g. 'Calculate', 'State', 'Explain'.

If you **get completely stuck** with a question, leave space in your answer book and return to it later.

If you do not understand what a question is asking, state your assumptions. Even if you do not answer in precisely the way the examining team hoped, you should be given some credit, provided that your assumptions are reasonable.

You should do everything you can to make things easy for the marker. The marker will find it easier to identify the points you have made if your answers are legible.

Computations: It is essential to include all your workings in your answers. Many computational questions require the use of a standard format. Be sure you know these formats thoroughly before the examination and use the layouts that you see in the answers given in this book and in model answers.

Adopt a logical approach and cross reference workings to the main computation to keep your answers tidy.

All sections

Don't skip parts of the syllabus. Spend time learning the rules and definitions.

Practice plenty of questions to improve your ability to apply the techniques and perform the calculations.

Spend the last five minutes reading through your answers and making any additions or corrections.

Method of examination

For examinations from September 2016, computer-based testing (CBT) will be available in respect of the ACCA Fundamental Skills Level papers (F5 – F9).

Students will have a choice of CBT or paper examinations.

The CBT and paper examinations will follow the same format, with the following exception:

OT questions in sections A and B of the paper examination will be of multiple choice style only. This means there will be four possible answers to choose from for each OT, with only one answer being correct.

OT questions in sections A and B of the CBT examination will be of varying styles. These styles include multiple choice, number entry, pull down list, multiple response, hot area, and drag and drop. A full explanation of these question types is included in the Kaplan Exam Kit.

Section C will be in the same format for both the CBT and paper examinations.

If you would like further information on sitting a CBT F5 examination please contact either Kaplan, or the ACCA.

You should do everything you can to make things easy for the marker. The marker will find it easier to identify the points you have made if your answers are legible.

Case studies: Most questions will be based on specific scenarios. To construct a good answer first identify the areas in which there are problems, outline the main principles/theories you are going to use to answer the question, and then apply the principles / theories to the case. It is essential that you tailor your comments to the scenario given.

Essay questions: Some questions may contain short essay-style requirements. Your answer should have a clear structure. It should contain a brief introduction, a main section and a conclusion. Be concise. It is better to write a little about a lot of different points than a great deal about one or two points.

Computations: It is essential to include all your workings in your answers. Many computational questions require the use of a standard format. Be sure you know these formats thoroughly before the exam and use the layouts that you see in the answers given in this book and in model answers.

Reports, memos and other documents: some questions ask you to present your answer in the form of a report or a memo or other document. So use the correct format – there could be easy marks to gain here.

Study skills and revision guidance

This section aims to give guidance on how to study for your ACCA exams and to give ideas on how to improve your existing study techniques.

Preparing to study

Set your objectives

Before starting to study decide what you want to achieve - the type of pass you wish to obtain. This will decide the level of commitment and time you need to dedicate to your studies.

Devise a study plan

Determine which times of the week you will study.

Split these times into sessions of at least one hour for study of new material. Any shorter periods could be used for revision or practice.

Put the times you plan to study onto a study plan for the weeks from now until the exam and set yourself targets for each period of study – in your sessions make sure you cover the course, course assignments and revision.

If you are studying for more than one paper at a time, try to vary your subjects as this can help you to keep interested and see subjects as part of wider knowledge.

When working through your course, compare your progress with your plan and, if necessary, re-plan your work (perhaps including extra sessions) or, if you are ahead, do some extra revision/practice questions.

Effective studying

Active reading

You are not expected to learn the text by rote, rather, you must understand what you are reading and be able to use it to pass the exam and develop good practice. A good technique to use is SQ3Rs – Survey, Question, Read, Recall, Review:

(1) **Survey the chapter** – look at the headings and read the introduction, summary and objectives, so as to get an overview of what the chapter deals with.

(2) **Question** – whilst undertaking the survey, ask yourself the questions that you hope the chapter will answer for you.

(3) **Read** through the chapter thoroughly, answering the questions and making sure you can meet the objectives. Attempt the exercises and activities in the text, and work through all the examples.

(4) **Recall** – at the end of each section and at the end of the chapter, try to recall the main ideas of the section/chapter without referring to the text. This is best done after a short break of a couple of minutes after the reading stage.

(5) **Review** – check that your recall notes are correct.

You may also find it helpful to re-read the chapter to try to see the topic(s) it deals with as a whole.

Note-taking

Taking notes is a useful way of learning, but do not simply copy out the text. The notes must:

- be in your own words
- be concise
- cover the key points
- be well-organised
- be modified as you study further chapters in this text or in related ones.

Trying to summarise a chapter without referring to the text can be a useful way of determining which areas you know and which you don't.

Three ways of taking notes:

Summarise the key points of a chapter.

Make linear notes – a list of headings, divided up with subheadings listing the key points. If you use linear notes, you can use different colours to highlight key points and keep topic areas together. Use plenty of space to make your notes easy to use.

Try a diagrammatic form – the most common of which is a mind-map. To make a mind-map, put the main heading in the centre of the paper and put a circle around it. Then draw short lines radiating from this to the main sub-headings, which again have circles around them. Then continue the process from the sub-headings to sub-sub-headings, advantages, disadvantages, etc.

Highlighting and underlining

You may find it useful to underline or highlight key points in your study text - but do be selective. You may also wish to make notes in the margins.

Revision

The best approach to revision is to revise the course as you work through it. Also try to leave four to six weeks before the exam for final revision. Make sure you cover the whole syllabus and pay special attention to those areas where your knowledge is weak. Here are some recommendations:

Read through the text and your notes again and condense your notes into key phrases. It may help to put key revision points onto index cards to look at when you have a few minutes to spare.

Review any assignments you have completed and look at where you lost marks – put more work into those areas where you were weak.

Practise exam standard questions under timed conditions. If you are short of time, list the points that you would cover in your answer and then read the model answer, but do try to complete at least a few questions under exam conditions.

Also practise producing answer plans and comparing them to the model answer.

If you are stuck on a topic find somebody (a tutor) to explain it to you.

Read good newspapers and professional journals, especially ACCA's Student Accountant – this can give you an advantage in the exam.

Ensure you know the structure of the exam – how many questions and of what type you will be expected to answer. During your revision attempt all the different styles of questions you may be asked.

Further reading

You can find further reading and technical articles under the student section of ACCA's website.

FORMULAE SHEET

Learning curve

$Y = ax^b$

Where	y	= cumulative average time per unit to produce × units
	a	= the time taken for the first unit of output
	x	= the cumulative number of units produced
	b	= the index of learning (log LR/log2)
	LR	= the learning rate as a decimal

Demand curve

$P = a - bQ$

$b = \frac{\text{Change in price}}{\text{Change in quantity}}$

a = price when Q = 0

$MR = a - 2bQ$

chapter

1

A Revision of F2 topics

Chapter learning objectives

The contents of this chapter are now assumed knowledge from the F2 syllabus.

Absorption, marginal and standard costing, and the basics of variance analysis, were encountered in F2, Management Accounting.

In the ACCA F5 paper, you will have to cope with the following:

- new, more advanced variances
- more complex calculations
- discussion of the results and implications of your calculations.

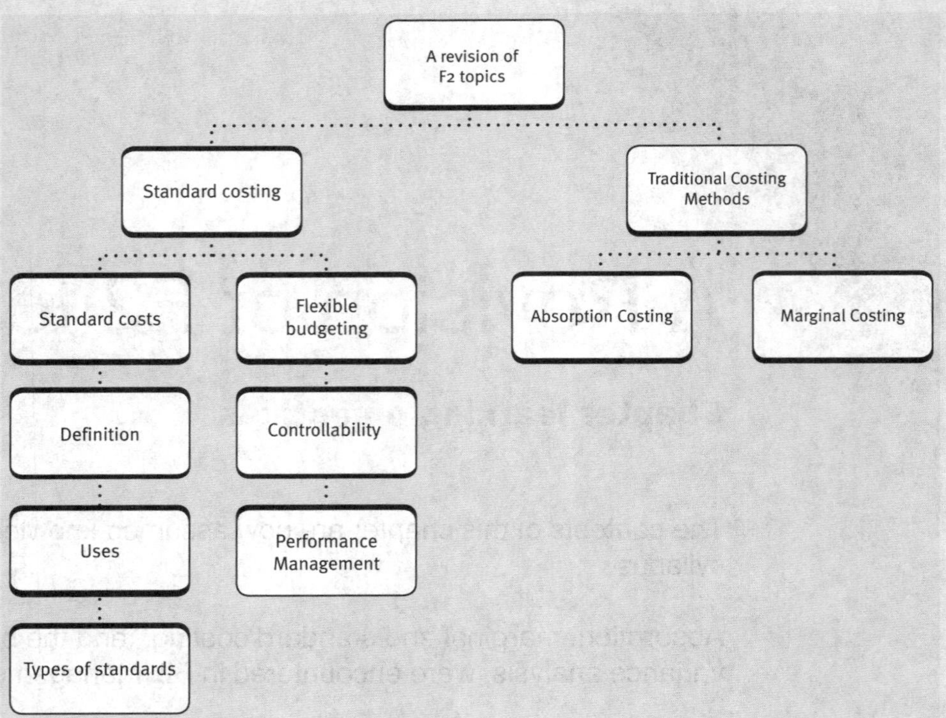

1 What is the purpose of costing?

In paper F2 we learnt how to determine the cost per unit for a product. We might need to know this cost in order to:

- Value inventory – the cost per unit can be used to value inventory in the statement of financial position (balance sheet).
- Record costs – the costs associated with the product need to be recorded in the income statement.
- Price products – the business will use the cost per unit to assist in pricing the product. For example, if the cost per unit is $0.30, the business may decide to price the product at $0.50 per unit in order to make the required profit of $0.20 per unit.
- Make decisions – the business will use the cost information to make important decisions regarding which products should be made and in what quantities.

How can we calculate the cost per unit? There are a number of costing methods available, most of them based on **standard costing**.

Standard costing

What is standard costing?

A standard cost for a product or service is a predetermined unit cost set under specified working conditions.

The uses of standard costs

The main purposes of standard costs are:

- **Control:** the standard cost can be compared to the actual costs and any differences investigated.
- **Planning:** standard costing can help with budgeting.
- **Performance measurement:** any differences between the standard and the actual cost can be used as a basis for assessing the performance of cost centre managers.
- **Inventory valuation:** an alternative to methods such as LIFO and FIFO.
- **Accounting simplification:** there is only one cost, the standard.

Standard costing is most suited to organisations with:

- mass production of homogenous products
- repetitive assembly work.

The large scale repetition of production allows the average usage of resources to be determined.

Standard costing is less suited to organisations that produce non-homogenous products or where the level of human intervention is high.

McDonaldisation

Restaurants traditionally found it difficult to apply standard costing because each dish is slightly different to the last and there is a high level of human intervention.

McDonalds attempted to overcome these problems by:

- Making each type of product produced identical. For example, each Big Mac contains a pre-measured amount of sauce and two gherkins. This is the standard in all restaurants.
- Reducing the amount of human intervention. For example, staff do not pour the drinks themselves but use machines which dispense the same volume of drink each time.

Test your understanding 1

Which of the following organisations may use standard costing?

(i) a bank

(ii) a kitchen designer

(iii) a food manufacturer

(a) (i), (ii) and (iii)

(b) (i) and (ii) only

(c) (ii) and (iii) only

(d) (i) and (iii) only

Preparing standard costs

A standard cost is based on the expected price and usage of material, labour and overheads.

Test your understanding 2

K Ltd makes two products. Information regarding one of those products is given below:

Budgeted output/sales for the year:	900 units
Standard details for one unit	
Direct materials	40 square metres at $5.30 per square metre
Direct wages	Bonding department: 24 hours at $5.00 per hour
	Finishing department: 15 hours at $4.80 per hour
Variable overhead	$1.50 per bonding labour hour
	$1 per finishing labour hour
Fixed production overhead	$36,000
Fixed non-production overhead	$27,000

Note: Variable overheads are recovered (absorbed) using hours, fixed overheads are recovered on a unit basis.

Required:

(a) Prepare a standard cost card for one unit and enter on the standard cost card the following subtotals:

(i) Prime cost

(ii) Variable production cost

(iii) Total production cost

(iv) Total cost.

(b) Calculate the selling price per unit allowing for a profit of 25% of the selling price.

Types of standard

There are four main types of standard:

Attainable standards

- They are based upon efficient (but not perfect) operating conditions.
- The standard will include allowances for normal material losses, realistic allowances for fatigue, machine breakdowns, etc.
- These are the most frequently encountered type of standard.
- These standards may motivate employees to work harder since they provide a realistic but challenging target.

Basic standards

- These are long-term standards which remain unchanged over a period of years.
- Their sole use is to show trends over time for such items as material prices, labour rates and efficiency and the effect of changing methods.
- They cannot be used to highlight current efficiency.
- These standards may demotivate employees if, over time, they become too easy to achieve and, as a result, employees may feel bored and unchallenged.

Current standards

- These are standards based on current working conditions.
- They are useful when current conditions are abnormal and any other standard would provide meaningless information.
- The disadvantage is that they do not attempt to motivate employees to improve upon current working conditions and, as a result, employees may feel unchallenged.

Ideal standards

- These are based upon perfect operating conditions.
- This means that there is no wastage or scrap, no breakdowns, no stoppages or idle time; in short, no inefficiencies.
- In their search for perfect quality, Japanese companies use ideal standards for pinpointing areas where close examination may result in large cost savings.
- Ideal standards may have an adverse motivational impact since employees may feel that the standard is impossible to achieve.

Preparing standard costs which allow for idle time and waste

Attainable standards are set at levels which include an allowance for:

- Idle time, i.e. employees are paid for time when they are not working.
- Waste, i.e. of materials.

Test your understanding 3

The fastest time in which a batch of 20 'spicy meat special' sandwiches has been made was 32 minutes, with no hold-ups. However, work studies have shown that, on average, about 8% of the sandwich makers' time is non-productive and that, in addition to this, setup time (getting ingredients together etc.), is 2 minutes.

If the sandwich-makers are paid $4.50 per hour, what is the attainable standard labour cost of one sandwich?

Flexible budgeting

Before introducing the concept of flexible budgeting it is important to understand the following terms:

- **Fixed budget:** this is prepared before the beginning of a budget period for a single level of activity.
- **Flexible budget:** this is also prepared before the beginning of a budget period. It is prepared for a number of levels of activity and requires the analysis of costs between fixed and variable elements.
- **Flexed budget:** this is prepared at the end of the budget period. It provides a more meaningful estimate of costs and revenues and is based on the actual level of output.

Budgetary control compares actual results against expected results. The difference between the two is called a variance.

The actual results may be better (favourable variance) or worse (adverse variance) than expected.

It can be useful to present these figures in a flexible budget statement. (**Note:** This is not the same as a flexible budget).

Test your understanding 4

A business has prepared the following standard cost card based on producing and selling 10,000 units per month:

	$
Selling price	10
Variable production costs	3
Fixed production cost	1
Profit per unit	6

Actual production and sales for month 1 were 12,000 units and this resulted in the following:

	$000
Sales	125
Variable production costs	40
Fixed production costs	9
Total profit	76

Required:

Using a flexible budgeting approach, prepare a table showing the original fixed budget, the flexed budget, the actual results and the total meaningful variances.

Controllability and performance management

A cost is controllable if a manager is responsible for it being incurred or is able to authorise the expenditure.

A manager should only be evaluated on the costs over which they have control.

It is worth emphasising that this concept of controllability is an important idea for F5, and will be revisited many times throughout the syllabus.

Test your understanding 5

The materials purchasing manager is assessed on:

- total material expenditure for the organisation
- the cost of introducing safety measures, regarding the standard and the quality of materials, in accordance with revised government legislation
- a notional rental cost, allocated by head office, for the material storage area.

Required:

Discuss whether these costs are controllable by the manager and if they should be used to appraise the manager.

Test your understanding 6

Explain whether a production manager should be accountable for direct labour and direct materials cost variances.

2 Traditional costing methods: AC and MC

The next chapter, Chapter 2, focuses on one of the modern costing techniques, ABC. However, in order to understand ABC and the benefits that it can bring, it is useful to start by reminding ourselves of the two main traditional costing methods : Absorption Costing (AC) and Marginal Costing (MC).

These will be referred to again in the *Advanced Variances* chapter.

Absorption costing

The aim of traditional absorption costing is to determine the full production cost per unit.

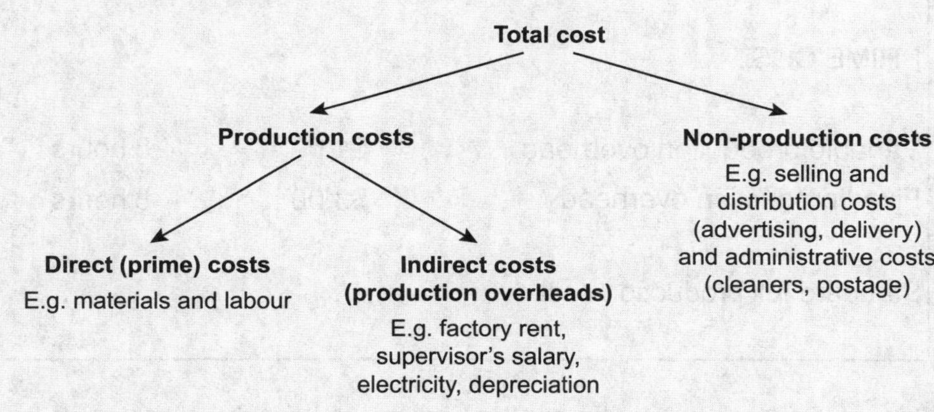

When we use absorption costing to determine the cost per unit, we focus on the production costs only. We can summarise these costs into a cost card:

Standard Cost Card

Product Widget, Ref. ABG56A

		Cost	Requirement	$
Direct materials				
	Material A	$2.00 per kg	6 kgs p.u.	12.00
	Material B	$3.00 per kg	2 kgs p.u.	6.00
	Material C	$4.00 per litre	1 litre	4.00
				22.00
Direct labour				
	Grade I labour	$4.00	3 hours p.u.	12.00
	Grade II labour	$5.40	5 hours p.u.	27.00
PRIME COST				61.00
Variable production overhead		$1.00	8 hours	8.00
Fixed production overhead		$3.00	8 hours	24.00
Standard full production cost				93.00

It is relatively easy to estimate the cost per unit for direct materials and labour. In doing so we can complete the first two lines of the cost card. Prime cost is the total of all direct costs.

However, it is much more difficult to estimate the production overhead per unit. This is an indirect cost and so, by its very nature, we do not know how much is contained in each unit.

Therefore, we need a method of attributing the production overheads to each unit. All production overheads must be absorbed into units of production, using a suitable basis, e.g. units produced, labour hours or machine hours.

The assumption underlying this method of absorption is that overhead expenditure is connected to the volume produced.

Illustration 1 – Absorption costing

Saturn, a chocolate manufacturer, produces three products:

- The Sky Bar, a bar of solid milk chocolate.
- The Moon Egg, a fondant filled milk chocolate egg.
- The Sun Bar, a biscuit and nougat based chocolate bar.

Information relating to each of the products is as follows:

	Sky Bar	**Moon Egg**	**Sun Bar**
Direct labour cost per unit ($)	0.07	0.14	0.12
Direct material cost per unit ($)	0.17	0.19	0.16
Actual production/sales (units)	500,000	150,000	250,000
Direct labour hours per unit	0.001	0.01	0.005
Direct machine hours per unit	0.01	0.04	0.02
Selling price per unit ($)	0.50	0.45	0.43
Annual production overhead = $80,000			

Required:

Using traditional absorption costing, calculate the full production cost per unit and the profit per unit for each product. Comment on the implications of the figures calculated.

Illustration – Solution

Solution

As mentioned, it is relatively easy to complete the first two lines of the cost card. The difficult part is calculating the production overhead per unit, so let's start by considering this. We need to absorb the overheads into units of production. To do this, we will first need to calculate an overhead absorption rate (OAR):

$$\text{OAR} = \frac{\text{Production overhead}}{\text{Activity level}} \quad \begin{matrix}\text{(this is \$80,000, as per the question)} \\ \text{(this must be chosen)}\end{matrix}$$

The activity level must be appropriate for the business. Saturn must choose between three activity levels:

- Units of production – This would not be appropriate since Saturn produces more than one type of product. It would not be fair to absorb the same amount of overhead into each product.
- Machine hours or labour hours – It is fair to absorb production overheads into the products based on the labour or machine hours taken to produce each unit. We must decide if the most appropriate activity level is machine or labour hours. To do this we can look at the nature of the process. Production appears to be more machine intensive than labour intensive because each unit takes more machine hours to produce than it does labour hours. Therefore, the most appropriate activity level is machine hours.
- To calculate the OAR we need to identify the total activity level for the period i.e. the total machine hours needed to produce all three products.

Working – OAR

$$\frac{\$80{,}000 \text{ production overhead}}{(0.01 \times 500\text{k}) + (0.04 \times 150\text{k}) + (0.02 \times 250\text{k}) \text{ hours}}$$

$$= \frac{\$80{,}000}{16{,}000 \text{ hours}}$$

= \$5 per machine hour

We can now absorb these into the units of production:

	Sky Bar	**Moon Egg**	**Sun Bar**
Production overheads (\$) = machine hours per unit × \$5	0.05	0.20	0.10

This is the difficult part done. We can now quickly complete the cost card and answer the question:

	Sky Bar	Moon Egg	Sun Bar
	$	$	$
Direct labour cost per unit	0.07	0.14	0.12
Direct material cost per unit	0.17	0.19	0.16
Production overhead per unit	0.05	0.20	0.10
Full production cost per unit	**0.29**	**0.53**	**0.38**
Selling price per unit	0.50	0.45	0.43
Profit/(loss) per unit	**0.21**	**(0.08)**	**0.05**

Outcome of absorption costing

Based on absorption costing, the Sky Bar and the Sun Bar are both profitable. However, the Moon Egg is loss making. Managers would need to consider the future of the Moon Egg. They may look at the possibility of increasing the selling price and/or reducing costs. If this is not possible, they may make the decision to stop selling the product.

However, this may prove to be the wrong decision because absorption costing does not always result in an accurate calculation of the full production cost per unit. Activity Based Costing (ABC) can be a more accurate method of calculating the full production cost per unit and as a result should lead to better decisions.

3 Under- and over-absorption

A predetermined overhead absorption rate is used to smooth out seasonal fluctuations in overhead costs, and to enable unit costs to be calculated quickly throughout the year.

$$\text{Pre-determined overhead absorption rate} = \frac{\text{Budgeted overhead}}{\text{Budgeted volume}}$$

'Budgeted volume' may relate to total units, direct labour hours, machine hours, etc. If either or both of the actual overhead cost or activity volume differ from budget, the use of this rate is likely to lead to what is known as under-absorption or over-absorption of overheads.

(a) Over absorption occurs if absorbed > actual

(b) Underabsorption occurs if absorbed < actual

To calculate over or under absorption, follow 3 steps:

(1) $\text{OAR} = \dfrac{\text{Budgeted overhead cost}}{\text{Budgeted level of activity}}$

(2) Overhead absorbed = actual activity × OAR

(3) Actual overhead incurred – Overhead absorbed (in Step 2) = Under/(Over) absorbed overheads

Illustration 2 – Under- and over-absorption of overheads

A company budgeted to produce 3,000 units of a single product in a period at a budgeted cost per unit as follows:

	$ per unit
Direct costs	17
Fixed overheads	9
Total costs	**26 per unit**

In the period covered by the budget, actual production was 3,200 units and actual fixed overhead expenditure was 5% above that budgeted. All other costs were as budgeted. What was the amount, if any, of over- or under-absorption of fixed overhead?

Illustration – Solution

Answer

The budgeted fixed overhead amounts to 3,000 units × $9 = $27,000.

Over/(under)absorption = Absorbed overheads – Incurred overheads.

	$
Fixed overhead absorbed (3,200 units × $9)	28,800
Fixed overhead incurred ($27,000 × 1.05)	28,350
Over-absorbed fixed overheads	**450**

What does this mean?

- During the period concerned, overheads will be accounted for as units are made.

- Thus by the end of the period $28,800 of overheads will have been incorporated. The precise location will depend on
  - whether the units concerned have been sold (in which case the costs will have ended up in cost of sales in the Profit and Loss account)
  - or are remaining in closing inventory (in which case the costs will have ended up in the valuation of closing inventory on the Statement of Financial Position).
- At the end of the period the company then determines that the actual overheads are $28,350 so recognise that they have accounted for $450 too many. This amount will need to be reversed out to ensure the correct costs are included.
- The simplest way of dealing with this adjustment is as a separate item in the Profit and Loss account. In this case the adjustment will be a CREDIT of $450.

4 Marginal costing

Marginal costing is the accounting system in which variable costs are charged to cost units and fixed costs of the period are written off in full against the aggregate contribution. Its special value is in recognising cost behaviour, and hence assisting in decision making.

The **marginal cost** is the extra cost arising as a result of making and selling one more unit of a product or service, or is the saving in cost as a result of making and selling one less unit.

Contribution is the difference between sales value and the variable cost of sales. It may be expressed per unit or in total. It is short for 'Contribution to fixed costs and profits'. Contribution is a key concept we will come back to time and time again in management accounting.

With marginal costing, contribution varies in direct proportion to the volume of the units sold. Profits will increase as sales volume rises, by the amount of extra contribution earned. Since fixed cost expenditure does not alter, marginal costing gives an accurate picture of how a firm's cash flows and profits are affected by changes in sales volumes.

Illustration 3 – Marginal costing

A company manufactures only one product called XY. The following information relates to the product:

	$
Selling price per unit	20
Direct material cost per unit	(6)
Direct labour cost per unit	(2)
Variable overhead cost per unit	(4)
Contribution per unit	**8**

Fixed costs for the period are $25,000.

Required:

Complete the following table:

Level of activity	**2,500 units**	**5,000 units**	**7,500 units**	**10,000 units**
Revenue				
Variable costs				
Total contribution				
Fixed costs				
Total profit/(loss)				
Contribution per unit				
Profit/(loss) per unit				

Solution

Level of activity	**2,500 units**	**5,000 units**	**7,500 units**	**10,000 units**
Revenue	50,000	100,000	150,000	200,000
Variable costs	30,000	60,000	90,000	120,000
Total contribution	20,000	40,000	60,000	80,000
Fixed costs	25,000	25,000	25,000	25,000
Total profit/(loss)	(5,000)	15,000	35,000	55,000
Contribution per unit	$8	$8	$8	$8
Profit/(loss) per unit	$(2)	$3	$4.67	$5.50

The table illustrates that contribution per unit remains constant at all levels of activity. However, profit per unit changes.

Hence marginal costing is a more useful method than absorption costing for decision making, say when trying to analyse and manage costs. However, marginal costing is less useful for financial reporting – for example, inventory needs to be valued at total production cost, not just variable cost.

5 Advantages and disadvantages of AC and MC

Absorption costing presents the following advantages:

- It includes an element of fixed overheads in inventory values, in accordance with IAS 2.
- Analysing under/over absorption of overheads is a useful exercise in controlling costs of an organisation.
- In small organisations, absorbing overheads into the cost of products is the best way of estimating job costs and profits on jobs.

The main disadvantage of absorption costing is that it is more complex to operate than marginal costing, and it does not provide any useful information for decision making, like marginal costing does.

Marginal costing presents the following advantages:

- Contribution per unit is constant, unlike profit per unit which varies with changes in sales volumes.
- There is no under or over absorption of overheads (and hence no adjustment is required in the income statement).
- Fixed costs are a period cost and are charged in full to the period under consideration.
- Marginal costing is useful in the decision-making process.
- It is simple to operate.

The main disadvantage of marginal costing is that closing inventory is not valued in accordance with IAS 2 principles, and that fixed production overheads are not shared out between units of production, but written off in full instead.

6 Chapter summary

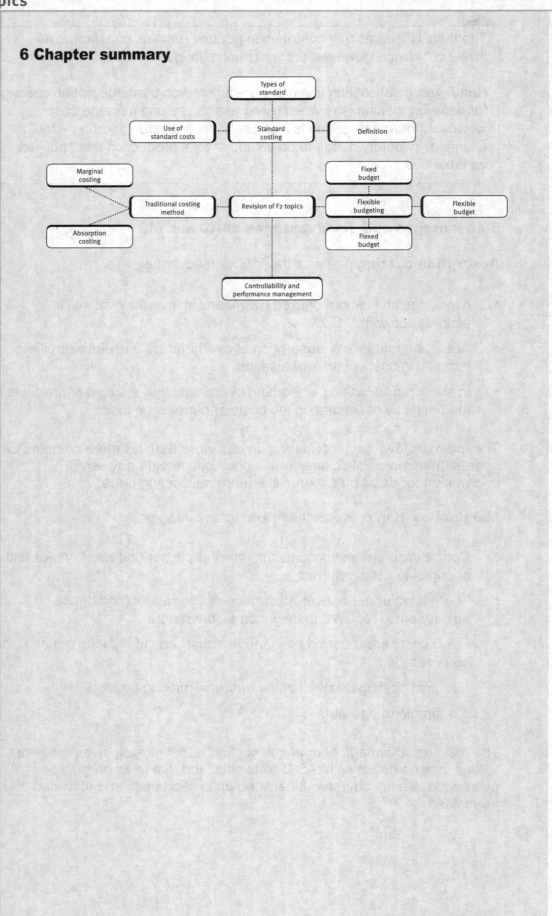

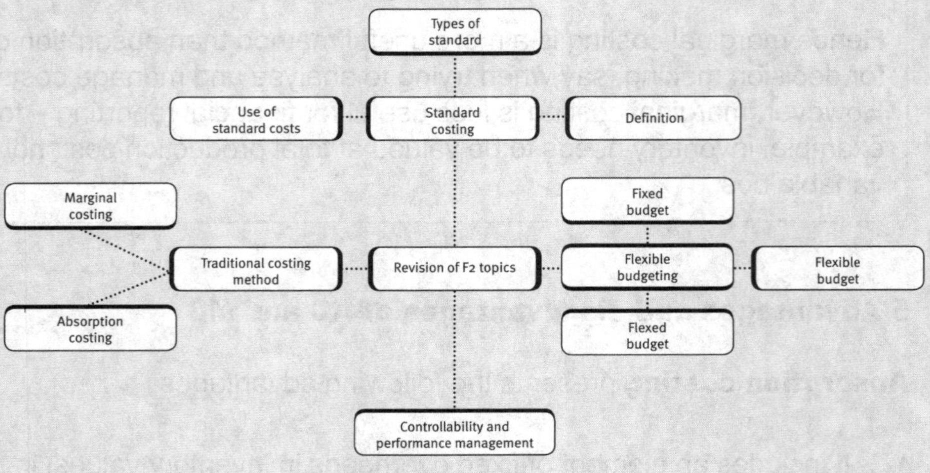

Revision of F2 topics

- Standard costing
  - Types of standard
  - Use of standard costs
  - Definition
- Flexible budgeting
  - Fixed budget
  - Flexible budget
  - Flexed budget
- Traditional costing method
  - Marginal costing
  - Absorption costing
- Controllability and performance management

Test your understanding answers

Test your understanding 1

D

A bank and a food manufacturer would have similar repetitive output for which standard costs could be calculated whereas a kitchen designer is likely to work on different jobs specified by the customer.

Test your understanding 2

(a)	$
Direct materials (40 × $5.30)	212
Direct labour:	
Bonding (24 hours × $5.00)	120
Finishing (15 hours at $4.80)	72
(i) **Prime cost**	404
Variable overhead:	
Bonding (24 hours at $1.50 per hour)	36
Finishing (15 hours at $1 per hour)	15
(ii) **Variable production cost**	455
Production overheads ($36,000 ÷ 900)	40
(iii) **Total production cost**	495
Non-production overheads ($27,000 ÷ 900)	30
(iv) **Total cost**	525
(b)	
Profit **(**(25/75) × 525**)**	175
Price ($525 + $175)	700

Test your understanding 3

		Per batch of 20
Ideal time	(92%)	32.0 minutes
Non-productive idle time	(8%)	2.8 minutes
	(100%)	34.8 minutes
Setup time		2.0 minutes
Total time		36.8 minutes
Total cost @ $4.50/hr		$2.76
Standard labour cost per sandwich ($2.76/20)		$0.138

Test your understanding 4

	Original fixed budget	Flexed budget	Actual results	Meaningful variance = flexed – actual
Based on production/ sales of:	10,000 units	12,000 units	12,000 units	–
Sales	10,000 units × $10/ unit = $100,000	12,000 units × $10/ unit = $120,000	$125,000	$5,000 Fav
Variable production cost	10,000 units × $3/ unit = $30,000	12,000 units × $3/ unit = $36,000	$40,000	$4,000 Adv
Fixed production cost	10,000 units × $1/ unit = $10,000	As per original budget = $10,000	$9,000	$1,000 Fav
Profit	$60,000	$74,000	$76,000	$2,000 Fav

Test your understanding 5

The total material expenditure for the organisation will be dependent partly on the prices negotiated by the purchasing manager and partly by the requirements and performance of the production department. If it is included as a target for performance appraisal the manager may be tempted to purchase cheaper material which may have an adverse effect elsewhere in the organisation.

The requirement to introduce safety measures may be imposed but the manager should be able to ensure that implementation meets budget targets.

A notional rental cost is outside the control of the manager and should not be included in a target for performance appraisal purposes.

Test your understanding 6

- The production manager will be responsible for managing direct labour and direct material usage.
- However, the manager may not be able to influence:
  - the cost of the material
  - the quality of the material
  - the cost of labour
  - the quality of labour.
- Performance should be measured against the element of direct cost which the manager can control.

[illegible]

The total material expenditure for the organisation will be determined partly by the prices negotiated by the purchasing manager, and partly by the requirements and performance of the production department. If it is included as a target for performance appraisal the manager may be tempted to purchase cheaper materials which may have an adverse effect elsewhere in the organisation.

The resources made to the departmental manager may be imposed but the manager should be able to ensure that implementation meets budget targets.

A notional amount of discussion the control of the manager, and should not be included in a target for performance appraisal purposes.

[illegible]

- The production manager will be responsible for managing direct labour and direct material usage.
- However, the manager may not be able to influence:
  - cost of the material
  - the quality of the material
  - cost of labour
  - the quality of labour.
- Performance should be measured against the elements of direct cost which the manager can control.

chapter

2

Advanced costing methods

Chapter learning objectives

Upon completion of this chapter you will be able to:

- explain what is meant by the term cost driver and identify appropriate cost drivers under activity-based costing (ABC)
- calculate costs per driver and per unit using (ABC)
- compare ABC and traditional methods of overhead absorption based on production units, labour hours or machine hours
- explain what is meant by the term 'target cost'
- derive a target cost in both manufacturing and service industries
- explain the difficulties of using target costing in service industries
- describe the target cost gap
- suggest how a target cost gap might be closed
- explain what is meant by the term 'life-cycle costing' in a manufacturing industry
- identify the costs involved at different stages of the life-cycle
- explain throughput accounting and the throughput accounting ratio (TPAR), and calculate and interpret, a TPAR
- suggest how a TPAR could be improved
- apply throughput accounting to a given multi-product decision-making problem
- discuss the issues a business faces in the management of environmental costs
- describe the different methods a business may use to account for its environmental costs.

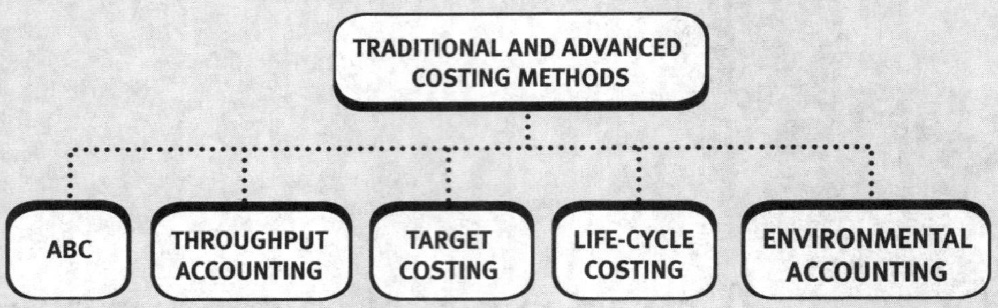

1 Reasons for the development of ABC

Absorption costing (covered in F2 and the previous chapter) is based on the principle that production overheads are driven by the level of production. This is because the activity level in the OAR calculation can be units, labour hours or machine hours.

These all increase as the level of production increases. This was true in the past, because businesses only produced one simple product or a few simple and similar products. The following points should be remembered:

- **Overheads used to be small in relation to other costs in traditional manufacturing**
  In addition, production overheads, such as machine depreciation, will have been a small proportion of overall costs. This is because production was more labour intensive and, as a result, direct costs would have been much higher than indirect costs. A rough estimate of the production overhead per unit was therefore fine.
- **Overheads are now a larger proportion of total costs in modern manufacturing**
  Manufacturing has become more machine intensive and, as a result, the proportion of production overheads, compared to direct costs, has increased. Therefore, it is important that an accurate estimate is made of the production overhead per unit.
- The nature of manufacturing has changed. Many companies must now operate in a highly competitive environment and, as a result, **the diversity and complexity of products has increased**.

2 Comparing ABC with traditional methods

Traditional systems measure accurately volume-related resources that are consumed in proportion to the number of units produced of the individual products. Such resources include direct materials, direct labour, energy, and machine-related costs.

However, many organisational resources exist for activities that are unrelated to physical volume. Non-volume related activities consist of support activities such as materials handling, material procurement, set-ups, production scheduling and first item inspection activities.

Traditional product-cost systems, which assume that products consume all activities in proportion to their production volumes, thus report distorted product costs.

So, although both traditional absorption costing and activity-based costing systems adopt a two-stage allocation process, the differences can be listed as follows:

(1) For **overhead allocation**, ABC establishes separate cost pools for support activities such as material handling. As the costs of these activities are assigned directly to products through cost driver rates, reapportionment of service department costs is avoided.

Traditional costing:

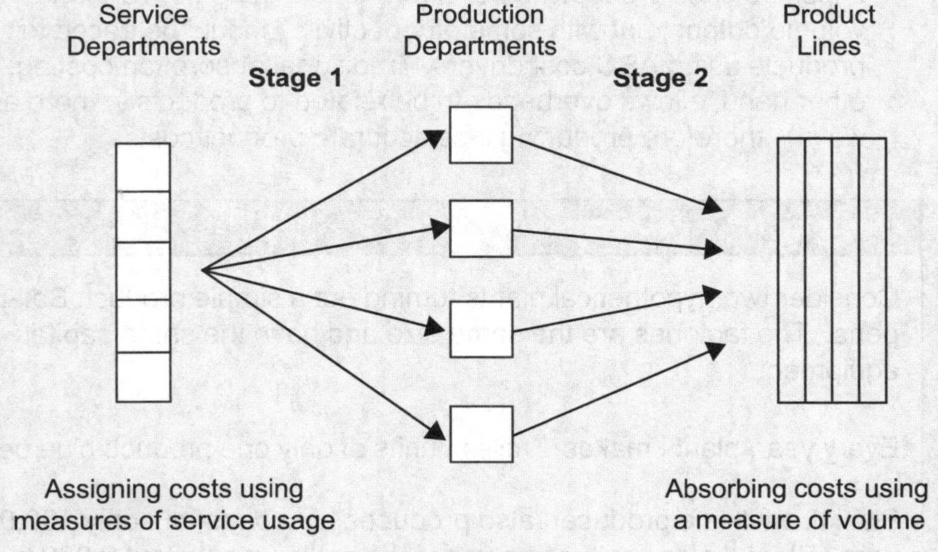

ABC:

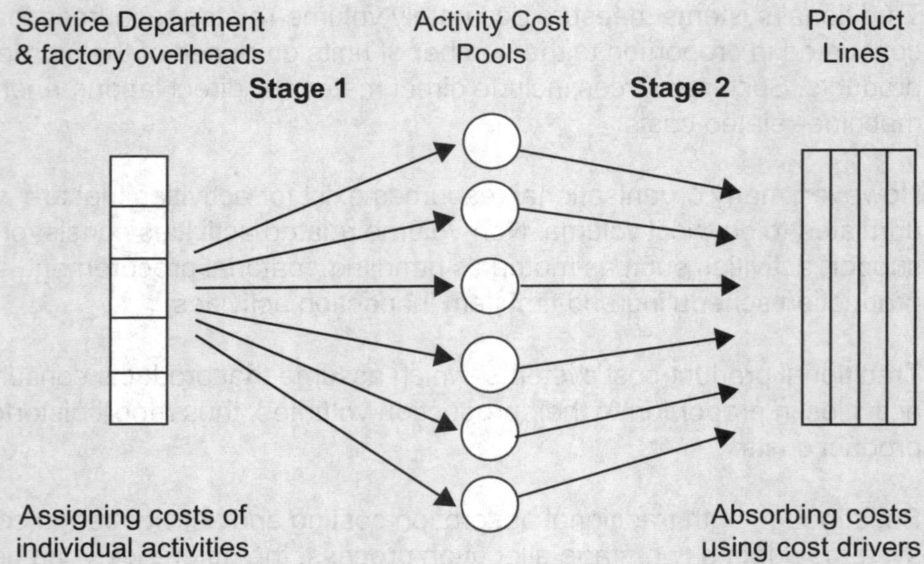

(2) **Overhead absorption** into products is where the main difference lies between ABC and traditional costing. Traditional absorption costing uses two absorption bases, (labour hours or machine hours) to charge overhead to products, whereas ABC uses many cost drivers as absorption bases (e.g. the number of orders, or the number of despatches.)

(3) The use of **cost drivers** is the main idea behind ABC as they highlight what causes costs to increase - for example, the number of orders to suppliers each product incurs. Overheads that do not vary with volume/output , but with some other activity, should be traced to products using ABC cost drivers. Traditional absorption costing, on the other hand, allows overheads to be related to products in more arbitrary ways – therefore producing less accurate product costs.

Illustration 1 – Pen factories

Consider two hypothetical plants turning out a simple product: Ball-point pens. The factories are the same size and have the same capital equipment.

Every year, plant I makes 1 million units of only one product: blue pens.

Plant II, a full-line producer, also produces blue pens, but only 100,000 a year. Plant II also produces a variety of similar products: 80,000 black pens, 30,000 red pens, 5,000 green pens, 500 lavender pens, and so on. In a typical year, plant II produces up to 1,000 product variations, with volumes ranging between 100 and 100,000 units. Its aggregate annual output equals the 1 million pens of plant I.

The first plant has a simple production environment and requires limited manufacturing support facilities. With its higher **diversity** and **complexity** of operations, the second plant requires a much larger support structure. For example 1,000 different products must be scheduled through the plant, and this requires more people for:

- scheduling the machines
- performing the set-ups
- inspecting items
- purchasing, receiving and handling materials
- handling a large number of individual requests.

Expenditure on support overheads will therefore be much higher in the second plant, even though the number of units produced and sold by both plants is identical. Furthermore, since the number of units produced is identical, both plants will have approximately the same number of direct labour hours, machine hours and material purchases. The much higher expenditure on support overheads in the second plant cannot therefore be explained in terms of direct labour, machine hours operated or the amount of materials purchased.

Traditional costing systems, however, use volume bases to allocate support overheads to products. In fact, if each pen requires approximately the same number of machine hours, direct labour hours or material cost, the reported cost per pen will be identical in plant II. Thus blue and lavender pens will have identical product costs, even though the lavender pens are ordered, manufactured, packaged and despatched in much lower volumes.

The small-volume products place a much higher relative demand on the support departments than low share of volume might suggest. Intuitively, it must cost more to produce the low-volume lavender pen than the high-volume blue pen. Traditional volume-based costing systems therefore tend to overcost high-volume products and undercost low-volume products. To remedy this discrepancy ABC expands the second stage assignment bases for assigning overheads to products.

Calculating the full production cost per unit using ABC

There are five basic steps:

Step 1: Group production overheads into activities, according to how they are driven.

A cost pool is an activity which consumes resources and for which overhead costs are identified and allocated.

For each cost pool, there should be a cost driver. The terms 'activity' and 'cost pool' are often used interchangeably.

Step 2: Identify cost drivers for each activity, i.e. what causes these activity costs to be incurred.

A cost driver is a factor that influences (or drives) the level of cost.

Step 3: Calculate an OAR for each activity.

The OAR is calculated in the same way as the absorption costing OAR. However, a separate OAR will be calculated for each activity, by taking the activity cost and dividing by the total cost driver volume.

Step 4: Absorb the activity costs into the product.

The activity costs should be absorbed back into the individual products.

Step 5: Calculate the full production cost and/ or the profit or loss.

Some questions ask for the production cost per unit and/ or the profit or loss per unit.

Other questions ask for the total production cost and/ or the total profit or loss.

Illustration 2 – ABC

In addition to the data from illustration 1 from Chapter 1 (Saturn), some supplementary data is now available for Saturn company:

	$
Machining costs	5,000
Component costs	15,000
Set-up costs	30,000
Packing costs	30,000
Production overhead (as per illustration 1)	80,000

Cost driver data:

	Sky Bar	Moon Egg	Sun Bar
Labour hours per unit	0.001	0.01	0.005
Machine hours per unit	0.01	0.04	0.02
Number of production set-ups	3	1	26
Number of components	4	6	20
Number of customer orders	21	4	25

Required:

Using ABC, calculate the full production cost per unit and the profit per unit for each product. Comment on the implications of the figures calculated.

Step-by-step approach

Step 1: Group production overheads into activities, according to how they are driven.

This has been done above. The $80,000 production overhead has been split into four different activities (cost pools).

Step 2: Identify cost drivers for each activity, i.e. what causes these activity costs to be incurred.

Activity	**Cost driver**
Machining costs	Number of machine hours
Component costs	Number of components
Set-up costs	Number of set-ups
Packing costs	Number of customer orders

Step 3: Calculate an OAR for each activity

OAR machining costs = $5,000 machining costs / 16,000 machine hours (as per former illustration)

= **$0.31 per machine hour**

OAR component costs = $15,000 component cost / (4 + 6 + 20) = 30 components

= **$500 per component**

$$\text{OAR set-up costs} = \frac{\$30{,}000 \text{ set-up costs}}{(3 + 1 + 26) \text{ set-ups}}$$

= **$1,000 per set-up**

$$\text{OAR packing costs} = \frac{\$30{,}000 \text{ packing costs}}{(21 + 4 + 25) \text{ orders}}$$

= **$600 per order**

Step 4: Absorb the activity costs into the product

	Sky Bar	**Moon Egg**	**Sun Bar**
	$	$	$
Machining costs ($) = $0.31 × machine hours	1,550	1,860	1,550
Component costs ($) = $500 × components	2,000	3,000	10,000
Set-up costs ($) = $1,000 × set-ups	3,000	1,000	26,000
Packing costs ($) = $600 × orders	12,600	2,400	15,000
Total production overhead ($)	**19,150**	**8,260**	**52,550**
Units produced	500,000	150,000	250,000
Production overhead per unit ($)	**0.04**	**0.06**	**0.21**

Step 5: Calculate the full production cost and the profit or loss, using Activity-Based Costing

	Sky Bar	**Moon Egg**	**Sun Bar**
	$	$	$
Direct labour cost per unit	0.07	0.14	0.12
Direct material cost per unit	0.17	0.19	0.16
Production overhead per unit	0.04	0.06	0.21
Full production cost per unit	**0.28**	**0.39**	**0.49**
Selling price per unit	0.50	0.45	0.43
Profit/(loss) per unit	**0.22**	**0.06**	**(0.06)**

In summary:

	Sky Bar	Moon Egg	Sun Bar
	$	$	$
Profit/loss per unit, using traditional Absorption costing	0.21	(0.08)	0.05
Profit/loss per unit, using traditional ABC	0.22	0.06	(0.06)

Outcome of ABC

When comparing the results of absorption costing and ABC, the Sky Bar is slightly more profitable. The real surprise is the results for the Moon Egg and the Sun Bar. The Moon Egg is now profitable and the Sun Bar is now loss making. This is because the production overheads have been absorbed in a more accurate way.

For example:

- There are twenty components in a Sun Bar, compared with only six in a Moon Egg. It is therefore fair that the Sun Bar receives more of the component cost.
- There are only four orders for the Moon Eggs but twenty five for the Sun Bar. It is therefore fair that the Sun Bar receives more of the packing costs.

ABC absorbs overheads more accurately and should therefore result in better decision making. The managers at Saturn should be concerned about the Sun Bar and not the Moon Egg, as was previously thought. They will now have to decide if it is possible to control the Sun Bar costs and/ or increase the selling price. If not, they may decide to stop selling the product.

Test your understanding 1

Cabal makes and sells two products, Plus and Doubleplus. The direct costs of production are $12 for one unit of Plus and $24 per unit of Doubleplus.

Information relating to annual production and sales is as follows:

	Plus	Doubleplus
Annual production and sales	24,000 units	24,000 units
Direct labour hours per unit	1.0	1.5
Number of orders	10	140
Number of batches	12	240
Number of setups per batch	1	3
Special parts per unit	1	4

Information relating to production overhead costs is as follows:

	Cost driver	Annual cost
		$
Setup costs	Number of setups	73,200
Special parts handling	Number of special parts	60,000
Other materials handling	Number of batches	63,000
Order handling	Number of orders	19,800
Other overheads	–	216,000
		432,000

Other overhead costs do not have an identifiable cost driver, and in an ABC system, these overheads would be recovered on a direct labour hours basis.

(a) Calculate the production cost per unit of Plus and of Doubleplus if the company uses traditional absorption costing and the overheads are recovered on a direct labour hours basis.

(b) Calculate the production cost per unit of Plus and of Doubleplus if the company uses ABC.

(c) Comment on the reasons for the differences in the production cost per unit between the two methods.

(d) What are the implications for management of using an ABC system instead of an absorption costing system?

3 Advantages and disadvantages of ABC

ABC has a number of advantages:

- It provides a more accurate cost per unit. As a result, pricing, sales strategy, performance management and decision making should be improved.
- It provides much better insight into what drives overhead costs.
- ABC recognises that overhead costs are not all related to production and sales volume.
- In many businesses, overhead costs are a significant proportion of total costs, and management needs to understand the drivers of overhead costs in order to manage the business properly. Overhead costs can be controlled by managing cost drivers.
- It can be applied to derive realistic costs in a complex business environment.
- ABC can be applied to all overhead costs, not just production overheads.
- ABC can be used just as easily in service costing as in product costing.

Disadvantages of ABC:

- ABC will be of limited benefit if the overhead costs are primarily volume related or if the overhead is a small proportion of the overall cost.
- It is impossible to allocate all overhead costs to specific activities.
- The choice of both activities and cost drivers might be inappropriate.
- ABC can be more complex to explain to the stakeholders of the costing exercise.
- The benefits obtained from ABC might not justify the costs. In some situations, ABC does not provide very different information from traditional absorption costing: see Question 5 from the December 2012 exam, 'Wash Co'. Overhead absorption techniques need to be carefully considered before recommending a company uses them.

4 ABC in the public sector

Background

The austerity measures introduced by many governments have meant that the public sector is under increasing pressure to deliver more services, for less money, and with greater transparency. Public sector organisations thus need to identify, allocate and control costs more than ever before. ABC is seen as one possible tool to help with this.

Reasons for introducing ABC

The main drivers for introducing ABC are:

- **Public responsibility** – responsible public organisations must have tight control of running costs at a time when resources provided by central government are strictly limited.
- **Public accountability** – many organisations are being challenged as to whether or not they spend taxpayer money wisely and feel a need to demonstrate this when the questions are asked.
- **Resource allocation within organisations** – there have been concerns in many organisations as to whether the services provided had an equitable distribution of scarce resource – or whether those who shouted loudest got the most resource.
- **Helping managers to manage** – managers ned a better awareness of what activities actually cost to provide before they can think which to cut.

Resistance

However, many public sector organisations have resisted the introduction of ABC.

To measure the cost of a service and take into account resource costs, the resource used must be measured – which often means recording time spent. Timesheets allow accountability for what people are actually doing, and for this cost then to be allocated to services. This is a challenge for the public sector, and for those that wish to use ABC or take a similar approach, a culture change is definitely required.

Illustration 3 – ABC in the CPS

The Crown Prosecution Service (CPS) in the UK has been using some activity based measures for allocating costs for over 10 years.

What does the CPS do?

- The Crown Prosecution Service is the British Government Department responsible for prosecuting criminal cases investigated by the police.
- The main "activity" is thus reviewing criminal cases, although some categories are much more complex than others and require more time.

Are all costs included within ABC?

- Only staff costs, which account for 3/4 of total costs, are dealt with via ABC.
- Standard ABC times for each type of case are determined, taking into account holidays, indirect work and rest.
- These are used to allocate costs to areas based on the volume of that type of case undertaken.

Claimed benefits include the following:

- The ability to use ABC data as part of the resource allocation exercise to help ensure a more equitable distribution of running cost resources/budgets to the 13 CPS Areas, based on their relative caseload and case type.
- Meaningful performance management information for managers at all levels within the organisation, and beyond.
- Operational costing information on all aspects of CPS casework performance, and costing support for any "what-if" scenarios, or policy changes.
- Contributes to assurances to government and other bodies on CPS cost efficiency.
- Costing of new proposals for CPS and support for business cases/benefits realisation work on all major change initiative projects and programmes.
- Identification and advice on the avoidance of inefficiencies within the CPS prosecution process.
- Essential information to other agencies – important in the Criminal Justice System where performance is often dependent upon other Agencies.

5 Throughput Accounting – background

There are two aspects of modern manufacturing that you need to be familiar with – Total Quality Management (TQM) and Just in Time (JIT).

Total Quality Management

TQM is the continuous improvement in quality, productivity and effectiveness through a management approach focusing on both the process and the product.

Fundamental features include:

- prevention of errors before they occur
- importance of total quality in the design of systems and products
- real participation of all employees
- commitment of senior management to the cause
- recognition of the vital role of customers and suppliers
- recognition of the need for continual improvement.

Just-In-Time (JIT)

JIT is a pull-based system of production, pulling work through the system in response to customer demand. This means that goods are only produced when they are needed, eliminating large stocks of materials and finished goods.

Key characteristics for successfully operating such a system are:

High quality: possibly through deploying TQM systems.

Speed: rapid throughput to meet customers' needs.

Reliability: computer-aided manufacturing technology will assist.

Flexibility: small batch sizes and automated techniques are used.

Low costs: through all of the above.

Standard product costs are associated with traditional manufacturing systems producing large quantities of standard items. Key features of companies operating in a JIT and TQM environment are:

- high level of automation
- high levels of overheads and low levels of direct labour costs
- customised products produced in small batches
- low stocks
- emphasis on high quality and continuous improvement.

6 Throughput accounting

Examiner's article: visit the ACCA website, www.accaglobal.com, to review the examiner's articles written on this topic (September 2014).

Throughput accounting aims to make the best use of a scare resource (bottleneck) in a JIT environment.

Throughput is a measure of profitability and is defined by the following equation:

Throughput = sales revenue – direct material cost

The aim of throughput accounting is to maximise this measure of profitability, whilst simultaneously reducing operating expenses and inventory (money is tied up in inventory).

The goal is achieved by determining what factors prevent the throughput from being higher. This constraint is called a *bottleneck*, for example there may be a limited number of machine hours or labour hours.

In the short-term the best use should be made of this bottleneck. This may result in some idle time in non-bottleneck resources, and may result in a small amount of inventory being held so as not to delay production through the bottleneck.

In the long-term, the bottleneck should be eliminated. For example a new, more efficient machine may be purchased. However, this will generally result in another bottleneck, which must then be addressed.

Main assumptions:

- The only totally variable cost in the short-term is the purchase cost of raw materials that are bought from external suppliers.
- Direct labour costs are not variable in the short-term. Many employees are salaried and even if paid at a rate per unit, are usually guaranteed a minimum weekly wage.
- Given these assumptions, throughput is effectively the same as contribution.

Goldratt and Cox describe the process of identifying and taking steps to remove the constraints that restrict output as the **Theory Of Constraints** (TOC). The process involves five steps:

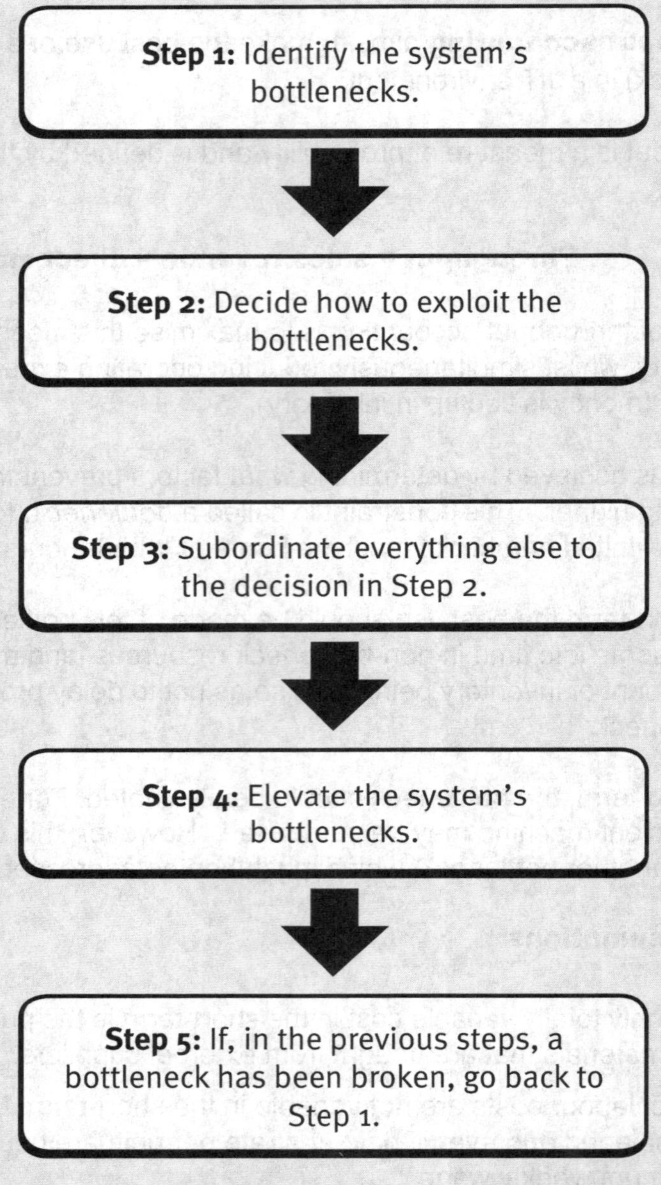

The bottleneck is the focus of management's attention. Decisions regarding the optimum mix of products must be undertaken.

Step 3 requires that the optimum production of the bottleneck activity determines the production schedule of the non-bottleneck activities. There is no point in a non-bottleneck activity supplying more than the bottleneck activity can consume. This would result in increased work-in-progress (WIP) inventories with no increased sales volume.

The TOC is a process of continuous improvement to clear the throughput chain of all the constraints. Thus, step 4 involves taking action to remove, or elevate, the constraint. This may involve replacing the bottleneck machine with a faster one, providing additional training for a slow worker or changing the design of the product to reduce the processing time required on the bottleneck activity. Once a bottleneck has been elevated it will generally be replaced by a new bottleneck elsewhere in the system. It then becomes necessary to return to Step 1.

Example 1 – Theory of constraints

Demand for a product made by P Ltd is 500 units per week. The product is made in three consecutive processes – A, B, and C. Process capacities are:

Process	*A*	*B*	**C**
Capacity per week	400	300	250

The long-run benefit to P Ltd of increasing sales of its product is a present value of $25,000 per additional unit sold per week.

Investigations have revealed the following possibilities:

(1) Invest in a new machine for process A, which will increase its capacity to 550 units per week. This will cost $1m.

(2) Replace the machine in process B with an upgraded machine, costing $1.5m. This will double the capacity of process B.

(3) Buy an additional machine for process C, costing $2m. This will increase capacity in C by 300 units per week.

Required:

What is P Ltd's best course of action?

Note: The above options are not mutually exclusive, so your answer should consider combinations as well as looking at them individually.

Throughput calculation

Hard Tiles recorded a profit of $120,000 in the accounting period just ended, using marginal costing. The contribution/sales ratio was 75%.

Material costs were 10% of sales value and there were no other variable production overhead costs. Fixed costs in the period were $300,000.

Required:

What was the value of throughput in the period?

Solution

	$
Profit	120,000
Fixed costs	300,000
Contribution	420,000
Contribution/sales ratio	75%
	$
Sales	560,000
Material costs (10% of sales)	56,000
Throughput	504,000

The Throughput Accounting Ratio

When there is a bottleneck resource, performance can be measured in terms of throughput for each unit of bottleneck resource consumed.

There are three inter-related ratios:

1. Throughput (return) per Factory Hour = $\frac{\text{Throughput per unit}}{\text{Product's time on the bottleneck resource}}$

2. Cost per Factory Hour = $\frac{\text{Total factory cost}}{\text{Total bottleneck resource time available}}$

3. Throughput Accounting Ratio (TPAR) = $\frac{\text{Return per factory hour}}{\text{Cost per factory hour}}$

Note: The *total factory cost* is the fixed production cost, including labour. The total factory cost may be referred to as 'operating expenses'.

Interpretation of TPAR

- TPAR>1 would suggest that throughput exceeds operating costs so the product should make a profit. Priority should be given to the products generating the best ratios.
- TPAR<1 would suggest that throughput is insufficient to cover operating costs, resulting in a loss.

Decision making in a Throughput Accounting environment

- When ranking products made within the same factory it is sufficient to look at their respective return per hour figures.
- However, if ranking products or divisions across the company it would be suitable to look at TPAR figures to reflect differences in costs between factories.

Criticisms of TPAR

- It concentrates on the short-term, when a business has a fixed supply of resources (i.e. a bottleneck) and operating expenses are largely fixed. However, most businesses can't produce products based on the short term only.
- It is more difficult to apply throughput accounting concepts to the longer-term, when all costs are variable, and vary with the volume of production and sales or another cost driver. The business should consider this long-term view before rejecting products with a TPAR < 1.
- In the longer-term an ABC approach might be more appropriate for measuring and controlling performance.

Test your understanding 2

X Limited manufactures a product that requires 1.5 hours of machining. Machine time is a bottleneck resource, due to the limited number of machines available. There are 10 machines available, and each machine can be used for up to 40 hours per week.

The product is sold for $85 per unit and the direct material cost per unit is $42.50. Total factory costs are $8,000 each week.

Calculate

(a) the return per factory hour

(b) the TPAR.

Additional example on TPAR

A business manufactures a single product that it sells for $10 per unit. The materials cost for each unit of product sold is $3. Total operating expenses are $50,000 each month.

Labour hours are limited to 20,000 hours each month. Each unit of product takes 2 hours to assemble.

Required:

Calculate the throughput accounting ratio (TPAR)

Solution

- Throughput per factory (assembly) hour = $(10 – 3)/2 hours = $3.50
- Cost per factory hour = $50,000/20,000 hours = $2.50

Note: The operating expenses of $50,000 are the total factory cost.

- Throughput accounting ratio = $3.50/$2.50 = 1.40

Improving the TPAR

Options to increase the TPAR include the following:

- increase the sales price for each unit sold, to increase the throughput per unit
- reduce material costs per unit (e.g. by changing materials or switching suppliers), to increase the throughput per unit
- reduce total operating expenses, to reduce the cost per factory hour
- improve the productivity of the bottleneck, e.g. the assembly workforce or the bottleneck machine, thus reducing the time required to make each unit of product. Throughput per factory hour would increase and therefore the TPAR would increase.

Improving the TPAR

Suppose in the illustration above the following changes were made:

- the sales price were increased from $10 to $13.5
- the time taken to make each product fell from 2 hours to 1.75 hours
- the operating expenses fell from $50,000 to $45,000.

The following changes would take place:

Throughput per factory hour = $(13.5 – 3)/1.75 hours = $6.0

Cost per factory hour = $45,000/20,000 hours = $2.25

TPAR = $6.0/$2.25 = 2.67

The TPAR would nearly double, increasing from 1.4 to 2.67.

Calculation 2 – Multi-product decision making

Throughput accounting may be applied to a multi-product decision making problem in the same way as conventional key factor analysis.

The usual objective in questions is to maximise profit. Given that fixed costs are unaffected by the production decision in the short run, the approach should be to maximise the throughput earned.

Step 1: identify the bottleneck constraint.

Step 2: calculate the throughput per unit for each product.

Step 3: calculate the throughput per unit of the bottleneck resource for each product.

Step 4: rank the products in order of the throughput per unit of the bottleneck resource.

Step 5: allocate resources using this ranking and answer the question.

Test your understanding 3

Justin Thyme manufactures four products, A, B, C and D. Details of sales prices, costs and resource requirements for each of the products are as follows.

	Product A	Product B	Product C	Product D
	$	$	$	$
Sales price	1.40	0.80	1.20	2.80
Materials cost	0.60	0.30	0.60	1.00
Direct labour cost	0.40	0.20	0.40	1.00
	Minutes	Minutes	Minutes	Minutes
Machine time per unit	5	2	3	6
Labour time per unit	2	1	2	5
	Units	Units	Units	Units
Weekly sales demand	2,000	2,000	2,500	1,500

Machine time is a bottleneck resource and the maximum capacity is 400 machine hours each week. Operating costs, including direct labour costs, are $5,440 each week. Direct labour costs are $12 per hour, and direct labour workers are paid for a 38-hour week, with no overtime.

(a) Determine the quantities of each product that should be manufactured and sold each week to maximise profit and calculate the weekly profit.

(b) Calculate the throughput accounting ratio at this profit-maximising level of output and sales.

Objective Test Case Question – CBF Throughput Accounting

(1) A division of CBF Co produces three types of small storage heaters, Alpha, Beta and Gamma. The production director has just read an article on Goldratt's Theory of Constraints, and is considering using throughput accounting in order to maximise the division's profits.

Which of the following statements regarding the Theory Of Constraints (TOC) are correct?

(1) It focuses on identifying stages of congestion in a process when production arrives more quickly than the next stage can handle.

(2) It uses a sequence of focusing steps to overcome a single bottleneck, at which point the improvement process is complete.

(3) It is based on the concept that organisations manage three key factors – throughput, operating expenses and inventory.

(4) It can be applied to the management of all limiting factors, both internal and external, which can affect an organisation.

A Statements (1) and (2)

B Statements (1), and (3)

C Statements (2) and (4)

D Statements (3) and (4)

(2) After manufacture, each heater has to go through three processes: 'Assembly', 'Quality Control' and 'Packaging'. The following information is available for the three heaters:

	Alpha	Beta	Gamma
Sales price per unit	$2.00	$2.25	$1.75
Direct materials cost per unit	$0.50	$0.81	$0.35
Direct labour cost per unit	$0.30	$0.60	$0.50
Machine time per unit:			
Assembly (in minutes)	2	3	2.5
Quality Control (in minutes)	3	4	2
Packaging (in minutes)	4	5	3
Weekly sales demand	1,000 units	1,500 units	850 units

Operating expenses, including labour, are $4,000. The maximum hours available for the machines are 150 hours (Assembly), 170 hours (Quality Control) and 250 hours (Packaging).

How many units of 'Beta' should be produced each week to maximise profit?

A 850 units

B 1,000 units

C 1,375 units

D 1,500 units

(3) In order to be able to meet increased demand, CBF Co bought another assembly machine, so doubling capacity. The quality control and packaging machines were also modified, so increasing their capacity by 70% and 40% respectively. The per unit factors of sales price, material cost and machine time remain unaltered.

The economy thrived and the maximum demand for each product rose to 1,500 Alpha, 2,750 Beta and 900 Gamma. Operating expenses increased by 30% and the packaging machine became the bottleneck. Weekly profit maximising output has been calculated as 1,500 Alpha, 2,460 Beta and 900 Gamma giving a weekly profit of $1852.40.

What is the throughput accounting ratio at this profit maximising level of output, to two decimal places?

A 1.36

B 0.356

C 1.76

D 0.46

(4) **Which of the following would increase CBF Co's throughput accounting ratio?**

A CBF Co purchasing another assembly machine

B The rates of the factory decreasing

C Reducing the sales price of Beta, due to demand

D Employ more skilled labour with increased productivity in the packaging department

(5) CBF Co uses cost-plus pricing.

Which of the following statements regarding cost-plus pricing strategies are correct?

(1) Marginal cost-plus pricing is easier where there is a readily identifiable variable cost.

(2) Full cost-plus pricing requires the budgeted level of output to be determined at the outset.

(3) Cost-plus pricing is a strategically focused approach as it accounts for external factors.

(4) Cost-plus pricing requires that the profit mark-up applied by an organisation is fixed.

A Statements (1) and (2)

B Statements (2), (3) and (4)

C Statements (1), (3) and (4)

D Statements (1), (2), (3) and (4)

7 Throughput accounting in the public sector

Throughput accounting principles can be applied in both the private and public sectors. Take the following example:

Throughput accounting in the public sector

A not-for-profit organisation performs a medical screening service in three sequential stages: 1)Take an X-ray, 2) interpret the result and 3) recall patients who need further investigation/tell others that all is fine.

The 'goal unit' of this organisation will be to progress a person through all three stages. The number of people who complete all the stages is the organisation's throughput, and the organisation should seek to maximise its throughput. The duration of each stage, and the weekly resource available, is as follows:

Process	Time per patient (hours)	Total hours available per week
Take an X-Ray	0.50	80
Interpret the result	0.20	40
Recall patients who need further investigation/tell others that all is fine	0.40	60

From the above table, the maximum number of patients (goal units) who can be dealt with in each process is as follows:

Take an X-Ray	80/0.50 =	160
Interpret the result	40/0.20 =	200
Recall patients who need further investigation/tell others that all is fine	60/0.40 =	150

Here, **the recall procedure is the bottleneck resource, or constraint**. Throughput, and thereby the organisation's performance, cannot be improved until that part of the process can deal with more people.

Therefore, to improve throughput, the following steps can be taken:

(1) Ensure there is no idle time in the bottleneck resource, as that will be detrimental to overall performance (idle time in a non-bottleneck resource is not detrimental to overall performance).

(2) See if less time could be spent on the bottleneck activity.

(3) Finally, increase the bottleneck resource available.

In this example, increasing the bottleneck resource, or the efficiency with which it is used, might be relatively cheap and easy to do because this is a simple piece of administration while the other stages employ expensive machinery or highly skilled personnel. There is certainly no point in improving the first two stages if things grind to a halt in the final stage; patients are helped only when the whole process is completed, and they are recalled if necessary.

8 Target costing

Target costing involves setting a target cost by subtracting a desired profit from a competitive market price. Real world users include Sony, Toyota and the Swiss watchmakers, Swatch.

In effect it is the opposite of conventional 'cost plus pricing'.

Illustration 4

Music Matters manufactures and sells cds for a number of popular artists. At present, it uses a traditional cost-plus pricing system.

Cost-plus pricing system

(1) The cost of the cd is established first. This is $14 per unit.

(2) A profit of $5 per unit is added to each cd.

(3) This results in the current selling price of $19 per unit.

(2) Required profit = $5 per cd	
(1) Cost = $14 per cd	(3) Selling price is $19 per cd

However, cost-plus pricing ignores:

- The price that customers are willing to pay – pricing the cds too high could result in low sales volumes and profits.
- The price charged by competitors for similar products – if competitor's are charging less than $19 per cd for similar cds then customers may decide to buy their cds from the competitor companies.
- Cost control – the cost of the cd is established at $14 but there is little incentive to control this cost.

Target costing

Music Matters could address the problems discussed above through the implementation of target costing:

(1) The first step is to establish a competitive market price. The company would consider how much customers are willing to pay and how much competitors are charging for similar products. Let's assume this is $15 per unit.

(2) Music Matters would then deduct their required profit from the selling price. The required profit may be kept at $5 per unit.

(3) A target cost is arrived at by deducting the required profit from the selling price, i.e. $15 – $5 = $10 per unit.

(4) The cost gap can then be identified. In this case the current cost per unit of $14 per unit must be reduced to the target cost of $10. A gap of $4 per unit must be closed.

(5) Steps must then be taken to close the target cost gap (see below for further details).

(2) Required profit = $5 per cd	
(1) Cost = $10 per cd	(3) Selling price is $15 per cd

Steps used in deriving a target cost (manufacturing industries)

Step 1: a target price is set, based on the customers' perceived value of the product. This will therefore be a market based price.

↓

Step 2: The required target operating profit per unit is then calculated. This may be based on either return on sales, or return on investment.

↓

Step 3: The target cost is derived by subtracting the target profit from the target price.

↓

Step 4: The cost gap is then calculated.

↓

Step 5: If there is a cost gap, attempts will be made to close the gap. Techniques such as value engineering may be performed, which looks at every aspect of the value chain business functions, with an objective of reducing costs whilst satisfying customer needs.

↓

Negotiation with customers may take place before deciding whether to go ahead with the project.

Closing the target cost gap

The target cost gap is established in step 4 of the target costing process.

Target cost gap = Estimated product cost – Target cost

It is the difference between what an organisation thinks it can currently make a product for, and what it needs to make it for, in order to make a required profit.

Alternative product designs should be examined for potential areas of cost reduction that will not compromise the quality of the products.

Questions that a manufacturer may ask in order to close the gap include:

- Can any materials be eliminated, e.g. cut down on packing materials?
- Can a cheaper material be substituted without affecting quality?
- Can labour savings be made without compromising quality, for example, by using lower skilled workers?
- Can productivity be improved, for example, by improving motivation?
- Can production volume be increased to achieve economies of scale?
- Could cost savings be made by reviewing the supply chain?
- Can part-assembled components be bought in to save on assembly time?
- Can the incidence of the cost drivers be reduced?
- Is there some degree of overlap between the product-related fixed costs that could be eliminated by combining service departments or resources?

A key aspect of this is to understand which features of the product are essential to customer perceived quality and which are not. This process is known as 'value analysis'. Attention should be focused more on reducing the costs of features perceived by the customer not to add value.

Note: Closing the cost gap by increasing the selling price is not a viable option as the price is determined by market forces rather than the company.

Value analysis

Value analysis, otherwise known as 'cost engineering' and 'value engineering', is a technique in which a firm's products, and maybe those of its competitors, are subjected to a critical and systematic examination by a small group of specialists. They can be representing various functions such as design, production, sales and finance.

Value analysis seeks to close the cost gap by asking of a product the following questions: does it need all of its features? Can a usable part be made better at lower cost?

A cost advantage may be obtained in many ways, e.g. economies of scale, the experience curve, product design innovations and the use of 'no-frills' product offering. Each provides a different way of competing on the basis of cost advantage.

9 Types of value

Cost value: this is the cost incurred by the firm incurring the product.

Exchange value: the amount of money that consumers are willing to exchange to obtain ownership of the product, i.e. its price.

Use value: this is related entirely to function, i.e. the ability of a product to perform its specific intended purpose. For example, a basic small car provides personal transport at a competitive price and is reasonably economic to run.

Esteem value: this relates to the status or regard associated with ownership. Products with high esteem value will often be associated with premium or even price-skimming prices.

'Value' is a function of both 'use' and 'esteem'. Value analysis aims to maintain the esteem value in a product, but at a reduced cost value. The result of value analysis is to achieve an improved value/cost relationship.

Test your understanding 4

The Swiss watchmaker Swatch reportedly used target costing in order to produce relatively low-cost, similar-looking plastic watches in a country with one of the world's highest hourly labour wage rates.

Suggest ways in which Swatch may have reduced their unit costs for each watch.

10 Target costing in service organisations

Target costing is as relevant to the service sector as the manufacturing sector. Key issues are similar in both: the needs of the market need to be identified and understood as well as its customers and users; and financial performance at a given cost or price (which does not exceed the target cost when resources are limited) needs to be ensured.

For example, if a firm of accountants was asked to bid for a new client contract, the partners or managers would probably have an idea of what kind of price is likely to win the contract. If staff costs are billed out at twice their hourly salary cost, say, this would help to determine a staff budget for the contract. It would then be necessary to work out the hours needed and play around with the mix of juniors/senior staff to get to that target cost.

There are ways in which target costing can be applied to service-oriented businesses, and the focus of target costing shifts from the product to the service delivery system.

Target costing in the NHS

In 2005, the National Audit Office and the Audit Commission identified the need for improvements in financial skills to meet the challenges facing the health service, as first-class financial management has a vital role in delivering improvements to patients. A number of healthcare providers in the United States had recently made significant improvements to patient care and resource utilisation by adopting approaches used in manufacturing businesses, including target costing principles, which is thought to have contributed towards significant benefits in improved quality of care, decreased mortality and cost reduction.

Target costing was thought of as a better method of costing services, in order to help NHS Trusts and hospitals to meet their financial responsibility to at least break-even, by ensuring that services are delivered within budgeted costs. Therefore, a move towards a new method of funding services was initiated, with NHS Trusts being paid a pre-set **national tariff** for each service they provide, rather than a price based on their own costs.

Take the example of Mrs Smith, who suffers from a medical condition requiring hospital care. She is booked into Guy's + St Thomas's hospital NHS Foundation Trust for a procedure this month. Lambeth PCT is the responsible commissioner for Mrs Smith's care, because she is registered with a GP practice there. The national tariff for the procedure amounts to £3,236, adjusted by two daily long stay payments at £740 a day. Therefore, the reimbursement from Lambeth PCT to St Guy's hospital for the procedure would amount to a total of £3,976.

It was hoped that target costing, with targets related to the national tariff and coupled with an emphasis on value-for-money performance indicators , might provide a discipline within which Trusts could manage costs to improve efficiency. In a case like Mrs Smith's, a target cost would hopefully encourage the hospital to perform the operation within this costs and promote better scheduling, use of cheaper drugs, etc.

11 Problems with target costing in service industries

Unlike manufacturing, service industries have the following characteristics which could make target costing more difficult:

(1) The **intangibility** of what is provided means that it is difficult to define the 'service' and attribute costs; in the NHS, it is challenging to define what a 'procedure' is. Clinical specialities cover a wide range of disparate treatments, and services include high levels of indirect cost. Consistent methods of cost attribution are needed, and this is not always straightforward. Direct charging is not always possible and there are different configurations of cost centres across providers. This may limit the consistency which can be achieved.

(2) **Inseparability**/simultaneity of production and consumption: although the manufacturer of a tangible good may never see the actual customer, customer often must be present during the production of a service, and cannot take the service home. No service exists until it is actually being experienced/consumed by the person who has brought it.

(3) **Heterogeneity** – The quality and consistency varies, because of an absence of standards or benchmarks to assess services against. In the NHS, there is no indication of what an excellent performance in service delivery would be, or any definition of unacceptable performance.

(4) **Perishability** – the unused service capacity from one time period cannot be stored for future use. Service providers and marketers cannot handle supply-demand problems through production scheduling and inventory techniques.

(5) **No transfer of ownership** – Services do not result in the transfer of property. The purchase of a service only confers on the customer access to or a right to use a facility.

12 Life-cycle costing

Traditional costing techniques based around annual periods may give a misleading impression of the costs and profitability of a product. This is because systems are based on the financial accounting year, and dissect the product's lifecycle into a series of annual sections. Usually, therefore, the management accounting systems would assess a product's profitability on a periodic basis, rather than over its entire life.

Lifecycle costing, however, tracks and accumulates costs and revenues attributable to each product **over its entire product lifecycle.**

$$\textbf{Lifecycle cost of Product A} = \frac{\textbf{Total costs of Product A over its entire lifecycle}}{\textbf{Total number of units of A}}$$

Then, the **total** profitability of any given product can be determined.

A product's costs are not evenly spread through its life.

According to Berliner and Brimson (1988), companies operating in an advanced manufacturing environment are finding that about **90% of a product's lifecycle costs are determined by decisions made early in the cycle**. In many industries, a large fraction of the life-cycle costs consists of costs incurred on product design, prototyping, programming, process design and equipment acquisition.

This had created a need to ensure that the tightest controls are at the design stage, i.e. before a launch, because most costs are committed, or 'locked-in', at this point in time.

Management Accounting systems should therefore be developed that aid the planning and control of product lifecycle costs and monitor spending and commitments **at the early stages of a product's life cycle.**

Test your understanding 5

The following details relate to a new product that has finished development and is about to be launched.

	Development	Launch	Growth	Maturity	Decline
Time period	Finished	1 year	1 year	1 year	1 year
R & D costs ($m)	20				
Marketing costs ($m)		5	4	3	0.9
Production cost per unit ($)		1.00	0.90	0.80	0.90
Production volume		1m	5m	10m	4m

The launch price is proving a contentious issue between managers. The marketing manager is keen to start with a low price of around $8 to gain new buyers and achieve target market share. The accountant is concerned that this does not cover costs during the launch phase and has produced the following schedule to support this:

Launch phase:		$ million
Amortised R&D costs	(20 ÷ 4)	5.0
Marketing costs		5.0
Production costs	(1 million × $1 per unit)	1.0
Total		11.0
Total production (units)		1 million
Cost per unit		$11.00

Prepare a revised cost per unit schedule looking at the whole lifecycle and comment on the implications of this cost with regards to the pricing of the product during the launch phase.

The product life-cycle

Most products have a distinct product life-cycle:

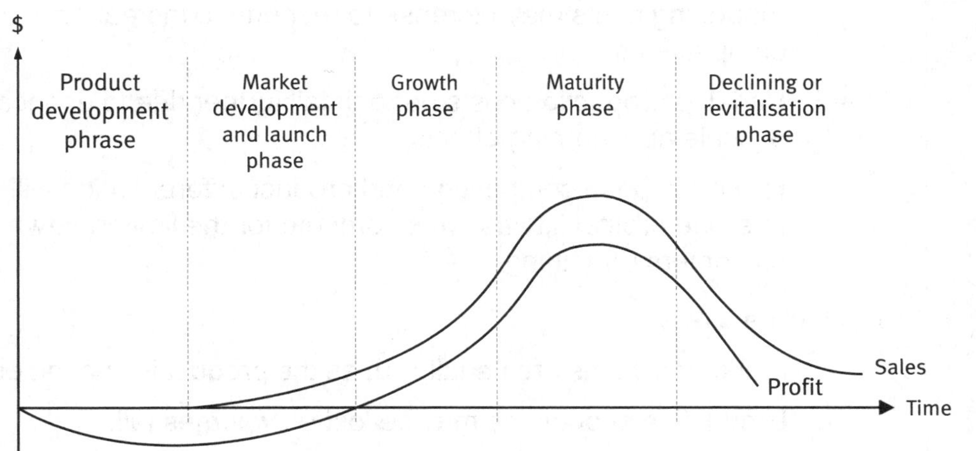

Specific costs may be associated with each stage.

(1) Pre-production/Product development stage
  - A high level of setup costs will be incurred in this stage (preproduction costs), including research and development (R&D), product design and building of production facilities.

(2) Launch/Market development stage
  - Success depends upon awareness and trial of the product by consumers, so this stage is likely to be accompanied by extensive marketing and promotion costs.
  - Production costs per unit will be extremely high due to the low volumes involved.

(3) Growth stage
  - Marketing and promotion will continue through this stage.
  - In this stage sales volume increases dramatically, and unit costs fall as fixed costs are recovered over greater volumes and variable production costs per unit fall due to economies of scale.

(4) Maturity stage

- Initially profits will continue to increase, as initial setup and fixed costs are recovered.
- Marketing and distribution economies are achieved but overall marketing costs may increase to respond to increased competition.
- Variable production costs per unit fall further due to economies of scale and learning effects.
- However, price competition and product differentiation will start to erode profitability as firms compete for the limited new customers remaining.

(5) Decline stage

- Marketing costs are usually cut as the product is phased out.
- Production economies may be lost as volumes fall.
- Meanwhile, a replacement product will need to have been developed, incurring new levels of R&D and other product setup costs.
- Alternatively additional development costs may be incurred to refine the model to extend the life-cycle (this is typical with cars where 'product evolution' is the norm rather than 'product revolution').

There are a number of factors that need to be managed in order to maximise a product's return over its lifecycle:

Design costs out of the product:

It was stated earlier that around 90% of a product's costs were often incurred at the design and development stages of its life. Decisions made then commit the organisation to incurring the costs at a later date, because the design of the product determines the number of components, the production method, etc. It is absolutely vital therefore that design teams do not work in isolation but as part of a cross-functional team in order to minimise costs over the whole life cycle.

Value engineering helps here; for example, Russian liquid-fuel rocket motors are intentionally designed to allow leak-free welding. This reduces costs by eliminating grinding and finishing operations (these operations would not help the motor to function better anyway.)

Minimise the time to market:

In a world where competitors watch each other keenly to see what new products will be launched, it is vital to get any new product into the marketplace as quickly as possible. The competitors will monitor each other closely so that they can launch rival products as soon as possible in order to maintain profitability. It is vital, therefore, for the first organisation to launch its product as quickly as possible after the concept has been developed, so that it has as long as possible to establish the product in the market and to make a profit before competition increases. Often it is not so much costs that reduce profits as time wasted.

Minimise the break-even point:

Firms may wish to try to minimise the time taken to achieve break-even for a new project. Leaving aside the cost aspects already discussed, this turns the focus to pricing strategies at launch:

- A low price would boost sales volumes more rapidly but at the expense of a lower contribution per unit.
- A higher price would boost the contribution per unit but potentially at the expense of sales volumes.

Such factors would have to be considered within the wider context of issues such as product strategy and objectives. For example, is the main objective to penetrate a market and gain market share, or to establish a high quality image?

Maximise the length of the life cycle itself:

Generally, the longer the life cycle, the greater the profit that will be generated, assuming that production ceases once the product goes into decline and becomes unprofitable. One way to maximise the life cycle is to get the product to market as quickly as possible because this should maximise the time in which the product generates a profit.

Another way of extending a product's life is to find other uses, or markets, for the product. Other product uses may not be obvious when the product is still in its planning stage and need to be planned and managed later on. On the other hand, it may be possible to plan for a staggered entry into different markets at the planning stage.

Many organisations stagger the launch of their products in different world markets in order to reduce costs, increase revenue and prolong the overall life of the product. A current example is the way in which new films are released in the USA months before the UK launch. This is done to build up the enthusiasm for the film and to increase revenues overall. Other companies may not have the funds to launch worldwide at the same moment and may be forced to stagger it. Skimming the market is another way to prolong life and to maximise the revenue over the product's life.

Illustration 5 – Lifecycle costing

Enrono is an accounting software package which has a six-year product lifecycle. The following are the yearly costs, estimated for the entire length of the package's life:

Costs – in $,000	Year 1	Year 2	Year 3	Year 4	Year 5	Year 6
Res. & Dev.	275					
Design		120				
Production costs			120	200	200	
Marketing costs			125	170	130	60
Distribution costs			20	20	15	10
Customer service costs			5	15	30	45

The lifecycle costs for the Enrono package can be added up as follows:

Lifecycle costs	**in $000**
Research and development	275
Design	120
Production costs	520
Marketing costs	485
Distribution costs	65
Customer Service costs	95
Total lifecycle costs	**1,560**

Lifecycle costing clearly takes into consideration the costs of the package incurred during the entire lifecycle – over $1.5 m. Accordingly, from lifecycle costing, the management can know whether the revenue earned by the product is sufficient to cover the whole costs incurred during its life cycle.

When viewed as a whole, there are opportunities for cost reduction and minimisation (and thereby scope for profit maximisation) in several categories of cost:

- For example, initiatives could be taken to reduce testing costs and therefore the 'Research and Development' category.
- Likewise, proper planning and a tight control on transportation & handling costs could minimise distribution costs.

These opportunities for cost reduction are unlikely to be found when management focuses on maximising profit in a period-by-period basis. **Only on knowing the lifecycle costs of a product can a business decide appropriately on its price.** This, coupled with planning of the different phases of the product's life, could give rise to the following tactics:

INTRODUCTION	**GROWTH**	**MATURITY**	**DECLINE**
High prices to recoup high development costs; high returns before competitors enter the market.	Competition increases; **reduce price** to remain competitive.	Sales slow down and level off; the market price is maintained. Upgrades and/or new markets should be considered.	Superior products appear – our prices must be cut to maintain sales.

Customer lifecycle costing

Not all investment decisions involve large initial capital outflows or the purchase of physical assets. The decision to serve and retain customers can also be a capital budgeting decision even though the initial outlay may be small. For example a credit card company or an insurance company will have to choose which customers they take on and then register them on the company's records. The company incurs initial costs due to the paperwork, checking creditworthiness, opening policies, etc. for new customers. It takes some time before these initial costs are recouped. Research has also shown that the longer a customer stays with the company the more profitable that customer becomes to the company.

Thus it becomes important to retain customers, whether by good service, discounts, other benefits, etc. A customer's 'life' can be discounted and decisions made as to the value of, say, a 'five-year-old' customer. Eventually a point arises where profit no longer continues to grow; this plateau is reached between about five years and 20 years depending on the nature of the business. Therefore by studying the increased revenue and decreased costs generated by an 'old' customer, management can find strategies to meet their needs better and to retain them.

Many manufacturing companies only supply a small number of customers, say between six and ten, and so they can cost customers relatively easily. Other companies such as banks and supermarkets have many customers and cannot easily analyse every single customer. In this case similar customers are grouped together to form category types and these can then be analysed in terms of profitability.

For example, the UK banks analyse customers in terms of fruits, such as oranges, lemons, plums, etc. Customers tend to move from one category to another as they age and as their financial habits change. Customers with large mortgages, for example, are more valuable to the bank than customers who do not have a large income and do not borrow money. Banks are not keen on keeping the latter type of customer.

Lifecycle costing in the service industry

A service organisation will provide services that have life cycles. For example, a company leasing heavy machinery to clients could use LCC to predict the total costs, resources, utilisation and productivity for an asset over its entire life cycle: thus, LCC is an excellent tool for assessing alternatives, which has made it very common in the procurement of large assets.

All pertinent cash flows that go to form the complete service over the life of the machine are important, and consideration should be given in advance as to how to carry them out so as to minimise the whole-life cost. A simple model is shown below:

in $000	Year 1	Year 2	Year 3	Year 4	Year 5	Total
Purchase cost of asset	$800					$800
Labour costs (operator)	$30	$31	$32	$33	$34	$160
Parts and materials	$10	$15	$15	$18	$18	$76
Fuel	$80	$96	$115.2	$138.24	$165.888	$595.328
Lubricants	$8	$8	$8	$8	$8	$40
Disposal					($100)	($100)
Total	**$928**	**$150**	**$170.2**	**$197.24**	**$125.888**	**$1,571.328**

The total cost of owning and operating the equipment is the sum of the individual cost elements. LCC also involves understanding the detail of the individual cost elements and building these up to the ultimate life cycle cost. Then, each cost can be broken down further. For example, the 'Parts and Materials' costs can be split as follows:

	Year 1	Year 2	Year 3	Year 4	Year 5	Total
Replacement of internal motor			$10,000			$10,000
Basic service	$5,000	$5,000	$2,000	$4,000	$4,000	$20,000
Direct administration costs	$1,500	$3,500	$1,500	$3,500	$3,500	$13,500
Wiring repairs	$3,500	$6,500	$1,500	$10,500	$10,500	$32,500
Total	**$10,000**	**$15,000**	**$15,000**	**$18,000**	**$18,000**	**$76,000**

For example, the internal motor change is scheduled to occur in Year 3. This is driven by an estimated life of the motor of X hours and an expected utilisation of the equipment of Y hours per year. If X or Y were to change, the model may provide a different result.

Assuming the LCC model above could be continuously updated, and the component costs automatically uploaded every time a maintenance task is performed, this would:

(1) Provide the company with more accurate and robust pricing information

(2) Provide a real time life cycle cost model

(3) Enable equipment managers to see and understand the impact of their decisions on the life cycle cost of the asset

(4) Allow the company to see the forward resource for parts, labour and materials

(5) Allow budgeting managers to plan cash outflows for the next 5 years and beyond.

13 Environmental management accounting

Examiner's article: visit the ACCA website, www.accaglobal.com, to review the examiner's article written on this topic (September 2014).

Organisations are beginning to recognise that environmental awareness and management are not optional, but are important for long-term survival and profitability. All organisations:

- are faced with increasing legal and regulatory requirements relating to environmental management
- need to meet customers' needs and concerns relating to the environment

- need to demonstrate effective environmental management to maintain a good public image
- need to manage the risk and potential impact of environmental disasters
- can make cost savings by improved use of resources such as water and fuel
- are recognising the importance of sustainable development, which is the meeting of current needs without compromising the ability of future generations to meet their needs.

EMA is concerned with the accounting information needs of managers in relation to corporate activities that affect the environment as well as environment-related impacts on the corporation. This includes:

- identifying and estimating the costs of environment-related activities
- identifying and separately monitoring the usage and cost of resources such as water, electricity and fuel and to enable costs to be reduced
- ensuring environmental considerations form a part of capital investment decisions
- assessing the likelihood and impact of environmental risks
- including environment-related indicators as part of routine performance monitoring
- benchmarking activities against environmental best practice.

14 Environmental concern and performance

Martin Bennett and Peter James ('The Green Bottom Line: Management Accounting for Environmental Improvement and Business Benefit', *Management Accounting*, November 1998), looked at the ways in which a company's concern for the environment can impact on its performance:

(a) Short-term savings through waste minimisation and energy efficiency schemes can be substantial.

(b) Companies with poor environmental performance may face increased cost of capital because investors and lenders demand a higher risk premium.

(c) There are a number of energy and environmental taxes, such as the landfill tax in the UK.

(d) Pressure group campaigns can cause damage to reputation, or additional costs.

(e) Environmental legislation may cause the 'sunsetting' of products and opportunities for 'sunrise' replacements.

(f) The cost of processing input which becomes waste is equivalent to 5–10% of some organisations' revenue.

(g) The phasing out of CFCs has led to markets for alternative products.

Achieving business and environmental benefits

Bennett and James ('The Green Bottom Line' 1998) went on to suggest six main ways in which business and environmental benefits can be achieved.

(a) Integrating the environment into capital expenditure decisions (by considering environmental opposition to projects which could affect cash flows, for example).

(b) Understanding and managing environmental costs. Environmental costs are often hidden in overheads, and environmental and energy costs are often not allocated to the relevant budgets.

(c) Introducing waste minimisation schemes.

(d) Understanding and managing life cycle costs. For many products, the greatest environmental impact occurs upstream (such as mining raw materials) or downstream from production (such as energy to operate equipment.) This has led to producers being made responsible for dealing with the disposal of products such as cars, and government and third party measures to influence raw material choices. Organisations therefore need to identify, control and make provision for environmental lifecycle costs and work with suppliers and customers to identify environmental cost reduction opportunities.

(e) Measuring environmental performance. Business is under increasing pressure to measure all aspects of environmental performance, both for statutory disclosure reasons and due to demands for more environmental data from customers.

(f) Involving management accountants in a strategic approach to environment-related management accounting and performance evaluation. A 'green accounting team' incorporating the key functions should analyse the strategic picture and identify opportunities for practical initiatives. It should analyse the short- medium-and long-term impact of possible changes in the following:

(1) Government policies, such as transport.

(2) Legislation and regulation.

(3) Supply conditions, such as fewer landfill sites.

(4) Market conditions, such as changing customer views.

(5) Social attitudes, such as to factory farming.

(6) Competitor strategies.

Possible **actions** include the following:

(1) Designating an 'environmental champion' within the strategic planning or accounting function to ensure that environmental considerations are fully taken into account.

(2) Assessing whether new data sources are needed to collect more (and better) data.

(3) Making comparisons between sites/offices to highlight poor performance and generate peer pressure for action.

(4) Developing checklists for internal auditors.

Such analysis and action should help organisations to better understand present and future environmental costs and benefits.

EM and effect on financial performance

There are a number of ways in which environmental issues can have an impact on the financial performance of organisations.

Improving revenue

Producing new products or services which meet the environmental needs or concerns of customers can lead to increased sales. It may also be possible to sell such products for a premium price. Improved sales may also be a consequence of improving the reputation of the business.

It is possible that in the future, rather than good environmental management resulting in improved sales, poor management will lead to losses. All businesses will be expected to meet a minimum standard related to environmental issues.

Cost reductions

Paying close attention to the use of resources can lead to reductions in cost. Often simple improvements in processes can lead to significant costs savings.

Increases in costs

There may be increases in some costs, for example the cost of complying with legal and regulatory requirements, and additional costs to improve the environmental image of the organisation. However some of these costs may be offset by government grants and this expenditure may save money in the long-term as measures taken may prevent future losses.

Costs of failure

Poor environmental management can result in significant costs, for example the cost of clean-up and fines following an environmental disaster.

Some EMA initiatives

Rolls-Royce Aerospace says up to a quarter of emissions can be cut by changes in airframe design. It adds that changes in its Environmentally Friendly Engine (EFE) programme will deliver up to another fifth and the remainder of the 50 per cent target can be met by changing the way the aircraft are operated.

Rolls are also developing fuel cell technology and alternatives to kerosene. A biofuel blended with kerosene will be used in one of the four Rolls-Royce RB211-524s powering an Air New Zealand Boeing 747-400 in the second half of 2008.

Another example of energy saving is **McCain Foods**, which buys an eighth of the UK's potatoes to make chips. It has cut its Peterborough plant's CO_2 footprint by two-thirds, says corporate affairs director Bill Bartlett. It invested £10m in three 3MW turbines to meet 60 per cent of its annual electricity demand. McCain spent another £4.5m on a lagoon to catch the methane from fermenting waste water and particulates, which generates another 10 per cent of the site's electricity usage. It also wants to refine its used cooking oil, either for its own vehicles fleet or for selling on. McCain want to become more competitive and more efficient.

The Hull factory of **Smith & Nephew Wound Management** makes single-use sterile wound dressings for injuries and operations. It saved £250,000 a year by replacing a large absorption chiller with a vapour compression chiller. It also replaced four 500kW chillers with a 'ring main' run from one 1MW chiller for the whole factory; in winter this runs at 250kW. Hull saved £50,000 by shutting down four of its eight compressors. These and other efforts have cut its energy use by 38 per cent to 48m kWh a year, saving £2m since 2003, says S&N energy and utilities manager Marc Beaumont, who adds: "And there's still more to go at." He says the main driver has been cost: "Energy prices are set to go only one way. If we can drive down costs we can increase our profits."

St Gobain are leaders in the design; production and distribution of materials for the construction; industrial and consumer markets. They used to pay contractors £75 a tonne for someone to take its cardboard away. Now it uses a baler that costs £238.33 a month to rent, maintain, operate and power. The baler crushes the cardboard into 500 kg bales that it sells to a paper mill for £30 a tonne.

McLenaghan has a long list of sellable wastes, from mobile phones to scrap metal to cutting-wheels, thermocouples, cutting tools and vending machine cups. They believe waste can be reused, reallocated or put into a revenue stream.

Xerox has announced 'green software' that allows its machines to spot pages with just a URL, banner, logo or legal jargon and refuse to print them.

Canon advertising says its copiers' on-demand fixing technology saved seven million tonnes of CO2 between 1999 and 2006. And in September 2007 Dell announced its aim to be carbon neutral.

15 Identifying and accounting for environmental costs

Management are often unaware of the extent of environmental costs and cannot identify opportunities for cost savings. Environmental costs can be split into two categories:

Internal costs

These are costs that directly impact on the income statement of a company. There are many different types, for example:

- improved systems and checks in order to avoid penalties/fines
- waste disposal costs
- product take back costs (i.e. in the EU, for example, companies must provide facilities for customers to return items such as batteries, printer cartridges etc. for recycling. The seller of such items must bear the cost of these "take backs")
- regulatory costs such as taxes (e.g. companies with poor environmental management policies often have to bear a higher tax burden)
- upfront costs such as obtaining permits (e.g. for achieving certain levels of emissions)
- back-end costs such as decommissioning costs on project completion.

External costs

These are costs that are imposed on society at large, but not borne by the company that generates the cost in the first instance. For example,

- carbon emissions
- usage of energy and water
- forest degradation
- health care costs
- social welfare costs.

However, governments are becoming increasingly aware of these external costs and are using taxes and regulations to convert them to internal costs. For example, companies might have to have a tree replacement programme if they cause forest degradation, or they receive lower tax allowances on vehicles that cause a high degree of harm to the environment. On top of this, some companies are voluntarily converting external costs to internal costs.

16 Other classifications

Other classification include:

(1) **Hansen and Mendoza:**

- (i) Environmental prevention costs: the costs of activities undertaken to prevent the production of waste. Examples include the costs of the design and operation of processes to reduce contaminants, training employees, recycling products and obtaining certification relating to meeting the requirements of national and international standards.
- (ii) Environmental detection costs: costs incurred to ensure that the organisation complies with regulations and voluntary standards. Examples include performing contamination tests and inspecting products to ensure regulatory compliance.
- (iii) Environmental internal failure costs: costs incurred from performing activities that have produced contaminants and waste that have **not** been discharged into the environment. Recycling scrap, or disposing of toxic materials, are examples.
- (iv) Environmental external failure costs: costs incurred on activities performed **after** discharging waste into the environment. Examples include the costs of cleaning up contaminated soil, oil spills, or restoring land to its natural state.

(2) **The US Environmental Protection Agency** makes a distinction between four types of costs:

- (i) Conventional costs : raw materials and energy costs having environmental relevance
- (ii) Potentially hidden costs: costs captured by accounting systems but then losing their identity in 'general overheads'
- (iii) Contingent costs: costs to be incurred at a future date, e.g. clean-up costs
- (iv) Image and relationship costs: costs that, by their nature, are intangible, for example the costs of preparing environmental reports.

(3) **The United Nations Division for Sustainable Development** describes environmental costs as comprising of costs incurred to protect the environment (for example, measures taken to prevent pollution) and costs of wasted material, capital and labour, i.e. inefficiencies in the production process.

Further examples of environmental costs

Regulatory	**Upfront**	**Voluntary (beyond compliance)**
Notification Reporting Monitoring/testing Studies/modelling Remediation Record keeping Plans Training Inspections Manifesting Labelling Preparedness Protective equipment Medical surveillance Environmental insurance Financial assurance Pollution control Spill response Storm water management Waste management Taxes/fees	Site studies Site preparation Permitting R&D Engineering and procurement Installation Conventional costs Capital equipment Materials Labour Supplies Utilities Structures Salvage value **Back-end** Closure/ decommissioning Disposal of inventory Post-closure care Site survey	Community relations/outreach Monitoring/testing Training Audits Qualifying suppliers Reports (e.g. annual environmental reports) Insurance Planning Feasibility studies Remediation Recycling Environmental studies R&D Habitat and wetland protection Landscaping Other environmental projects Financial support to environmental groups and/or researchers

17 EMA techniques

The most appropriate management accounting techniques for the identification and allocation of environmental costs are those identified by the United Nations Division for Sustainable Development. These include (Source: *Student Accountant,* Issue 15):

(1) **Input/outflow analysis**

This technique records material inflows and balances this with outflows on the basis that what comes in, must go out.

For example, if 100 kg of materials have been bought and only 80 kg of materials have been produced, then the 20 kg difference must be accounted for in some way. It may be, for example, that 10% of it has been sold as scrap and 90% of it is waste. By accounting for outputs in this way, both in terms of physical quantities, and, at the end of the process, in monetary terms too, businesses are forced to focus on environmental costs.

(2) **Flow cost accounting**

This technique uses not only material flows, but also the organisational structure. It makes material flows transparent by looking at the physical quantities involved, their costs and their value. It divides the material flows into three categories : material, system and delivery and disposal. The values and costs of each of these three flows are then calculated. The aim of flow cost accounting is to reduce the quantity of materials which, as well as having a positive effect on the environment, should have a positive effect on a business' total costs in the long run.

(3) **Activity-based costing**

ABC allocates internal costs to cost centres and cost drivers on the basis of the activities that give rise to the costs. In an environmental accounting context, it distinguishes between environment-related costs, which can be attributed to joint cost centres, and environment-driven costs, which tend to be hidden on general overheads.

(4) **Lifecycle costing**

Within the context of environmental accounting, lifecycle costing is a technique which requires the full environmental consequences, and, therefore, costs, arising from the production of a product to be taken account across its whole lifecycle, literally 'from cradle to grave'.

18 EMA: Advantages and disadvantages

Advantages of environmental costing	Disadvantages
• better/fairer product costs	• time consuming
• improved pricing – so that products that have the biggest environmental impact reflect this by having higher selling prices	• expensive to implement
• better environmental cost control	• determining accurate costs and appropriate costs drivers is difficult
• facilitates the quantification of cost savings from "environmentally-friendly" measures	• external costs not experienced by the company (e.g. carbon footprint) may still be ignored/unmeasured
• should integrate environmental costing into the strategic management process	• some internal environmental costs are intangible (e.g. impact on employee health) and these are still ignored
• reduces the potential for cross-subsidisation of environmentally damaging products	• a company that incorporates external costs voluntarily may be at a competitive disadvantage to rivals who do not do this

19 Chapter summary

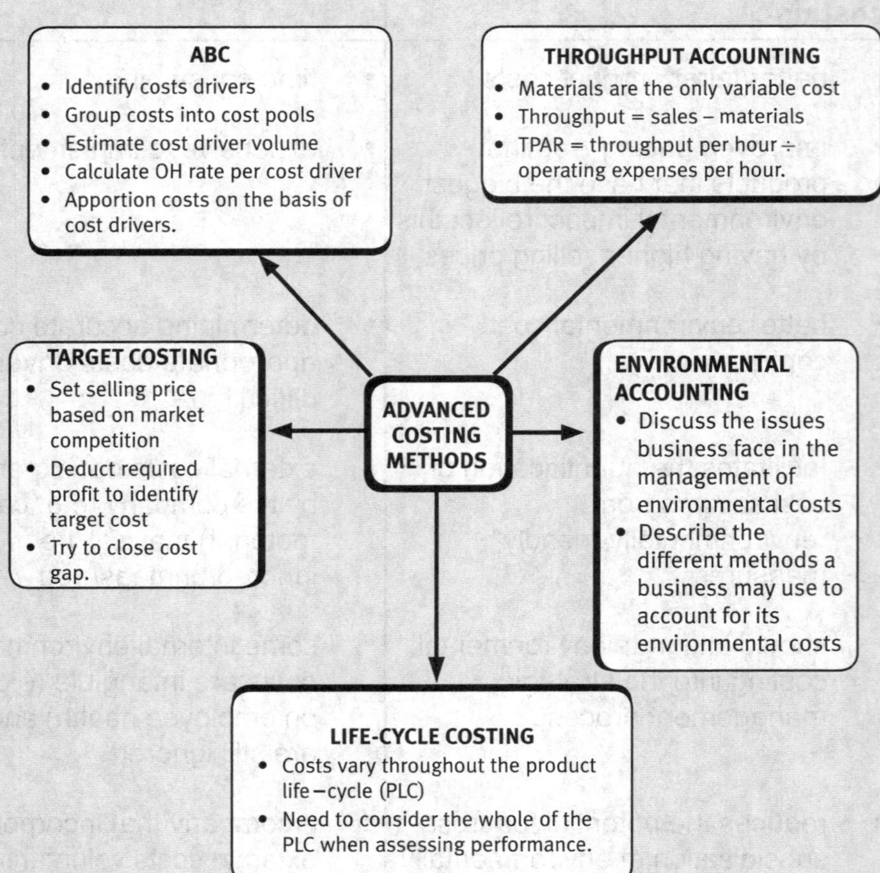

ABC
• Identify costs drivers
• Group costs into cost pools
• Estimate cost driver volume
• Calculate OH rate per cost driver
• Apportion costs on the basis of cost drivers.
THROUGHPUT ACCOUNTING
• Materials are the only variable cost
• Throughput = sales – materials
• TPAR = throughput per hour ÷ operating expenses per hour.
TARGET COSTING
• Set selling price based on market competition
• Deduct required profit to identify target cost
• Try to close cost gap.
ADVANCED COSTING METHODS
ENVIRONMENTAL ACCOUNTING
• Discuss the issues business face in the management of environmental costs
• Describe the different methods a business may use to account for its environmental costs
LIFE-CYCLE COSTING
• Costs vary throughout the product life–cycle (PLC)
• Need to consider the whole of the PLC when assessing performance.

Test your understanding answers

Test your understanding 1

(a) **Traditional absorption costing**

Budgeted direct labour hours (24,000 × 1.0) + (24,000 × 1.5)		60,000
Budgeted overhead costs		$432,000
Recovery rate per direct labour hour		$7.20
	Plus	**Doubleplus**
	$	$
Direct costs	12.00	24.00
Production overhead	7.20	10.80
Full production cost	19.20	34.80

(b) **ABC**

Workings

	Plus	Doubleplus	Total
Batches	12	240	252
Setups	12	720	732
Special parts	24,000	96,000	120,000
Orders	10	140	150
Direct labour hours	24,000	36,000	60,000

Cost driver rates

Setup costs	$73,200/732	$100 per setup
Special parts handling	$60,000/120,000	$0.50 per part
Order handling	$19,800/150	$132 per order
Materials handling	$63,000/252	$250 per batch
Other overheads	$216,000/60,000	$3.60 per hour

	Plus	Doubleplus	Total
	$	$	$
Setup costs	1,200	72,000	73,200
Special parts handling costs	12,000	48,000	60,000
Order handling costs	1,320	18,480	19,800
Materials handling costs	3,000	60,000	63,000
Other overheads	86,400	129,600	216,000
	103,920	328,080	432,000
Number of units	24,000	24,000	
	$	$	
Direct cost	12.00	24.00	
Overhead cost per unit	4.33	13.67	
Full cost	16.33	37.67	

Note: In the example above the full production costs were:

	Plus	Doubleplus
Using traditional absorption costing	$19.20	$34.80
Using ABC	$16.33	$37.67
Assume the selling prices are	$25.00	$40.00
Using absorption costing sales margins are	23.2%	13.0%
ABC sales margins are	34.7%	5.8%

(c) **The reasons for the difference in the production cost per unit between the two methods**

- The allocation of overheads under absorption costing was unfair. This method assumed that all of the overheads were driven by labour hours and, as a result, the Double Plus received 1.5 times the production overhead of the Plus.
- However, this method of absorption is not appropriate. The overheads are in fact driven by a number of different factors. There are five activity costs, each one has its own cost driver. By taking this into account we end up with a much more accurate production overhead cost per unit.

- Using ABC, the cost per unit of a Double Plus is significantly higher. This is because the Double Plus is a much more complex product than the Plus. For example, there are 140 orders for the Double Plus but only 10 for the Plus and there are 4 special parts for the Double Plus compared to only one for the Plus. As a result of this complexity, the Double Plus has received more than three times the overhead of the Plus.
- This accurate allocation is important because the production overhead is a large proportion of the overall cost.

(d) **The implications of using ABC**

- Pricing – pricing decisions will be improved because the price will be based on more accurate cost data.
- Decision making – this should also be improved. For example, research, production and sales effort can be directed towards the most profitable products.
- Performance management – should be improved. ABC can be used as the basis of budgeting and forward planning. The more realistic overhead should result in more accurate budgets and should improve the process of performance management. In addition, an improved understanding of what drives the overhead costs should result in steps being taken to reduce the overhead costs and hence an improvement in performance.
- Sales strategy – this should be more soundly based. For example, target customers with products that appeared unprofitable under absorption costing but are actually profitable, and vice versa.

Example 1 – Theory of constraints

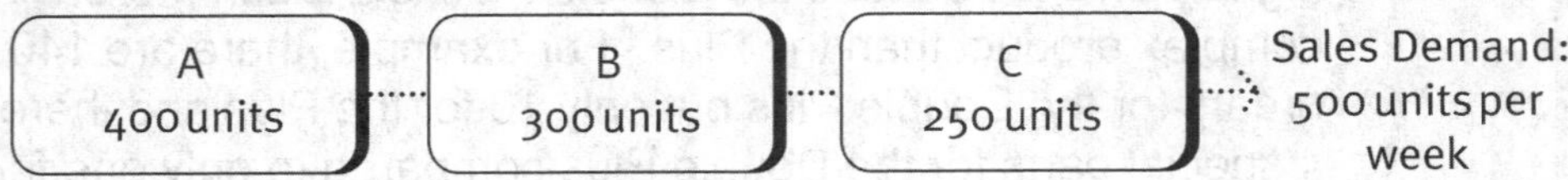

We can see from the above diagram that the bottleneck is at 'C', the slowest operation. The best course of action would be to maximise sales by releasing the bottleneck in Process C.

	A	*B*	*C*	*Demand*
Current Capacity per week	400	300	250*	500
Buy C – Capacity per week	400	300*	550	500
Buy C & B – Capacity per week	400*	600	550	500
Buy C, B, & A – Capacity per week	550	600	550	500*

* = Bottleneck

Financial viability

First, buy additional machine for 'C', and increase capacity by 300

Additional sales = 50

	$000
Benefit = 50 additional sales units × $25,000	1,250
Increase in costs	2,000
Net cost	750

Secondly, buy additional machine for 'B' and increase capacity by 300 units. This removes a second bottleneck at 'B'.

Additional sales from current position = 150

	$000
Benefit = 150 × $25,000	3,750
Cumulative costs ($2m + $1.5m)	3,500
Net benefit	250

Buy then an additional machine for A

Additional sales from current position = 250

	$000
Benefit = 250 × $25,000	6,250
Cumulative costs ($2m +$1.5m +$1m)	4,500
Net benefit	1,750

The company will benefit by $1,750,000 by investing in all three machines.

Test your understanding 2

Return per factory hour = ($85 – $42.50)/1.5 hours = $28.33

Cost per factory hour = $8,000/(10 × 40 hours) = $20

TPAR = $28.33/$20 = 1.4165

Test your understanding 3

(a)

Step 1: Determine the bottleneck constraint.

The bottleneck resource is machine time. 400 machine hours available each week = 24,000 machine minutes.

Step 2: Calculate the throughput per unit for each product.

	A	**B**	**C**	**D**
	$	$	$	$
Sales price	1.40	0.80	1.20	2.80
Materials cost	0.60	0.30	0.60	1.00
Throughput/unit	0.80	0.50	0.60	1.80

Step 3: Calculate the throughput per machine minute

Machine time per unit	5 minutes	2 minutes	3 minutes	6 minutes
Throughput per minute	$0.16	$0.25	$0.20	$0.30

Step 4: Rank

Rank	4th	2nd	3rd	1st

Step 5: Allocate resources using this ranking and answer the question.

The profit-maximising weekly output and sales volumes are as follows.

Product	Units	Machine minutes	Throughput per unit	Total throughout
			$	$
D	1,500	9,000	1.80	2,700
B	2,000	4,000	0.50	1,000
C	2,500	7,500	0.60	1,500
		20,500		
A (balance)	700	3,500	0.80	560
		24,000		5,760
Operating expenses				5,440
Profit				320

(b) Throughput per machine hour: $5,760/400 hours = $14.40

Cost (operating expenses) per machine hour: $5,440/400 hours = $13.60.

TPAR: $14.40/$13.60 = 1.059.

Objective Test Case Question – CBF Throughput Accounting

(1) **B**

Statement (1) is correct: The Theory of Constraints is focused on identifying bottlenecks in a process, and how to manage that bottleneck.

Statement (2) is not correct: the process is not complete once the bottleneck has been overcome. In fact, it is an ongoing process of improvement, as once the bottleneck has been elevated, it is probable that another bottleneck will appear, and the process will continue.

Statement (3) is correct. Statement (4) is not correct: some limiting factors, particularly those external to the organisation, may be out of the organisation's control.

(2) **C**

First, we establish the bottleneck:

The 'Assembly' hours needed for maximum production are 143.75. This is less than the 150 hours available. The 'Quality Control' hours needed for maximum production are 178.33 , which is greater than the 170 hours available. So, 'quality control hours' is the limiting resource/bottleneck. The 'Packaging' hours needed for maximum production are 234.17. This is less than the 250 hours available.

Then, we calculate the throughput per unit:

	Alpha	**Beta**	**Gamma**
Sales price per unit	\$2.00	\$2.25	\$1.75
Direct materials cost per unit	\$0.50	\$0.81	\$0.35
Throughput per unit	\$1.50	\$1.44	\$1.40

Then, we calculate the throughput per machine hour:

	Alpha	**Beta**	**Gamma**
Throughput per unit	\$1.50	\$1.44	\$1.40
Machine time per unit – quality control	3 minutes	4 minutes	2 minutes
Throughput per minute	\$0.50	\$0.36	\$0.70

Then, we rank our products:

	Alpha	Beta	Gamma
Rank	2	3	1

Allocate resources

	Units made	Quality Control time taken (minutes)	Quality Control time left (minutes)
Make Gamma first	850	1,700	8,500
Then Alpha	1,000	3,000	5,500
Finally Beta	1,375	5,500	

(3) **A**

Total throughput = 1,500 × 1.5 + 2,460 × 1.44 + 900 × 1.4 = $7052.40

Throughput per machine hour = $7052.40/(250 × 1.4) = $20.15

Cost per machine hour = $4,000 × 1.3/350 = $14.86

TPAR = 20.15/14.86 = 1.36

Option B uses profit to calculate the throughput per machine hour i.e. [($7,052.40 – $5,200)/350]/14.86 = 0.356. Option C does not increase the operating expenses [(7,052.40/350)/(4,000/350)] = 1.76. Option D uses profit and do not increase the operating expenses i.e. (1,852.40/350)/11.43 = 0.46

(4) **B**

Assembly is not a binding constraint, so increasing the capacity would not increase output. We are already making all we can of Beta, so increasing demand will not increase throughput. Despite labour having greater productivity, the packaging machine can do no more work, so no more units can be made.

(5) **B**

Test your understanding 4

Your answer may include:

- Simplification of the production process allowing cheaper unskilled labour to be used in place of more highly paid skilled labour.
- Using plastics instead of metal for components.
- Using less packaging – e.g. expensive boxes replaced with plastic sheaths.
- Sharing components between models can result in economies of scale. (This is widely used in the car industry and has helped to reduce costs dramatically.)
- Reduce stockholding costs through the introduction of a just-in-time system.
- Using cheaper overseas labour.

Test your understanding 5

Lifecycle costs		$ million
Total R&D costs		20.0
Total Marketing costs	(5 + 4 + 3 + 0.9)	12.9
Total Production costs	(1 × 1 + 5 × 0.9 + 10 × 0.8 + 4 × 0.9)	17.1
Total Lifecycle costs		50.0
Total production (units)	(1 + 5 + 10 + 4)	20 million
Cost per unit	(50 ÷ 20)	$2.50

Comment

- The cost was calculated at $11 per unit during the launch phase. Based on this cost, the accountant was right to be concerned about the launch price being set at $8 per unit.
- However, looking at the whole life-cycle the marketing manager's proposal seems more reasonable.
- The average cost per unit over the entire life of the product is only $2.50 per unit. Therefore, a starting price of $8 per unit would seem reasonable and would result in a profit of $5.50 per unit.

chapter

3

Cost volume profit analysis

Chapter learning objectives

Upon completion of this chapter you will be able to:

- explain the nature of CVP analysis
- calculate and interpret break-even point and margin of safety
- calculate the contribution to sales ratio, in single and multi-product situations, and demonstrate an understanding of its use
- calculate target profit or revenue in single and multi-product situations, and demonstrate an understanding of its use
- prepare break even charts and profit volume charts and interpret the information contained within each, including multi-product situations
- discuss the limitations of CVP analysis for planning and decision making.

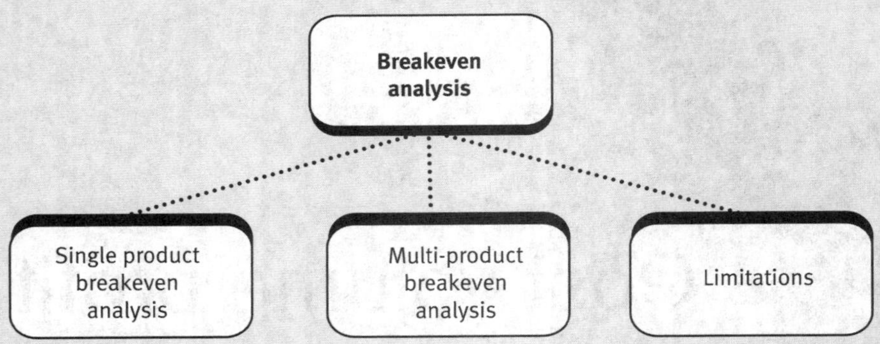

1 Break-even analysis

Also known as CVP analysis, or cost-volume-profit analysis. Break-even analysis is the study of the effects on future profit of changes in fixed cost, variable cost, sales price, quantity and mix.

CVP analysis is a particular example of *'what if?'* analysis. A business sets a budget based upon various assumptions about revenues, costs, product mixes and overall volumes. CVP analysis considers the impact on the budgeted profit of changes in these various factors.

2 Single product break-even analysis

The breakeven point is the level of activity at which there is neither profit, nor loss.

Finding the breakeven point is simple. In the following illustration, each unit sells for $200 and contributes $160 towards covering fixed costs of $600,000:

Selling price per unit	$200
Less: Variable cost per unit	($40)
Contribution per unit	$160
Total fixed costs	$600,000
Profit	?

In order to breakeven, we need to cover our fixed costs. Here, the breakeven point = Total fixed costs divided by the unit contribution: $600,000/$160 = 3,750 units.

A further example will be used to illustrate the basic formulae and calculations.

Test your understanding 1 – Break-even analysis

The following data relate to Product PQ:

Selling price	£25 per unit
Variable cost	£20 per unit

Fixed costs are £50,000.

(a) Calculate the number of units that must be made and sold in order to break even.

$$\text{Break-even point in units} = \frac{\text{Fixed cost}}{\text{Contribution per unit}}$$

(b) Calculate the level of activity that is required to generate a profit of £40,000.

$$\text{Level of activity to earn a required profit} = \frac{\text{Required profit + Fixed costs}}{\text{Contribution per unit}}$$

(c) The company budgets to sell 13,000 units of Product PQ.

Calculate the margin of safety.

The margin of safety is the difference between the budgeted level of activity and the break-even level of activity. It may be expressed in terms of units, sales value or as a percentage of the original budget.

(d) Calculate the contribution/sales ratio for Product PQ.

The C/S ratio is normally expressed as a percentage. It is constant at all levels of activity. The C/S ratio reveals the amount of contribution that is earned for every £1 worth of sales revenue.

$$\text{C/S ratio} = \frac{\text{Contribution}}{\text{Sales}}$$

(e) Calculate the break-even point again, this time expressed in terms of sales revenue.

$$\text{Breakeven point in sales revenue} = \frac{\text{Fixed costs}}{\text{C/S ratio}}$$

(f) Calculate the sales revenue that is required to generate a profit of £40,000.

$$\text{Sales revenue to earn a required profit} = \frac{\text{Required profit + Fixed costs}}{\text{C/S ratio}}$$

3 Drawing a basic breakeven chart

A basic breakeven chart records costs and revenues on the vertical axis (y) and the level of activity on the horizontal axis (x). Lines are drawn on the chart to represent costs and sales revenue.

The breakeven point can be read off where the total sales revenue line cuts the total cost line. We will use a basic example to demonstrate how to draw a breakeven chart. The data is:

Selling price	$50 per unit
Variable cost	$30 per unit
Fixed costs	$20,000 per month
Forecast sales	1,700 units per month

The completed graph is shown below:

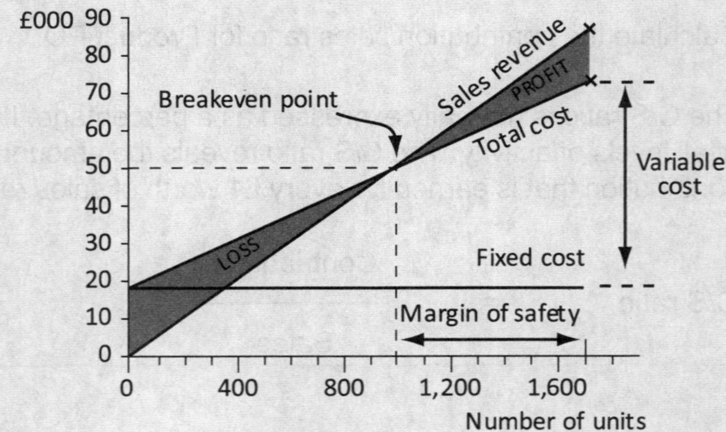

Learning to draw a chart to scale will provide a firm foundation for your understanding of breakeven charts. To give yourself some practice, it would be a good idea to follow the step-by-step guide which follows to produce your own chart on a piece of graph paper.

- **Step 1:** *Select appropriate scales for the axes and draw and label them.* Your graph should fill as much of the page as possible. This will make it clearer and easier to read. You can make sure that you do this by putting the extremes of the axes right at the end of the available space.

The furthest point on the vertical axis will be the monthly sales revenue, that is,

1,700 units × $50 = $ 85,000

The furthest point on the horizontal axis will be monthly sales volume of 1,700 units.

Make sure that you do not need to read data for volumes higher than 1,700 units before you set these extremes for your scales.

- **Step 2:** *Draw the fixed cost line and label it.* This will be a straight line parallel to the horizontal axis at the $20,000 level.

The $20,000 fixed costs are incurred in the short term even with zero activity.

- **Step 3:** *Draw the total cost line and label it.* The best way to do this is to calculate the total costs for the maximum sales level, which is 1,700 units in our example. Mark this point on the graph and join it to the cost incurred at zero activity, that is, $20,000.

	$
Variable costs for 1,700 units (1,700 × $30)	51,000
Fixed costs	20,000
Total cost for 1,700 units	71,000

- **Step 4:** *Draw the revenue line and label it.* Once again, the best way is to plot the extreme points. The revenue at maximum activity in our example is 1,700 × $50 = $85,000. This point can be joined to the origin, since at zero activity there will be no sales revenue.

- **Step 5:** *Mark any required information on the chart and read off solutions as required*. You can check that your chart is accurate by reading off the breakeven point and then check this against the calculation for breakeven:

$$\textbf{Breakeven point in units} = \frac{\textbf{Fixed costs}}{\textbf{Contribution per unit}}$$

= 20,000/(50–30) = **1,000 units.**

The margin of safety can be seen as the area to the right of the breakeven point up to the forecast sales level of 1,700. The margin of safety is the difference the budgeted level of activity (1,700 units), and the breakeven level of activity (1,000 units): a margin of safety of 700 units.

The margin of safety may also be expressed as a percentage of the original budget:

$$\textbf{Margin of safety (\%)} = \frac{\textbf{Budgeted sales – Breakeven sales}}{\textbf{Budgeted sales}} \times \textbf{100\%}$$

$$\textbf{Margin of safety (as a \%)} = \frac{\textbf{1,700 units – 1,000 units}}{\textbf{1,700 units}} \times \textbf{100\%}$$

Margin of safety (as a %) = 41%

The contribution breakeven chart

One of the problems with the conventional or basic breakeven chart is that it is not possible to read contribution directly from the chart. A contribution breakeven chart is based on the same principles but it shows the variable cost line instead of the fixed cost line. The same lines for total cost and sales revenue are shown so the breakeven point and profit can be read off in the same way as with a conventional chart. However, it is also possible also to read the contribution for any level of activity.

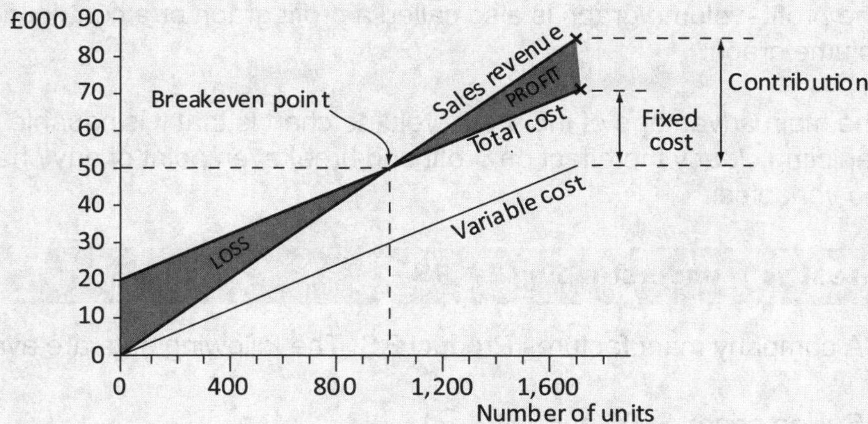

Using the same basic example as for the conventional chart, the total variable cost for an output of 1,700 units is 1,700 x $30 = $51,000. This point can be joined to the origin since the variable cost is nil at zero activity.

The contribution can be read as the difference between the sales revenue line and the variable cost line.

This form of presentation might be used when it is desirable to highlight the importance of contribution and to focus attention on the variable costs.

Ensure you are familiar with these charts and that you are able to identify all the component parts.

4 The profit–volume chart

Another form of breakeven chart is the profit–volume chart. This chart plots a single line depicting the profit or loss at each level of activity. The breakeven point is where this line cuts the horizontal axis. A profit–volume graph for our example is shown below.

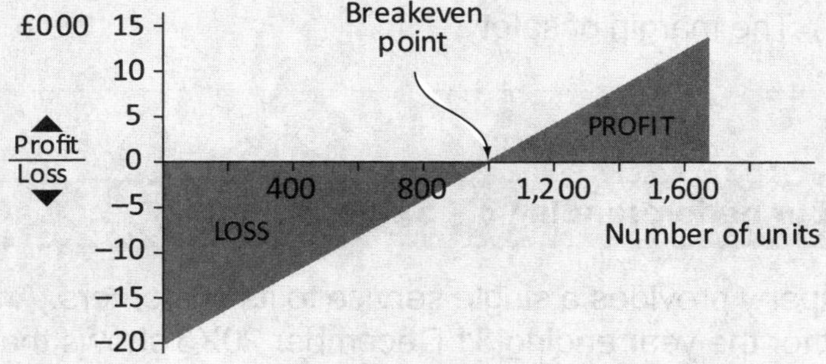

The vertical axis shows profits and losses and the horizontal axis is drawn at zero profit or loss.

At zero activity the loss is equal to $20,000, that is, the amount of fixed costs. The second point used to draw the line could be the calculated breakeven point or the calculated profit for sales of 1,700 units.

The profit–volume graph is also called a profit graph or a contribution–volume graph.

The main advantage of the profit–volume chart is that it is capable of depicting clearly the effect on profit and breakeven point of any changes in the variables.

Test your understanding 2 – RS

A company manufactures Product RS. The following data are available:

Selling price: $100 per unit
Variable cost: $60 per unit.

Fixed costs are $250,000. The company budgets to produce 12,000 units in the next period.

Required:

(a) Scenario I – Calculate:
   (i) The break-even point (expressed in units and $ of revenue).
   (ii) The level of activity required to generate a profit of $90,000 (expressed in units).
   (iii) The margin of safety as a percentage.

(b) Using graph paper, draw a profit-volume chart for scenario I.

(c) Scenario II – Using the graph drawn in (b), illustrate and explain the impact of a change in selling price to $120 per unit, on:
   (i) The break-even point (expressed in units and $ of revenue)
   (ii) The level of activity required to generate a profit of $90,000 (expressed in units)
   (iii) The margin of safety.

Test your understanding 3 – Single product

R Company provides a single service to its customers. An analysis of its budget for the year ending 31 December 20X5 shows that, in Period 3, when the budgeted activity was 6,570 service units with a sales value of $72 each, the margin of safety was 21.015%.

The budgeted contribution to sales ratio of the service is 35%.

Required:

Calculate the budgeted fixed costs in period 3.

5 Multi-product break-even analysis

The basic breakeven model can be used satisfactorily for a business operation with only one product. However, most companies sell a range of different products, and the model has to be adapted when one is considering a business operation with several products.

CVP Analysis assumes that, if a range of products is sold, sales will be in accordance with a **pre-determined sales mix**.

When a pre-determined sales mix is used, it can be depicted in the CVP Analysis by assuming average revenues and average variable costs for the given sales mix.

However, the assumption has to be made that the sales mix remains **constant**. This is defined as the relative proportion of each product's sale to total sales. It could be expressed as a ratio such as 2:3:5, or as a percentage as 20%, 30%, 50%.

The calculation of breakeven point in a multi-product firm follows the same pattern as in a single product firm. While the numerator will be the same fixed costs, the denominator now will be the **weighted average contribution margin**.

In multi-product situations, a weighted average C/S ratio is calculated by using the formula:

$$\textbf{Weighted average C/S ratio} = \frac{\textbf{Total contribution}}{\textbf{Total revenue}}$$

The weighted average C/S ratio is useful in its own right, as it tells us what percentage each $ of sales revenue contributes towards fixed costs; it is also invaluable in helping us to quickly calculate the breakeven point in sales revenue:

$$\textbf{Breakeven revenue} = \frac{\textbf{Fixed costs}}{\textbf{Weighted average C/S ratio}}$$

Weighted average contribution to sales ratio

Company A produces Product X and Product Y. Fixed overhead costs amount to $200,000 every year. The following budgeted information is available for both products for next year:

	Product X	Product Y
Sales price	$50	$60
Variable cost	$30	$45
Contribution per unit	$20	$15
Budgeted sales (in units)	20,000	10,000

In order to calculate the breakeven revenue for the next year, using the budgeted sales mix, we need the weighted average C/S ratio as follows:

$$\text{Weighted average C/S ratio} = \frac{\text{Total contribution}}{\text{Total revenue}}$$

$$\text{Weighted average C/S ratio} = \frac{(20{,}000 \times \$20) + (\$10{,}000 \times \$15)}{(20{,}000 \times \$50) + (\$10{,}000 \times \$60)}$$

$$\text{Weighted average C/S ratio} = 34.375\%$$

The breakeven revenue can now be calculated this way for company A:

$$\text{Breakeven revenue} = \frac{\text{Fixed costs}}{\text{Weighted average C/S ratio}}$$

$$\text{Breakeven revenue} = \frac{\$200{,}000}{0.34375}$$

$$\text{Breakeven revenue} = \$581{,}819$$

Calculations in the illustration above provide only estimated information because they assume that products X and Y are sold in a constant mix of 2X to 1Y. In reality, this constant mix is unlikely to exist and, at times, more Y may be sold than X. Such changes in the mix throughout a period, even if the overall mix for the period is 2:1, will lead to the actual breakeven point being different than anticipated.

6 Establishing a target profit for multiple products

The approach is the same as in single product situations, but the weighted average contribution to sales ratio is now used so that:

$$\textbf{Target profit} = \frac{\textbf{Fixed costs + required profit}}{\textbf{Weighted average C/S ratio}}$$

Target profit in Company A

To achieve a target profit of $300,000 in Company A:

Sales revenue required for profit of $300,000 = (Fixed costs + required profit) / W.A. C/S ratio

Sales revenue required for profit of $300,000 = ($200,000 + $300,000) / 0.34375

Sales revenue required for profit of $300,000 = $1,454,545

7 Margin of safety calculations

The basic breakeven model for calculating the margin of safety can be adapted to multi-product environments. Calculating the margin of safety for multiple products is exactly the same as for single products, but we use the standard mix. The easiest way to see how it's done is to look at an example below:

Illustration

Murray Ltd produces and sells two types of sports equipment items for children, balls (in batches) and miniature racquets.

A batch of balls sells for $8 and has a variable cost of $5. Racquets sell for $4 per unit and have a unit variable cost of $2.60.

For every 2 batches of balls sold, one racquet is sold. Murray budgeted fixed costs are $407,000 per period. Budgeted sales revenue for next period is $1,250,000 in the standard mix.

To calculate the margin of safety, the following steps must be followed:

Step 1 – Calculate contribution per unit:

	Balls	Racquets
	$ per batch	$ per unit
Selling price	$8	$4
Variable cost	$5	$2.60
Contribution	$3	$1.40

Step 2 – Calculate contribution per mix:

($3 × 2 batches) + ($1.40 × 1 racquet) =$7.40

Step 3 – Calculate the breakeven point in terms of the number of mixes:

Breakeven point = Fixed costs/Contribution per mix

Breakeven point = $407,000/$7.40 = 55,000 mixes

Step 4 – Calculate the breakeven point in terms of the units of the products:

55,000 mixes × 2 = 110,000 balls

55,000 mixes × 1 = 55,000 racquets

Step 5 – Calculate the breakeven point in terms of revenue

($8 × 110,000 batches) + ($4 × 55,000 racquets) =$1,100,000

Step 6 – Calculate the margin of safety:

Budgeted sales – breakeven sales =$1,250,000 – $1,100,000 = $150,000

Or, as a percentage, ($1,250,000 – $1,100,000)/$1,250,000 = 12%

8 The multi-product profit-volume graph – Step-by-step

In a multi-product environment, two lines must be shown on the profit-volume graph:

(1) One **straight** line, where a constant mix between the products is assumed

(2) One **bow shaped** line, to see how the individual products contribute to profit rather than as a constant mix. It is assumed that the company sells its most profitable product first and then its next most profitable product, and so on.

Step 1: Calculate the C/S ratio of each product being sold, and rank the products in order of profitability (in other words, products are ranked in decreasing order based on the size of their C/S ratio with the highest C/S ratio product ranked first.)

Step 2: Draw the graph, showing cumulative sales on the x-axis. The products are shown individually on a graph from left to right, in order of the size of their C/S ratio (and therefore based on the Step 1 ranking above.) For example, if we assume 3 products X, Y and Z, then the following graph could be drawn , with 'V' representing the total sales. At an output of 0, the profit earned will amount to the company's fixed costs, represented by point *k* on the chart.

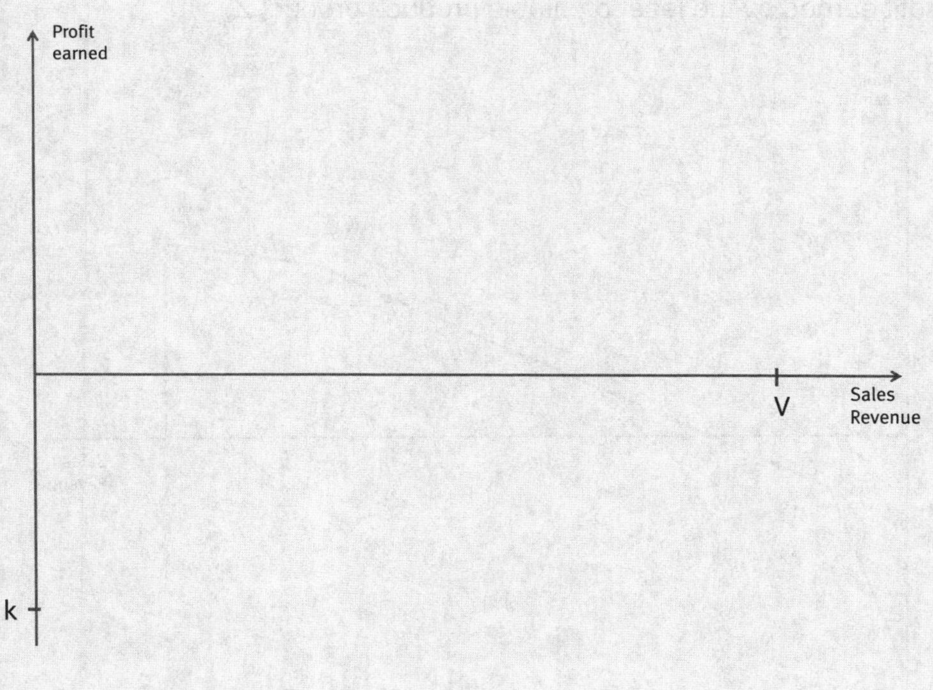

Step 3: Draw the line *km*, that represents the profit earned by product X – the slope of the line is determined by the contribution per unit earned on sales of that product.

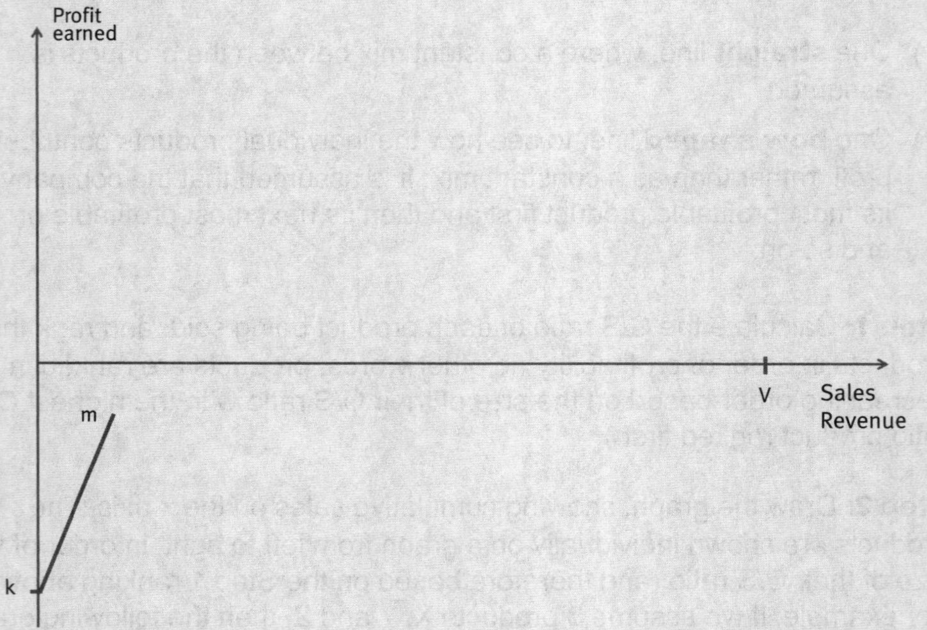

Step 4: Draw the line *mn*, that represents the profit earned by product y, which has a lower contribution per unit than product X. The line *nj* is the profit earned by the least profitable product, product Z.

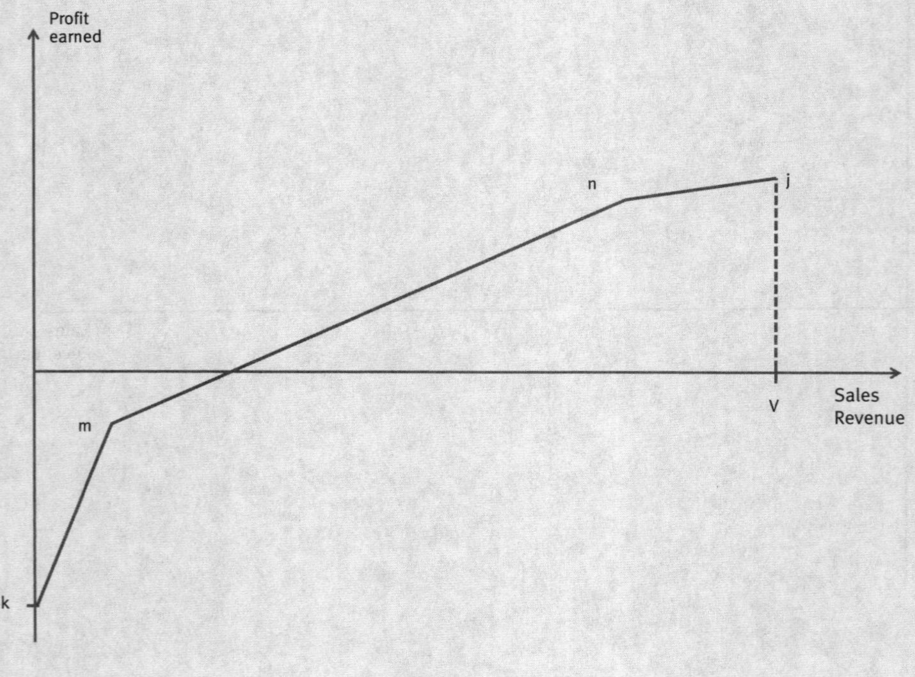

Step 5: Draw the line joining points *k* and *j*: it reflects the average profitability of the three products, and each point on that line represents the profit earned for the associated output, assuming that the three products are sold in the standard product mix, i.e. the mix implied in the construction of the chart. Accordingly, the indicated breakeven point only applies if the products are sold in the standard product mix.

It can also be seen that breakeven can also occur at lower levels of output, provided the proportions of the products are changed. For example, the point B where the line *kmnj* crosses the horizontal axis indicates a possible breakeven point.

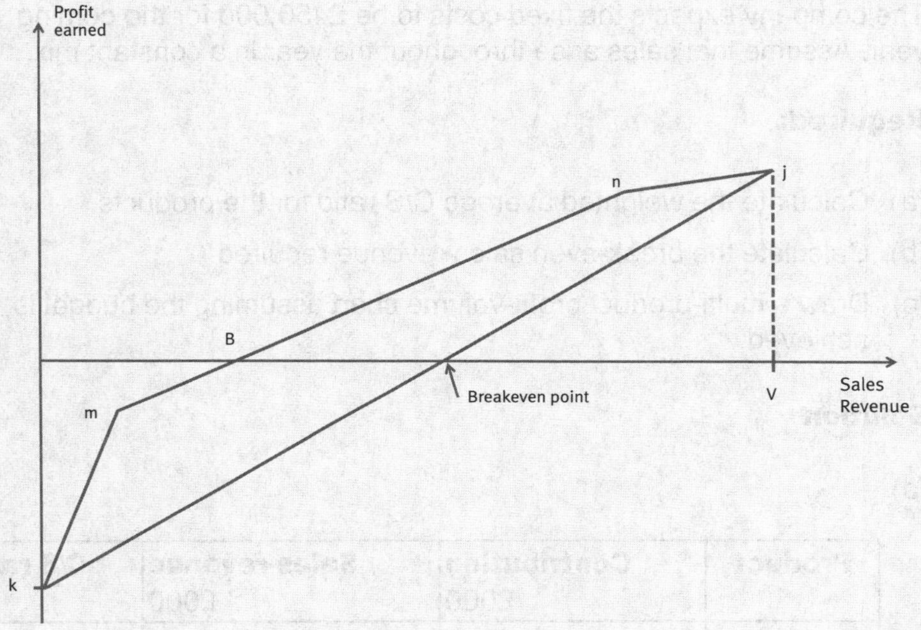

Plotting products individually may present the following **benefits** in a decision-making process:

- In order to improve overall profitability, it may be worth considering an increase in the sales of the product with the highest C/S ratio, even if it means as decrease in the least profitable product.
- It helps managers decide which products should be continued or abandoned.
- It also helps management focus on the price of products and whether some prices should be raised in order to improve the individual product's C/S ratio.
- Last, it clarifies what changes in selling prices and sales volumes will have on breakeven points and profits.

Multi-product break even graph

BJS Ltd produces and sells the following three products:

Product	X	Y	Z
Selling price per unit	£16	£20	£10
Variable cost per unit	£5	£15	£7
Contribution per unit	£11	£5	£3
Budgeted sales volume	50,000 units	10,000 units	100,000 units

The company expects the fixed costs to be £450,000 for the coming year. Assume that sales arise throughout the year in a constant mix.

Required:

(a) Calculate the weighted average C/S ratio for the products.

(b) Calculate the break-even sales revenue required.

(c) Draw a multi-product profit-volume chart assuming the budget is achieved.

Solution

(a)

Product	Contribution £000	Sales revenue £000	C/S ratio
X	550	800	0.6875
Y	50	200	0.25
Z	300	1,000	0.30
Total	900	2,000	

$$\text{Weighted average contribution to sales ratio} = \frac{\text{Total contribution}}{\text{Total sales}}$$

$$= \frac{£900,000}{£2,000,000}$$

$$= 0.45 \text{ or } 45\%$$

(b)

$$\text{Breakeven sales revenue required} = \frac{\text{Fixed costs}}{\text{C/S ratio}}$$

$$= \frac{£450,000}{45\%}$$

$$= £1,000,000$$

(c) **Break even graph**

Firstly, products must be ranked according to their C/S ratios. This gives X > Z > Y. Then assume that the products are sold in the order of highest C/S ratio first to generate co-ordinates to plot on the graph.

The first point on the graph is where sales volume = 0

- Cumulative Revenue = 0
- Profit/loss = loss equal to the fixed costs of £450k.
- Co-ordinates (in £000s) = (0, – 450)

To get the next point we include the sales of 50,000 units of product X.

- Total cumulative revenue = 50,000 × 16 = 800k
- Additional contribution = 50,000 × 11 = 550k
- Net cumulative profit = –450 + 550 = +100k
- Co-ordinates = (800, 100)

Next we sell 100,000 units of product Z

- Additional revenue = 100 × 10 = 1,000k
- Total cumulative revenue = 800 + 1,000 = 1,800k
- Additional contribution = 100 × 3 = 300k
- Net cumulative profit = 100 + 300 = 400k
- Co-ordinates = (1800, 400)

Finally we sell 10,000 units of product Y

- Additional revenue = 10 × 20 = 200k
- Total cumulative revenue = 1,800 + 200 = 2,000k
- Additional contribution = 10 × 5 = 50k
- Net cumulative profit = 400 + 50 = 450k
- Co-ordinates = (2000, 450)

This can be summarised in the following table:

Product	**Contribution** £000	**Cumulative Profit/(Loss)** £000	**Revenue** £000	**Cumulative revenue** £000
None	–	(450)	–	0
X	550	100	800	800
Z	300	400	1,000	1,800
Y	50	450	200	2,000

The chart is, essentially, a profit/volume chart. Cumulative profit is plotted against cumulative sales revenue. Like P/V charts for single products the line drawn starts at the fixed costs below the line.

Multi-product profit-volume chart

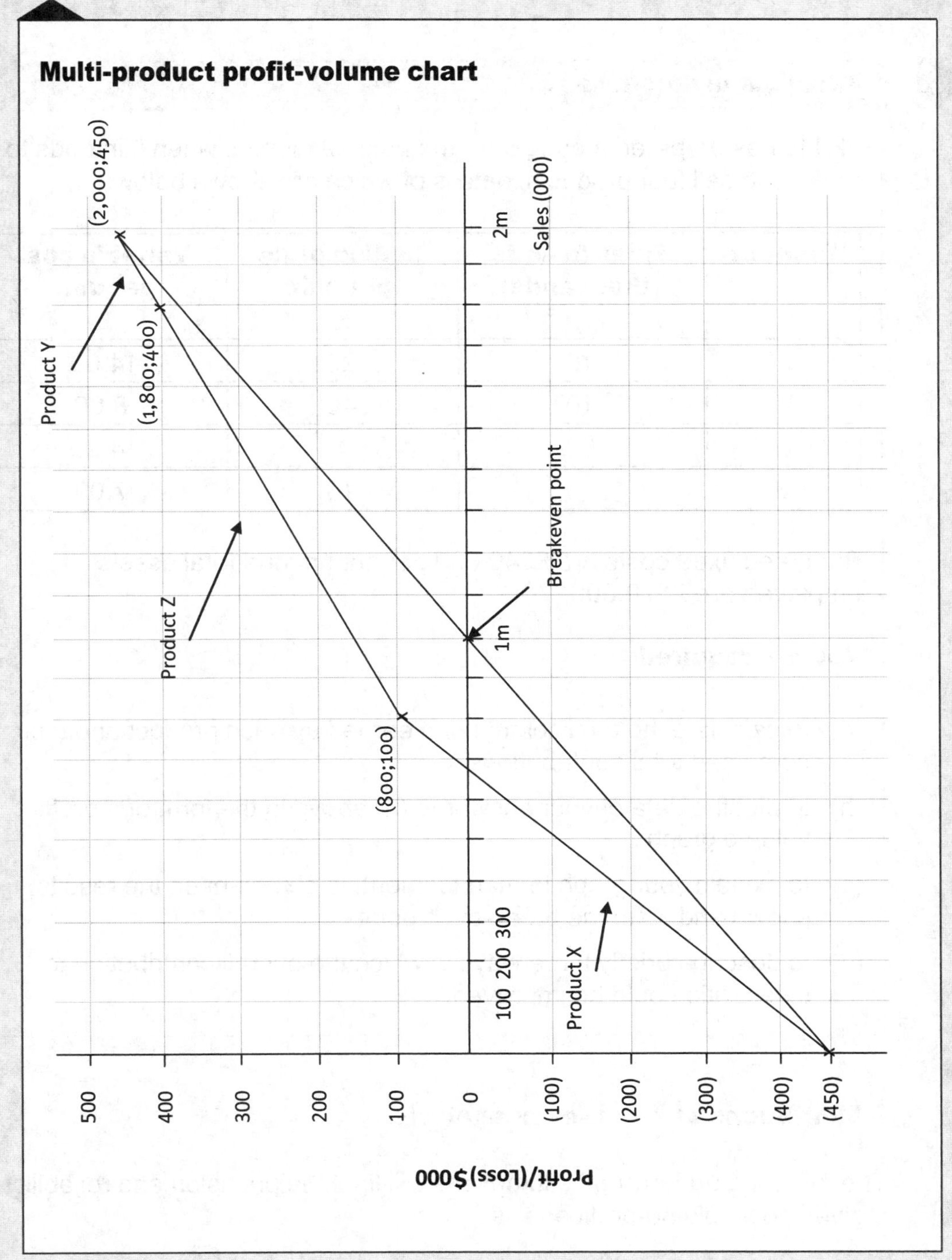

Test your understanding 4

JK Ltd has prepared a budget for the next 12 months when it intends to make and sell four products, details of which are shown below:

Product	Sales in units (thousands)	Selling price per unit £	Variable cost per unit £
J	10	20	14.00
K	10	40	8.00
L	50	4	4.20
M	20	10	7.00

Budgeted fixed costs are £240,000 per annum and total assets employed are £570,000.

You are required:

(a) to calculate the total contribution earned by each product and their combined total contributions

(b) to plot the data of your answer to (a) above in the form of a profit-volume graph

(c) to explain your graph to management, to comment on the results shown and state the break-even point

(d) to describe briefly three ways in which the overall contribution to sales ratio could be improved.

9 Limitations of break-even analysis

The following underlying assumptions will limit the precision and reliability of a given cost-volume-profit analysis.

(1) The behaviour of total cost and total revenue has been reliably determined and is linear over the relevant range.

(2) All costs can be divided into fixed and variable elements.

(3) Total fixed costs remain constant over the relevant volume range of the CVP analysis.

(4) Total variable costs are directly proportional to volume over the relevant range.

(5) Selling prices are to be unchanged.

(6) Prices of the factors of production are to be unchanged (for example, material, prices, wage rates).

(7) Efficiency and productivity are to be unchanged.

(8) The analysis either covers a single product or assumes that a given sales mix will be maintained as total volume changes.

(9) Revenue and costs are being compared on a single activity basis (for example, units produced and sold or sales value of production).

(10) Perhaps the most basic assumption of all is that volume is the only relevant factor affecting cost. Of course, other factors also affect costs and sales. Ordinary cost-volume-profit analysis is a crude oversimplification when these factors are unjustifiably ignored.

(11) The volume of production equals the volume of sales, or changes in beginning and ending inventory levels are insignificant in amount.

Test your understanding 5

H Limited manufactures and sells two products – J and K. Annual sales are expected to be in the ratio of J:1 K:3. Total annual sales are planned to be £420,000. Product J has a contribution to sales ratio of 40% whereas that of product K is 50%. Annual fixed costs are estimated to be £120,000.

Required:

What is the budgeted break-even sales value?

Test your understanding 6

PER plc sells three products. The budgeted fixed cost for the period is £648,000. The budgeted contribution to sales ratio (C/S ratio) and sales mix are as follows:

Product	C/S ratio	Mix
P	27%	30%
E	56%	20%
R	38%	50%

Required:

What is the breakeven sales revenue?

10 Chapter summary

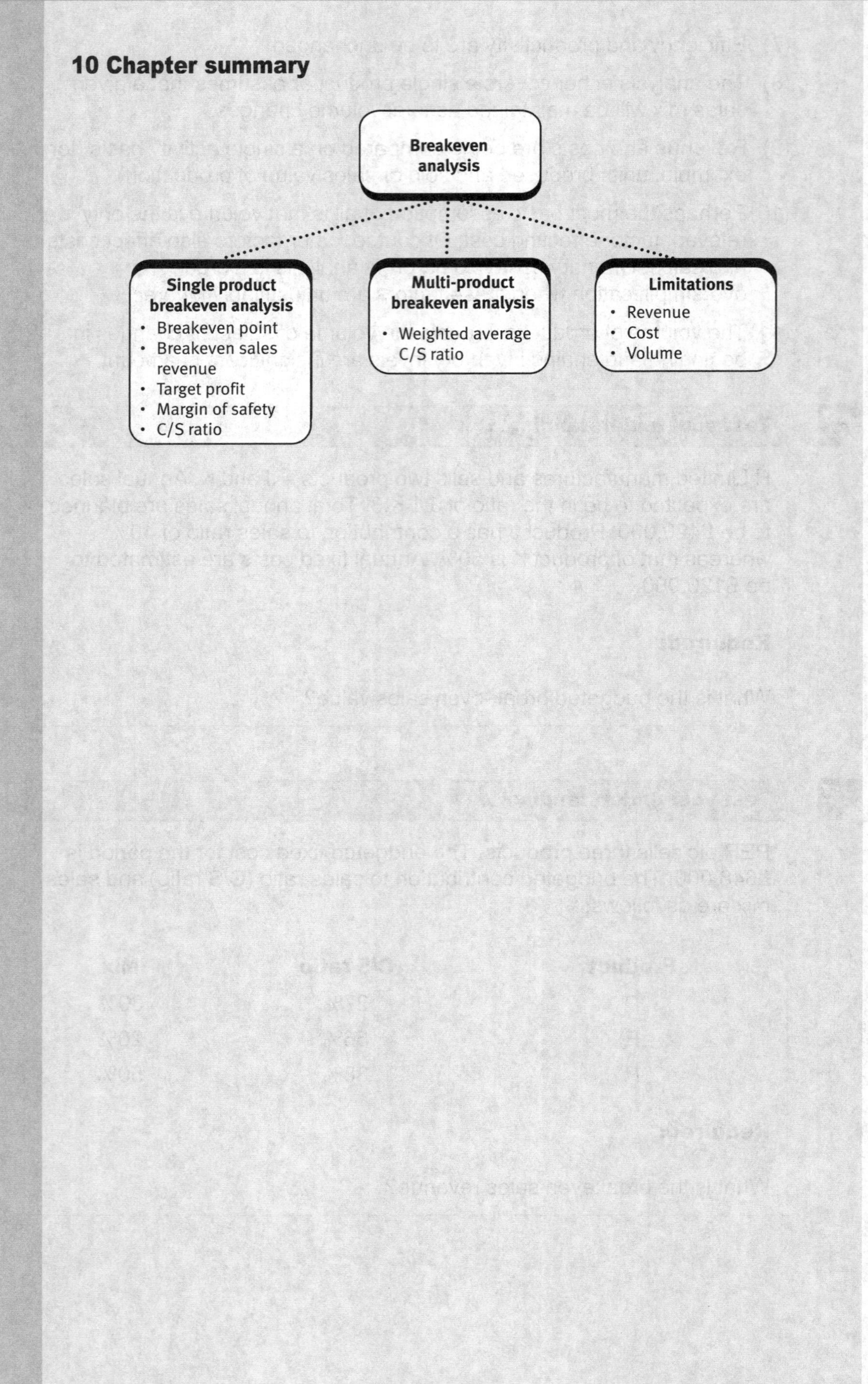

Test your understanding answers

Test your understanding 1 – Break-even analysis

(a) Contribution per unit = £25 – £20 = £5 per unit

$$\text{Break-even point in units} = \frac{\text{Fixed cost}}{\text{Contribution per unit}}$$

BEP = £50,000 ÷ £5 = 10,000 units

(b)

$$\textbf{Level of activity to earn a required profit} = \frac{\textbf{Required profit + Fixed costs}}{\textbf{Contribution per unit}}$$

Number of units = (£40,000 + £50,000) ÷ £5 = 18,000 units

(c)

Margin of safety = 13,000 – 10,000 = 3,000 units
In terms of sales revenue this is 3,000 × £25 = £75,000

$$\text{As a percentage of the budget} = \frac{3,000}{13,000} \times 100\%$$

= 23.1%

(d)

$$\textbf{C/S ratio} = \frac{\textbf{Contribution}}{\textbf{Sales}}$$

$$\text{C/S ratio} = \frac{£5}{£25}$$

C/S ratio = 20%

(e)

$$\text{Breakeven point in sales revenue} = \frac{\text{Fixed costs}}{\text{C/S ratio}}$$

BEP (in £) = £50,000 ÷ 0.20

BEP = £250,000

(f)

$$\text{Sales revenue to earn a required profit} = \frac{\text{Required profit + Fixed costs}}{\text{C/S ratio}}$$

Required sales = (£40,000 + £50,000) ÷ 0.20

i.e. **£450,000.**

Test your understanding 2 – RS

(a) **Scenario I**

(i)	Contribution per unit	= $100 – $60	= $40 per unit
	BEP (units)	= $250,000 ÷ $40	= 6,250 units
	C/S ratio	= $40/$100	= 0.40
	BEP ($ revenue)	= $250,000 ÷ 0.40	= $625,000
(ii)	Level of activity	= ($90,000 + $250,000) ÷ $40	= 8,500 units
	Level of activity	= ($90,000 + $250,000) ÷ 0.40	= $850,000
(iii)	Margin of safety	= 12,000 – 6,250	= 5,750 units
	Or expressed in $ revenue		= $575,000.

Margin of safety expressed as a % of the budget: 5,750 units/12,000 units = 48% approx.

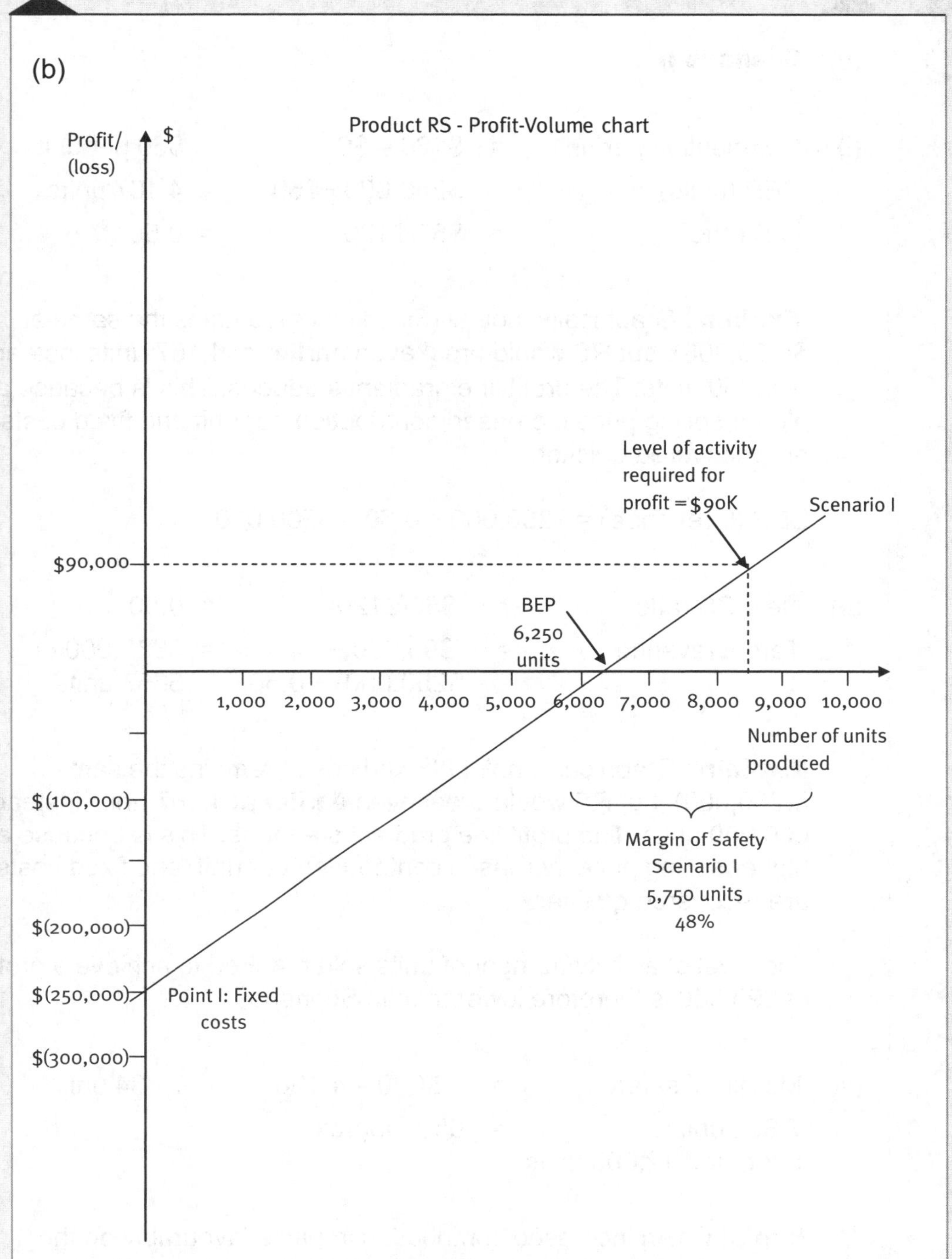

(b)
Product RS - Profit-Volume chart
Profit/ (loss)
$
Level of activity required for profit = $90K
Scenario I
$90,000
BEP 6,250 units
1,000 2,000 3,000 4,000 5,000 6,000 7,000 8,000 9,000 10,000
Number of units produced
$ (100,000)
Margin of safety Scenario I 5,750 units 48%
$(200,000)
$(250,000)
Point I: Fixed costs
$(300,000)

(c) **Scenario II**

(i)	Contribution per unit	=	$120 – $60	= $60 per unit
	BEP (units)	=	$250,000 ÷$60	= 4,167 units
	C/S ratio	=	$60/$120	= 0.50

'Explain': Graphically, point I (Fixed costs) remains the same at $(250,000), but RS would breakeven **earlier** at 4,167 units instead of 6,250 units. The profit line gradient steepens. This is because a higher selling price increased contribution per unit and fixed costs are recovered quicker.

BEP ($ revenue) = $250,000 ÷ 0.50 = $500,000

(ii)	New CS ratio	=	$60/$120	= 0.50
	Target revenue	=	($90,000 + $250,000) ÷ 0.50	= $680,000 or 5667 units

'Explain': Graphically, point I (Fixed costs) remains the same at $(250,000), but RS would breakeven **earlier** at 4,167 units instead of 6,250 units. The profit line gradient steepens. This is because a higher selling price increases contribution per unit, and fixed costs are recovered quicker.

The level of activity/number of units sold required to achieve a profit of £90,000 is therefore lower than in Scenario I.

(iii)	Margin of safety	=	12,000 – 4,166	= 7,834 units
	7,834 units ÷ budgeted 12,000 units	=	65% approx.	

'Explain' : An increased contribution impacts favourably on the margin of safety. Sales need to fall 65% short of budget before RS starts making a loss – compared with 48% in scenario I.

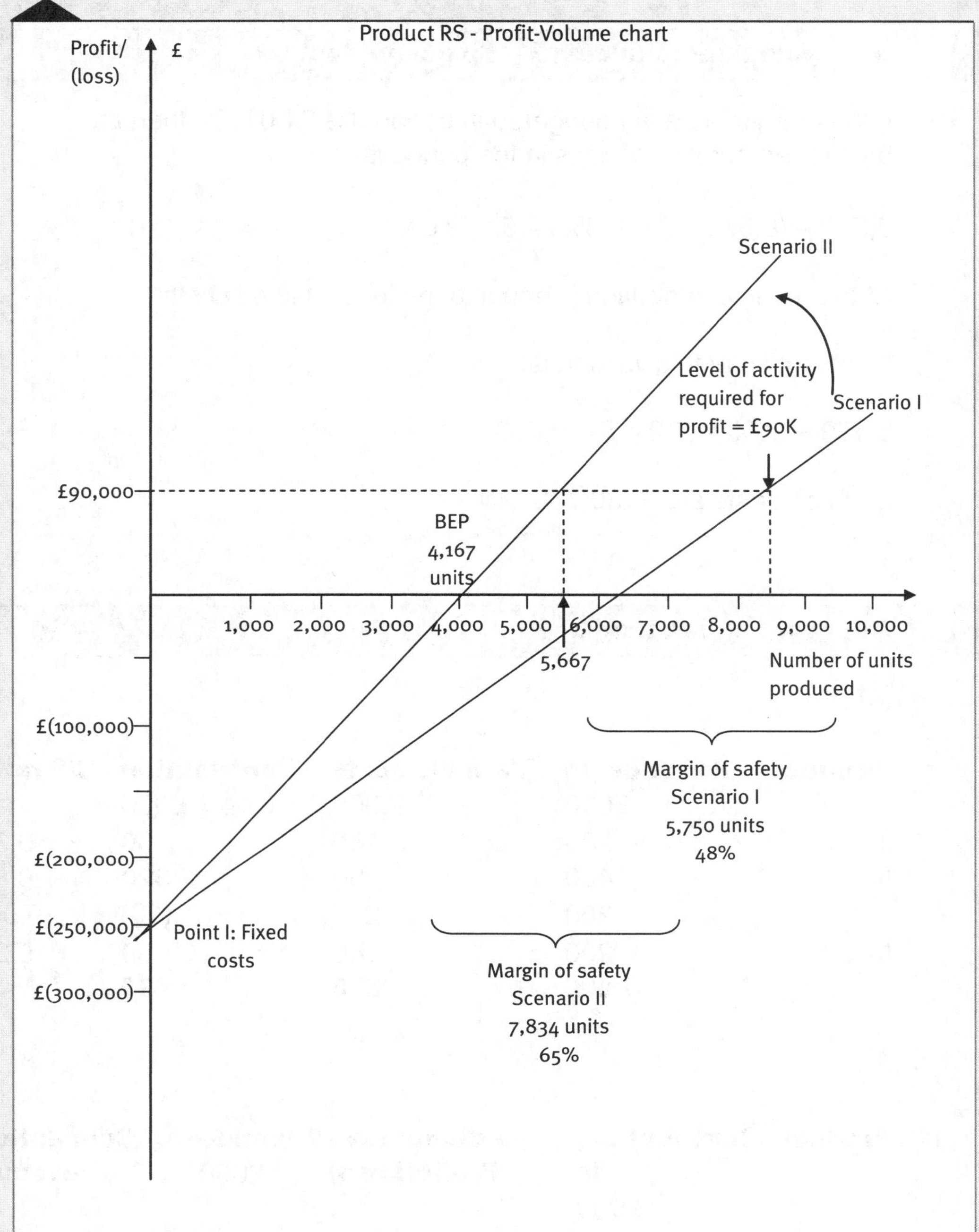

Product RS - Profit-Volume chart
Profit/ (loss)
£
Scenario II
Scenario I
Level of activity required for profit = £90K
£90,000
BEP 4,167 units
1,000 2,000 3,000 4,000 5,000 6,000 7,000 8,000 9,000 10,000
5,667
Number of units produced
£(100,000)
£(200,000)
£(250,000)
£(300,000)
Point I: Fixed costs
Margin of safety Scenario I 5,750 units 48%
Margin of safety Scenario II 7,834 units 65%

Test your understanding 3 – Single product

If the margin of safety budgeted in period 3 is 21.015%, then the breakeven number of units in the period is:

6,570 – (6,570 × 21.015%) = 5,189 units

At this level, contribution is equal to the level of fixed costs.

Contribution at this volume is:

5,189 × 35% × $72 = $130,763.

So fixed costs are $130,763.

Test your understanding 4

(a)

Product	**Revenue, in**	**Variable costs**	**Contribution**	**C/S ratio**
	£000	£000	£000	
J	200	140	60	0.30
K	400	80	320	0.80
L	200	210	(10)	(0.05)
M	200	140	60	0.30
	1,000	**570**	**430**	

(b)

Product	**Contribution, in** £000	**Cumulative Profit/(Loss)**	**Revenue** £000	**Cumulative revenue**
		(240)		0
K	320	80	400	400
J	60	140	200	600
M	60	200	200	800
L	(10)	190	200	1,000

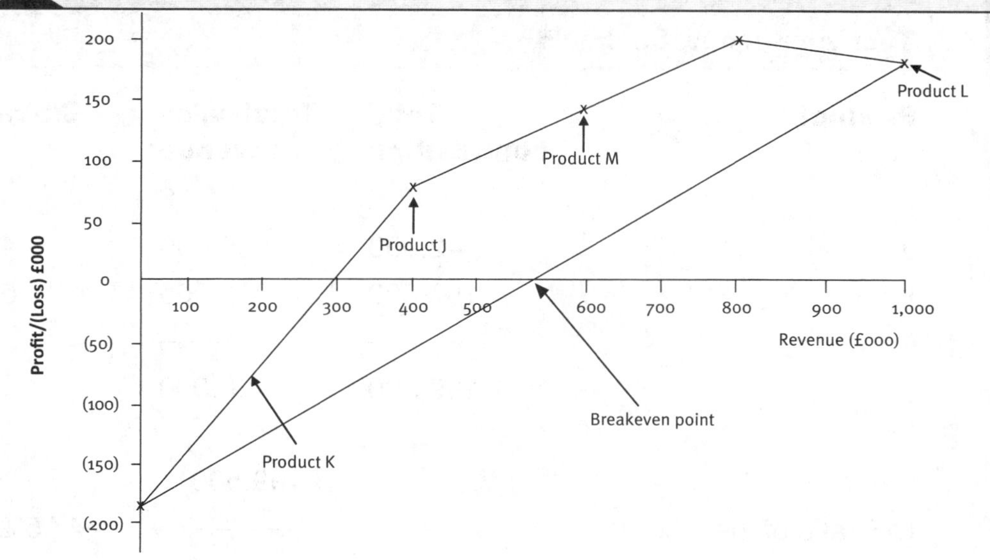

(c) The products are plotted in the order of their C/S ratios. The fixed costs of the company are £240,000. The chart reveals that if only product K is produced, the company will generate a profit of £80,000. The profit of the company is maximised at £200,000. This is achieved by producing Products K, J and M only.

If all four products are produced then JK Ltd can expect a profit of £190,000 from sales revenue of £1,000,000. If all four products are sold in the budget sales mix then the company will break even when revenue reaches £558,140. This point has been indicated on the graph. This point can also be calculated. Thus:

Average contribution/sales ratio = 430/1,000 = 43%

$$\text{Break-even point} = \frac{\text{Fixed costs}}{\text{Average C/S ratio}}$$

$$= \frac{£240,000}{0.43} = £558,140$$

(d) The overall C/S ratio could be improved by:

- Changing the product mix in favour of products with above-average C/S ratios. In this example that would mean increasing production of Product K.
- Increasing sales revenue.
- Deleting product L.

Test your understanding 5

Product	**Total contribution**	**Total sales revenue**	**C/S ratio**
	£	£	
J	42,000	105,000	40%
K	157,500	315,000	50%
	199,500	420,000	

$$\text{C/S ratio of the mix} = \frac{£199{,}500}{£420{,}000} = 47.5\%$$

$$\text{Break-even point} = \frac{£120{,}000}{47.5\%} = £252{,}632$$

OR

$$\text{C/S ratio of the mix} = \frac{(1 \times 40\%) + (3 \times 50\%)}{1 + 3}$$

$$= 47.5\%$$

$$\text{Breakeven point} = \frac{£120{,}000}{47.5\%}$$

$$= \mathbf{£252{,}000}$$

Test your understanding 6

$$\text{Breakeven point in £} = \frac{\text{Fixed cost}}{\text{C/S ratio of the mix}}$$

C/S ratio of the mix = (0.3 × 27%)+(0.2 × 56%)+(0.5 × 38%) = 38.3%

$$\text{Therefore, BEP} = \frac{£648{,}000}{38.3\%}$$

= £1,691,906

chapter

4

Planning with limiting factors

Chapter learning objectives

Upon completion of this chapter you will be able to:

- select an appropriate technique, where there is one limiting factor/key factor, to achieve desired organisational goals
- determine the optimal production plan where an organisation is restricted by a single limiting factor, including within the context of 'make' or 'buy' decisions (covered separately in Chapter 5)
- select an appropriate technique, where there are several limiting factors/key factors, to achieve desired organisational goals
- formulate a linear programming problem involving two products
- determine the optimal solution to a linear programming problem using a graphical approach
- use simultaneous equations to determine where the two lines cross to solve a multiple scarce resource problem
- explain shadow prices (dual prices) and discuss their implications on decision making and performance management in multiple limited resource situations
- calculate shadow prices (dual prices) and discuss their specific implications on decision making and performance management
- explain the implications of the existence of slack, in multiple limited resource situations, for decision making and performance management
- calculate slack and explain the specific implications of the existence of the slack for decision making and performance management.

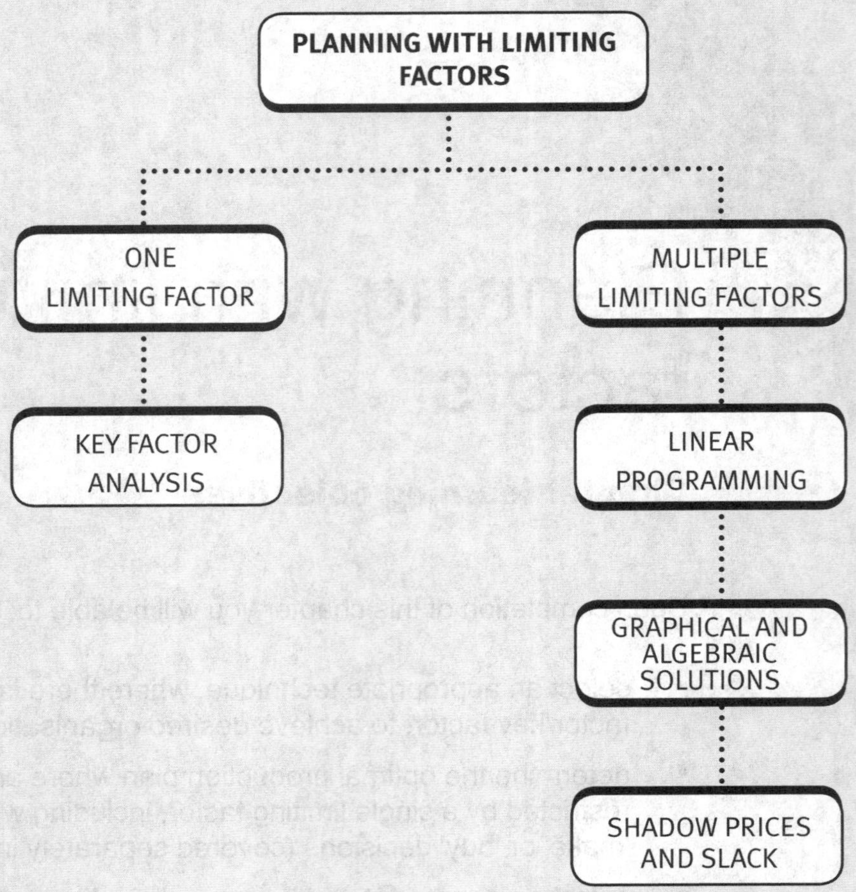

1 Introduction

Limiting factor analysis was covered in F2. In F5 the main difference is that the examination contains written questions so issues can be examined in more depth with scope for discussion. With linear programming the F5 syllabus also includes new aspects not seen before in F2.

Limiting factors

Firms face many constraints on their activity and plan accordingly:

- limited demand
- limited skilled labour and other production resources
- limited finance ('capital rationing').

Examination questions will focus on the problem of scarce resources that prevent the normal plan being achieved.

For example, a firm is facing a labour shortage this month due to sickness and, as a result, cannot produce the number of units that it would like to. How should its production plan be revised?

2 Planning with one limiting factor

The usual objective in questions is to maximise profit. Given that fixed costs are unaffected by the production decision in the short run, the approach should be to maximise the contribution earned. We have covered a similar approach in Chapter 2, with Throughput Accounting.

If there is one limiting factor, then the problem is best solved using key factor analysis:

Step 1: identify the scarce resource.

Step 2: calculate the contribution per unit for each product.

Step 3: calculate the contribution per unit of the scarce resource for each product.

Step 4: rank the products in order of the contribution per unit of the scarce resource.

Step 5: allocate resources using this ranking and answer the question.

Test your understanding 1

X Ltd makes three products, A, B and C, for which unit costs, machine hours and selling prices are as follows:

	Product A	**Product B**	**Product C**
Machine hours	10	12	14
	$	$	$
Direct materials			
@ 50c per kg	7 (14 kg)	6 (12 kg)	5 (10 kg)
Direct wages			
@ $7.50 per hour	9 (1.2 hours)	6 (0.8 hours)	3 (0.4 hours)
Variable overheads	3	3	3
Marginal cost	19	15	11
Selling price	25	20	15
Contribution	6	5	4

Sales demand for the period is limited as follows.

Product A	4,000
Product B	6,000
Product C	6,000

Company policy is to produce a minimum of 1,000 units of Product A.

The supply of materials in the period is unlimited, but machine hours are limited to 200,000 and direct labour hours to 5,000.

Required:

Indicate the production levels that should be adopted for the three products in order to maximise profitability, and state the maximum contribution.

The value of additional resources

For any scarce resource we can consider the value to the firm of gaining or losing units of that scarce resource.

For example, in TYU1 above it was determined that labour hours were the limiting factor and with 5,000 hours available the maximum contribution that could be earned was $38,750 based on selling 1,000A, 1,750B and 6,000C.

Suppose one additional labour hour became available. This would allow the company to make and sell more units of product B (Note that this was the product being made when the labour hours ran out).

- Each unit of B takes 0.8 hours, so one additional hour would enable us to make 1.25 additional units of B
- Each unit of B generates contribution of $5, so one additional hour would generate additional contribution of 1.25 × 5 = $6.25
- Note that this is contribution so has already deducted the cost of the labour at $7.50 per hour
- Thus the firm would be willing to pay up to 7.50 + 6.25 – $13.75 an hour for additional labour

This concept is discussed further below under the topic of shadow prices.

3 Several limiting factors – linear programming

When there is only one scarce resource, the method above (key factor analysis) can be used to solve the problem. However where there are two or more resources in short supply which limit the organisation's activities, then linear programming is required to find the solution.

In examination questions linear programming is used to:

- maximise contribution and/or
- minimise costs.

Formulating a linear programming problem involving two variables

The steps involved in linear programming are as follows:

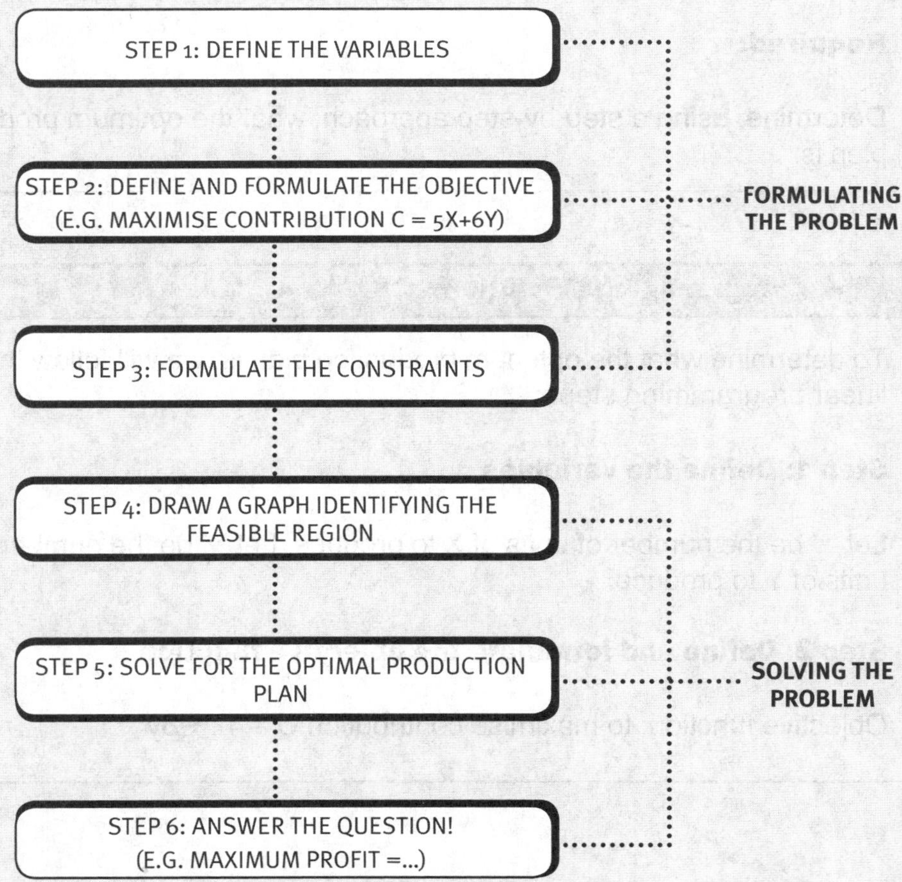

Note: Linear programming calculations will only involve two variables in exam questions.

Illustration 1 – Linear programming

A company produces two products in three departments. Details are shown below regarding the time per unit required in each department, the available hours in each department and the contribution per unit of each product:

	Product X: hours per unit	Product Y: hours per unit	Available hours
Department A	8	10	11,000
Department B	4	10	9,000
Department C	12	6	12,000
Contribution p.u.	$4	$8	

There is unlimited demand for Product X, but demand for Product Y is limited to 600 units per annum.

Required:

Determine, using a step-by-step approach, what the optimum production plan is.

Linear programming – Solution

To determine what the optimum production plan is, we will follow the linear programming steps:

Step 1: Define the variables

Let 'x' be the number of units of X to produce; Let 'y' be the number of units of Y to produce.

Step 2: Define and formulate the objective function

Objective function: to maximise contribution C = 4x + 8y

Step 3: Formulate the constraints

Subject to:

- In Department A, $8x + 10y \leq 11{,}000$ hours
- In Department B, $4x + 10y \leq 9{,}000$ hours
- In Department C, $12x + 6y \leq 12{,}000$ hours
- Non-negativity constraint: $0 \leq x, y$.

Sales demand for Product Y is also a constraint, that can be expressed by the inequality $y \leq 600$.

Step 4: Draw a graph identifying the feasible region

All the constraints are straight lines so each can be drawn by joining two points. In LP questions it is often easiest to get the two end points – i.e. where the lines cross the x and y axes.

To draw Constraint 1 (constraint in Department A), we take the inequality '$8x + 10y \leq 11{,}000$ hours' and turn it into an equation : $8x + 10y = 11{,}000$. To draw this constraint, we need two points.

- If X = 0, Y = 11,000 ÷ 10 so Y = 1,100
- Likewise, if Y = 0, X = 11,000 ÷ 8 so X = 1,375

To draw Constraint 2 (Department B):

- If X =0, Y = 900 and
- If Y = 0, X =2,250

To draw Constraint 3 (Department C):

- If X = 0 , Y = 2,000 and
- If Y = 0, X = 1,000

To draw the final constraint (maximum demand for Product Y), we draw the line y = 600 for any value of x:

- If X = 0 , Y = 600 and
- If X = 100, Y = 600

For each constraint line, we then need to consider whether the acceptable (feasible) co-ordinates are below or above the line. All of the constraints here are " ≤ " types, so acceptable solutions are to the left/below the lines giving the feasible region ABCDE.

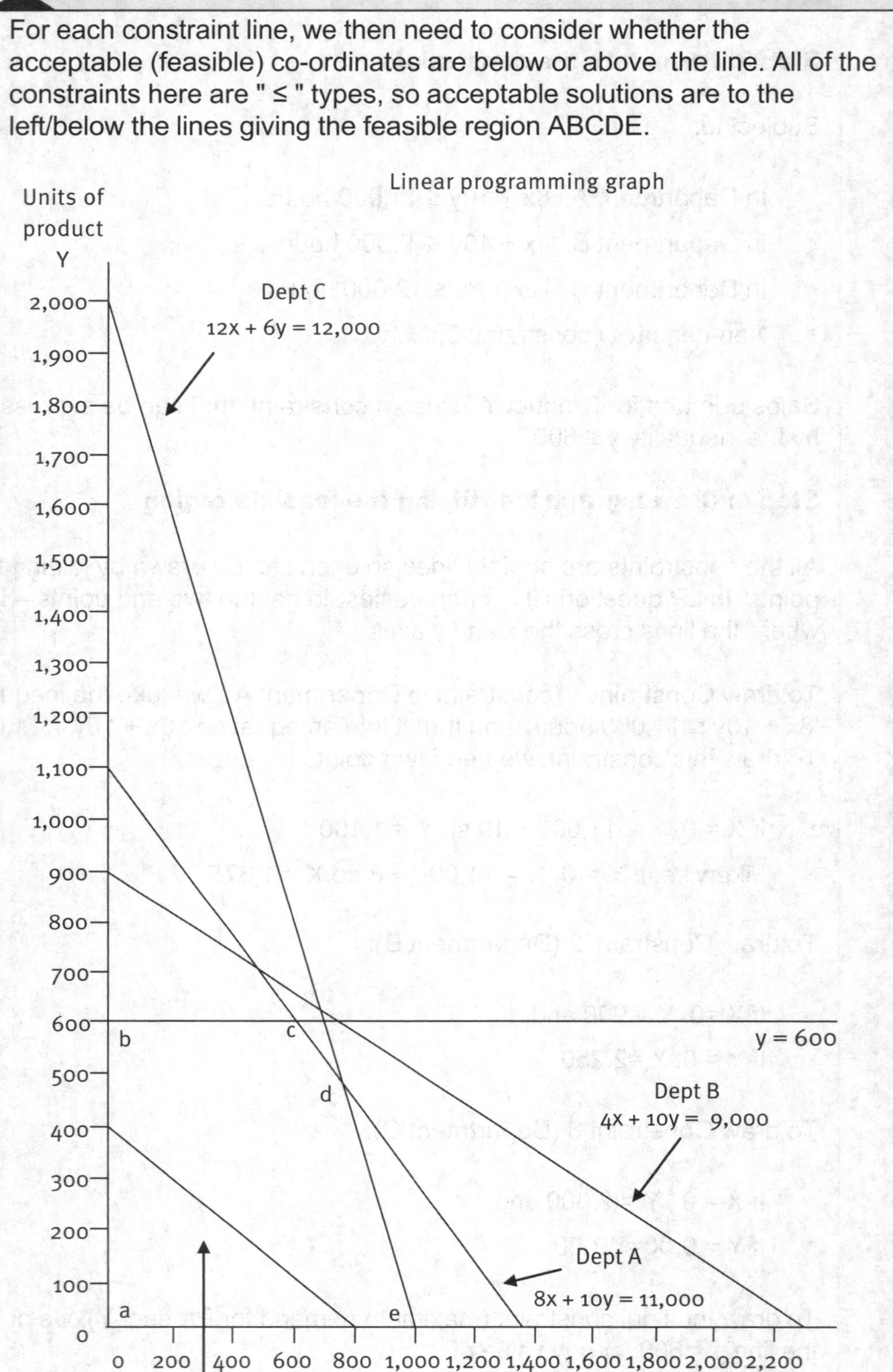

Step 5: Finding the optimum solution – Using the iso-contribution line

We do not know the maximum value of the objective function; however, we can draw an iso-contribution (or 'profit') line that shows all the combinations of x and y that provide the same total value for the objective function.

If, for example, we need to maximise contribution \$4x + \$8y, we can draw a line on a graph that shows combination of values for x and y that give the same total contribution, when x has a contribution of \$4 and y has a contribution of \$8.

Any total contribution figure can be picked, but a multiple of \$4 and \$8 is easiest.

- For example, assume 4x + 8y = 4,000. This contribution line could be found by joining the points on the graph x = 0, y = 500 and x = 1,000 and y = 0.
- Instead, we might select a total contribution value of 4x + 8y = \$8,000. This contribution line could be found by joining the points on the graph x = 0, y = 1,000 and x = 2,000 and y = 0.
- When drawing both of these contribution lines on a graph, we find that the two lines are parallel and the line with the higher total contribution value for values x and y (\$8,000) is further away from the origin of the graph (point 0).
- This can be used to identify the solution to a linear programming problem. Draw the iso-contribution line showing combinations of values for x and y that give the same total value for the objective function.
- Look at the slope of the contribution line and, using a ruler, identify which combination of values of x and y within the feasible area for the constraints is furthest away from the origin of the graph. This is the combination of values for x and y where an iso-contribution line can be drawn as far to the right as possible that just touches one corner of the feasible area. This is the combination of values of x and y that provides the solution to the linear programming problem.

Optimum corner is Corner C, the intersection of:

8x + 10y = 11,000 and y = 600
At this corner, x = 625 and y = 600.

The optimum production plan is to produce 625 units of Product X and 600 units of Product Y; The contribution at this point is maximised C = (625 × \$4) + (600 × \$8) = \$7,300.

Test your understanding 2 – Steps 1 to 3

Hebrus Inc manufactures summerhouses and garden sheds. Each product passes through a cutting process and an assembly process. One summerhouse, which makes a contribution of $50, takes six hours' cutting time and four hours' assembly time; while one shed makes a contribution of $40, and takes three hours' cutting time and eight hours' assembly time. There is a maximum of 36 cutting hours available each week and 48 assembly hours.

Cutters are paid $10 per hour and assembly workers $15 per hour.

Required:

Formulate the linear programming problem.

Step 4: Drawing the graph and identifying the feasible region

Drawing the graph

- Step 4 of the linear programming model is to represent the constraints as straight lines on a graph.
- In order to plot the constraints it is normally best to compute the intercepts of the equalities on the horizontal and vertical axes. Thus, x and y are each set equal to zero in turn and the value of y and x computed in these circumstances.

Revision of graphing a straight line

Step 4 of the linear programming model is to represent the constraints as straight lines on a graph. We do this below. In the meantime, this section contains basic revision for students who are not familiar with the process of graphing a straight line.

To begin with, we must have a linear relationship between two measurements.

Examples	y	=	3x + 1
	y	=	2x + 42 etc.

Note:

(1) To recognise a linear relationship the equation must have only 'x' not 'x' to the power of anything, e.g. x^2.

(2) A straight line has two characteristics:

(i) a slope or gradient – which measures the 'steepness' of the line

(ii) a point at which it cuts the y axis – this is called the intercept:

y = (slope × x) + intercept

e.g. y = 2x + 3

Therefore, the gradient is 2 and the point at which the line cuts the y axis is 3.

To draw a straight line graph we only need to know two points that can then be joined.

Consider the following two equations:

(i) y = 2x + 3

(ii) y = 2x – 2

In order to draw the graphs of these equations it is necessary to decide on two values for x and then to calculate the corresponding values for y. Let us use x = 0 and 3. These calculations are best displayed in tabular form.

(i) (x = 0, y = 3) and (x = 3, y = 9)

(ii) (x = 0, y = –2) and (x = 3, y = 4)

So to draw the first line we plot the points (0, 3) and (3, 9) and simply join them up. Similarly, for the second line we plot the points (0, –2) and (3, 4) and join them up.

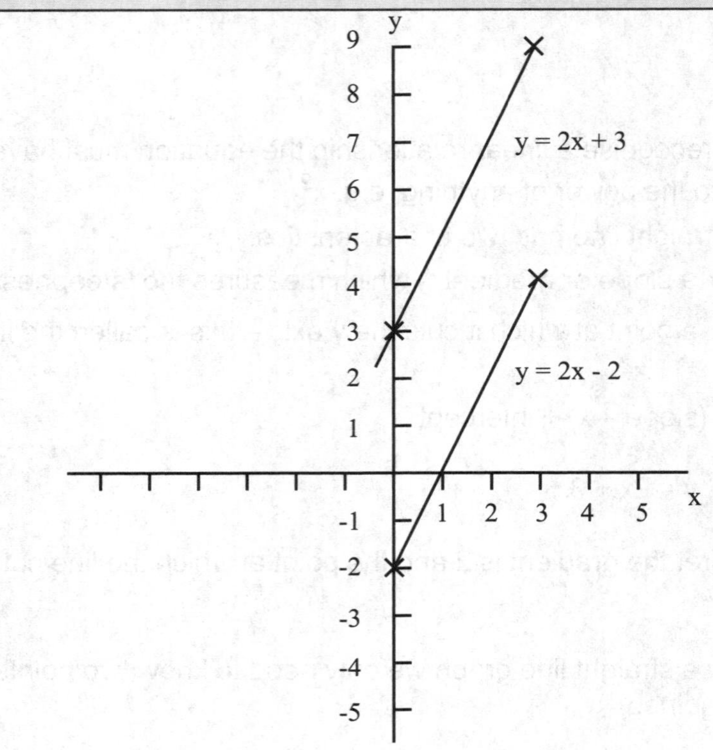

Note: The lines are parallel because the equations have the same gradient of 2.

Test your understanding 3 – Step 4

Using the information from the Hebrus example (TYU 2) you are required to plot the constraints on a graph and indicate on the graph the feasible region.

Identifying the feasible region

- Having inserted the straight lines in the graph, we are then ready to work out what is called the feasible region.
- The feasible region shows those combinations of variables which are possible given the resource constraints.
- In the TYU above the original constraints were '≤' types, so the feasible region is shown by the area bounded by the thick black line on the graph. Production can be anywhere in this area.
- The lines drawn on the graph represent equations where the LHS equals the RHS. However, the original constraint was either '≤' or '≥'.
- A '≤' type constraint is represented by all points on the line AND all points in the area below the line (i.e. nearer to the origin – the point x = 0,y = 0).

- A '≥' type constraint is represented by all points on the line AND all points in the area above the line (i.e. away from the origin).
- Watch out in the examination for constraints that show minimum amounts required as well as maximum amounts of constraints available. Typically in questions these tend to be a government quota that a minimum amount of one of the output needs to be produced.

Step 5: Finding the optimal solution using the graph

Having found the feasible region the problem now is to find the optimal solution within this feasible region.

There are two approaches to this final stage.

- **By inspection** it is clear that the maximum contribution will lie on one of the corners of the feasible region. The optimal solution can be reached simply by calculating the contributions at each corner. This approach is not recommended in the exam since it tends to be quite time consuming.
- **By drawing an iso-contribution line** (an objective function for a particular value of C), which is a line where all points represent an equal contribution. This is the recommended approach, particularly for more complex problems.

Drawing the iso-contribution line

We do not know the maximum value of the objective function; however, we can draw an iso-contribution (or 'profit') line that shows all the combinations of x and y that provide the same total value for the objective function.

If, for example, we need to maximise contribution \$4x + \$8y, we can draw a line on a graph that shows combination of values for x and y that give the same total contribution, when x has a unit contribution of \$4 and y has a unit contribution of \$8. Any total contribution figure can be picked, but a multiple of \$4 and \$8 is easiest.

- For example, assume 4x + 8y = 4,000. This contribution line could be found by joining the points on the graph x = 0, y = 500 and x = 1,000 and y = 0.
- Instead, we might select a total contribution value of 4x + 8y = \$8,000. This contribution line could be found by joining the points on the graph x = 0, y = 1,000 and x = 2,000 and y = 0.

- When drawing both of these contribution lines on a graph, we find that the two lines are parallel and the line with the higher total contribution value for values x and y ($8,000) is further away from the origin of the graph (point 0).
- This can be used to identify the solution to a linear programming problem. Draw the iso-contribution line showing combinations of values for x and y that give the same total value for the objective function.
- Look at the slope of the contribution line and, using a ruler, identify which combination of values of x and y within the feasible area for the constraints is furthest away from the origin of the graph. This is the combination of values for x and y where an iso-contribution line can be drawn as far to the right as possible that just touches one corner of the feasible area. This is the combination of values of x and y that provides the solution to the linear programming problem.

Test your understanding 4 – Steps 5 and 6

Using the Hebrus example again (TYU 2 and 3) you are required to find the optimal solution using the graph (Step 5).

Calculate the contribution at this point (Step 6).

Solving the problem using simultaneous equations

You may consider that the whole process would be easier by solving the constraints as sets of simultaneous equations and not bothering with a graph. This is possible and you may get the right answer, but such a technique should be used with caution and is not recommended until you have determined graphically which constraints are effective in determining the optimal solution.

Furthermore, if the question asks for a graphical solution, then a graph must be used.

The technique can, however, be used as a check, or to establish the exact quantities for the optimal solution when the graph does not give sufficient accuracy.

Test your understanding 5 – Simultaneous equations

Using the Hebrus example again (TYU 2 – 4) you are required to use simultaneous equations to verify the optimal point.

You will need the linear programming graph to see which constraints intersect, and Hebrus' graph has been correctly drawn as follows:

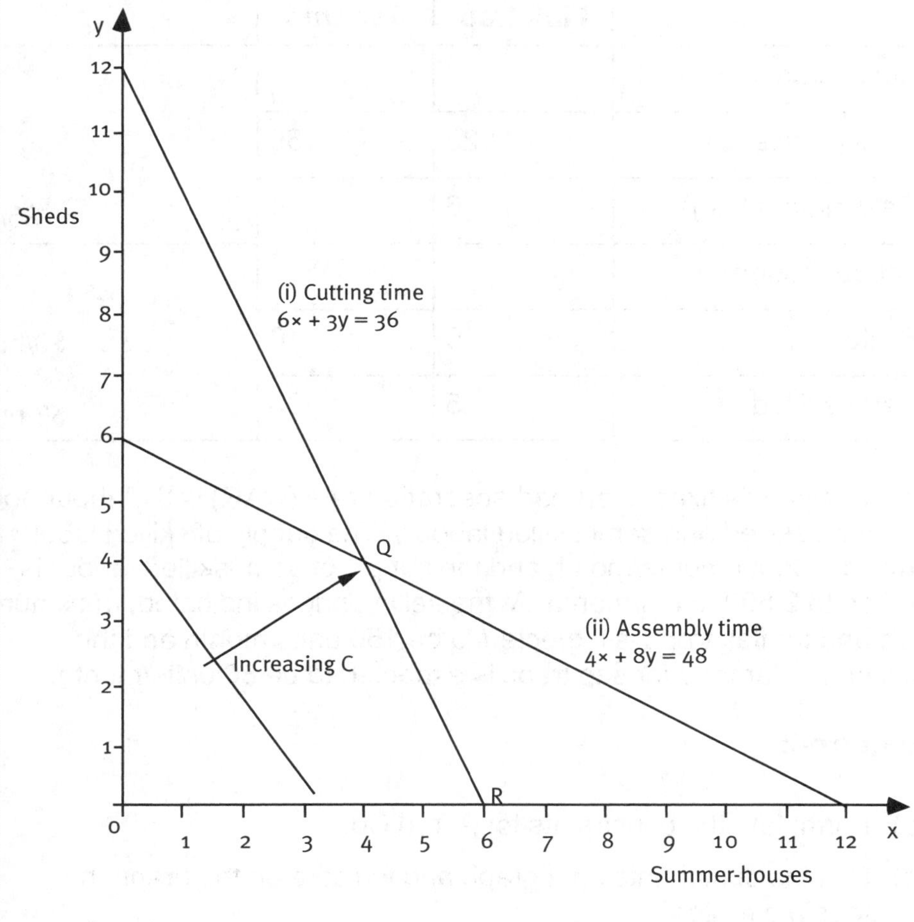

Test your understanding 6 – Additional example

Alfred Co is preparing its production plan for the coming month. It manufactures two products, the flak trap and the sap trap. Details are as follows.

	Product		**Price/wage rate**
	Flak trap	**Sap trap**	
Amount/unit			
Selling price ($)	125	165	
Raw material (kg)	6	4	$5/kg
Labour hours:			
Skilled	10	10	$3/hour
Semi-skilled	5	25	$3/hour

The company's fixed overhead absorption rate (OAR) is $1/labour hour (for both skilled and semi-skilled labour). The supply of skilled labour is limited to 2,000 hours/month and the supply of semi-skilled labour is limited to 2,500 hours/month. At the selling prices indicated, maximum demand for flak traps is expected to be 150 units/month and the maximum demand for sap traps is expected to be 80 units/month.

Required:

(a) Formulate the constraints for Alfred Co.

(b) Plot the constraints on a graph and indicate on the graph the feasible region.

(c) Using the graph find the optimal production plan.

(d) Use simultaneous equations to accurately calculate the quantities produced at the optimal point and calculate the maximum contribution at this point.

Test your understanding 7 – Minimising costs

J Farms Ltd can buy two types of fertiliser which contain the following percentage of chemicals:

	Nitrates	Phosphates	Potash
Type X	18	5	2
Type Y	3	2	5

For a certain crop the following minimum quantities (kg) are required:

Nitrates 100 | Phosphates 50 | Potash 40

Type X costs £10 per kg and type Y costs £5 per kg. J Farms Ltd currently buys 1,000 kg of each type and wishes to minimise its expenditure on fertilisers.

(a) Write down the objective function and the constraints for J Farms Ltd.

(b) Draw a graph to illustrate all the constraints (equations/inequalities), shading the feasible region.

(c) Recommend the quantity of each type of fertiliser which should be bought and the cost of these amounts.

(d) Find the saving J Farms Ltd can make by switching from its current policy to your recommendation.

Limiting factor analysis – discussion aspects

Assumptions

- There is a single quantifiable objective – e.g. maximise contribution. In reality there may be multiple objectives such as maximising return while simultaneously minimising risk.
- Each product always uses the same quantity of the scarce resource per unit. In reality this may not be the case. For example, learning effects may be enjoyed.
- The contribution per unit is constant. In reality this may not be the case:
  - the selling price may have to be lowered to sell more
  - there may be economies of scale, for example a discount for buying in bulk.

- Products are independent – in reality:
  - customers may expect to buy both products together
  - the products may be manufactured jointly together.
- The scenario is short term. This allows us to ignore fixed costs.

The assumptions apply to the analysis used when there is one limiting factor or if there are multiple limiting factors.

Shadow prices and slack

When discussing constraints, **slack** is the amount by which a resource is under-utilised, i.e. slack occurs when the maximum availability of a resource is not used. Graphically speaking, it will occur when the optimum point does not fall on a given resource line.

- The optimal solution will typically occur where two ("critical") constraint lines cross. There will be no slack for these constraints/resources as they will be fully utilised.
- For other constraint lines, the fact that the optimal solution is not on these lines means that the resources are not fully utilised, so there will be slack.

Slack is important for two reasons

- For critical constraints (zero slack), then gaining additional units of these scarce resources will allow the optimal solution to be improved (e.g. higher contribution earned). Similarly if another department wants these resources then it will result in lower contribution.
- For non-critical constraints, gaining or losing a small number of units of the scarce resource will have no impact on the optimal solution.

To determine how much this makes scarce resources worth to the business, see the section below on "shadow prices"

Note: The term 'slack' can also apply to a product i.e. there can be unfulfilled demand.

Illustration 2 – Slack

Illustration 1

In Illustration 1 we solved the following problem:

Objective function: to maximise contribution C = 4x + 8y

Subject to:

- Department A time, 8x + 10y ≤ 11,000
- Department B time, 4x + 10y ≤ 9,000
- Department C time, 12x + 6y ≤ 12,000
- Non-negativity constraint: 0 ≤ x, y.

The optimal solution (x = 625, y = 600) was found where the department A and Product B constraints crossed.

We can therefore say:

- Department A time is a critical constraint with no slack.
- Product Y constraint is a critical constraint with no slack.
- For Department B time, actual amount used = 4x + 10y = 4 × 625 + 10 × 600 = 8,500. The maximum amount available was 9,000 giving slack of 500 hours.
- For Department C time, actual amount used = 12x + 6y = 12 × 625 + 6 × 600 = 11,100. The maximum amount available was 12,000 giving slack of 900 hours.

Hebrus (TYU 2 – 5)

In the Hebrus example, the optimum point Q lies on both the cutting and assembly time lines.

Therefore both resources are fully utilised and are referred to as critical constraints.

Alfred Co (TYU 6)

In the Alfred Co example, the optimum point D (x = 150, y = 50) lies on the intersection of the skilled labour line (10x + 10y = 2,000) and the maximum demand line for flak traps (x = 150).

At this point there is unutilised semi-skilled labour. This means that slack exists for semi-skilled labour.

The amount of semi-skilled labour used = 5x + 25y = 5 × 150 + 25 × 50 = 2,000 compared to a maximum available of 2,500 thus giving slack of 500 hours.

Semi-skilled labour is a non-critical constraint and this unutilised resource should be used elsewhere in the business to generate contribution.

Shadow (or dual) prices

The shadow price or dual price of a limiting factor is the increase in contribution created by the availability of one additional unit of the limiting factor at the original cost.

- The shadow price of a resource can be found by calculating the increase in value (usually extra contribution) which would be created by having available one additional unit of a limiting resource at its original cost.
- It therefore represents the maximum premium that the firm should be willing to pay for one extra unit of each constraint. This aspect is discussed in more detail below.
- Non-critical constraints will have zero shadow prices as slack exists already.

Calculating shadow prices

The simplest way to calculate shadow prices for a critical constraint is as follows:

Step 1: Take the equations of the straight lines that intersect at the optimal point. Add one unit to the constraint concerned, while leaving the other critical constraint unchanged.

Step 2: Use simultaneous equations to derive a new optimal solution.

Step 3: Calculate the revised optimal contribution. The increase is the shadow price for the constraint under consideration.

Test your understanding 8 – Shadow prices

In Hebrus the optimal solution was determined to be x = 4 and y = 4 giving an optimal contribution of $360. This solution was at the intersection of the lines:

Cutting	6x + 3y	=	36
Assembly	4x + 8y	=	48

Required:

Suppose one extra hour was available for the cutting process. Calculate the shadow price for this additional hour of cutting time.

Additional example on shadow prices

Using the following data, calculate the shadow price for machining time.

Maximise C = 80x + 75y (contribution), subject to

(i) 20x + 25y ≤ 500 (machining time)

(ii) 40x + 25y ≤ 800 (finishing time)

The optimal solution at the intersection of the above constraints is: x = 15, y = 8.

Solution

Step 1: Machining time – the constraints become:

(i) 20x + 25y ≤ 501

(ii) 40x + 25y ≤ 800

Step 2: Subtracting (i) from (ii) gives 20x = 299 and thus x = 14.95

Inserting into (i) gives

(20 × 14.95) + 25y = 501

25y = 202

y = 8.08

Step 3: Original contribution = (15 × $80) + (8 × $75) = $1,800.

Amended contribution = (14.95 × $80) + (8.08 × $75) = $1,802.

The shadow price per machine hour is thus $2.

Implications of shadow prices

- Management can use shadow prices as a measure of the maximum premium that they would be willing to pay for one more unit of the scarce resource.
- However, the shadow price should be considered carefully. For example, the shadow price of labour may be calculated as $20 per hour. However, it may be possible to negotiate a lower shadow price than this.
- In addition, if more of the critical constraint is obtained, the constraint line will move outwards altering the shape of the feasible region. After a certain point there will be little point in buying more of the scarce resource since any non-critical constraints will become critical.

Additional example on linear programming

Suppose a linear programming problem gives the following results.

Constraint	Normal cost	Shadow price
Skilled labour	$20/hour	$12/hour
Unskilled labour	$10/hour	zero
Materials	$5/kg	$3/kg

Required:

(a) Which two constraints give rise to the optimal solution?

(b) Overtime is paid at 'time-and-a-half'. Is it worth paying overtime to help relax constraints?

(c) A new product has been proposed with the following proposed costs and revenues.

	$
Selling price	80
Skilled labour – 2 hours @ $20/hour	(40)
Unskilled labour – 1 hour @ $10/hour	(10)
Materials – 3 kg @ $5/kg	(15)
Profit per unit	15

Assuming that the constraints cannot be relaxed, should the new product be manufactured?

Solution

(a) Critical constraints have non-zero dual prices, so the optimal solution will be at the intersection of skilled labour and materials.

(b) For skilled labour overtime will cost $30 per hour and the benefit will be 20 + 12 = $32 per hour. The overtime is thus worthwhile and will generate a net $2 per hour benefit.

For unskilled labour there is already slack so overtime is not worthwhile.

(c) The profit statement can be revised using as follows:

	$
Selling price	80
Skilled labour – 2 hours @ (20+12)	(64)
Unskilled labour – 1 hour @ 10	(10)
Materials – 3 kg @ (5+3)	(24)
Loss per unit	(18)

Incorporating the contribution lost elsewhere by reallocating scarce resources, the new product is not viable.

4 Chapter summary

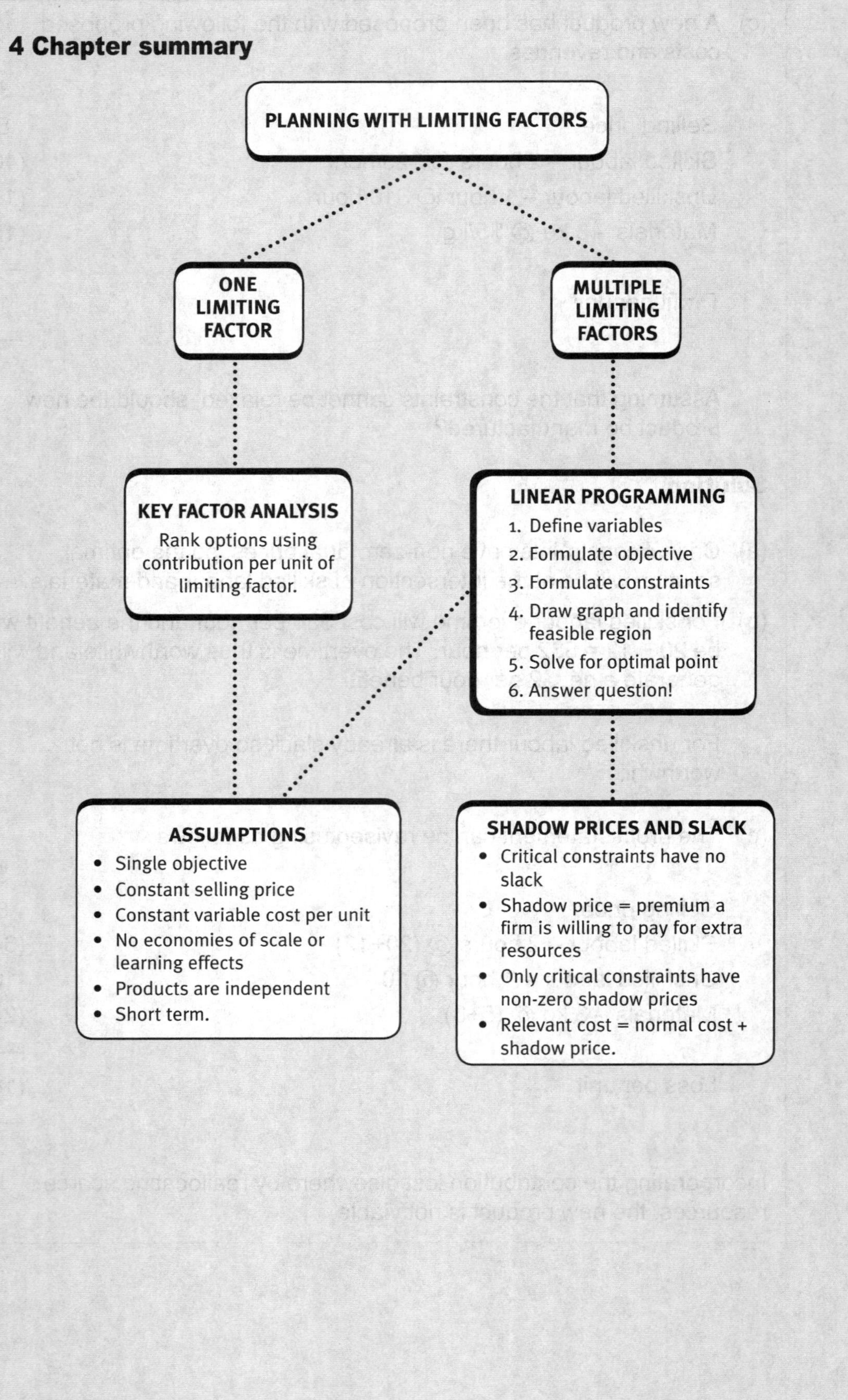

PLANNING WITH LIMITING FACTORS
ONE LIMITING FACTOR
MULTIPLE LIMITING FACTORS
KEY FACTOR ANALYSIS
Rank options using contribution per unit of limiting factor.
LINEAR PROGRAMMING
1. Define variables
2. Formulate objective
3. Formulate constraints
4. Draw graph and identify feasible region
5. Solve for optimal point
6. Answer question!
ASSUMPTIONS
• Single objective
• Constant selling price
• Constant variable cost per unit
• No economies of scale or learning effects
• Products are independent
• Short term.
SHADOW PRICES AND SLACK
• Critical constraints have no slack
• Shadow price = premium a firm is willing to pay for extra resources
• Only critical constraints have non-zero shadow prices
• Relevant cost = normal cost + shadow price.

Test your understanding answers

Test your understanding 1

Step 1: Identify the scarce resource (this may be done for you in examination questions).

At potential sales level:

	Sales potential units	Total machine hours	Total labour hours
Product A	4,000	40,000	4,800
Product B	6,000	72,000	4,800
Product C	6,000	84,000	2,400
		196,000	**12,000**

Thus, labour hours are the limiting factor.

Step 2: calculate the contribution per unit for each product.

This has been done for us in the question.

Step 3: calculate the contribution per unit of the scarce resource for each product, i.e. per labour hour.

Product A $6/1.2 = $5.00

Product B $5/0.8 = $6.25

Product C $4/0.4 = $10.00

Step 4: rank the products in order of the contribution per unit of the scarce resource.

Thus, production should be concentrated first on C, up to the maximum available sales, then B, and finally A.

However, a minimum of 1,000 units of A must be produced.

Step 5: allocate resources using this ranking and answer the question, i.e. state the maximum contribution.

Taking these factors into account, the production schedule becomes:

	Units produced	Labour hours	Cumulative labour hours	Limiting factor
Product A	1,000	1,200	1,200	Policy to produce 1,000 units
Product C	6,000	2,400	3,600	Sales
Product B	1,750	1,400	5,000	Labour hours

The maximum contribution is therefore as follows.

	$
A (1,000 × $6)	6,000
B (1,750 × $5)	8,750
C (6,000 × $4)	24,000
	38,750

Test your understanding 2 – Steps 1 to 3

Step 1 – define the variables
Let x = the number of summerhouses produced each week

y = the number of garden sheds produced each week.

(**Note:** Be careful to specify the time periods involved.)

Step 2 – define and formulate the objective function.

The objective here is to maximise contribution C, given by:
Maximise contribution = 50x + 40y

Step 3 – formulate the constraints.

The constraints (limitations) here are the amounts of cutting and assembly time available.

If 1 summerhouse requires 6 hours' cutting time,

x summerhouses require 6x hours' cutting time.

If 1 shed requires 3 hours' cutting time,

y sheds require 3y hours' cutting time.

Hence total cutting time required = 6x + 3y hours.

Similarly, if one summerhouse and one shed require 4 and 8 hours' assembly time respectively, the total assembly time for x summerhouses and y sheds will be 4x + 8y.

The conventional way of setting out the constraints is to place the units **utilised** on the left, and those **available** on the right; the inequality sign is the link.

Constraint		**Utilised**		**Available**
Cutting time	(i)	6x + 3y	≤	36
Assembly time	(ii)	4x + 8y	≤	48

In addition, two other logical constraints must be stated, i.e. $x \geq 0$ and $y \geq 0$

These simply state that negative amounts of garden sheds or summerhouses cannot be made.

Test your understanding 3 – Step 4

The cutting time constraint is an inequality 6x + 3y ≤ 36 which represents a region on the graph. To identify this region we draw the line 6x + 3y = 36 (equality) and then determine which side of the line is feasible. This process is repeated for each constraint.

For the equation 6x + 3y = 36 – cutting time constraint

when x = 0, y = 36/3 = 12

when y = 0, x =36/6 = 6

To graph this constraint, we draw a straight line between the points (0, 12) and (6, 0).

For the equation 4x + 8y = 48 – assembly time constraint

when x = 0, y = 48/8 = 6

when y = 0, x =48/4 = 12

To graph this constraint, we draw a straight line between the points (0, 6) and (12, 0).

The constraints can now be represented graphically:

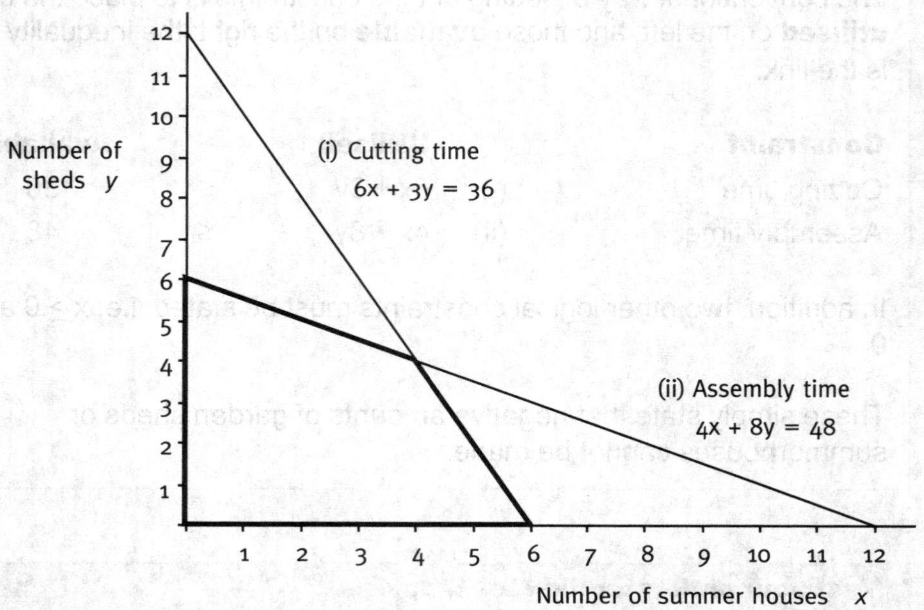

The original constraints were '≤' types, so the feasible region is shown by the area bounded by the thick black line on the graph. Production can be anywhere in this area.

Test your understanding 4 – Steps 5 and 6

Step 5: Finding the optimal solution using the graph.

Let's first consider what we mean by an iso-contribution line.

An iso-contribution line is a line where all the points represent an equal contribution.

The contribution for Hebrus is given by the equation, C = 50x + 40y (from Step 2).

- If we choose a contribution of, say, \$200 we can draw an iso-contribution line 200 = 50x + 40y

  when x = 0, y = 200/40 = 5

  when y = 0, x = 200/50 = 4

  To graph the line, we draw a straight line between the points (0, 5) and (4, 0). This line is shown on the graph below.

- If we choose another contribution of, say, \$240 we can draw an iso-contribution line 240 = 50x + 40y

  when x = 0, y = 240/40 = 6

  when y = 0, x = 240/50 = 4.8

  To graph the line, we draw a straight line between the points (0, 6) and (4.8, 0). This line is shown on the graph below.

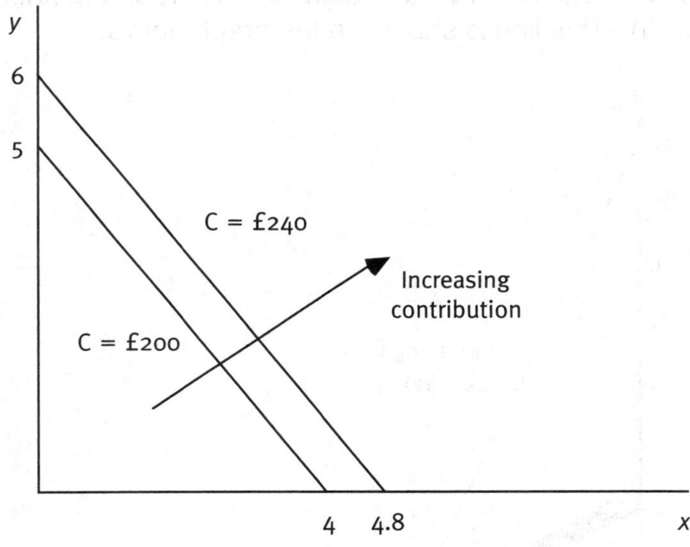

The iso-contribution lines move to and from the origin in parallel; the arrow indicates increasing contribution. The object is to get on the highest contribution line within (just touching) the binding constraints.

The optimum point is found by drawing an example of an iso-contribution line on the diagram (any convenient value of C will do), and then placing a ruler against it. Then, by moving the ruler away from the origin (in the case of a maximisation problem) or towards the origin (in the case of a minimisation problem) but keeping it parallel to the iso-contribution line, the last corner of the feasible solution space which is met represents the optimum solution.

To find the optimal point for Hebrus we have used an iso-contribution line for a contribution of $165. However, either of the iso-contribution lines discussed above, or another iso-contribution line, could have been used instead.

165 = 50x + 40y

when x = 0, y = 165/40 = 4.125

when y = 0, x = 165/50 = 3.3

To graph the line, we draw a straight line between the points (0, 4.125) and (3.3, 0). This line is shown on the graph below.

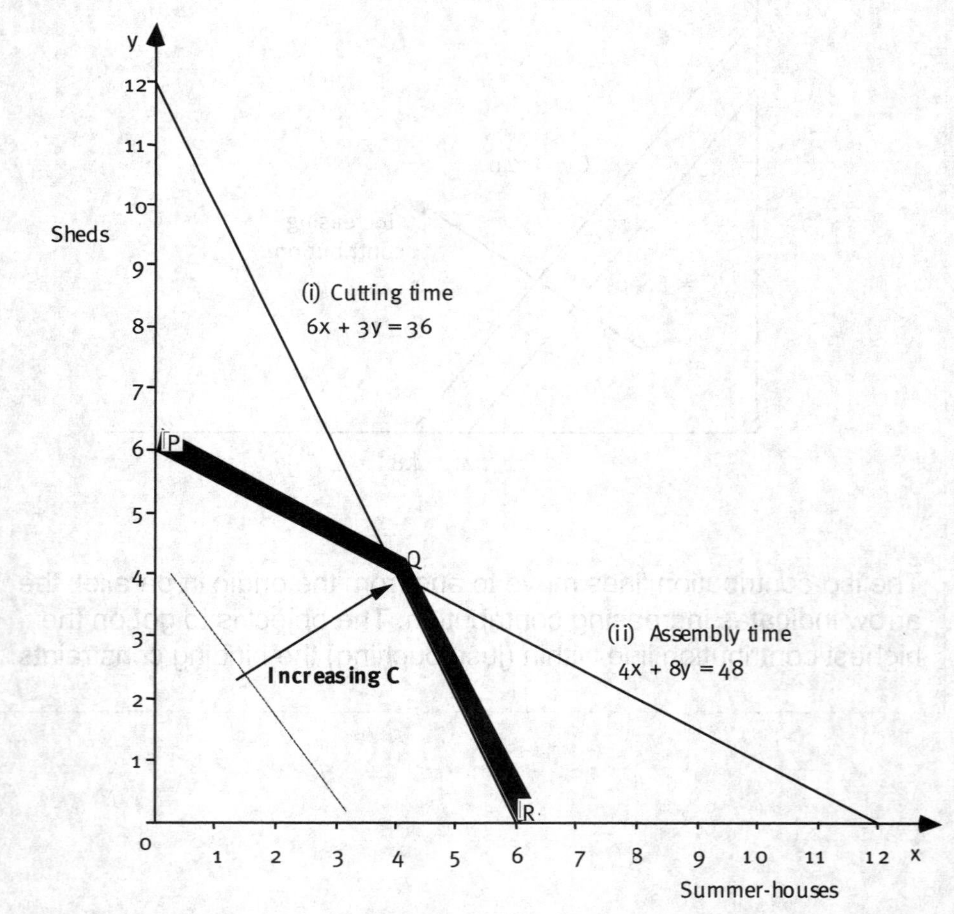

Optimal point: The highest available iso-contribution line occurs at point Q.

Step 6: Answer the question, i.e. calculate the contribution at the optimal point.

Reading from the graph, at point Q x = 4 and y = 4. This gives a maximum contribution of C = (50 × 4) + (40 × 4) = $360.

Test your understanding 5 – Simultaneous equations

Step 1: Take the equations of the two constraints that cross at the optimal point.

The optimal point is point Q. This is at the intersection of the two constraint lines:

4x + 8y = 48 this will be called (a)

6x + 3y = 36 this will be called (b)

Step 2: Multiply both equations in order to get the same number of x's or y's in each equation.

(a) multiplied by 3 gives 12x + 24y = 144

(b) multiplied by 2 gives 12x + 6y = 72

Step 3: Subtract one equation from the other to eliminate either x or y.

(a) 12x + 24y = 144

minus (b) 12x + 6y = 72

gives 0x + 18y = 72

Therefore, y = 72/18 = 4 (this is the same number of garden sheds found using the graph).

Step 4: Use any equation to find the missing value, i.e. either x or y.

Using the value y = 4 we can find the value of x. Any of the equations above can be used. For example:

$4x + 8y = 48$

$4x + (8 \times 4) = 48$

$4x = 16$

x = 16/4 = 4 (this is the same number of summerhouses found using the graph).

Step 5: Answer the question.

The optimal point is at x = 4 and y = 4. This gives a maximum contribution of C = (50 × 4) + (40 × 4) = $360 (as per TYU4).

Test your understanding 6 – Additional example

(a) **Step 1: define variables**

Let x = the number of units of flak traps produced per month.

y = the number of units of sap traps produced per month.

Step 2: objective function

The objective is to maximise contribution, C, given by C = 50x + 40y (Working)

Working:

Contribution per flak trap = 125 – (6 × 5) – (10 × 3) – (5 × 3) = 50

Contribution per sap trap = 165 – (4 × 5) – (10 × 3) – (25 × 3) = 40

Step 3: constraints

Skilled labour	10x + 10y	≤	2,000
Semi-skilled labour	5x + 25y	≤	2,500
Max demand	x	≤	150
	y	≤	80
Non-negativity	x,y	≥	0

(b) **Step 4: draw a graph and identify the feasible region**

Skilled labour: x = 0, y = 2,000/10 = 200

y = 0, x = 2,000/10 = 200

We simply join up the points (0, 200) and (200, 0).

Semi-skilled labour: x = 0, y = 2,500/25 = 100

y = 0, x = 2,500/5 = 500

We join up the points (0, 100) and (500, 0)

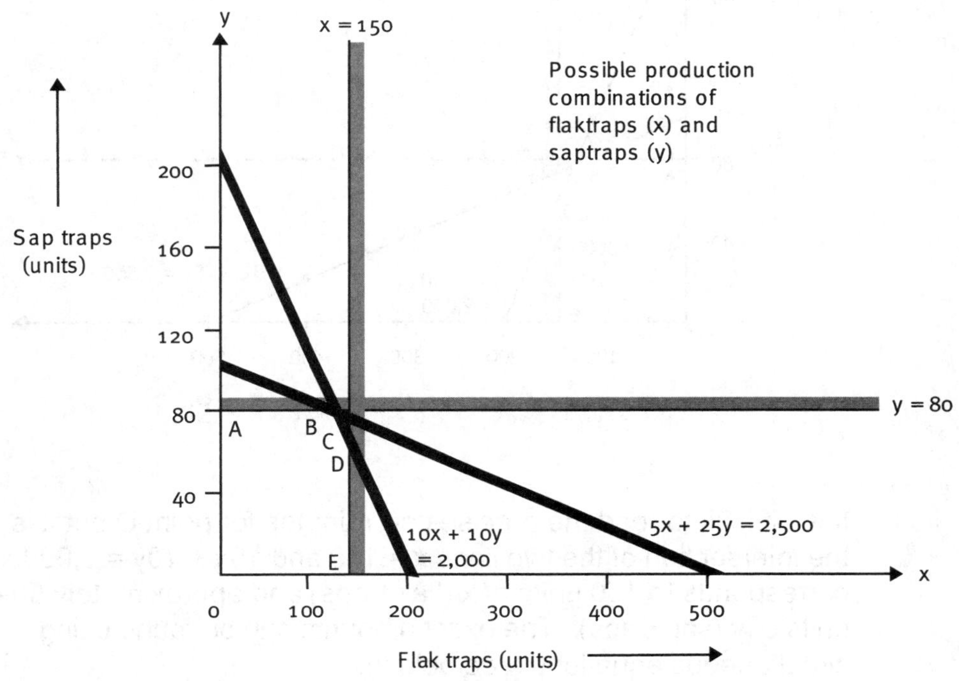

This gives a feasibility region of 0ABCDE.

(c) **Step 5: use the graph to solve the optimal production plan**

Objective is to maximise contribution C = 50x + 40y.

The iso-contribution line C=2,000 has been drawn to establish the gradient and identify the optimal solution at point D:

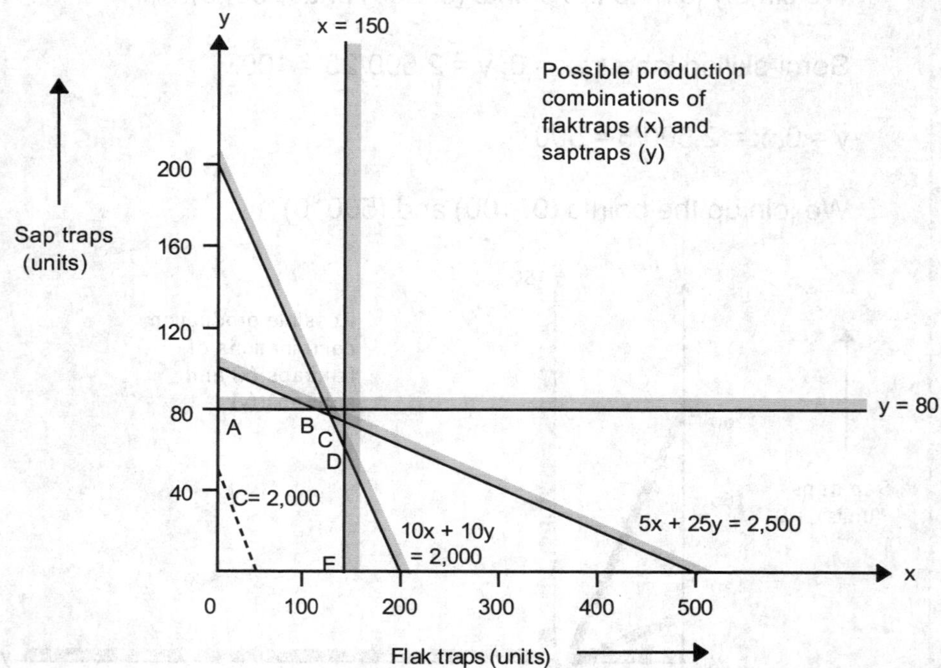

It is difficult to read the precise co-ordinates for point D but it is at the intersection of the two lines x = 150 and 10x + 10y = 2,000. This corresponds to 150 units of x (flak traps) and approximately 50–60 units of y (sap traps). The exact amounts can be found using simultaneous equations (see below).

(d) **Use simultaneous equations to accurately calculate the quantities produced at the optimal point and calculate the maximum contribution at this point.**

Take the equations of the two constraints that cross at the optimal point.

The optimal point is point D. This is at the intersection of the two constraint lines:

x = 150 this will be called (a)

10x + 10y = 2,000 this will be called (b)

Find the value of x

The solution is slightly easier here since we already know that x = 150, i.e. we should produce 150 flak traps.

Use any equation to find the missing value, i.e. y

Using the value x = 150 we can find the value of y.

$10x + 10y = 2,000$

$(10 \times 150) + 10y = 2,000$

$10y = 500$

y = 500/10 = 50, i.e. we should produce 50 sap traps

Step 6: answer the question

The optimal point is at x = 150 and y = 50. This gives a maximum contribution of C = (50 × 150) + (40 × 50) = $9,500

Test your understanding 7 – Minimising costs

(a) The chemicals are given in percentage terms that are converted to decimals.

Step 1: define the variables

Let x = number of kg of X purchased

Let y = number of kg of Y purchased

Step 2: define and formulate the objective function

Total cost: z = 10x + 5y, the objective function which has to be minimised.

Step 3: formulate the constraints

The constraints exist on the chemical composition of the fertilisers:

Nitrates:	$0.18x + 0.03y$	≥	100
Phosphates:	$0.05x + 0.02y$	≥	50
Potash:	$0.02x + 0.05y$	≥	40
Non-negativity:	$x \geq 0, y \geq 0$		

(b) **Step 4: draw the graph and identify the feasible region**

In this example, all the points where the lines cut the axes are required, so that the easiest way to draw the constraints is to calculate these points.

Constraint	End points	
0.18x + 0.03y = 100	x = 0, y = 100/0.03 = 3,333.3	y = 0, x = 100/0.18 = 555.5
0.05x + 0.02y = 50	x = 0, y = 50/0.02 = 2,500	y = 0, x = 50/0.05 = 1,000
0.02x + 0.05y = 40	x = 0, y = 40/0.05 = 800	y = 0, x = 40/0.02 = 2,000

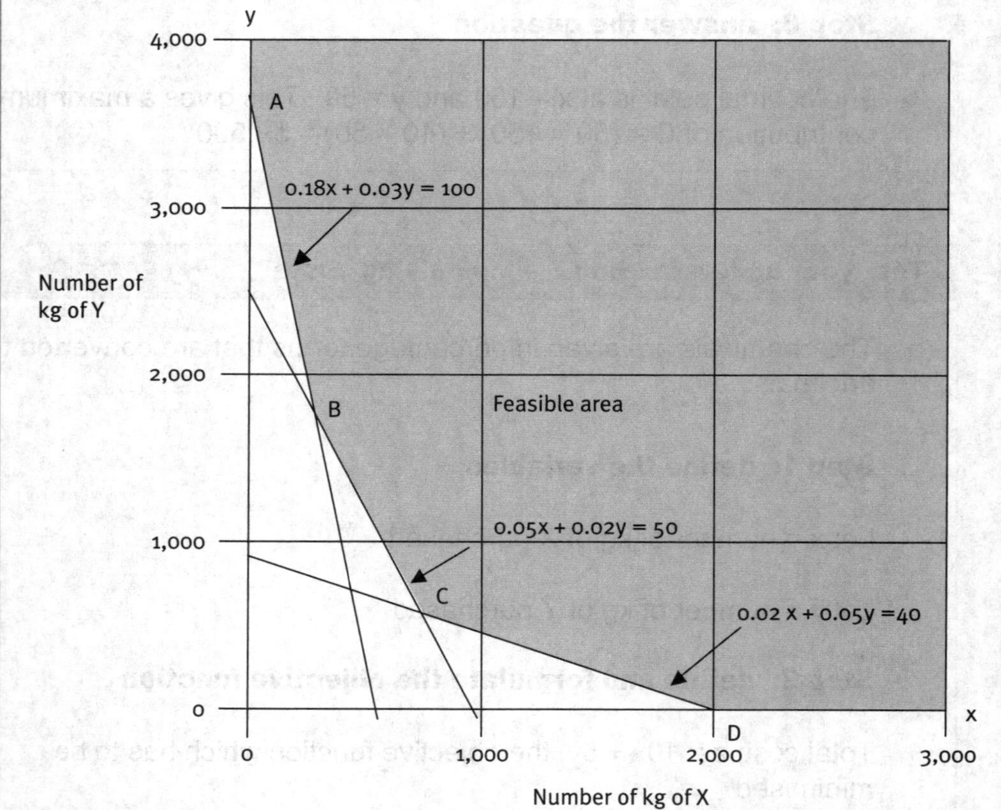

(c) **Step 5: find the optimal solution using the graph**

The inspection method has been used here, for illustration purposes only.

Considering the vertices (i.e. corners) of the feasible area.

A: $x = 0$ $y = 3{,}333.3$
$z = 10x + 5y = 10(0) + 5(3{,}333.3) = \$16{,}666.50$

B: Solving $0.18x + 0.03y = 100$ and $0.05x + 0.02y = 50$
gives $x = 238.1$ and $y = 1{,}904.8$
$z = 10(238.1) + 5(1{,}904.8) = \$11{,}905$

C: Solving $0.05x + 0.02y = 50$ and $0.02x + 0.05y = 40$
gives $x = 809.5$ and $y = 476.2$
$z = 10(809.5) = 5(476.2) = \$10{,}476$

D: $x = 2{,}000$ $y = 0$
$z = 10(2{,}000) + 5(0) = \$20{,}000$

Step 6: answer the question

Thus C gives the point of minimum cost with x = 809.5 and y = 476.2, i.e. 809.5 kg of X and 476.2 kg of Y, total cost $10,476.

or:

Alternatively, an iso-cost line for z = 20,000 (say) could be plotted and moved downwards. This would identify point C as the optimum point on the graph, and the values of x and y could be determined using simultaneous equations as above. This would be quicker in the exam and the method should give the same answer.

(d) The current policy costs: 1,000 ($10) + 1,000 ($5) = $15,000, so the saving made is of $(15,000 – 10,476) = $4,524.

Test your understanding 8 – Shadow prices

Step 1: Take the equations of the straight lines that intersect at the optimal point. Add one unit to the constraint concerned, while leaving the other critical constraint unchanged.

We would then need to solve:

Cutting	6x + 3y	=	37
Assembly	4x + 8y	=	48

Step 2: Use simultaneous equations to derive a new optimal solution

The simultaneous equations above can be solved in the same way as was seen in the previous TYU's. This gives and optimum vale of y = 3.888… and x = 4.222…

Step 3: Calculate the revised optimal contribution. The increase is the shadow price for the constraint under consideration.

The contribution. C = 50x + 40y.

At the revised optimal point this gives a revised contribution of C = (50 × 4.222…) + (40 × 3.888…) = $366.67 .

The increase of $6.67 ($366.67 – $360) is the shadow price for cutting time per hour. This represents the premium that the firm would be willing to pay for each extra hour of cutting time. The current cost is $10 per hour and therefore the maximum price that would be paid for an extra hour of cutting time is $16.67.

Note: A similar calculation can be done for assembly time giving a shadow price of $2.50 per hour.

chapter

5

Pricing

Chapter learning objectives

Upon completion of this chapter you will be able to:

- explain the factors that influence the pricing of a product or service, e.g. costs, demand and competition
- define and explain the price elasticity of demand
- from supplied data, derive and manipulate a straight-line demand equation
- from supplied data, derive an equation for the total cost function excluding or including volume-based discounts
- using data supplied or equations derived, advise on whether or not to increase production and sales levels considering incremental costs, incremental revenues and other factors
- explain, using a simple example, all forms of cost-plus pricing strategy
- calculate, for given data, a price using a cost-plus strategy
- explain different pricing strategies
- identify suitable pricing strategies for given situations from skimming, penetration, complementary product, product-line, volume discounting
- explain, using a simple example, a price-discrimination pricing strategy
- explain, using a simple example, a relevant-cost pricing strategy
- calculate, for given data, a price using a relevant cost strategy.

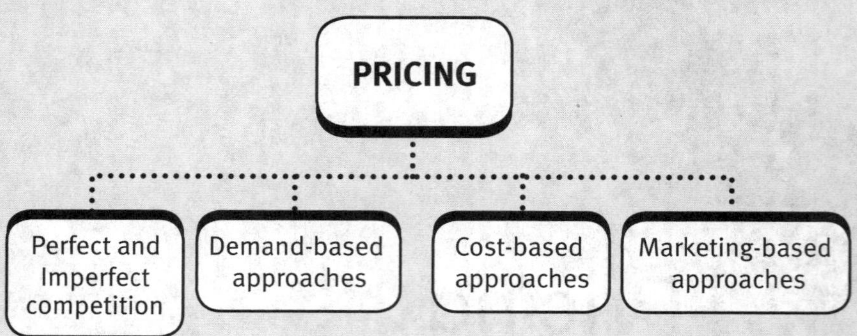

1 Introduction

Pricing is important because:

- It makes a pivotal contribution to profit maximisation – the overriding aim of most businesses.
- Businesses make profits by selling goods and services at a price higher than their cost.
- The amount that they are able to sell will often be determined by the price charged for the goods and services.

2 Different types of market structures

The price that a business can charge for its products or services will be determined by the market in which it operates.

In a **perfectly competitive** market, every buyer or seller is a 'price taker', and no participant influences the price of the product it buys or sells. Other characteristics of a perfectly competitive market include:

- **Zero entry/Exit barriers** – It is relatively easy to enter or exit as a business in a perfectly competitive market.
- **Perfect Information** – Prices and quality of products are assumed to be known to all consumers and producers.
- **Companies aim to maximise profits** – Firms aim to sell where marginal costs meet marginal revenue, where they generate the most profit.
- **Homogeneous products** – The characteristics of any given market good or service do not vary across suppliers.

Imperfect competition refers to the market structure that does not meet the conditions of perfect competition. Its forms include:

- **Monopoly**, in which there is only one seller of a good. The seller dominates many buyers and can use its market power to set a profit-maximising price. Microsoft is usually considered a monopoly.

- **Oligopoly**, in which a few companies dominate the market and are inter-dependent: firms must take into account likely reactions of their rivals to any change in price, output or forms of non-price competition. For example, in the UK, four companies (Tesco, Asda, Sainsbury's and Morrisons) share 74.4% of the grocery market.
- **Monopolistic competition**, in which products are similar, but not identical. There are many producers ('price setters') and many consumers in a given market, but no business has total control over the market price.

Illustration 1 – Monopolistic competition

For example, there are many different brands of soap on the market today. Each brand of soap is similar because it is designed to get the user clean; however, each soap product tries to differentiate itself from the competition to attract consumers. One soap might claim that it leaves you with soft skin, while another that it has a clean, fresh scent. Each participant in this market structure has some control over pricing, which means it can alter the selling price as long as consumers are still willing to buy its product at the new price. If one product costs twice as much as similar products on the market, chances are most consumers will avoid buying the more expensive product and buy the competitors' products instead. Monopolistic products are typically found in retailing businesses. Some examples of monopolistic products and/or services are shampoo products, extermination services, oil changes, toothpaste, and fast-food restaurants.

3 Three broad approaches to pricing

Pricing decisions may be separated into three broad approaches:

(1) Demand-based approaches

(2) Cost-based approaches

(3) Marketing-based approaches.

4 Demand-based approaches (The Economists' viewpoint)

Most firms recognise that there exists a relationship between the selling price of their product or service and the demand. By investigating and analysing this relationship it is possible, in theory, to establish an optimum price, i.e. a price that will maximise profits.

This relationship can often be described by an inverse, linear relationship:

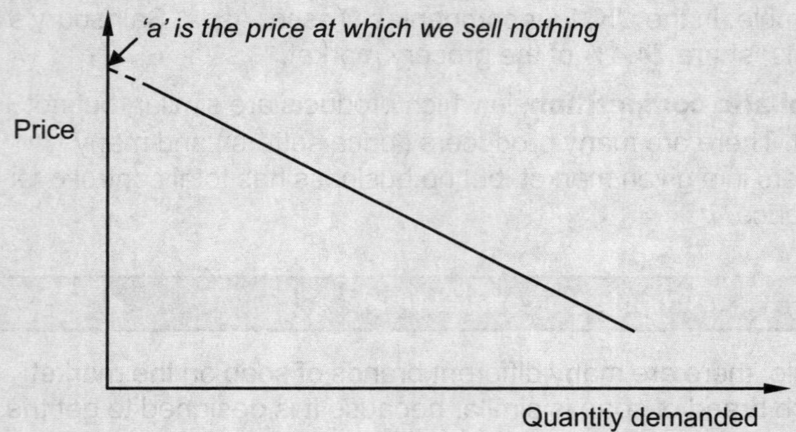
'a' is the price at which we sell nothing
Price
Quantity demanded

Note: "a" can also be viewed as the theoretical maximum possible price that could be charged before demand fell to zero.

There are two methods of solution to problems investigating the relationship between price and demand: the algebraic approach, and the tabular approach.

5 The algebraic approach

Economic theory states that the monopolist maximises profit when Marginal cost = Marginal revenue.

Illustration 2 – The MR= MC

Marginal revenue is the additional revenue from selling one extra unit, for example:

Quantity	Price	Revenue	Marginal revenue
1	$70	$70	$70
2	$60	$120	$50
3	$50	$150	$30
4	$40	$160	$10
5	$30	$150	$(10)

Marginal cost is the cost from making one more unit. It is usually just the variable cost, e.g. MC = $30.

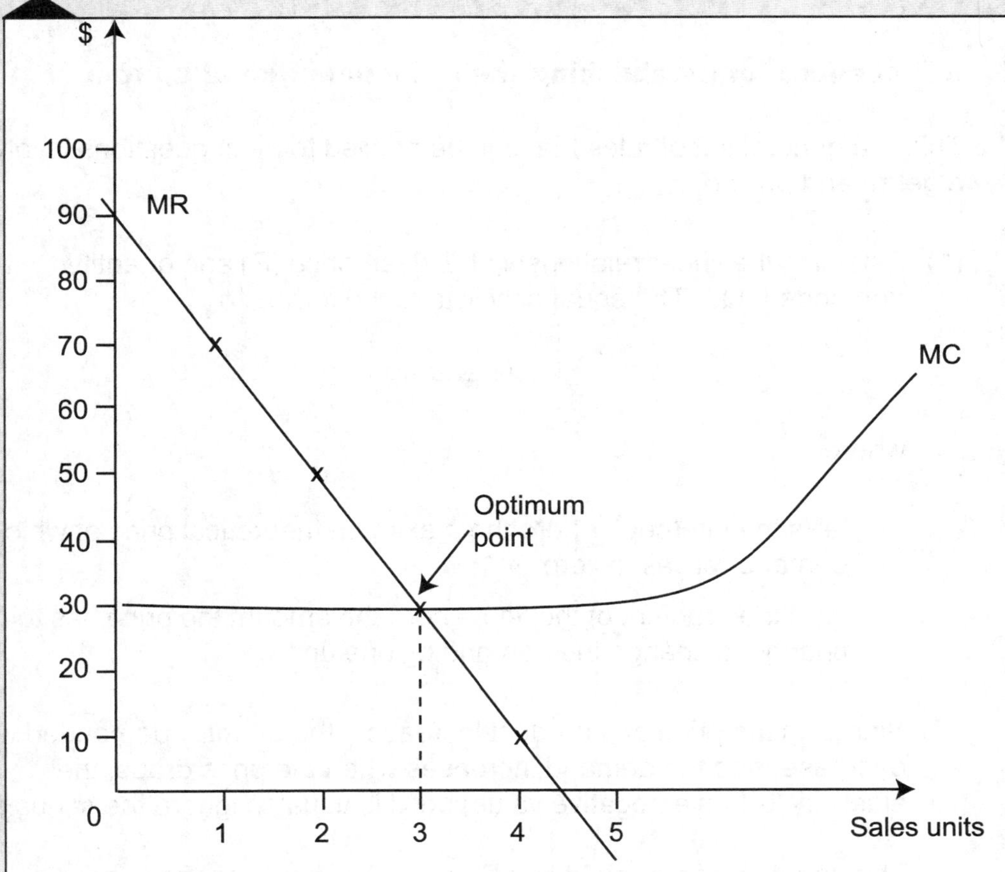

The optimum price is $50. At output less than Q = 3, the extra cost of making a unit is less than the extra revenue from selling it – so it is worth selling it.

At output greater than Q = 3, the extra costs of making a unit exceed the revenue from selling it.

6 Procedure for establishing the optimum price of a product

This is a general set of rules that can be applied to most questions involving algebra and pricing.

(1) Establish the linear relationship between price (P) and quantity demanded (Q). The equation will take the form:

$$P = a - bQ$$

where

- 'a' is the intercept – here the maximum theoretical price at which demand will fall to zero
- 'b' is the gradient of the line – here the amount the price has to change to change the demand by one unit.

Since, as the price of a product increases, the quantity demanded will decrease; and the demand increases when the price drops, the elasticity 'b' has a negative value, but it is usual to ignore the minus sign.

The equation of a straight line P= a – bQ can be used to show the demand for a product at a given price:

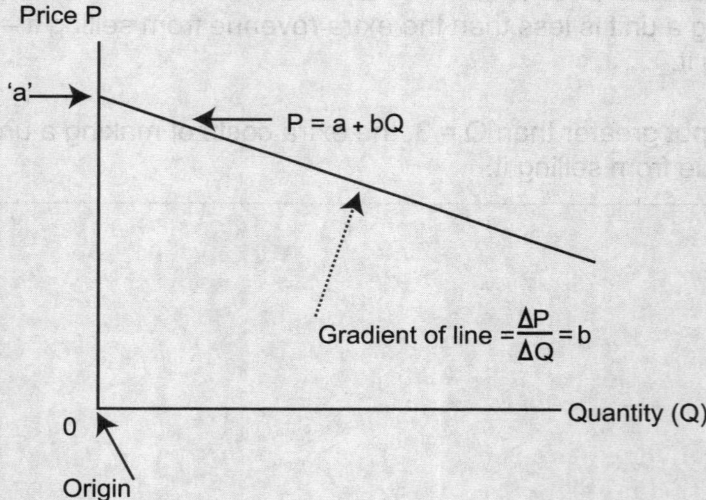

Note: 'b' is always negative because of the inverse relationship between price and quantity.

(2) Double the gradient to find the marginal revenue: **MR = a – 2bQ.**

(3) Establish the **marginal cost MC**. This will simply be the variable cost per unit.

(4) To maximise profit, **equate MC and MR** and solve to find Q.

(5) Substitute this value of Q into the price equation to find the optimum price.

(6) It may be necessary to calculate the maximum profit.

The price elasticity of demand

When a business proposes to change the price of a product or service the key question is: 'to what degree will demand be affected?'

Calculation

Price elasticity measures how *responsive* demand is to a change in price.

The price elasticity of demand measures the proportional or percentage change in demand as a result of a corresponding proportional or percentage change in price.

It can be calculated as follows:

$$\text{Price elasticity of demand} = \frac{\text{Change in quantity demanded, as a percentage of demand}}{\text{Change in price, as a percentage of the price}}$$

Example: assume that the sales of a retailer fall from 20 per day to 12 per day when the price of a chocolate bar goes up from 40c to 60c. The price elasticity can be calculated as follows:

%change in price = (increase in price of 20/original price of 40) × 100 = +50%

%change in demand =(decrease in demand of – 8/original demand of 20) × 100 = – 40%

PED = – 40/+50 = – 0.8

The negative sign should be ignored in the PED calculation. Therefore the **PED = 0.8.**

Interpretation of PED

Elastic demand

If the % change in demand > the % change in price, then price elasticity > 1.

Demand is 'elastic', i.e. very responsive to changes in price.

- Total revenue increases when price is reduced.
- Total revenue decreases when price is increased.

Therefore, price increases are not recommended but price cuts are recommended.

Inelastic demand

If the % change in demand < the % change in price, then price elasticity < 1.

Demand is 'inelastic', i.e. not very responsive to changes in price.

- Total revenue decreases when price is reduced.
- Total revenue increases when price is increased.

Therefore, price increases are recommended but price cuts are not recommended.

Additional example on straight-line demand equation

(a) Find the linear relationship between price (P) and the quantity demanded (Q) in relation to the following sales and demand data:

– Selling price of $300 = sales of 500 units per month.

– Selling price of $330 = sales of 400 units per month.

(b) Using the price equation in (a) and assuming the variable cost per unit is $90, calculate the optimum price and output.

(c) Calculate the maximum contribution.

Solution

(a)
- $P = a - bQ$
- $- b$ (gradient) $= (330 - 300) \div (400 - 500) = - 0.3$
- remembering that price (P) = 300 when 500 units are sold and substituting 0.3 for b
- $300 = a - (0.3 \times 500)$
- $300 = a - 150$
- $a = 300 + 150 = 450$
- So the linear relationship (or demand function equation) is: $P = 450 - 0.3Q$.

(b) $MR = 450 - 0.6Q$
MC = VC so equating MR = MC: $90 = 450 - 0.6Q$
So Q = 600
And substituting Q into Price function, P = $270

(c) Contribution per unit = $270 – $90 = $180
Total contribution = $180 × 600 units = $108,000

Note that if there were fixed costs in the question, and the examiner asked for the maximum **profit,** these fixed costs would need to be deducted from the maximum contribution.

Test your understanding 1

Find the linear relationship between price (P) and the quantity demanded (Q), i.e. find the straight-line demand equation, in relation to the following sales and demand data:

- Selling price of $200 = sales of 1,000 units per month.
- Selling price of $220 = sales of 950 units per month.

Required:

(a) Use this equation to predict the quantity demanded per month if the selling price is $300.

(b) Using the price equation in (a) and assuming the variable cost per unit is $100, calculate the optimum price and output.

(c) Calculate the maximum contribution.

Test your understanding 2

The total fixed costs per annum for a company that makes one product are $100,000, and a variable cost of $64 is incurred for each additional unit produced and sold over a very large range of outputs.

The current selling price for the product is $160. At this price, 2,000 units are demanded per annum.

It is estimated that for each successive increase in price of $5 annual demand will be reduced by 50 units. Alternatively, for each $5 reduction in price, demand will increase by $50 units.

Required:

(a) Calculate the optimum output and price, assuming that if prices are set within each $5 range there will be a proportionate change in demand.

(b) Calculate the maximum profit.

7 The tabular approach

A tabular approach to price setting involves different prices and volumes of sales being presented in a table.

When data in the exam is given in tabular form and there is no indication about the demand function, and/or when there is no simple linear relationship between output and profit – the tabular approach is likely to be the best to define optimum profit and the associated selling price.

Then, it makes sense to calculate the profit for each price and quantity combination, and finally select the price at which the level of profit is maximised.

Illustration 3 – Tabular approach

XYZ Ltd is a car manufacturer introducing a new type of car in a market where there is imperfect competition, so that to sell more units of output, it must reduce the sales price of all the units it sells. The following data is available for prices, and costs (all in $000):

Price per unit	Demand/output units	Total cost
50.00	1	44.00
47.00	2	56.00
44.00	3	71.00
41.00	4	85.00
38.00	5	95.00
35.00	6	110.00
32.00	7	122.00
29.00	8	135.00
26.00	9	145.00

Required:

Complete the table below to determine the output level and price at which the organisation would maximise its profits.

Price per unit	Demand/output units	Total revenue	MR	Total cost	MC	Profit
50.00	1					
47.00	2					
44.00	3					
41.00	4					
38.00	5					
35.00	6					
32.00	7					
29.00	8					
26.00	9					

Tabular approach – Solution

Price per unit	Demand/output units	Total revenue	MR	Total cost	MC	Profit
50.00	1	50.00	50.00	44.00	44.00	6.00
47.00	2	94.00	44.00	56.00	12.00	38.00
44.00	3	132.00	38.00	71.00	15.00	61.00
41.00	4	164.00	32.00	85.00	14.00	79.00
38.00	5	190.00	26.00	95.00	10.00	95.00
35.00	6	210.00	20.00	110.00	15.00	100.00
32.00	7	224.00	14.00	122.00	12.00	102.00
29.00	8	232.00	8.00	135.00	13.00	97.00
26.00	9	234.00	2.00	145.00	10.00	89.00

As the price per unit declines, so demand expands. Total revenue rises, but at a decreasing rate as shown by the column showing marginal revenue.

Profit increases every time the level of output increases, because the marginal revenue from selling units is greater than the marginal cost of producing them.

However, once marginal cost is greater than marginal revenue (at 8 units in our example), total profits start to fall.

The profit is maximised at 7 units of output and a price of $32,000, when MR is most nearly equal to MC.

8 Equation for the total cost function

Cost equations are derived from historical cost data. Once a cost equation has been established (using methods such as the high/low method which will be revised later in the course) it can be used to estimate future costs. In the exam, cost functions will be linear:

$y = a + bx$

- 'a' is the fixed cost per period (the intercept)
- 'b' is the variable cost per unit (the gradient)
- 'x' is the activity level (the independent variable)
- 'y' is the total cost = fixed cost + variable cost (the dependent variable).

Suppose a cost has a cost equation of y = $5,000 + 10x, this can be shown graphically as follows:

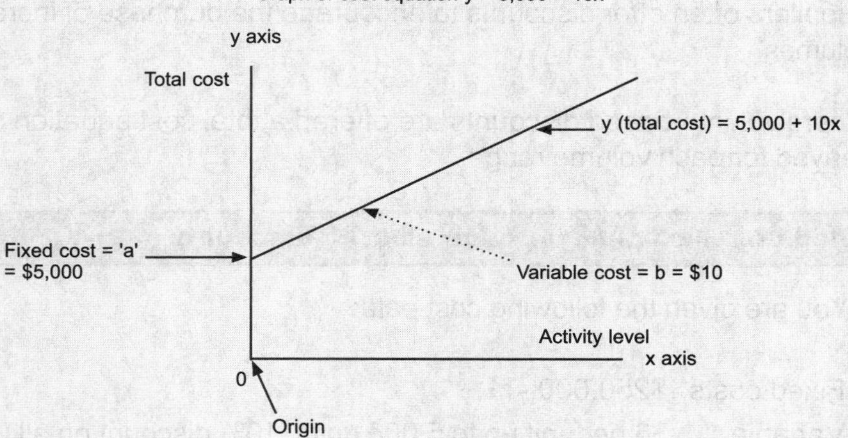

Test your understanding 3

- Fixed costs $100,000.
- Variable costs per unit $5 for volumes up to 1,000 units.
- Volumes above 1,000 units receive 5% discount on all units.

Required:

Derive the two equations for the total cost function.

Additional example on the total cost function

Consider the linear function y = 1,488 + 20x and answer the following questions.

(a) The line would cross the y axis at the point

(b) The gradient of the line is

(c) The independent variable is

(d) The dependent variable is

Solution

(a) The line would cross the y axis at the point	1,488
(b) The gradient of the line is	20
(c) The independent variable is	x
(d) The dependent variable is	y

9 Cost equations including volume-based discounts

Suppliers often offer discounts to encourage the purchase of increased volumes.

Where volume-based discounts are offered a total cost equation can be derived for each volume range.

Additional example on volume-based discounts

You are given the following cost data:

Fixed costs	$250,000.
Variable costs	$6 per unit up to 5,000 units. 10% discount on all units purchased over 5,000 units.

Required:

Derive equations for the total cost function.

Solution

$y = 250,000 + 6x$ for $x \leq 5,000$.

$y = 250,000 + 5.4x$ for $x > 5,000$.

10 Increasing sales and production levels

When an opportunity to increase sales and production levels arises in a business the key question to answer is:

- will the increased contribution (sales less variable costs) generated by the increased sales exceed any additional fixed costs that will be incurred as a result of the increased sales level?

If the answer is 'yes' the opportunity should normally be pursued.

Test your understanding 4

An opportunity arises to increase sales by 10,000 units:

- Selling price of additional units = $10
- Variable cost of additional units = $6
- Fixed costs will increase by = $50,000

Required:

Should the opportunity be accepted?

Additional example on increasing volumes

A company produces and sells one product and its forecast for the next financial year is as follows:

	$000	$000
Sales 100,000 units @ $8		800
Variable costs:		
Material	300	
Labour	200	
		500
Contribution ($3 per unit)		300
Fixed costs		150
Net profit		150

In an attempt to increase net profit, two proposals have been put forward:

(a) To launch an advertising campaign costing $14,000. This will increase the sales to 150,000 units, although the price will have to be reduced to $7.

(b) To produce some components at present purchased from suppliers. This will reduce material costs by 20% but will increase fixed costs by $72,000.

Required:

Decide whether these proposals should be pursued.

Solution

Proposal (a) will increase the sales revenue but the increase in costs will be greater:

	$000
Sales (150,000 @ $7)	1,050
Variable costs (150,000 @ $5)	750
	300
Fixed costs plus advertising	164
Net profit	136

This is lower than the current forecast.

Proposal (b)

- reduces variable costs by $60,000 ($300,000 × 20%)
- but increases fixed costs by $72,000 and is therefore not to be recommended unless the total volume increases as a result of the policy (e.g. if the supply of the components were previously a limiting factor).

Conclusion

Neither proposal should be accepted.

11 Cost plus pricing

Many businesses adopt simple cost-plus pricing techniques:

Price = cost per unit + chosen margin or mark-up

There is a difference between a mark-up and a margin.

A mark-up is the profit expressed as a percentage of cost (cost is 100%).

A margin is the profit expressed as a percentage of the sales price (sales is 100%).

Which cost to use?

When using cost-plus pricing the following options are available:

- *Actual or standard cost*

  The advantage of using standard costing is that prices can be set in advance and fixed for the period concerned. This makes marketing simpler and may attract customers who value knowing exactly how much they will pay. The main disadvantage is that if significant variances occur, then the price may have been set too low and a loss ensues.

  The main advantage of using actual costs is that a profit is guaranteed. However, there is less incentive for the supplier to control costs as inefficiencies can be passed on to customers. Such a contract may discourage some customers from dealing with the firm concerned.

  Examples where actual costs are used include large military contracts (where cost overruns often become a matter of political debate), tradesmen (e.g. builders) and car repairs, where the mark-up is incorporated into the hourly labour rate used by the garage.

- *Marginal or full cost*

  The use of marginal cost is simpler as there is no need for the absorption of fixed overheads and could be argued to be more consistent with the use of contribution in decision making. The main difficulty lies in setting an appropriate margin or mark-up as this will need to ensure that fixed costs are covered. In practice the danger is often that prices are set too low. Marginal costing is particularly useful in short-term decisions concerning the use of excess capacity or one off contracts.

  The use of full cost ensures that all costs are incorporated into the pricing decision, so should ensure a profit is made, provided the target volume is achieved. However, to calculate the fixed cost per unit an assumption must be made concerning sales volumes, which in turn depends on the price, which depends on the cost per unit. A further criticism is that the method of absorbing overheads is somewhat arbitrary, so the prices obtained may not be very realistic when compared with what customers are willing to pay.

- *Relevant costs*

  The principles of relevant costing were met in paper F2 and will be reviewed in more detail in a later chapter.

  Relevant costs can be used to arrive at a minimum tender price for a one-off tender or contract. The minimum price should be equal to the total of all of the relevant cash flows.

  The use of relevant costs is only suitable for a one-off decision since:

  – fixed costs may become relevant in the long run

  – there are problems estimating incremental cash flows

  – there is a conflict between accounting measures such as profit and this approach.

Example of cost-plus pricing

When using a cost-plus pricing strategy a business should work through a step by step approach. For example:

Step 1: Establish the cost per unit. For example, if full cost is used this may be:

• raw materials	$40 per unit
• variable production costs	$40 per unit
• fixed costs based on planned volumes	$20 per unit
• total cost	$100 per unit

Step 2: Add the target profit to arrive at the selling price. For example:

- 20% mark-up = selling price of $120 per unit
- 20% sales margin = selling price of $125 per unit

Step 3: Consider how realistic the target profit is. This will depend upon:

- accurate knowledge of costs
- the selling price arrived at being one which customers are prepared to pay
- selling the planned volume of goods.

Advantages and disadvantages of cost-plus pricing

Advantages of cost-plus pricing	Disadvantages of cost-plus pricing
• Widely used and accepted. • Simple to calculate if costs are known. • Selling price decision may be delegated to junior management. • Justification for price increases. • May encourage price stability – if all competitors have similar cost structures and use similar mark-up.	• Ignores the economic relationship between price and demand. • No attempt to establish optimum price. • Different absorption methods give rise to different costs and hence different selling prices. • Does not guarantee profit – if sales volumes are low fixed costs may not be recovered. • Must decide whether to use full cost, manufacturing cost or marginal cost. • This structured method fails to recognise the manager's need for flexibility in pricing. • Circular reasoning – for example, a price increase will reduce volume, thus increasing unit costs, resulting in pressure to increase the price further.

Objective Test Case Question – Greenfields

(1) Greenfields Ltd manufactures three products, W, X and Y. Each product uses the same materials and the same type of direct labour, but in different quantities. The company currently uses a full cost-plus basis to determine the selling price of its products. This is based on full cost, using an overhead absorption rate per direct labour hour.

The direct costs of the three products are shown below:

	Product W	Product X	Product Y
Budgeted annual production, in units	15,000	24,000	20,000
Direct materials ($ per unit)	$35	$45	$30
Direct labour ($10 per hour)	$40	$30	$50

In addition to the above direct costs, Greenfields incurs annual indirect production costs of $1,044,000.

What is the full cost per unit of each product, using Greenfields's current method of absorption costing?

A $18 for W, $75 for X and $22.50 for Y

B $75 for W, $75 for X and $100.50 for Y

C $93 for W, $88.50 for X and $102.50 for Y

D $93 for W, $90.50 for X and $102.50 for Y

(2) An analysis of the company's indirect production costs shows the following:

	$	Cost drivers
Material ordering costs	220,000	Number of supplier orders
General facility costs	824,000	Number of labour hours

The following additional data relate to each product:

	Product W	Product X	Product Y
Suppliers orders per line of products	120	180	100

What is the full cost per unit of each product, using ABC?

A $14.21 for W, $10.66 for X and $17.76 for Y

B $93.61 for W, $99.16 for X and $100.50 for Y

C $93.61 for W, $89.79 for X and $100.51 for Y

D $107.21 for W, $99.16 for X and $120.25 for Y

(3) The company currently uses a full cost plus basis to determine the selling price of its products.

Which of the following statements regarding the current full cost-plus pricing approach strategy are correct?

(1) The use of absorption costing means that the price is dependent at least in part on the method used to absorb the costs into each cost unit.

(2) The use of absorption costing suggests that this is the cost of the individual item whereas, in fact, it includes costs that would continue to be incurred if the item were not produced.

(3) A manager may reject a sale because the customer is only prepared to pay a price which is less than the absorption cost.

(4) Full cost-plus pricing requires that the profit mark-up applied by a company is fixed.

A Statements (2) and (4)

B Statements (1), (2) and (3)

C Statements (1), (3) and (4)

D Statements (1), (2), (3) and (4)

(4) The managing director is concerned that the company may be losing sales because of its approach to setting prices. He thinks that a marginal cost-plus costing approach may be more appropriate, particularly since the workforce is guaranteed a minimum weekly wage and has a three month notice period.

Which of the following statements regarding a marginal cost-plus pricing approach strategy are correct?

(1) The use of marginal costing identifies the variable cost of the item produced and thus provides a clear indication of the maximum price that should be charged so as to avoid a negative contribution.

(2) A marginal cost-plus approach may mean that managers are persuaded to sell items at too low a price, so that the contribution earned is insufficient to cover the fixed costs of the business.

(3) It is very difficult to increase the price for a subsequent sale of the same item to the same customer, so the company may find it difficult to break out of the low price arena once they have entered it.

(4) Marginal cost-plus pricing is easier where there is a readily identifiable variable cost.

A Statements (1) and (2)

B Statements (3) and (4)

C Statements (1), (3) and (4)

D Statements (2), (3) and (4)

(5) **Which of the following statements regarding the use of ABC in pricing decisions are correct?**

(1) The management of Greenfields can use the information provided by the activity-based costing approach to identify potential cost savings by changing the method of operation within the company.

(2) It may be appropriate to consider investing in new machines to automate production processes and increase the number of labour hours.

(3) The effect of activity-based costing is often to identify costs as being more controllable because their cause has now been identified.

(4) While some facility costs will remain and are truly fixed as they are not driven by any particular future activity, many of the other costs will now become variable depending on the number of times an activity is performed.

A Statements (1) and (2)

B Statements (2), (3) and (4)

C Statements (1), (3) and (4)

D Statements (1), (2), (3) and (4)

Customer based pricing – the marketer's approach

Customer-based pricing reflects customers' perceptions of the benefits they will enjoy from purchasing the product, e.g. convenience, status. The product is priced to reflect these benefits.

This approach has regard to costs but reflects a belief that the greater understanding you have of your customer the better placed you are to price the product.

Illustration 4 – Customer-based pricing

On a remote beach in a hot country, the offer of food and drink to tourists on the beach will be perceived by them as being of significant benefit and they are likely to be prepared to pay a significant amount in excess of cost.

Competition-based pricing

Competition-based pricing means setting a price based upon the prices of competing products.

Competing products can be classified as:

- The same type of product which is not easily distinguished from one's own products. For example, petrol sold at two competing petrol stations.
  - price changes by competitors will have a material impact.
- Substitute products which are different products but fulfil the same need, e.g. you may buy ice cream instead of soft drinks on a hot day.
  - impact of price changes will depend on relative price/performance of substitute.

Test your understanding 5

Of the three approaches to pricing discussed above:

- cost-based
- customer-based
- competition-based.

Which is the least likely to maximise profits and why?

12 Different pricing strategies

There are a number of different pricing strategies available to a business:

- Cost-plus pricing
- Market-skimming
- Penetration pricing
- Complementary product pricing
- Product-line pricing
- Volume discounting.
- Price discrimination
- Relevant cost pricing

Cost-plus pricing was covered earlier. The other strategies will now be reviewed in turn.

13 Market-skimming pricing strategy

Market skimming involves charging high prices when a product is first launched in order to maximise short-term profitability. Initially high prices may be charged to take advantage of the novelty appeal of a new product when demand is initially inelastic.

Once the market becomes saturated the price can be reduced to attract that part of the market that has not been exploited.

Conditions suitable for a market-skimming strategy

- Where the product is new and different and has little direct competition. This is the most common reason for using a market-skimming strategy.
- Where products have a short life cycle, and there is a need to recover their development costs quickly and make a profit.
- Where the strength of demand and the sensitivity of demand to price are unknown. From a psychological point of view it is far better to begin with a high price, which can then be lowered if the demand for the product appears to be more price sensitive than at first thought.
- A firm with liquidity problems may use market-skimming in order to generate high cash flows early on.

With high prices being charged potential competitors will be tempted to enter the market. For skimming to be sustained one or more significant barriers to entry must be present to deter these potential competitors. For example, patent protection, strong brand loyalty.

Test your understanding 6

What products may be priced using a market-skimming strategy?

14 Penetration pricing strategy

- **Penetration pricing** is the charging of low prices when a new product is initially launched in order to gain rapid acceptance of the product.
- Once market share is achieved, prices are increased.
- It is an alternative to market skimming when launching a new product.

Circumstances which favour a penetration policy

- If the firm wishes to increase market share.
- A firm wishes to discourage new entrants from entering the market.
- If there are significant economies of scale to be achieved from high-volume output, and so a quick penetration into the market is desirable.
- If demand is highly elastic and so would respond well to low prices.

Illustration 5 – Penetration pricing strategy

The 2006 launch of Microsoft's anti-virus product, Windows Live OneCare, was described by commentators as an example of penetration pricing. Microsoft's competitors in this market (e.g. Symantec and McAfee) reportedly lost material market share within a few months of its launch.

15 Complementary-product pricing

A **complementary product** is one that is normally used with another product. An example is razors and razor blades – if sales of razors increase more razor blades will also be bought.

Other examples of complementary products are:

- game consoles and associated games
- printers and printer cartridges.

Complementary goods provide suppliers with additional power over the consumer.

Illustration 6 – What is complementary-product pricing?

A complementary-product pricing strategy can take two forms:

- The major product (e.g. a printer or a camera) is priced at a relatively low figure – to encourage the purchase and lock the consumer into subsequent purchases of relatively high price consumables (e.g. printer cartridges or memory cards). This is the most common form.
- The major product (e.g. membership of a fashionable sports or golf club) is priced at a relatively high figure – to create a barrier to entry and exit and the consumer is locked into subsequent purchases of relatively low-price facilities (e.g. court fees or green fees).

16 Product-line pricing strategy

A product line is a range of products that are related to one another.

Product line pricing occurs when setting the price steps between various products in a product line, based on:

- Cost differences between the products
- Customer evaluations of different features
- Competitors prices.

In other words, product line pricing occurs when a company must decide the price differences between the upgrades of a product or service.

Illustration 7 – Product-line pricing strategy

A basic car wash may be shown as one price, a super wash with wash and wax will cost a little more, and a full-service premium wash will be the most expensive.

17 Volume-discounting pricing strategy

Volume discounting means offering customers a lower price per unit if they purchase a particular quantity of a product.

It takes two main forms:

- Quantity discounts – for customers that order large quantities.
- Cumulative quantity discounts – the discount increases as the cumulative total ordered increases. This may appeal to those who do not wish to place large individual orders but who purchase large quantities over time.

Benefits to the business of using a volume discounting strategy

- Increased customer loyalty – cumulative quantity discounts 'lock in' the customer since further purchases can be made at a lower cost per unit.
- Attracting new customers – an exceptional level of discount can be offered to new customers on a one-off basis, enabling the supplier to 'get his foot in the door'.
- Lower sales processing costs – an increased proportion of his sales take the form of bulk orders.

- Lower purchasing costs – high sales volumes enable the business to enjoy discounts from their suppliers, creating a virtuous circle.
- Discounts help to sell items that are bought primarily on price.
- Clearance of surplus stock or unpopular item through the use of discounts.
- Discounts can be geared to particular off-peak periods.

Conditions suitable for a volume-discounting pricing strategy

- Sales margin is substantial allowing profits to be made even after discounting.
- The product is bought on price and it is difficult to distinguish it from competing products.
- Products with a limited shelf life (for example, fashion items) may be discounted to shift them.

Recap of pricing strategies for a given situation

Situation	Pricing strategy
• Product is new and different (e.g. new electronic product). • 'Early adopters' are prepared to pay high prices to achieve ownership. • Significant barriers to entry exist (e.g. patent protection, high capital investment, or unusually strong brand loyalty) to deter competition – in order that skimming can be sustained. • The product has a short life cycle so there is a need to recover development costs and make a profit quickly. • The business has a liquidity problem and may be attracted by the high initial cash flows available in the early stages of a product's life. • Strength of demand and the sensitivity of demand to price are unknown. It is much easier to lower prices than to increase them.	Skimming

• The business wishes to discourage newcomers from entering the market. • The business wishes to shorten the initial period of the product's life cycle in order to enter the growth and maturity stages as quickly as possible. • There are significant economies of scale to be achieved from high-volume output, and so a quick penetration into the market is desirable in order to gain those unit cost reductions. • Demand is highly elastic and so would respond well to low prices.	Penetration
• A range of products is being marketed – the products within a product line are related but may vary in terms of style, colour, quality, etc. (e.g. dinner services, cutlery sets). • Consumers will tend to buy a number of items within the range and be prepared to pay a relatively high price for the less essential items in order to build up a matching set.	Product-line
• The sales margin is substantial, allowing good profits to be made even after significant discounting (e.g. consumer software products). • The product is traditionally bought on price – it is difficult to distinguish from competing products (e.g. car tyres). • Products with a limited shelf life (e.g. fashion items).	Volume discounting

18 Price-discrimination pricing strategy

A price-discrimination strategy is where a company sells the same product or services at different prices in different markets, for reasons not associated with costs.

Conditions required for a price-discrimination strategy

- The seller must have some degree of monopoly power, or the price will be driven down.
- Customers can be segregated into different markets.

- Customers cannot buy at the lower price in one market and sell at the higher price in the other market.
- Price discrimination strategies are particularly effective for services.
- There must be different price elasticities of demand in each market so that prices can be raised in one and lowered in the other to increase revenue.

Dangers of price-discrimination as a strategy

- A black market may develop allowing those in a lower priced segment to resell to those in a higher priced segment.
- Competitors join the market and undercut the firm's prices.
- Customers in the higher priced brackets look for alternatives and demand becomes more elastic over time.

Test your understanding 7

Which products or services lend themselves to a price-discrimination strategy?

Test your understanding 8 – Recap of pricing strategies

(1) Which pricing strategies are aimed at the start of the product life cycle?

(2) Which pricing strategies seek to attract sales by offering a product at a relatively low price?

(3) Which pricing strategies lure the customer in with a relatively low-priced product in order to lock the customer in to subsequent additional purchases of similar items that are relatively highly priced?

(4) Which pricing strategy is appropriate to items that are bought primarily on price.

19 Chapter summary

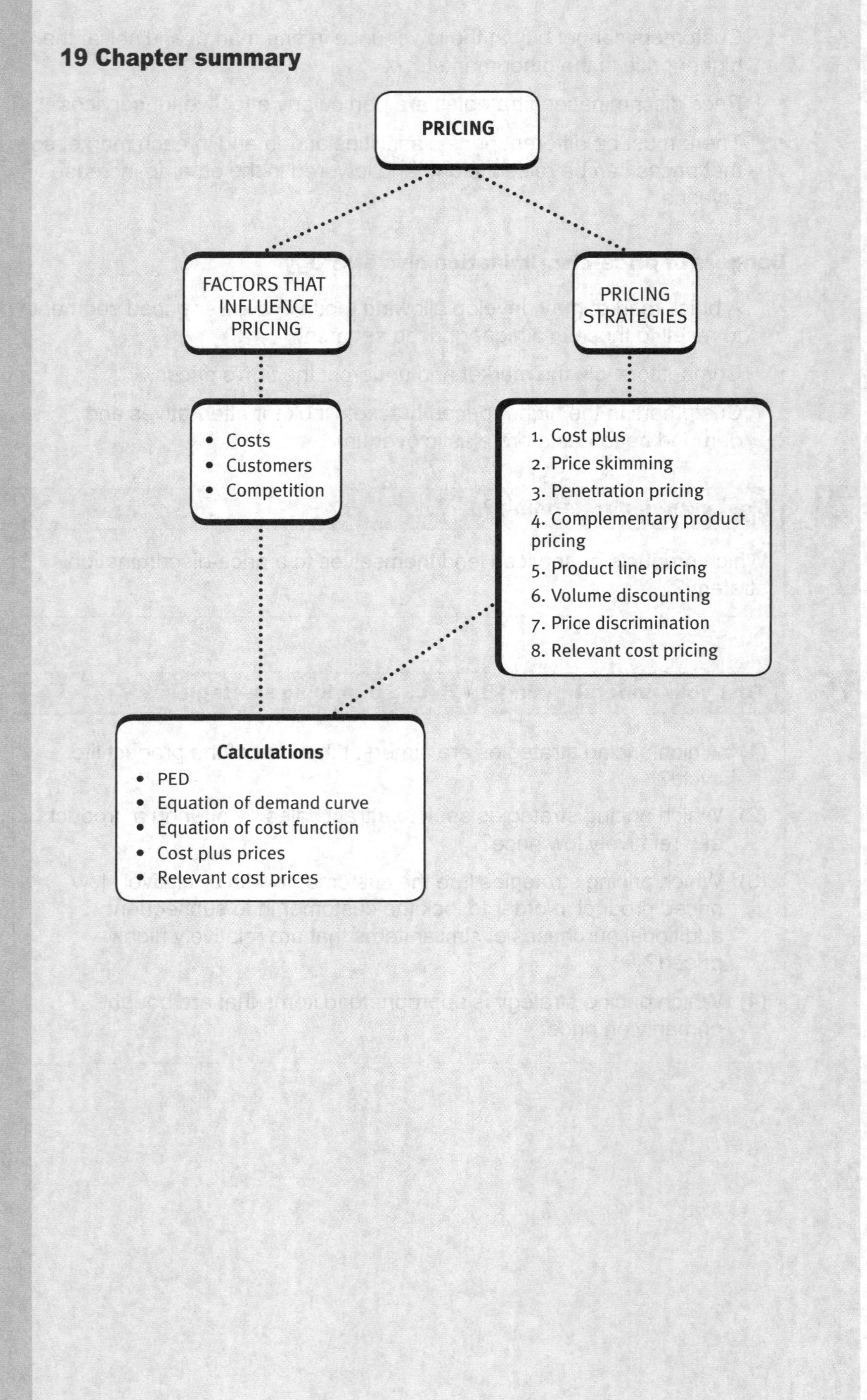
PRICING
FACTORS THAT INFLUENCE PRICING
PRICING STRATEGIES
• Costs
• Customers
• Competition
1. Cost plus
2. Price skimming
3. Penetration pricing
4. Complementary product pricing
5. Product line pricing
6. Volume discounting
7. Price discrimination
8. Relevant cost pricing
Calculations
• PED
• Equation of demand curve
• Equation of cost function
• Cost plus prices
• Relevant cost prices

Test your understanding answers

Test your understanding 1

(a) **Step 1: Find the gradient, b**

The question provides us with two selling prices and the respective level of demand at these selling prices. Therefore, we can begin by calculating the gradient of the straight line, b.

b (gradient) = change in price/change in quantity
= (220 – 200)/(950 – 1000) = – 0.4

Step 2: Calculate the intersect, a

Once the gradient is known the intersect can be found using either of the selling prices and demand levels given in the question.

For example, price (P) = 200 when 1000 units (Q) are sold and substituting – 0.4 for b

200 = a – (0.4 × 1,000)

200 = a – 400

a = 200 + 400 = 600

Step 3: Straight-line demand equation

So the equation is: P = 600 – 0.4Q.

Step 4: Forecast the demand at a given selling price

At a price of $300

300 = 600 – 0.4Q

0.4Q = 300

Q = 300/0.4

Quantity demanded (Q) = 750 units per month

(b) MR = 600 – 0.8Q

MC = VC so equating MR = MC: 100 = 600 – 0.8Q

So Q = 625

And substituting Q into Price function, P = $350

(b) Contribution per unit = $350 – $100 = $250

Total contribution = $250 × 625 units = $156,250

Test your understanding 2

(a) Let Q = quantity produced/sold

Gradient 'b'=

$$b = \frac{\text{Change in price}}{\text{Change in quantity}} = \frac{\$5}{\$50}$$

b = – 0.1

Price = a – 0.1Q; $160 = a – 0.1 (2,000) therefore **a = $360**

P = $360 – 0.1Q
MR = $360 – 0.2Q
MC = $64

(b) To maximise profit, MR = MC. Therefore, $360 – 0.2Q = $64

Q	= (360 – 64) ÷ 0.2	= 1,480	units
P	= 360 – 0.1 (1,480)	= $212	
Revenue	= $212 × 1,480	= $313,760	
Less Costs	= ($64 × 1,480) + $100,000	= ($194,720)	
Maximum profit	=	$119,040	

Test your understanding 3

- Y = 100,000 + 5x for x ≤1,000
- Y = 100,000 + 4.75x for x >1,000.

Test your understanding 4

The effect of the increased sales would be to reduce net profits by $10,000.

- $100,000 increased sales ($10 × 10,000 units)
- $60,000 increased variable costs ($6 × 10,000 units) = $40,000 additional contribution
- less additional fixed costs of $50,000 = $10,000 reduction in net profit.

Based on this analysis, the opportunity should be rejected. However, other factors need to be considered such as:

- the impact on future sales beyond the current period
- the impact of rejection on customer goodwill
- whether the extra sales would help build the firm's brand.

Objective Test Case Question – Greenfields

(1) **C**

The full cost per unit includes all production costs, including a share of fixed overheads.

$$\text{OAR} = \frac{\text{Budgeted production overhead (\$1,044,000, per question)}}{\text{Activity level (Total number of labour hours)}}$$

$$\text{OAR} = \frac{\$1,044,000}{\text{232,000 labour hours (W1)}}$$

OAR = $4.50 per labour hour

	Product W	Product X	Product Y
Material costs per unit, as per question	$35	$45	$30
Labour costs per unit, as per question	$40	$30	$50
Fixed overhead cost per unit	$4.50 × 4 hours = $18	$4.50 × 3 hours = $13.50	$4.50 × 5 hours = $22.50
Total = full cost per unit	**$93**	**$88.50**	**$102.50**

(2) **C**

	Product W	Product X	Product Y
Material costs per unit, as per question	$35	$45	$30
Labour costs per unit, as per question	$40	$30	$50
Material ordering costs per unit (W2)	$4.40	$4.125	$2.75
General running costs per unit (W3)	$14.21	$10.655	$17.759
Total cost per unit using ABC	**$93.61**	**$89.79**	**$100.51**

(3) **B**

Statement (4) is not correct. The mark-up percentage does not have to be fixed: it may vary and be adjusted to reflect market conditions.

(4) **D**

All statements are correct, apart from statement (1), which should refer to the minimum (not the maximum) price: The use of marginal costing identifies the variable cost of the item produced and thus provides a clear indication of the **minimum** price that should be charged so as to avoid a negative contribution.

(5) **C**

Statement 2 is not correct. Investing in new machines would hopefully reduce the number of labour hours.

Workings

(W1)	Product W	Product X	Product Y
Direct labour hours per unit	4 hours	3 hours	5 hours
Total number of units	15,000 units	24,000 units	20,000 units
Total number of hours: 232,000 hours	60,000 hours	72,000 hours	100,000 hours

(W2)

The 'material ordering costs' activity will be associated with the number of supplier orders. There are (120 + 180 + 100) = 400 supplier orders in total.

Cost per supplier order = $\frac{\$220,000}{400 \text{ orders}}$ = \$550 per supplier order

	Product W	Product X	Product Y
Material ordering costs per unit	(\$550 per order × 120)/15,000 = \$4.40 per unit	(\$550 per order × 180)/24,000 = \$4.125 per unit	(\$550 per order × 100)/20,000 = \$2.75 per unit

(W3)

The 'General running costs' activity will be associated with the number of labour hours.

Cost per order = $\frac{\$824,000}{232,000 \text{ lab. hours}}$ = \$3.551 per labour hour

	Product W	Product X	Product Y
General running costs per unit @ \$3.551 per labour hour	\$14.21	\$10.655	\$17.759

Test your understanding 5

Customer-based and competition-based pricing are most likely to maximise profits since they take into account the behaviour of customers and competitors, as well as the need to recover costs or obtain a particular margin on sales. Cost-based pricing, in contrast, simply reflects the objective of cost recovery or achieving a margin on sales and ignores the potential to exploit the level of customers' interest in the product or the strength of the product in the marketplace relative to competitors.

Test your understanding 6

Market skimming is often used in relation to electronic products when a new range (e.g. DVD players, plasma TV screens) are first released onto the market at a high price.

The target is the 'early adopters' of such products; their price sensitivity is relatively low because their interest in the product is substantial or they have a stronger appreciation of the qualities offered by the product.

Test your understanding 7

Examples of price discrimination include:

- lower admission prices for children at certain sporting and entertainment events
- discounts for Senior Citizens in some pubs and restaurants
- concessionary rail fares for students
- lower admission prices for females at some nightclubs.

Test your understanding 8 – Recap of pricing strategies

(1) Skimming and the penetration-pricing strategies.

(2) Penetration and volume discounting rely substantially on relatively low-price offers; this is also true to a lesser extent of complementary and product line pricing strategies.

(3) Complementary and product-line pricing strategies.

(4) Volume discounting.

chapter

6

Relevant costing

Chapter learning objectives

Upon completion of this chapter you will be able to:

- explain the practical issues surrounding make versus buy and outsourcing decisions
- for given data, calculate and compare 'make' costs with 'buy-in' costs
- for given data, compare in-house costs and outsource costs of completing tasks and consider other issues surrounding this decision
- for given data, apply relevant costing principles in situations involving make or buy, shut down, one-off contracts and joint product further processing decisions.

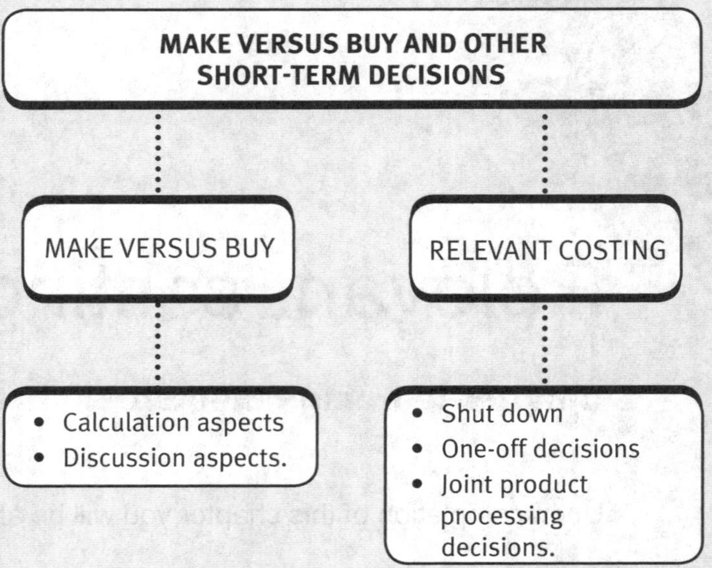

1 Introduction

This chapter will focus on a number of short-term decisions that are typically made by a business:

- Make versus buy decisions
- Shut-down decisions
- One-off contract decisions
- Further processing decisions.

Each of these decisions is based on relevant costing principles. Therefore, a recap of relevant costing will be useful before looking at each of the decisions in turn.

2 Relevant costs and revenues

Decision making involves making a choice between two or more alternatives. When a business is making one of the short-term decisions mentioned it should only consider the relevant cash flows that arise as a result of this decision:

Cash position if accept proposal	A	
		Relevant cash flow = A–B
Cash position if reject proposal (and do next best alternative instead)	B	

A relevant cash flow is a 'future incremental cash flow'.

- **Future**

  Only future cash flows that occur as a result of the decision should be considered, e.g. any future costs or revenue.

  Sunk costs (i.e. costs that have already been incurred in the past) are not relevant to the decision and should therefore be ignored – we cannot change the past.

- **Incremental**

  Only extra cash flows that occur as a result of the decision should be considered, e.g. extra costs or revenues.

  Fixed costs should be ignored unless there is an incremental fixed cost as a result of the decision.

  Committed costs (i.e. costs that are unavoidable in the future) are not affected by the decision and should therefore be ignored.

  Opportunity costs should be included – look at the next best alternative use of a resource.

- **Cash flows**

  Only cash items are relevant to the decision.

  For example, depreciation is not relevant since it is not a cash flow.

Test your understanding 1 – Relevant costs

Identify which of the following costs are relevant to the decisions specified:

(a) The salary to be paid to a market researcher who will oversee the development of a new product. This is a new post to be created especially for the new product but the £12,000 salary will be a fixed cost.

Is this cost relevant to the decision to proceed with the development of the product?

(b) The £2,500 additional monthly running costs of a new machine to be purchased to manufacture an established product. Since the new machine will save on labour time, the fixed overhead to be absorbed by the product will reduce by £100 per month.

Are these costs relevant to the decision to purchase the new machine?

(c) Office cleaning expenses of £125 for next month. The office is cleaned by contractors and the contract can be cancelled by giving one month's notice.

Is this cost relevant to a decision to close the office?

(d) Expenses of £75 paid to the marketing manager. This was to reimburse the manager for the cost of travelling to meet a client with whom the company is currently negotiating a major contract.

Is this cost relevant to the decision to continue negotiations?

3 Opportunity cost

Opportunity cost is an important concept for decision-making purposes. It is the value of the best alternative that is foregone when a particular course of action is undertaken. It emphasises that decisions are concerned with choices and that by choosing one plan, there may well be sacrifices elsewhere in the business.

Opportunity costs

A new project requires the use of an existing machine that would otherwise be sold.

Information concerning the machine is as follows:

- Original purchase price = $20,000
- Current net book value (NBV) = $5,000
- Estimated current sales value = $4,000

Required:

What is the relevant cost (if any) if using the machine in the project?

Solution

- The original purchase price is sunk so is not relevant.
- The NBV is a combination of the purchase price (sunk) and depreciation (not a cash flow) so is not relevant.
- By undertaking the project we miss out on the opportunity of selling the asset and thus have an opportunity cost of ($4,000).

Cash position if accept proposal	NIL	
		Relevant cash flow = ($4,000)
Cash position if reject proposal (and do next best alternative instead)	Receive $4,000	

Test your understanding 2 – Opportunity cost

A company which manufactures and sells one single product is currently operating at 85% of full capacity, producing 102,000 units per month. The current total monthly costs of production amount to £330,000, of which £75,000 are fixed and are expected to remain unchanged for all levels of activity up to full capacity.

A new potential customer has expressed interest in taking regular monthly delivery of 12,000 units at a price of £2.80 per unit.

All existing production is sold each month at a price of £3.25 per unit. If the new business is accepted, existing sales are expected to fall by 2 units for every 15 units sold to the new customer.

What is the overall increase in monthly profit which would result from accepting the new business?

4 The relevant cost of materials

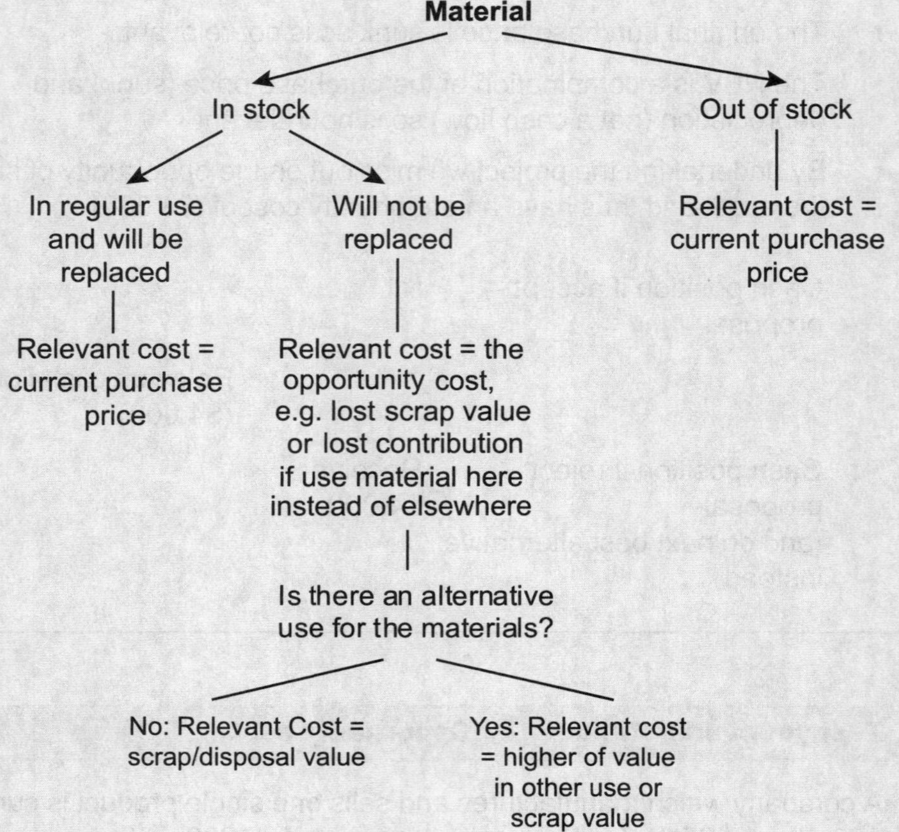

Any historic cost given for materials is **always a sunk cost** and **never relevant** unless it happens to be the same as the current purchase price.

Note: The above diagram assumes that it is possible to buy more materials if required. This may not always be the case.

- If a material is in short supply, then the only way a proposal can be undertaken would be by denying another part of the organisation that resource.
- In this case the relevant cost = normal materials cost + lost contribution in the other department.

5 The relevant cost of labour

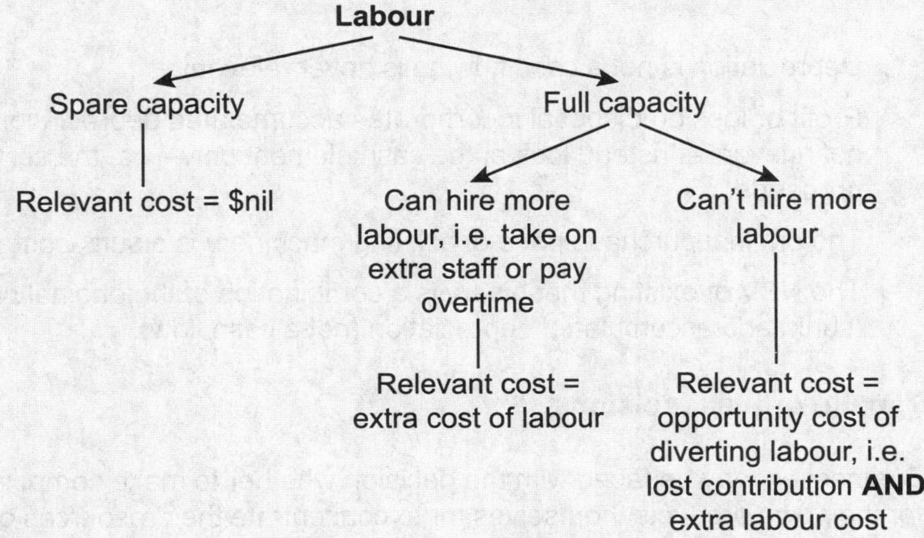

6 Relevant costs associated with non-current assets

Based on the comments above we can summarise the relevant costs associated with non-current assets as follows:

Typical relevant cash flows

- The purchase price of any new machinery that needs to be bought.
- If an existing machine is to be used in the project that would otherwise have been sold, then there is an opportunity cost equal to the proceeds foregone.
- Scrap/disposal proceeds on new assets bought.
- If we need to take an existing machine from another department and it is not replaced (either by choice or because a replacement is not available), then there is an opportunity cost equal to the lost contribution from the other department would need to be included.

Items that are not relevant

- Depreciation is not a cash flow so is never relevant.
- Profit or loss on disposal incorporates accumulated depreciation so is not relevant – instead look at the cash element only – i.e. the scrap proceeds.
- The original purchase price of existing machinery is a sunk cost.
- The NBV of existing machinery is a combination of the original price (sunk) and accumulated depreciation (not a cash flow).

7 Make or buy decisions

Businesses may be faced with the decision whether to make components for their own products themselves, or to concentrate their resources on assembling the products, obtaining the components from outside suppliers instead of making them 'in house'.

If the resources are bought in, their purchase cost is wholly marginal (i.e. direct). However, if it is decided to manufacture the components internally, the comparative costs of doing so will be the direct materials and wages costs, plus the variable factory overhead.

If the total variable costs of internally manufactured components is seen to be greater than the cost of obtaining similar components elsewhere, it is obviously uneconomic to produce these items internally.

There are two types of make vs. buy decisions:

- Make or buy decisions with no limiting factors
- Make or buy decisions with limiting factors.

Make or buy decisions with no limiting factors

In a make or buy decision with no limiting factors, the relevant costs are the differential costs between the two options.

Test your understanding 3 – Make vs buy

KRS Ltd is considering whether to administer its own purchase ledger or to use an external accounting service. It has obtained the following cost estimates for each option:

Internal service department

	Cost	**Volume**
Purchase hardware/software	$320 pa	
Hardware/software maintenance	$750 pa	
Accounting stationery	$500 pa	
Part-time account clerk	$6,000 pa	

External services

Processing of invoices/credit notes	$0.50 per document	5,000 pa
Processing of cheque payments	$0.50 per cheque	4,000 pa
Reconciling supplier accounts	$2.00 per supplier per month	150 suppliers

Determine the cost effectiveness of outsourcing the accounting activities and identify the qualitative factors involved.

8 Make or buy with a limiting factor

In the presence of a limiting factor, the following step-by-step approach could be adopted with a make vs. buy question:

(1) The saving per unit of each product is calculated. Saving = Purchases price – VC to make.

(2) Divide this by the amount of scarce resource (a.k.a. limiting factor) each product uses. This gives the saving per unit of the limiting factor (LF).

(3) Rank products. The higher the saving per unit of LF, the greater the priority to make that should be given to the product.

(4) Once the priorities have been decided, the scarce resource is allocated to the products in the order of the priorities, until it is fully used up.

(5) Any products with unsatisfied demand can be satisfied by buying from the external source.

Test your understanding 4 – Make Or Buy with a limiting factor

A company manufactures four components (L, M, N and P) which are incorporated into different products. All the components are manufactured using the same general purpose machinery. The following production cost and machine hour data are available, together with the purchase prices from an outside supplier.

	L	*M*	*N*	*P*
Production cost:	$	$	$	$
Direct material	12	18	15	8
Direct labour	25	15	10	8
Variable overhead	8	7	5	4
Fixed overhead	10	6	4	3
Total	**55**	**46**	**34**	**23**
Purchase price from outside supplier	$57	$55	$54	$50
	Hours	Hours	Hours	Hours
Machine hours per unit	3	5	4	6

Manufacturing requirements show a need for 1,500 units of each component per week. The maximum number of general purpose machinery hours available per week is 24,000.

What number of units should be purchased from the outside supplier?

Make vs. buy: other issues to consider

In addition to the relative cost of buying externally compared to making in-house, management must consider a number of other issues before a final decision is made.

- **Reliability of external supplier:** can the outside company be relied upon to meet the requirements in terms of:
  - quantity required
  - quality required
  - delivering on time
  - price stability.
- **Specialist skills:** the external supplier may possess some specialist skills that are not available in-house.
- **Alternative use of resource:** outsourcing will free up resources which may be used in another part of the business.

- **Social:** will outsourcing result in a reduction of the workforce? Redundancy costs should be considered.
- **Legal:** will outsourcing affect contractual obligations with suppliers or employees?
- **Confidentiality:** is there a risk of loss of confidentiality, especially if the external supplier performs similar work for rival companies.
- **Customer reaction:** do customers attach importance to the products being made in-house?

9 Outsourcing pros and cons

Advantages	Disadvantages
Greater flexibility	Possibility of choosing wrong supplier
Lower investment risk	Loss of visibility and control over process
Improved cash flow	Possibility of increased lead times
Concentrates on core competence	
Enables more advanced technologies to be used without making investment	

10 Shut-down decisions

Part of a business, for example a department or a product, may appear to be unprofitable. The business may have to make a decision as to whether or not this area should be shut down.

The quantifiable cost or benefit of closure

The relevant cash flows associated with closure should be considered. For example:

- the lost contribution from the area that is being closed (= relevant cost of closure)
- savings in specific fixed costs from closure (= relevant benefit of closure)
- known penalties and other costs resulting from the closure, e.g. redundancy, compensation to customers (= relevant cost of closure)
- any known reorganisation costs (= relevant cost of closure)
- any known additional contribution from the alternative use for resources released (= relevant benefit of closure).

If the relevant benefits are greater than the relevant costs of closure then closure may occur. However, before a final decision is made the business should also consider the non-quantifiable factors discussed below.

Non-quantifiable costs and benefits of closure

- Some of the costs and benefits discussed above may be non-quantifiable at the point of making the shut-down decision:
  - penalties and other costs resulting from the closure (e.g. redundancy, compensation to customers) may not be known with certainty
  - reorganisation costs may not be known with certainty
  - additional contribution from the alternative use for resources released may not be known with certainty.
- Knock-on impact of the shut-down decision. For example, supermarkets often stock some goods which they sell at a loss. This is to get customers through the door, who they then hope will purchase other products which have higher profit margins for them. If the decision is taken to stop selling these products, then the customers may no longer come to the store.

Test your understanding 5

The management of Fiona Co is considering the closure of one of its operations, department 3, and the financial accountant has submitted the following report.

Department	**1**	**2**	**3**	**Total**
Sales (units)	5,000	6,000	2,000	13,000
Sales ($)	150,000	240,000	24,000	414,000
Cost of sales ($)				
Direct material	75,000	150,000	10,000	235,000
Direct labour	25,000	30,000	8,000	63,000
Production overhead	5,769	6,923	2,308	15,000
Gross profit ($)	44,231	53,077	3,692	101,000
Expenses ($)	15,384	18,461	6,155	40,000
Net profit ($)	28,847	34,616	(2,463)	61,000

Additional information:

- production overheads of $15,000 have been apportioned to the three departments on the basis of unit sales volume
- expenses are head office overheads, again apportioned to departments on sales volume.

As management accountant, you further ascertain that, on a cost driver basis:

- 50% of the production overheads can be directly traced to departments and so could be allocated on the basis 2:2:1.
- Similarly 60% of the expenses can be allocated 3:3:2, with the remainder not being possible to allocate.
- 80% of the so-called direct labour is fixed and cannot be readily allocated. The remaining 20% is variable and can be better allocated on the basis of sales volume.

(a) Restate the financial position in terms of the contribution made by each department and, based on these figures, make a clear recommendation.

(b) Discuss any other factors that should be considered before a final decision is made.

Additional example on shut-down decisions

Harolds fashion store comprises three departments – Men's Wear, Ladies' Wear and Unisex. The store budget is as follows:

	Men's	**Ladies'**	**Unisex**	**Total**
	$	$	$	$
Sales	40,000	60,000	20,000	120,000
Direct cost of sales	20,000	36,000	15,000	71,000
Department costs	5,000	10,000	3,000	18,000
Apportioned store costs	5,000	5,000	5,000	15,000
Profit/(loss)	10,000	9,000	(3,000)	16,000

It is suggested that Unisex be closed to increase the size of Men's and Ladies' Wear.

Required:

Determine what information is relevant or required.

Solution

Possible answers are as follows:

(a) Unisex earns $2,000 net contribution (apportioned costs will still be incurred and thus reapportioned to other departments).

(b) Possible increase in Men's/Ladies' sales volume.

(c) Will Unisex staff be dismissed or transferred to Men's/Ladies'?

(d) Reorganisation costs, e.g. repartitioning, stock disposal.

(e) Loss of custom because Unisex attracts certain types of customer who will not buy in Men's/Ladies'.

11 One-off contracts

When a business is presented with a one-off contract, it should apply relevant costing principles to establish the cash flows associated with the project in order to help set a price.

The minimum contract price = the total net relevant cash flow associated with the contract.

Comments on the method used

- The minimum price is effectively a break-even price, so will give the firm no gain or loss.
- If the contract price does not cover these cash flows then it should be rejected as the company will have less cash if it accepts the contract.
- Any price higher than the minimum will mean that the company is better-off accepting the contract than rejecting it.

Further considerations:

- The price may be acceptable for a one-off contract but not for pricing all contracts and products – for example, when viewing a one-off contract fixed costs will probably be ignored as unavoidable. However, if every manager ignores fixed costs, then the company will end up making a loss.

- The minimum price obtained using relevant costing may be much lower than typical market prices. A firm may thus be reluctant to accept this price if it might affect the prices of other contracts in the future – for example, other customers may hear about the low prices offered and demand similar lower prices on their contracts.
- On the other hand a company may be willing to accept a loss on this contract if it increases the chances of winning subsequent contracts (albeit at what price?).

Test your understanding 6

Mr Smith has been asked to quote a price for a special contract. He has already prepared his tender but has asked you to review it for him.

He has pointed out to you that he wants to quote the minimum price as he believes this will lead to more lucrative work in the future.

Mr Smith's tender

		$
Material:	A 2,000 kgs @ $10 per kg	20,000
	B 1,000 kgs @ $15 per kg	15,000
	C 500 kgs @ $40 per kg	20,000
	D 50 litres @ $12 per litre	600
Labour:	Skilled 1,000 hrs @ $25 per hr	25,000
	Semi-skilled 2,000 hrs @ $15 per hr	30,000
	Unskilled, 500 hrs @ $10 per hr	5,000
Fixed overheads 3,500 hrs @ $12 per hr		42,000
Costs of preparing the tender:		
Mr Smith's time		1,000
other expenses		500
Minimum profit (5% of total costs)		7,955
Minimum tender price		167,055

Other information

Material A

- 1,000 kgs of this material is in stock at a cost of $5 per kg.
- Mr Smith has no alternative use for his material and intends selling it for $2 per kg.
- However, if he sold any he would have to pay a fixed sum of $300 to cover delivery costs.
- The current purchase price is $10 per kg.

Material B

- There is plenty of Material B in stock and it cost $18 per kg.
- The current purchase price is $15 per kg.
- The material is constantly used by Mr Smith in his business.

Material C

- The total amount in stock of 500 kgs was bought for $10,000 some time ago for another one-off contract that never happened.
- Mr Smith is considering selling it for $6,000 in total or using it as a substitute for another material, constantly used in normal production.
- If used in this latter manner it would save $8,000 of the other material.
- Current purchase price is $40 per kg.

Material D

- There are 100 litres of this material in stock.
- It is dangerous and if not used in this contract will have to be disposed of at a cost to Mr Smith of $50 per litre.
- The current purchase price is $12 per litre.

Skilled labour

- Mr Smith only hires skilled labour when he needs it.
- $25 per hour is the current hourly rate.

Semi-skilled labour

- Mr Smith has a workforce of 50 semi-skilled labourers who are currently not fully utilised.
- They are on annual contracts and the number of spare hours currently available for this project are 1,500. Any hours in excess of this will have to be paid for at time-and-a-half.
- The normal hourly rate is $15 per hour.

Unskilled labour

- These are currently fully employed by Mr Smith on jobs where they produce a contribution of $2 per unskilled labour hour.
- Their current rate is $10 per hour, although extra could be hired at $20 an hour if necessary.

Fixed overheads

- This is considered by Mr Smith to be an accurate estimate of the hourly rate based on his existing production.

Costs of preparing the tender

- Mr Smith has spent 10 hours working on this project at $100 per hour, which he believes is his charge-out rate.
- Other expenses include the cost of travel and research spent by Mr Smith on the project.

Profit

- This is Mr Smith's minimum profit margin which he believes is necessary to cover 'general day-to-day expenses of running a business'.

Required:

Calculate and explain for Mr Smith what you believe the minimum tender price should be.

Additional example on one-off contracts

A research contract, which to date has cost the company $150,000, is under review.

If the contract is allowed to proceed:

- it will be completed in approximately one year
- the results would then be sold to a government agency for $300,000.

Shown below are the additional expenses which the managing director estimates will be necessary to complete the work.

Materials

- This material for the contract has just been purchased at a cost of $60,000.
- It is toxic; if not used in this contract it must be disposed of at a cost of $5,000.

Labour

- Skilled labour is hard to recruit.
- The workers concerned were transferred to the contract from a production department, and at a recent meeting, the production manager claimed that if the men were returned to him they could generate sales of $150,000 in the next year.
  - The prime cost of these sales would be $100,000, including $40,000 for the labour cost itself.
  - The overhead absorbed into this production would amount to $20,000.

Research staff

- It has been decided that when work on this contract ceases, the research department will be closed.
- Research wages for the year are $60,000, and redundancy and severance pay has been estimated at $15,000 now, or $35,000 in one year's time.

Equipment

- The contract utilises a special microscope which cost $18,000 three years ago.
- It has a residual value of $3,000 in another two years, and a current disposal value of $8,000.
- If used in the contract it is estimated that the disposal value in a year's time will be $6,000.

Share of general building services

- The contract is charged with $35,000 pa to cover general building expenses.
- Immediately after the contract is discontinued, the space occupied could be sub-let for an annual rental of $7,000.

Required:

Advise the managing director as to whether the contract should be allowed to proceed, explaining the reasons for the treatment of each item.

(**Note:** Ignore the time value of money.)

Solution	$
Relevant costs and revenues of proceeding with the contract	
(1) Costs to date of $150,000 sunk – ignore.	–
(2) Materials – in stock and will not be replaced There is an opportunity benefit of the disposal costs saved.	5,000
(3) Labour cost – no spare capacity and additional labour can't be hired. Opportunity cost is lost contribution of $50,000 ($150k – $100k) plus the direct cost of labour of $40,000. The overhead will be incurred anyway and so should be ignored.	(90,000)
(4) Research staff costs:	
Wages for the year (cost would be saved if contract did not go ahead)	(60,000)
Increase in redundancy pay due to the delay in closure of the department ($35,000 – $15,000)	(20,000)

(5)	Equipment:	
	Deprival value if used in the project = disposal value	(8,000)
	Disposal proceeds in one year	6,000
	(All book values and depreciation figures are irrelevant)	
(6)	General building services	
	Apportioned costs – irrelevant	
	Opportunity costs of rental foregone	(7,000)
	Total relevant cash flows associated with the contract	(174,000)
	Sales value of contact	300,000
	Increased contribution from contract	126,000

Advice. Proceed with the contract.

Objective Test Case Questions – Relevant costs

(1) Z Co is pricing a new contract. The new contract requires the use of 50 tonnes of metal ZX. There are 25 tonnes of ZX in inventory at the moment, which were bought for $200 per tonne. Z Co no longer has any use for metal ZX. The current purchase price is $210 per tonne, and the metal could be disposed of for net scrap proceeds of $150 per tonne.

What cost should be charged to the new contract for metal ZX?

A $5,250

B $6,500

C $9,000

D $10,500

(2) 100 hours of unskilled labour, currently paid at $5.50 per hour, are needed for the contract. Z Co has no surplus capacity at the moment , but additional temporary staff could be hired at $6.50 per hour.

What is the relevant cost of the unskilled labour on the contract?

A $0

B $550

C $600

D $650

(3) 100 hours of skilled labour are needed for a contract. The company currently has 300 hours worth of spare capacity. There is a union agreement in place that there are no lay-offs. The workers are paid $8.50 per hour.

What is the relevant cost of the skilled labour on the contract?

A $0

B $650

C $850

D $2,550

(4) Equipment owned by Z Co has a net book value of $1,800 and has been idle for some months. It could now be used on the new contract. If not used on this contract, the equipment could be sold for a net amount of $2,000. After use on the contract, the equipment would have no resale value, and would be dismantled.

What is the total relevant cost of the equipment to the contract?

A $0

B $200

C $1,800

D $2,000

(5) **Which of the following statements about relevant costing are true?**

(1) The opportunity cost is represented by the forgone potential benefit from the best rejected course of action.

(2) Materials can never have an opportunity cost, whereas labour can.

(3) The annual depreciation charge is not a relevant cost.

(4) Fixed costs would have a relevant cost element if a decision causes a change in their total expenditure.

(5) Notional costs are always relevant, as they make the estimate more realistic.

A Statements (1) and (2)

B Statements (1), (3) and (4)

C Statements (1), (3) and (5)

D Statements (1), (4) and (5)

12 Further processing decisions

A further processing decision will be tested in the context of joint products in the exam.

Revision of joint product costing

Joint product costing was introduced in paper F2:

- Joint products arise where the manufacture of one product inevitably results in the manufacture of other products.
- The specific point at which individual products become identifiable is known as the split-off point.
- Costs incurred before the split-off point are called joint costs and must be shared between joint products produced.
- After separation products may be sold immediately or may be processed further. Any further processing costs are allocated directly to the product on which they are incurred.

The basis of apportionment of joint costs to products is usually one of the following:

(i) Sales value of production (also known as 'market value')

(ii) Production units

(iii) Net realisable value.

Illustration 1 – Valuation of joint products

Products A and B are two joint products with information as follows:

	Kgs produced	Kgs sold	Selling price per kg	Joint cost
Product A	100	80	$5	
				$750
Product B	200	150	$2	

(a) **Apportionment by production units**

$$\frac{\text{Joint cost}}{\text{Kgs produced}} = \frac{\$750}{300} = \$2.50 \text{ per kg for A and B}$$

Trading results are as follows:

	Product A		Product B		Total
Sales	80 × $5.00	$400	150 × $2.00	$300	$700
Cost of sales	80 × $2.50	($200)	150 × $2.50	($375)	($575)
Profit/(loss)		$200		($75)	$125
Value of closing stock	20 × $2.50	$50	50 × $2.50	$125	

The production ratio is 100 : 200 which means that in order to obtain 1 kg of A , it is necessary to produce 2 kgs of B. For exam purposes, you should assume that the ratio of output is fixed.

(b) **Apportionment by market value at point of separation**

	Sales value of production	Proportion	Joint cost apportionment	Per kg
A : 100 × $5	$500	5/9	$417	$4.17
B : 200 × $2	$400	4/9	$333	$1.67
			750	

Trading results:

	A	**B**	**Total**
Sales	400	300	700
Cost of sales	333.6	250.5	585.1
Profit	66.4	49.5	114.9
Profit/Sales ratio	16.6%	16.5%	
Closing inventory	(20 × 4.17) = $83	(50 × $1.67) = $83	

Note that the apportionment is on the basis of proportionate sales value of production; Profit per unit will be the same (with a small rounding difference.)

(c) **Apportionment by Net Realisable Value**

This approach should be used in situations where the sales value at the split-off point is not known – either because the product is not saleable, or if the examiner does not tell us.

Further information is needed:

	Further processing costs	Selling price after further processing
Product A	$280 + $ 2.00 per kg	$8.40
Product B	$160 + $1.40 per kg	$4.50

Apportionment of joint costs:

	Product A	Product B
Final sales value of production (100 × $8.40; 200 × $4.50)	$840	$900
Further processing cost (280 + 100 × $2; 160 + 200 × $1.40)	$480	$440
Net realisable value	$360	$460
Joint cost apportionment (360;460)	329	421
Joint cost per kg	$3.29	$2.10

Trading results (for common process only)			
Sales			$700
Joint costs		$750	
Less closing inventory			
A : 20 × $3.29	$66		
B : 50 × $2.10	$105		
	171		
Cost of sales			$579
Profit			$121

Test your understanding 7

The following is relevant for a production process for Period 1:

Direct material cost	$10,000
Direct labour cost	$5,000
Overheads	$3,000
Total costs	$18,000

The process produces joint products A and B, which are then sold at the prices given below. The output figure represents all of the output from the process:

	Product A	Product B
Units of output	2,000	8,000
Price per unit	$5	$2.50

Required:

Calculate the cost of sales, and gross profit for products A and B assuming:

(i) joint costs are apportioned by market value

(ii) joint costs are apportioned by production units.

Further processing decision

When deciding whether to process a particular product further or to sell after split-off only future incremental cash flows should be considered:

- Any difference in revenue and any extra costs.
- Joint costs are sunk at this stage and thus not relevant to the decision. (Note: if we are considering the viability of the whole process, then the joint costs would be relevant).

Test your understanding 8

A firm makes three joint products, X, Y and Z, at a joint cost of $400,000. Joint costs are apportioned on the basis of weight. Products X and Z are currently processed further.

Product	**Weight at split-off**	**Further processing costs (variable)**	**Sales**
	(tonnes)	$000	$000
X	600	800	980
Y	200	–	120
Z	200	400	600

An opportunity has arisen to sell all three products at the split-off point for the following prices.

X	$200,000
Y	$120,000
Z	$160,000

Which of the products, if any, should the firm process further?

13 Chapter summary

MAKE VERSUS BUY AND OTHER SHORT-TERM DECISIONS

MAKE VERSUS BUY

Calculation aspects

- Compare incremental costs of manufacture versus buy
- Does spare capacity exist?

Discussion aspects

- Quality
- Skills/competences
- Alternative use of resources
- Social/legal aspects
- Confidentiality
- Operating gearing
- Scheduling
- Customer reaction
- Re-badging.

RELEVANT COSTING

Shut down

- Are fixed overheads avoided?
- Will staff be sacked or relocated?
- Include redundancy and other closure costs.

One-off decisions

- Only include incremental cash flows in calculations
- Discuss wider implications – e.g. effect on long term sales.

Joint product processing decisions

- Joint costs are not relevant.

Test your understanding answers

Test your understanding 1 – Relevant costs

(a) The salary is a relevant cost of £12,000. Do not be fooled by the mention of the fact that it is a fixed cost, it is a cost that is relevant to the decision to proceed with the future development of the new product. This is an example of a directly attributable fixed cost. A directly attributable fixed cost may also be called a product-specific fixed cost.

(b) The £2,500 additional running costs are relevant to the decision to purchase the new machine. The saving in overhead absorption is not relevant since we are not told that the total overhead expenditure will be altered. The saving in labour cost would be relevant but we shall assume that this has been accounted for in determining the additional monthly running costs.

(c) This is not a relevant cost for next month since it will be incurred even if the contract is cancelled today. If a decision is being made to close the office, this cost cannot be included as a saving to be made next month. However, it will be saved in the months after that so it will become a relevant cost saving from month 2 onwards.

(d) This is not a relevant cost of the decision to continue with the contract. The £75 is sunk and cannot be recovered even if the company does not proceed with the negotiations.

Test your understanding 2 – Opportunity cost

100% capacity	= 102,000 ÷ 0.85	=	120,000 units

Spare capacity amounts to 18,000 units. So there is sufficient slack to meet the new order.

Variable costs	= £330,000 less £75,000	=	£255,000
Variable cost per unit	= £255,000 ÷ 102,000	=	£2.50
Contribution per unit from existing product		=	£3.25 – £2.50 = £0.75
Contribution per unit from new product		=	£2.80 – £2.50 = £0.30

	£
Increase in contribution from new product:	
£0.30 × 12,000 units	3,600
Fall in contribution from existing product:	
£0.75 × (12,000 ÷ 15) × 2	
£0.75 × 1,600	(1,200)
Net Gain in contribution	**2,400**

Test your understanding 3 – Make vs buy

Annual internal processing costs

Hardware and software	$320	
Hardware/software annual maintenance	$750	
Accounting stationery	$500	
Part time accounts clerk	$6,000	
Total	$7,570	
Annual outsourcing costs		
Processing of invoices/credit notes	$2,500	5,000 × $0.50
Processing of cheque payments	$2,000	4,000 × $0.50
Reconciling supplier accounts	$3,600	150 × $2 × 12
Total	$8,100	

It would not be cost effective to outsource the accounting activities. The present costs of $7,570 would rise to $8,100 pa

Qualitative factors include:

- predicted volumes – higher volumes will make outsourcing more expensive
- the quality of supply – will the external supplier make more errors?
- security of information.

Test your understanding 4 – Make Or Buy with a limiting factor

The following method could be adopted in this example:

(1) The saving per unit of each product is calculated. Saving = Purchases price – VC to make.

(2) Divide this by the amount of scarce resource (a.k.a. limiting factor) each product uses. This gives the saving per unit of limiting factor (LF).

(3) Rank. The higher the saving per unit of LF the greater the priority to make that should be given to the product.

(4) Once the priorities have been decided, the scarce resource is allocated to the products in the order of the priorities until it is fully used up.

(5) Any products with unsatisfied demand can be satisfied by buying from the external source.

(1) Calculate saving = Purchases price – VC to make:

	L	*M*	*N*	*P*
External purchase price	$57	$55	$54	$50
Variable costs to make	$45	$40	$30	$20
Saving	$12	$15	$24	$30

(2) Calculate the saving per unit of limiting factor/scarce resource:

	L	*M*	*N*	*P*
Saving	$12	$15	$24	$30
Scarce resource (machine hours) per unit	3 hours	5 hours	4 hours	6 hours
Saving per unit of the scarce resource	$4	$3	$6	$5

(3) Rank

	L	*M*	*N*	*P*
Saving per unit of the scarce resource	$4	$3	$6	$5
Ran: product to make in priority	3	4	1	2

(4) Allocate scarce resource of 24,000 machine hours to production

Make all Ns (1,500 units). This will use up 1,500 × 4 hours = 6,000 hours.

Then, make all Ps (1,500 units). This will use up 1,500 × 6 hours = 9,000 hours. The cumulative total is 6,000 + 9,000 = 15,000 hours.

Then, make all Ls (1,500 units). This will use up 1,500 × 3 hours = 4,500 hours. The cumulative total is 15,000 + 4,500 = 19,500 hours.

This leaves (24,000 – 19,500) = 4,500 hours, in which to make

$$\frac{4,500}{5} = 900 \text{ units of Product M}$$

(5) Unsatisfied demand = 1,500 Ms – 900 Ms = 600 Ms. These will have to be bought externally.

	L	**M**	**N**	**P**
Variable production cost	$45	$40	$30	$20
External cost	$57	$55	$54	$50
Incremental cost	$**12**	$**15**	$**24**	$**30**
Hours per unit	÷ 3	÷ 5	÷ 4	÷ 6
Incremental cost per hour	**$4**	**$3**	**$6**	**$5**
Cheapest per hour	2nd	1st	4th	3rd

The analysis shows that it is actually cheaper to try and make ALL the components within the factory.

Hours required to make 1,500 units of each component:

(1,500 × 3) + (1,500 × 5) + (1,500 × 4) + (1,500 × 6) = 27,000 hours

The company only has 24,000 hours available. So, 3,000 hours of work must be sub-contracted. The CHEAPEST component per hour must be bought externally. This is component M.

3,000 hours of time on M equates to 3,000 ÷ 5 = **600 units of M.**

Test your understanding 5

(a) First of all we must restate the figures so that they present the situation in its true light. Only relevant cash flows should be considered. This will enable each department to be readily evaluated on its locally controllable performance.

Department	**1**	**2**	**3**	**Total**
Sales volume (units)	5,000	6,000	2,000	13,000
Sales value ($)	150,000	240,000	24,000	414,000
Cost of sales: ($)				
Direct material	75,000	150,000	10,000	235,000
Direct labour (note 1)	4,846	5,815	1,939	12,600
Prodn overhead (note 2)	3,000	3,000	1,500	7,500
Expenses (note 3)	9,000	9,000	6,000	24,000
Contribution ($)	58,154	72,185	4,561	134,900
Other costs ($):				
Labour (note 4)				(50,400)
Overhead (note 5)				(7,500)
Expenses (note 6)				(16,000)
Net profit				61,000

Notes

(1) 80% of the labour cost is fixed and is therefore excluded from the contribution calculation. The remaining 20% has been allocated on the basis of sales volume.

(2) Only 50% of the production overheads can be directly allocated to the departments. This has been allocated in the ratio 2:2:1.

(3) Only 60% of the expenses can be directly traced to the departments. This has been allocated in the ratio 3:3:2.

(4) Fixed cost of labour is 80%.

(5) This is the remaining 50% of overheads that can't be allocated to departments.

(6) This is the remaining 40% of expenses that can't be allocated to departments.

Conclusion

From the restated figures department 3 should be kept open since:

- The department is making a contribution of $4,561 to the overall profit of the business.
- The apparent loss arises purely from inappropriate apportionment of overheads and expenses.
- If the department were closed:
  - there would be a loss of $4,561 contribution to the business and
  - on the assumption there would be no further saving on fixed costs, the profit would be reduced to $56,439.

(b) Consideration must be given to the following factors which may be non-quantifiable at present:

- Redundancy costs or costs relating to the disposal of equipment if department 3 is closed.
- The possible loss of business due to products from department 3 being unavailable to customers who buy from other departments at the same time.
- The reorganisation costs that may arise from the closure of department 3.
- Additional benefits of closure of department 3 such as labour and machinery being used to generate contribution elsewhere in the business.

Test your understanding 6

		$	$
Material A (note 1)	1,000 kgs @ $2 – $300	1,700	
	1,000 kgs @ $10	10,000	
			11,700
Material B (note 2)	1,000 kgs @$15		15,000
Material C (note 3)	500 kgs – opportunity cost		8,000
Material D (note 4)	50 litres @ $50		(2,500)
Skilled labour (note 5)	1,000 hrs @ $25		25,000
Semi-skilled labour (note 6)	500 hrs @ $22.50		11,250
Unskilled labour (note 7)	500 hrs @ $12 (opportunity cost)		6,000
Minimum tender price = total of relevant cash flows			74,450

Notes

(1) There are 1,000 kgs in stock and these will not be replaced. These would otherwise be sold at a net gain of $1,700. This gain is therefore foregone as a result of using this material in the contract. The other 1,000 kgs are out of stock and therefore the relevant cost is the current purchase price of $10 per kg.

(2) The material is in stock but will be replaced and therefore the relevant cost is the current purchase price of $15 per kg.

(3) The material is in stock and there are two options if this material is not used for the contract:

Option 1 – Sell it for $6,000.

Option 2 – Use it as a substitute and save $8,000.

Option 2 is preferable. This is therefore the opportunity cost of using it in the contract.

(4) The material is in stock and will not be replaced. The cost of disposing of 50 litres will be saved (@ $50/litre, i.e. $2,500). Saving this cost is a relevant benefit.

(5) The incremental cost of paying for the labour needed.

(6) 1,500 spare hours have already been paid for as the workforce are on annual contracts. The additional cash flow is therefore the extra 500 hours that are needed at time-and-a-half.

(7) For each hour diverted from their normal jobs contribution of $2 will be foregone. This together with the cost of paying the workers to do the project amounts to a relevant cost of $12 per kg. They would not be hired at $20 per hour as this is more expensive.

(8) Fixed overheads can be ignored as they are not incremental.

(9) Costs of preparing the tender are all sunk costs and hence must be ignored.

(10) Profit element should be ignored since a minimum contract price is being calculated.

Objective Test Case Questions – Relevant costs

(1) **C**

The only alternative use for the material held in inventory is to sell it for scrap. To use 25 tonnes on the contract is to give up the opportunity of selling it for 25 x $150 = $3,750. Z Co must then purchase a further 25 tonnes, and assuming this is in the near future, it will cost $210 per tonne. Therefore, the contract must be charged with

25 tonnes × $150	$3,750
25 tonnes × $210	$5,250
	$9,000

(2) **D**

Spare capacity does not exist, but extra employees may be hired , therefore the relevant cost is the cost of hiring temporary staff at $6.50 per hour, i.e. 100 hours × $6.50 = $650.

(3) **A**

The relevant cost of the semi-skilled labour on the contract is NIL. Spare capacity exists, and therefore the relevant cost of the semi-skilled labour is $0.

(4) **D**

The asset will not be replaced, but it could now be sold for $2,000. If not sold now, it would have no other value. Therefore the relevant cost is the opportunity cost now, i.e. $2,000.

(5) **B**

Statement 2 is not correct: materials can have an alternative use that can exceed their value in the project being considered.

Statement 5 is not correct either: notional costs are used to make cost estimates more realistic; however, they are not real cash flows and are not considered to be relevant.

Test your understanding 7

(a) **Market value basis**

	Product A	**Product B**	**Total**
Sales value	$10,000	$20,000	$30,000
Joint costs apportioned (W1)	$6,000	$12,000	$18,000
Gross profit	$4,000	$8,000	$12,000

Working:

Joint costs allocated to Product A $= \frac{10,000}{30,000} \times \$18,000 = \$6,000$

Joint costs allocated to Product B $= \frac{20,000}{30,000} \times \$18,000 = \$12,000$

(b) **Production units basis**

	Product A	**Product B**	**Total**
Sales value	$10,000	$20,000	$30,000
Joint costs apportioned (W1)	$3,600	$14,400	$18,000
Gross profit	$6,400	$5,600	$12,000

Working:

Total output units = 2,000 + 8,000 = 10,000

Joint costs allocated to Product A $= \frac{2,000}{10,000} \times \$18,000 = \$3,600$

Joint costs allocated to Product B $= \frac{8,000}{10,000} \times \$18,000 = \$14,400$

Test your understanding 8

The pre-separation (i.e. "joint") costs are not incremental and so can be ignored. The only incremental cash flows are as follows:

Product	**X**	**Y**	**Z**
	$000	$000	$000
Additional revenue from further processing	780	n/a	440
Additional costs from further processing	800	n/a	400
Benefit/(cost) of further processing	(20)		40

Thus only Z should be processed further.

chapter

7

Risk and uncertainty

Chapter learning objectives

Upon completion of this chapter you will be able to:

- describe generally available research techniques to reduce uncertainty, e.g. focus groups, market research
- suggest for a given situation, suitable research techniques for reducing uncertainty
- explain, using a simple example, the use of simulation
- explain, calculate and demonstrate the use of expected values and sensitivity analysis in simple decision-making situations
- for given data, apply the techniques of maximax, maximin and minimax regret to decision making problems including the production of profit tables
- calculate the value of perfect information
- calculate the value of imperfect information.

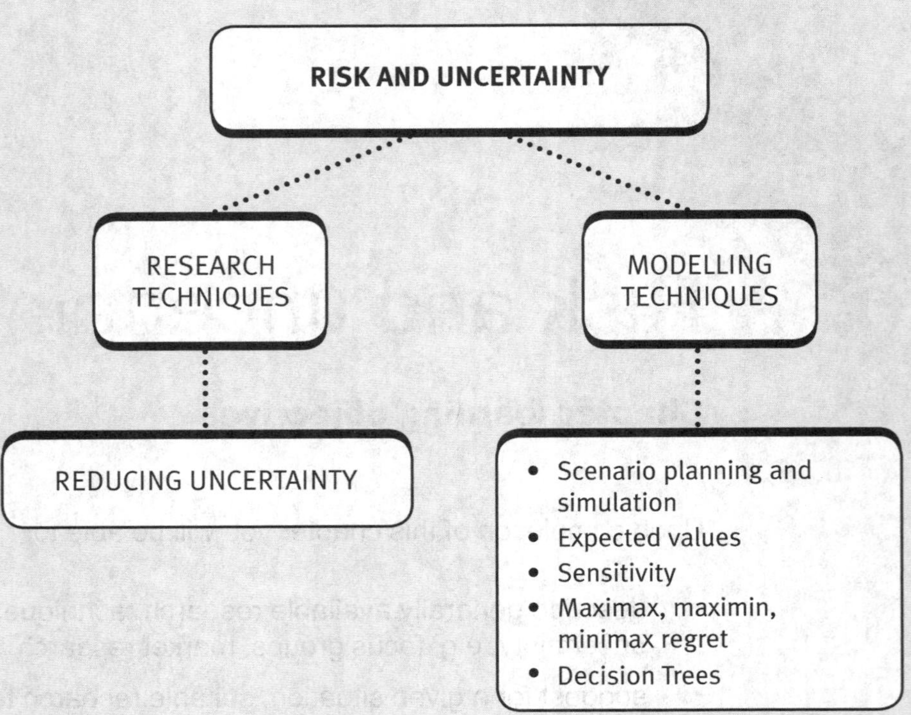

1 Introduction

All businesses face risk. **Risk** is the variability of possible returns.

Risk management is important in a business. It is the process of understanding and managing the risks that an organisation is inevitably subject to.

Distinction between risk and uncertainty

Risk: there are a number of possible outcomes and the probability of each outcome is known.

For example, based on past experience of digging for oil in a particular area, an oil company may estimate that they have a 60% chance of finding oil and a 40% chance of not finding oil.

Uncertainty: there are a number of possible outcomes but the probability of each outcome is not known.

For example, the same oil company may dig for oil in a previously unexplored area. The company knows that it is possible for them to either find or not find oil but it does not know the probabilities of each of these outcomes.

The role of market research techniques

Market research is an important means of assessing and reducing uncertainty. For example, about the likely responses of customers to new products, new advertising campaigns and price changes.

A number of research techniques are available:

- Focus Groups
- Desk research (secondary research).
- Field research (primary research). This includes:
  - motivational and
  - measurement research.

Each method will be reviewed in turn.

Focus groups

Focus groups are a common market research tool involving small groups (typically eight to ten people) selected from the broader population. The group is interviewed through facilitator-led discussions in an informal environment in order to gather their opinions and reactions to a particular subject.

For example, a supermarket may use a focus group before a product launch decision is made in order to gather opinions on a new range of pizzas.

Problems with focus groups

- Results are qualitative.
- The small sample size means that results may not be representative.
- Individuals may feel under pressure to agree with other members or to give a 'right' answer.
- Their cost and logistical complexity is frequently cited as a barrier, especially for smaller companies. On-line focus groups are becoming more popular and help to address this issue.

Desk research

- The information is collected from secondary sources.
- It obtains existing data by studying published and other available sources of information. For example, press articles, published accounts, census information.
- It can often eliminate the need for extensive field work.

Factors to consider when using desk research

- It may not be exactly what the researcher wants and may not be totally up to date or accurate.
- However, it is quicker and cheaper than field research.

There are three main types of information that can be collected by desk research:

- Economic intelligence can be defined as information relating to the economic environment within which a company operates. It is concerned with such factors as gross national product (GNP), investment, expenditure, population, employment, productivity and trade. It provides an organisation with a picture of past and future trends in the environment and with an indication of the company's position in the economy as a whole. A great deal of information is freely available in this area from sources such as government ministries, the nationalised industries, universities and organisations such as the OECD.
- Market intelligence is information about a company's present or possible future markets. Such information will be both commercial and technical, for example, the level of sales of competitors' products recorded by the Business Monitor or Census of Production; the product range offered by existing or potential competitors; the number of outlets forming the distribution network for a company's products; the structure of that network by size, location and relation to the end user; and the best overseas markets for a company.
- Internal company data is perhaps the most neglected source of marketing information. Companies tend to record their sales information for accountancy purposes or for the management of the sales force. Conversely, many companies, especially blue-chips and public services, can often be seen to produce reams of data for no apparent reason, or because 'we always have done'. Rarely is the information collected in a form in which it can readily be used by marketing management.

Field research

- Information is collected from primary sources by direct contact with a targeted group.
- Although it is more expensive and time consuming than desk research the results should be more accurate, relevant and up to date.
- There are two types of field research:
  - motivational research
  - measurement research.

Motivational research – the objective is to understand factors that influence why consumers do or do not buy particular products.

Motivational research techniques

Some of the more common techniques in motivational research are:

- Depth interviewing – undertaken at length by a trained person who is able to appreciate conscious and unconscious associations and motivations and their significance.
- Group interviewing – where between six and ten people are asked to consider the relevant subject (object) under trained supervision.
- Word association testing – on being given a word by the interviewer, the first word that comes into the mind of the person being tested is noted.
- Triad testing – where people are asked which out of a given three items they prefer. If the three are brands of a given type of product (or three similar types), replies may show a great deal about which features of a product most influence the buying decision.

Measurement research – the objective here is to build on the motivation research by trying to quantify the issues involved.

- Sample surveys are used to find out how many people buy the product, what quantity each type of buyer purchases, and where and when the product is bought.
- This sort of information can also be collected in retail environments at the point of sale, for example, through the use of loyalty cards.

Types of measurement research

It is also possible (less accurately) to assess roughly the importance of some reasons for buying or not buying a product. The main types of measurement are:

Random sampling – where each person in the target population has an equal chance of being selected. Such samples are more likely to be representative, making predictions more reliable. However, the technique may be unfeasible in practice.

Quota sampling – where samples are designed to be representative with respect to pre-selected criteria.

- For example, if the target population is 55% women and 45% men, then a sample of 200 people could be structured so 110 women and 90 men are asked, rather than simply asking 200 people and leaving it up to chance whether or not the gender mix is typical.
- The main disadvantage of quota sampling is that samples may still be biased for non-selected criteria.

Panelling – where the sample is kept for subsequent investigations, so trends are easier to spot.

Surveying by post – the mail shot method. Unfortunately the sample becomes self-selecting and so may be biased.

Observation – e.g. through the use of cameras within supermarkets to examine how long customers spend on reading the nutritional information on food packaging.

2 Other methods of dealing with risk and uncertainty

In addition to the research techniques discussed, the following methods can be used to address risk or uncertainty.

- Sensitivity analysis
- Simulation
- Expected values
- Maximax, maximin and minimax regret
- Decision Trees.

Each method will be reviewed in turn.

3 Sensitivity analysis

Sensitivity analysis takes each uncertain factor in turn, and calculates the change that would be necessary in that factor before the original decision is reversed. Typically, it involves posing 'what-if' questions.

By using this technique it is possible to establish which estimates (variables) are more critical than others in affecting a decision.

The process is as follows:

- Best estimates for variables are made and a decision arrived at.
- Each of the variables is analysed in turn to see how much the original estimate can change before the original decision is reversed. For example, it may be that the estimated selling price can fall by 5% before the original decision to accept a project is reversed.
- Estimates for each variable can then be reconsidered to assess the likelihood of the estimate being wrong. For example, what is the chance of the selling price falling by more than 5%?
- The maximum possible change is often expressed as a percentage. This formula only works for total cash flows. It cannot be used for individual units, selling prices, variable cost per unit, etc.

Illustration 1 – Sensitivity analysis

A manager is considering a make v buy decision based on the following estimates:

	If made in-house	If buy in and re-badge
	$	$
Variable production costs	10	2
External purchase costs	–	6
Ultimate selling price	15	14

You are required to assess the sensitivity of the decision to the external purchase price.

Solution

Step 1: What is the original decision?

Comparing contribution figures, the product should be bought in and re-badged:

	If made in-house	**If buy in and re-badge**
	$	$
Contribution	5	6

Step 2: Calculate the sensitivity (to the external purchase price)

For indifference, the contribution from outsourcing needs to fall to $5 per unit. Thus the external purchase price only needs to increase by $1 per unit (or $1/$6 = 17%). If the external purchase price rose by more than 17% the original decision would be reversed.

Strengths of sensitivity analysis

- There is no complicated theory to understand.
- Information will be presented to management in a form which facilitates subjective judgement to decide the likelihood of the various possible outcomes considered.
- It identifies areas which are crucial to the success of the project. If the project is chosen, those areas can be carefully monitored.

Weaknesses of sensitivity analysis

- It assumes that changes to variables can be made independently, e.g. material prices will change independently of other variables. Simulation allows us to change more than one variable at a time.
- It only identifies how far a variable needs to change; it does not look at the probability of such a change.
- It provides information on the basis of which decisions can be made but it does not point to the correct decision directly.

4 Simulation

Simulation is a modelling technique that shows the effect of more than one variable changing at the same time.

It is often used in capital investment appraisal.

The Monte Carlo simulation method uses random numbers and probability statistics. It can include all random events that might affect the success or failure of a proposed project – for example, changes in material prices, labour rates, market size, selling price, investment costs or inflation.

The model identifies key variables in a decision: costs and revenues, say. Random numbers are then assigned to each variable in a proportion in accordance with the underlying probability distribution. For example, if the most likely outcomes are thought to have a 50% probability, optimistic outcomes a 30% probability and pessimistic outcomes a 20% probability, random numbers, representing those attributes, can be assigned to costs and revenues in those proportions.

A powerful computer is then used to repeat the decision many times and give management a view of the likely range and level of outcomes. Depending on the management's attitude to risk, a more informed decision can be taken.

This helps to model what is essentially a one-off decision using many possible repetitions. It is only of any real value, however, if the underlying probability distribution can be estimated with some degree of confidence.

Illustration 2 – The MP Organisation

The MP Organisation is an independent film production company. It has a number of potential films that it is considering producing, one of which is the subject of a management meeting next week. The film which has been code named CA45 is a thriller based on a novel by a well respected author.

The expected revenues from the film have been estimated as follows: there is a 30% chance it may generate total sales of $254,000; 50% chance sales may reach $318,000 and 20% chance they may reach $382,000.

Expected costs (advertising, promotion and marketing) have also been estimated as follows: there is a 20% chance they will reach approximately $248,000; 60% chance they may get to $260,000 and 20 % chance of totalling $272,000.

In a Monte Carlo simulation, these revenues and costs could have random numbers assigned to them:

Sales revenue	Probability	Assign random numbers (assume integers)
$254,000	0.30	00–29
$318,000	0.50	30–79
$382,000	0.20	80–99
Costs		
$248,000	0.20	00–19
$260,000	0.60	20–79
$272,000	0.20	80–99

A computer could generate 20-digit random numbers such as 98125602386617556398. These would then be matched to the random numbers assigned to each probability and values assigned to 'Sales Revenues' and 'Costs' based on this. The random numbers generated give 5 possible outcomes in our example:

Random number	Sales revenue in $000	Random number	Costs in $000	Profit
98	382	12	248	134
56	318	02	248	70
38	318	66	260	58
17	254	55	260	(6)
63	318	98	272	46

Illustration 3 – Simulation

[***Note:*** *The illustration below is only here to show how a simulation works. You only need to be able to explain how one works, in the exam – not use one.*]

A business is choosing between two projects, project A and project B. It uses simulation to generate a distribution of profits for each project.

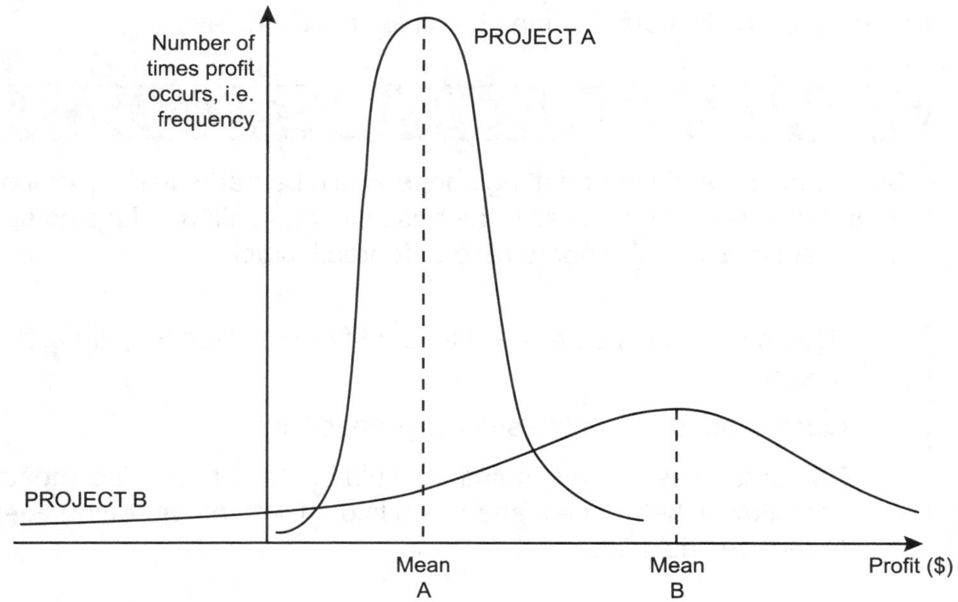

Required:

Which project should the business invest in?

Solution

Project A has a lower average profit but is also less risky (less variability of possible profits).

Project B has a higher average profit but is also more risky (more variability of possible profits).

There is no correct answer. All simulation will do is give the business the above results. It will not tell the business which is the better project.

If the business is willing to take on risk, they may prefer project B since it has the higher average return.

However, if the business would prefer to minimise its exposure to risk, it would take on project A. This has a lower risk but also a lower average return.

There are major **drawbacks** of simulation:

- It is not a technique for making a decision, only for obtaining more information about the possible outcomes.
- Models can become extremely complex.
- The time and costs involved in their construction can be more than is gained from the improved decisions.
- Probability distributions may be difficult to formulate.

Simulation in a chain of betting shops

Simulation for a chain of betting shops would be particularly useful on an operational level for analysing the possible implications of a single event, such as a major horse race or football match:

- Possible outcomes are easy to identify (e.g. win, lose, draw, 2–1,3–0, etc)
- Quoted odds can help estimate probabilities
- The outcomes of the simulation could be used to assess impact on cash flow, whether bets should be laid off with other betting agents to reduces risk, etc.

Simulation could also be used for wider strategic analysis such as for assessing the possibility and implications of stricter anti-gambling legislation.

5 Expected values (EVs)

An expected value is a weighted average of all possible outcomes. It calculates the average return that will be made if a decision is repeated again and again. In other words, it is obtained by multiplying the value of each possible outcome (x), by the probability of that outcome (p), and summing the results.

The formula for the expected value is **EV = Σpx**

Illustration 4 – Calculating EVs

An organisation is considering launching a new product. It will do so if the expected value of the total revenue is in excess of $1,000. It is decided to set the selling price at $10. After some investigation a number of probabilities for different levels of sales revenue are predicted; these are shown in the following table:

Units sold	Revenue	Probability	Pay-off
	$		$
80	800	0.15	120
100	1,000	0.50	500
120	1,200	0.35	420
		1.00	EV = 1,040

The expected sales revenue at a selling price of $10 per unit is $1,040, that is [800 × 0.15] + [1,000 × 0.50] + [1,200 × 0.35]. In preparing forecasts and making decisions management may proceed on the assumption that it can expect sales revenue of $1,040 if it sets a selling price of $10 per unit. The actual outcome of adopting this selling price may be sales revenue that is higher or lower than $1,040. And $1,040 is not even the most likely outcome; the most likely outcome is $1,000, since this has the highest probability.

Since the expected value shows the long run average outcome of a decision which is repeated time and time again, it is a useful decision rule for a **risk neutral decision maker**. This is because a risk neutral investor neither seeks risk or avoids it; he is happy to accept an average outcome.

Advantages and disadvantages of EVs

Advantages:

- Takes uncertainty into account by considering the probability of each possible outcome and using this information to calculate an expected value.
- The information is reduced to a single number resulting in easier decisions.
- Calculations are relatively simple.

Disadvantages:

- The probabilities used are usually very subjective.
- The EV is merely a weighted average and therefore has little meaning for a one-off project.
- The EV gives no indication of the dispersion of possible outcomes about the EV, i.e. the risk.
- The EV may not correspond to any of the actual possible outcomes.

Pay-off tables

A profit table (pay-off table) can be a useful way to represent and analyse a scenario where there is a range of possible outcomes and a variety of possible responses. A pay-off table simply illustrates all possible profits/losses.

Illustration 5 – Geoffrey Ramsbottom

Geoffrey Ramsbottom runs a kitchen that provides food for various canteens throughout a large organisation. A particular salad is sold to the canteen for $10 and costs $8 to prepare. Therefore, the contribution per salad is $2.

Based upon past demands, it is expected that, during the 250-day working year, the canteens will require the following daily quantities:

On 25 days of the year	40 salads
On 50 days of the year	50 salads
On 100 days of the year	60 salads
On 75 days	70 salads
Total 250 days	

The kitchen must prepare the salad in batches of 10 meals. Its staff has asked you to help them decide how many salads it should supply for each day of the forthcoming year.

Solution – Geoffrey Ramsbottom

Constructing a pay-off table:

- With pay-off tables it is common to put the decision variable across the top of the payoff table (i.e. columns) and the risk variable down the side (rows)
- If 40 salads will be required on 25 days of a 250-day year, the probability that demand = 40 salads is:

P(Demand of 40) = 25 days ÷ 250 days

P(Demand of 40) = 0.1

- Likewise, P(Demand of 50) = 0 .20; P(Demand of 60 = 0.4) and P (Demand of 70 = 0.30).
- Now let's look at the different values of profit or losses depending on how many salads are supplied and sold. For example, if we supply 40 salads and all are sold, our profits amount to 40 × $2 = 80.
- If however we supply 50 salads but only 40 are sold, our profits will amount to 40 × $2 – (10 unsold salads × $8 unit cost) = 0.

We can now construct a pay-off table as follows:

			Daily supply			
		Probability	**40 salads**	**50 salads**	**60 salads**	**70 salads**
Daily demand	40 salads	0.10	$80	$0	($80)	($160)
	50 salads	0.20	$80	$100	$20	($60)
	60 salads	0.40	$80	$100	$120	$40
	70 salads	0.30	$80	$100	$120	$140

6 Maximax, maximin and minimax regret

When probabilities are not available, there are still tools available for incorporating uncertainty into decision making.

Maximax

The maximax rule involves selecting the alternative that maximises the maximum pay-off achievable.

This approach would be suitable for an optimist, or 'risk-seeking' investor, who seeks to achieve the best results if the best happens.

Illustration 6 – The Maximax rule

Following up from the pay-off table example, Geoffrey Ramsbottom's table looks as follows:

			Daily supply			
		Probability	**40 salads**	**50 salads**	**60 salads**	**70 salads**
Daily demand	40 salads	0.10	$80	$0	($80)	($160)
	50 salads	0.20	$80	$100	$20	($60)
	60 salads	0.40	$80	$100	$120	$40
	70 salads	0.30	$80	$100	$120	$140

The manager who employs the maximax criterion is assuming that whatever action is taken, the best will happen; he/she is a risk-taker. How many salads will he decide to supply?

Answer

Here, the highest maximum possible pay-off is $140. We should therefore decide to supply 70 salads a day.

Test your understanding 1 – Applying maximax

A company is choosing which of three new products to make (A, B or C) and has calculated likely pay-offs under three possible scenarios (I, II or III), giving the following pay-off table.

Profit (loss)		**Product chosen**	
Scenario	**A**	**B**	**C**
I	20	80	10
II	40	70	100
III	50	(10)	40

Required:

Using maximax, which product would be chosen?

Maximin

The maximin rule involves selecting the alternative that maximises the minimum pay-off achievable.

The investor would look at the worst possible outcome at each supply level, then selects the highest one of these. The decision maker therefore chooses the outcome which is guaranteed to minimise his losses. In the process, he loses out on the opportunity of making big profits.

This approach would be appropriate for a risk-averse pessimist who seeks to achieve the best results if the worst happens.

Test your understanding 2 – Applying maximin

Required:

Using the information from the previous TYU apply the maximin rule to decide which product should be made.

Illustration 7 – The 'Maximin' rule

Following up from the pay-off table example, Geoffrey Ramsbottom's table looks as follows:

			Daily supply			
		Probability	**40 salads**	**50 salads**	**60 salads**	**70 salads**
Daily demand	40 salads	0.10	$80	$0	($80)	($160)
	50 salads	0.20	$80	$100	$20	($60)
	60 salads	0.40	$80	$100	$120	$40
	70 salads	0.30	$80	$100	$120	$140

How many salads should we supply, using the Maximin rule?

Answer

If we decide to supply 40 salads, the minimum pay-off is $80.

If we decide to supply 50 salads, the minimum pay-off is $0.

If we decide to supply 60 salads, the minimum pay-off is ($80).

If we decide to supply 70 salads, the minimum pay-off is ($160).

The highest minimum payoff arises from supplying **40 salads**.

The Minimax Regret rule

The minimax regret strategy is the one that minimises the maximum regret. It is useful for a risk-averse decision maker. Essentially, this is the technique for a 'sore loser' who does not wish to make the wrong decision.

'Regret' in this context is defined as the opportunity loss through having made the wrong decision.

Illustration 8 – The 'Minimax Regret' rule

Following up from the pay-off table example, Geoffrey Ramsbottom's table looks as follows:

			Daily supply			
		Probability	**40 salads**	**50 salads**	**60 salads**	**70 salads**
Daily demand	40 salads	0.10	$80	$0	($80)	($160)
	50 salads	0.20	$80	$100	$20	($60)
	60 salads	0.40	$80	$100	$120	$40
	70 salads	0.30	$80	$100	$120	$140

How many salads should we decide to supply if the minimax regret rule is applied?

Answer

Following up from the pay-off table example, Geoffrey Ramsbottom's table looks as follows:

			Daily supply			
		Probability	**40 salads**	**50 salads**	**60 salads**	**70 salads**
Daily demand	40 salads	0.10	$80	$0	($80)	($160)
	50 salads	0.20	$80	$100	$20	($60)
	60 salads	0.40	$80	$100	$120	$40
	70 salads	0.30	$80	$100	$120	$140

If the minimax regret rule is applied to decide how many salads should be made each day, we need to calculate the 'regrets'. This means we need to find the biggest pay-off for each demand row, then subtract all other numbers in this row from the largest number.

For example, if the demand is 40 salads, we will make a maximum profit of $80 if they all sell. If we had decided to supply 50 salads, we would achieve a nil profit. The difference, or 'regret' between that nil profit and the maximum of $80 achievable for that row is $80.

Regrets can be tabulated as follows:

		Daily supply			
		40 salads	**50 salads**	**60 salads**	**70 salads**
Daily demand	40 salads	$0	$80	$160	$240
	50 salads	$20	$0	$80	$160
	60 salads	$40	$20	$0	$80
	70 salads	$60	$40	$20	$0
	Maximum regret	**$60**	**$80**	**$160**	**$240**

A manager employing the minimax regret criterion would want to minimise that maximum regret, and therefore supply 40 salads only.

7 Decision trees

Examiner's article: visit the ACCA website, www.accaglobal.com, to review the examiner's article written on this topic (September 2014).

A decision tree is a diagrammatic representation of a multi-decision problem, where all possible courses of action are represented, and every possible outcome of each course of action is shown.

Decision trees should be used where a problem involves a series of decisions being made and several outcomes arise during the decision-making process. Decision trees force the decision maker to consider the logical sequence of events. A complex problem is broken down into smaller, easier to handle sections.

The financial outcomes and probabilities are shown separately, and the decision tree is 'rolled back' by calculating expected values and making decisions.

Three step method

Step 1: Draw the tree from left to right, showing appropriate decisions and events/outcomes.

Some common symbols can be used: a **square** is used to represent a decision point (i.e. where a choice between different courses of action must be taken. A **circle** is used to represent a *chance* point. The branches coming away from a circle with have probabilities attached to them. All probabilities should add up to '1'.

Label the tree and relevant cash inflows/outflows and probabilities associated with outcomes.

Step 2: Evaluate the tree from right to left carrying out these two actions:

(a) Calculate an EV at each outcome point.

(b) Choose the best option at each decision point.

Step 3: Recommend a course of action to management.

e.g

Decision trees

A university is trying to decide whether or not to advertise a new post-graduate degree programme.

The number of students starting the programme is dependent on economic conditions:

- If conditions are poor it is expected that the programme will attract 40 students without advertising. There is a 60% chance that economic conditions will be poor.
- If economic conditions are good it is expected that the programme will attract only 20 students without advertising. There is a 40% chance that economic conditions will be good.

If the programme is advertised and economic conditions are poor, there is a 65% chance that the advertising will stimulate further demand and student numbers will increase to 50. If economic conditions are good there is a 25% chance the advertising will stimulate further demand and numbers will increase to 25 students.

The profit expected, before deducting the cost of advertising of $15,000, at different levels of student numbers are as follows:

Number of students	**Profit in $**
15	(10,000)
20	15,000
25	40,000
30	65,000
35	90,000
40	115,000
45	140,000
50	165,000

Required:

Demonstrate, using a decision tree, whether the programme should be advertised.

Answer – University advertising decision tree

Step 1: Draw the tree from left to right. A **square** is used to represent a decision point (i.e. whether to advertise the programme, or not advertise.)

For both options, a **circle** is used to represent a *chance* point – a poor economic environment, or a good economic environment.

Label the tree and relevant cash inflows/outflows and probabilities associated with outcomes:

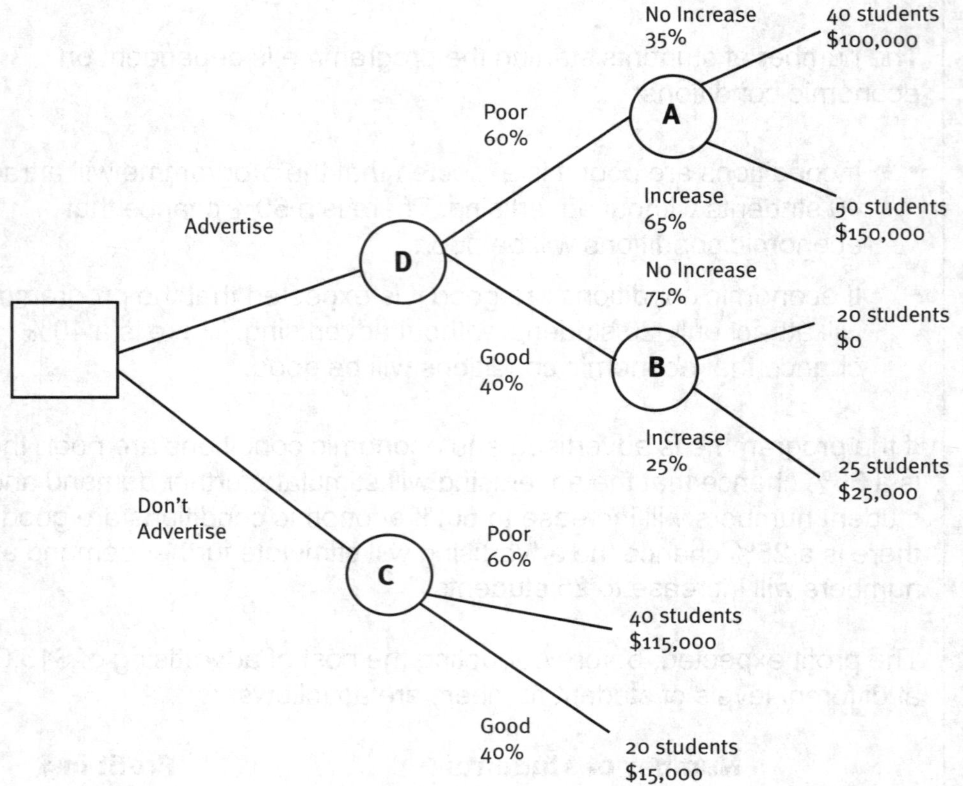

Note: The advertising costs have been deducted where relevant in arriving at the figures used on the tree.

For example, the gain for the top right outcome for 40 students = 115,000 – 15,000 = 100,000

Step 2: Evaluate the tree from right to left carrying out these two actions:

(a) Calculate an Expected Value at each outcome point. Working from top to bottom, we can calculate the EVs as follows:

EV (Outcome Point A) = (35% × $100,000) + (65% × $150,000) = $132,500

EV (Outcome Point B) = (0% × $0) + (25% × $25,000) = $6,250

EV (Outcome Point C) = (60% × $115,000) + (40% × $15,000) = $75,000

EV (Outcome Point D) = (60% × $132,500) + (40% × $6,250) = $82,000

(b) Choose the best option at each decision point and **recommend** a course of action to management.

At the first (and only) decision point in our tree, we should choose the option to advertise as EV ('D') is $82,000 and EV ('C) is $75,000.

Test your understanding 3 – The 'Duke of York' cinema

The 'Duke of York' is an independent cinema in Brightville. It is considering whether or not to hire a movie to show in its cinema for one week. If the management decides to hire the movie, it will be screened 20 times during the week. The cost of hiring the movie for the week is $70,000.

You work as the cinema's accountant, and you have been asked to evaluate the financial effects of the decision to hire the movie. You have made the following estimates:

(1) **Customers**

The entrance fee for every customer is $10. The number of customers watching the movie at each screening is uncertain, but has been estimated as follows: there is a 50% probability 200 customers will attend the screening; a 30% probability 250 customers will attend, and 20% probability 150 customers will come.

(2) **Customer contribution for each sale of refreshments**

The average contribution per customer earned from the sale of refreshments is also uncertain but has been estimated as follows:

Probability	**$ average contribution per customer**
40% probability	$10 per customer
25% probability	$12 per customer
35% probability	$8 per customer

Required:

Prepare a decision tree to show the total contributions which could be generated from the above scenario. Based on the expected values, determine if the movie should be hired.

8 The value of perfect information

In many questions the decision makers receive a forecast of a future outcome (for example a market research group may predict the forthcoming demand for a product). This forecast may turn out to be correct or incorrect. The question often requires the candidate to calculate the value of the forecast.

Perfect information The forecast of the future outcome is always a correct prediction. If a firm can obtain a 100% accurate prediction they will always be able to undertake the most beneficial course of action for that prediction.

Imperfect information The forecast is usually correct, but can be incorrect. Imperfect information is not as valuable as perfect information.

The value of information (either perfect or imperfect) may be calculated as follows:

Expected profit (outcome) WITH the information LESS Expected profit (outcome) WITHOUT the information

Test your understanding 4 – Geoffrey Ramsbottom

A new ordering system is being considered, whereby customers must order their salad online the day before. With this new system Mr Ramsbottom will know for certain the daily demand 24 hours in advance. He can adjust production levels on a daily basis.

How much is this new system worth to Mr Ramsbottom?

9 The value of imperfect information

Perfect information is only rarely accessible. In fact, information sources such as market research or industry experts are usually subject to error. Market research findings, for example, are likely to be reasonably accurate – but they can still be wrong.

Therefore, our analysis must extend to deal with imperfect information. The question is as follows: **how much would it be worth paying for such imperfect information**, given that we are aware of how right or wrong it is likely to be?

The value of imperfect information

(a) You have the mineral rights to a piece of land that you believe may have oil underground. There is only a 10% chance that you will strike oil if you drill, but the profit is $200,000.

It costs $10,000 to drill. The alternative is not to drill at all, in which case your profit is zero.

Should you drill? Draw a decision tree to represent your problem.

(b) Before you drill, you may consult a geologist who can assess the promise of the piece of land. She can tell you whether the prospects are good or poor, but she is not a perfect predictor. If there is oil, the probability that she will say there are good prospects is 95%. If there is no oil, the probability that she will say prospects are poor is 85%.

Draw a decision tree and calculate the value of imperfect information for this geologist. If the geologist charges $7,000, would you use her services?

Solution

(a)

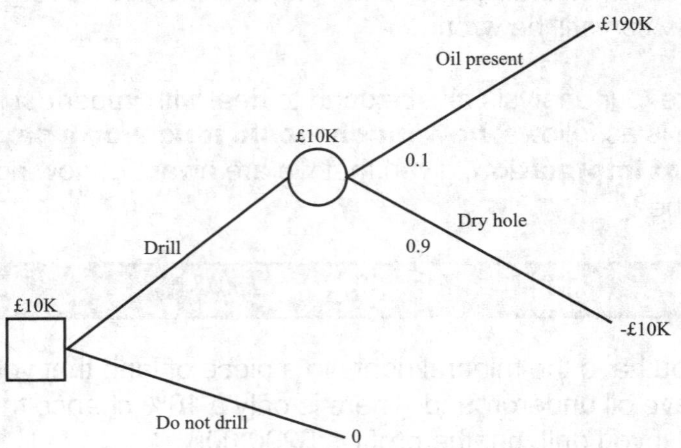

EV ('Drill') = (\$190K × 0.1) + (–\$10K × 0.9) so EV ('Drill') = \$10K.

We should drill, because the expected value from drilling is \$10K, versus nothing for not drilling.

(b) We will calculate the Expected Value of profits if we employ the geologist.

If this exceeds \$10,000, the geologist would be worth employing **as long as the benefit of employing her exceeds her charge of \$7,000.**

If we employ the geologist, the probabilities of her possible assessments can be tabulated as follows (assume 1,000 drills in total):

	Oil present	**No oil**	**Total**
Geologist says 'Prospects are good'	95% × 100 = 95 drills	15% × 900= 135 drills	230 drills
Geologist says 'Prospects are poor'	5% × 100 = 5 drills	85% × 900= 765 drills	770 drills
	100 drills	**900 drills**	**1,000 drills**

A decision tree can be drawn to calculate the expected value of profits if a geologist is employed:

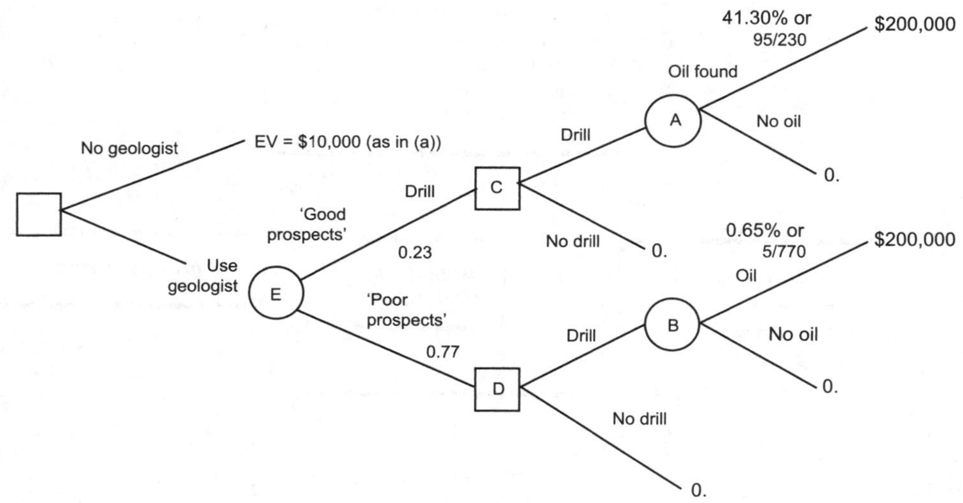

Working from right to left:

EV(A) = (41.30% × $200,000) – $10,000 drilling costs = $72,600. The decision at 'C' should be to drill, as this generates higher benefits than not drilling.

EV(B) = (0.65% × $200,000) – $10,000 drilling costs = –$8,700. The decision at 'D' should be not to drill.

EV(E) = 0.23 × $72,600 = $16,698. This is the expected value of profits if a geologist is employed and exceeds the EV of profits if she is not employed.

Expected Value of Imperfect Information = $16,698 – $10,000 = $6,698. Since this is less than the cost of buying the information ($7,000), we should not employ the geologist.

10 Chapter summary

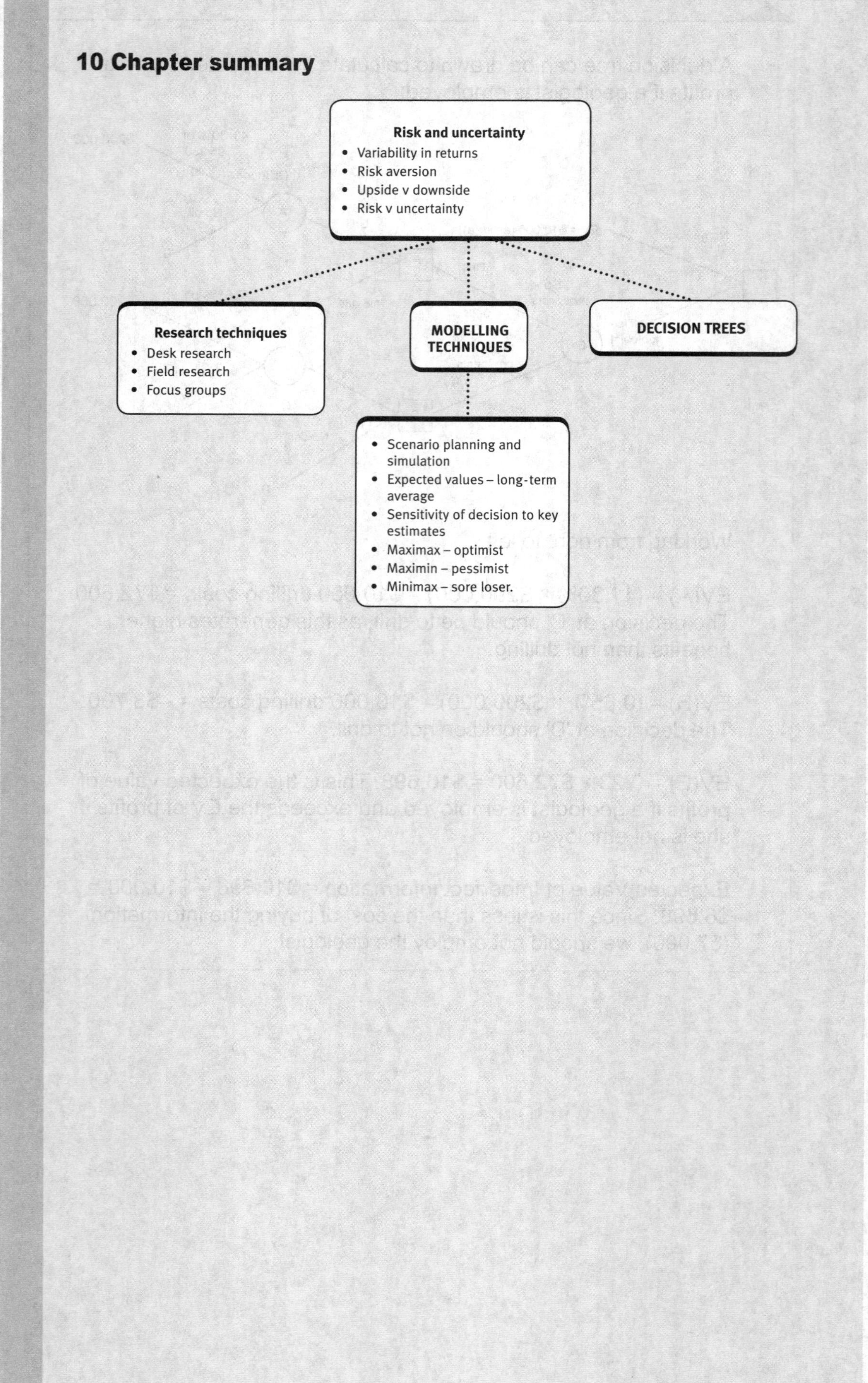
Risk and uncertainty
• Variability in returns
• Risk aversion
• Upside v downside
• Risk v uncertainty
Research techniques
• Desk research
• Field research
• Focus groups
MODELLING TECHNIQUES
DECISION TREES
• Scenario planning and simulation
• Expected values – long-term average
• Sensitivity of decision to key estimates
• Maximax – optimist
• Maximin – pessimist
• Minimax – sore loser.

Test your understanding answers

Test your understanding 1 – Applying maximax

Using maximax, an optimist would consider the best possible outcome for each product and pick the product with the greatest potential.

Here C would be chosen with a maximum possible gain of 100.

Test your understanding 2 – Applying maximin

- Using maximin, a pessimist would consider the poorest possible outcome for each product and would ensure that the maximum pay-off is achieved if the worst result were to happen.
- Therefore, product A would be chosen resulting in a minimum pay-off of 20 compared to a minimum pay-off of 10 for products B and C.

Test your understanding 3 – The 'Duke of York' cinema

Step 1: In order to reach a decision about whether or not the movie should be hired, a decision tree could be laid out as follows:

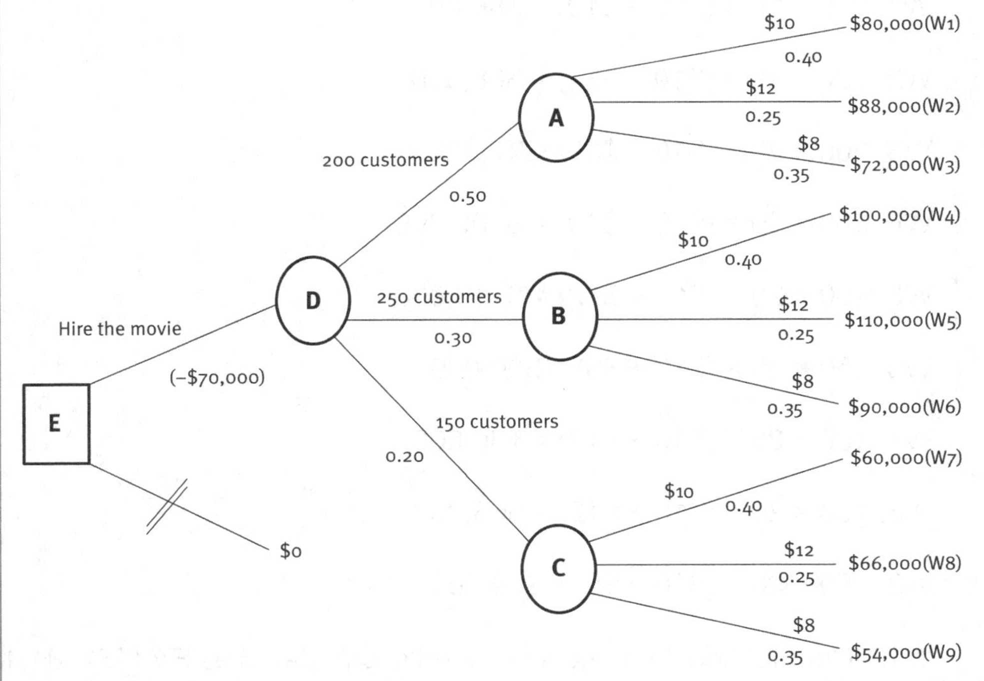

Step 2: Calculate an expected value at each outcome point

EV (Outcome point A) = (40% × \$80,000) + (25% × \$88,000) + (35% × \$72,000) = \$79,200

EV (Outcome point B) = (40% × \$100,000) + (25% × \$110,000) + (35% × \$90,000) = \$99,000

EV (Outcome point C) = (40% × \$60,000) + (25% × \$66,000) + (35% × \$54,000) = \$59,400

EV (Outcome point D) = (50% × \$79,200) + (30% × \$99,000) + (20% × \$59,400) = \$81,180

Step 3: Choose the best option at each decision point and recommend a course of action to management

At the first and only decision point in our tree 'E', we should choose the option to hire the movie as EV (D) is equal to a positive contribution of \$11,180 (See Working 10) and not hiring the movie does not generate any contribution at all.

Contribution generated – Workings

We can calculate those customers × 20 screenings × (\$10 entrance fee + refreshment contribution)

W1: 200 × 20 × (\$10 + \$10) = \$80,000

W2: 200 × 20 × (\$10 + \$12) = \$88,000

W3: 200 × 20 × (\$10 + \$8) = \$72,000

W4: 250 × 20 × (\$10 + \$10) = \$100,000

W5: 250 × 20 × (\$10 + \$12) = \$110,000

W6: 250 × 20 × (\$10 + \$8) = \$90,000

W7: 150 × 20 × (\$10 + \$10) = \$60,000

W8: 150 × 20 × (\$10 + \$12) = \$66,000

W9: 150 × 20 × (\$10 + \$8) = \$54,000

W10: Contribution if the movie is hired is calculated as EV ('D') \$81,180 – \$70,000 cost of hiring = \$11,180.

Test your understanding 4 – Geoffrey Ramsbottom

Supply = demand	X Pay off	P Probability	px
40	$80	0.1	8
50	$100	0.2	20
60	$120	0.4	48
70	$140	0.3	42
			118

E.V. with perfect information	= $118
E.V. without perfect information (Working 1)	= $90
Value of perfect information	$28 per day

Working 1:

According to the pay-off table from Illustration 5, the Expected Value of Profits if **40 salads** are supplied can be calculated as (0.10 × $80) + (0.20 × $80) + (0.40 × $80) + (0.30 × $80) = **$80.**

Likewise:

EV ('**50 salads** daily supply') =	($0 × 10%) =	$0
	+ ($100 × 20%) =	$20
	+ ($100 × 40%) =	$40
	+ ($100 × 30%) =	$30
		$90
EV ('**60 salads** daily supply') =	(– $80 × 10%) =	($8)
	+ ($20 × 20%) =	$4
	+ ($120 × 40%) =	$48
	+ ($120 × 30%) =	$36
		$80
EV ('**70 salads** daily supply') =	(– $160 × 10%) =	($16)
	+ (– $60 × 20%) =	($12)
	+ ($40 × 40%) =	$16
	+ ($140 × 30%) =	$42
		$30

Profits are therefore maximised at 50 salads and amount to $90.

chapter

8

Budgeting

Chapter learning objectives

Upon completion of this chapter you will be able to:

- explain why organisations use budgeting
- explain how budgetary systems fit within the performance hierarchy
- describe the factors which influence behaviour at work
- discuss the issues surrounding setting the difficulty level for a budget
- explain the benefits and difficulties of the participation of employees in the negotiation of targets
- explain and evaluate 'top down' and 'bottom up' budgetary systems; 'rolling', 'activity-based', 'incremental' and 'zero-based' budgetary systems.
- explain and evaluate 'feed-forward' budgetary control
- select and justify an appropriate budgetary system for a given organisation
- describe the information used in various budgetary systems and the sources of the information needed
- explain the difficulties of changing a budgetary system and type of budget used
- explain how budget systems can deal with uncertainty in the environment
- explain the major benefits and dangers in using spreadsheets in budgeting.

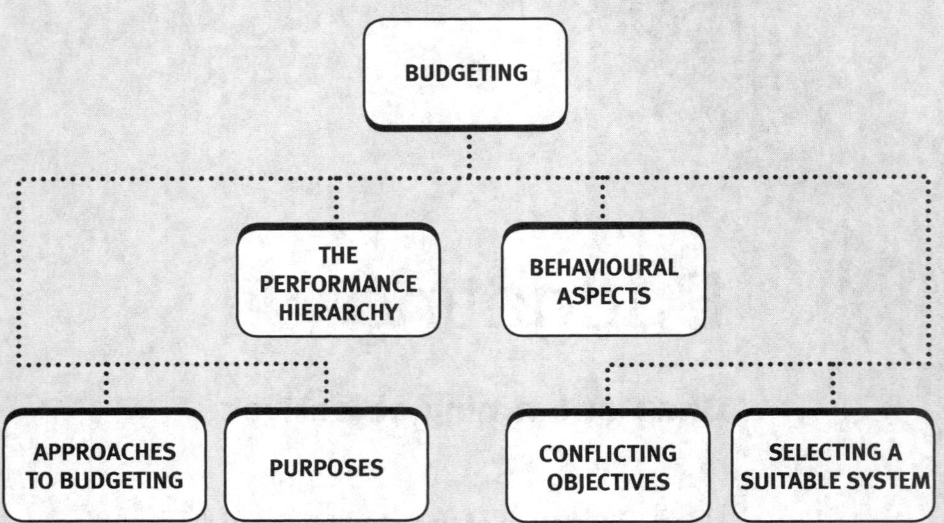

1 Purpose of budgets

A budget is a quantitative plan prepared for a specific time period. It is normally expressed in financial terms and prepared for one year.

Budgeting serves a number of purposes:

- **Planning**

  A budgeting process forces a business to look to the future. This is essential for survival since it stops management from relying on ad hoc or poorly co-ordinated planning.

- **Control**

  Actual results are compared against the budget and action is taken as appropriate.

- **Communication**

  The budget is a formal communication channel that allows junior and senior managers to converse.

- **Co-ordination**

  The budget allows co-ordination of all parts of the business towards a common corporate goal.

- **Evaluation**

  Responsibility accounting divides the organisation into budget centres, each of which has a manager who is responsible for its performance. The budget may be used to evaluate the actions of a manager within the business in terms of the costs and revenues over which they have control.

- **Motivation**

  The budget may be used as a target for managers to aim for. Reward should be given for operating within or under budgeted levels of expenditure. This acts as a motivator for managers.

- **Authorisation**

  The budget acts as a formal method of authorisation to a manager for expenditure, hiring staff and the pursuit of plans contained within the budget.

- **Delegation**

  Managers may be involved in setting the budget. Extra responsibility may motivate the managers. Management involvement may also result in more realistic targets.

2 Budgets and performance management

Budgets contribute to performance management by providing benchmarks against which to compare actual results (through variance analysis), and develop corrective measures. They take many forms and serve many functions, but most provide the basis for:

- detailed sales targets
- staffing plans
- production
- cash investment and borrowing
- capital expenditure.

Budgets give managers "preapproval" for execution of spending plans, and allow them to provide forward looking guidance to investors and creditors. For example, budgets are necessary to convince banks and other lenders to extend credit.

Even in a small business, an robust business plan/budget can often result in anticipating and avoiding disastrous outcomes.

Medium and larger organisations invariably rely on budgets. This is equally true in businesses, government, and not-for-profit organizations. The budget provides a formal quantitative expression of expectations. It is an essential facet of the planning and control process. Without a budget, an organisation will be highly inefficient and ineffective.

Test your understanding 1 – Evaluation of managers

A wage award for production staff is agreed which exceeds the allowance incorporated in the budget. Discuss whether the performance of the production manager should be linked to the wage cost.

3 The performance hierarchy

As you may recall from paper F1, firms have a planning hierarchy:

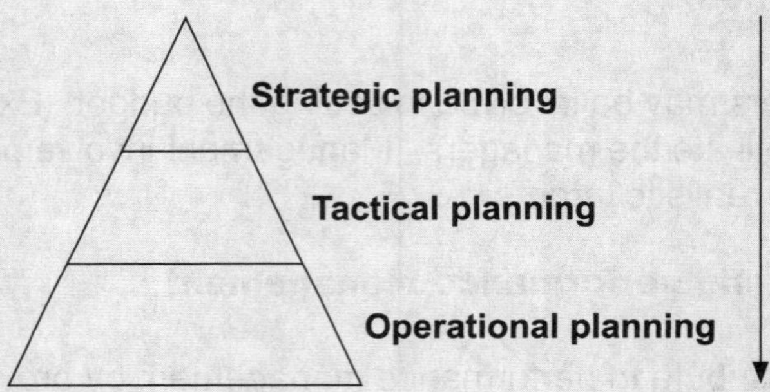

- Strategic planning is long term, looks at the whole organisation and defines resource requirements. For example, to develop new products in response to changing customer needs.
- Tactical planning is medium term, looks at the department/divisional level and specifies how to use resources. For example, to train staff to deal with the challenges that this new product presents.
- Operational planning is very short term, very detailed and is mainly concerned with control. Most budgeting activities fall within operational planning and control. For example, a budget is set for the new product to include advertising expenditure, sales forecasts, labour and material expenditure etc.

The aim is that if a manager achieves short-term budgetary targets (operational plans) then there is more chance of meeting tactical goals and ultimately success for strategic plans.

The achievement of budgetary plans will impact on the eventual achievement of the tactical and strategic plans. However, budgets should also be flexible in order to meet the changing needs of the business.

4 Behavioural aspects of budgeting

Individuals react to the demands of budgeting and budgetary control in different ways and their behaviour can damage the budgeting process.

Behavioural problems are often linked to management styles, and include dysfunctional behaviour and budget slack.

Management styles (Hopwood)

Research was carried out by Hopwood (1973) into the manufacturing division of a US steelworks, involving a sample of more than 200 managers with cost centre responsibility. Hopwood identified three distinct styles of using budgetary information to evaluate management performance.

Management style	Performance evaluation	Behavioural aspects
(1) Budget constrained style	• Manager evaluated on ability to achieve budget in the short term	• Job related pressure • May result in short-term decision making at the expense of long term goals
	• Manager will be criticised for poor results. For example, if spending exceeds the limit set	• Can result in poor working relations with colleagues • Can result in manipulation of data
(2) Profit conscious style	• Manager evaluated on ability to reduce costs and increase profit in the long term	• Less job related pressure
	• For example, a manager will be prepared to exceed the budgetary limit in the short term if this will result in an increase in long term profit	• Better working relations with colleagues • Less manipulation of data

(3)	Non-accounting style	• Manager evaluated mainly on non-accounting performance indicators such as quality and customer satisfaction	• Similar to profit conscious style but there is less concern for accounting information • Requires significant and stringent monitoring of performance against budget

5 Setting the difficulty level of a budget

Budgetary targets will assist motivation and appraisal if they are at the right level.

An **expectations** budget is a budget set at current achievable levels. This is unlikely to motivate managers to improve but may give more accurate forecasts for resource planning, control and performance evaluation.

An **aspirations** budget is a budget set at a level which exceeds the level currently achieved. This may motivate managers to improve if it is seen as attainable but may also result in an adverse variance if it is too difficult to achieve. This must be managed carefully.

Test your understanding 2

A manager is awarded a bonus for achieving monthly budgetary targets. State three possible behavioural implications of this policy. What should be done to try to improve the process?

Test your understanding 3

A sales manager has achieved $550,000 of sales in the current year. Business is expected to grow by 10% and price inflation is expected to be 3%.

Suggest a suitable budget target for the forthcoming year.

6 Approaches to budgeting

There are a number of different budgetary systems:

- Top down vs bottom up budgeting
- Incremental budgeting
- Zero-based budgeting (ZBB)

- Rolling budgets
- Activity-based budgeting
- Feed-forward control.

Each system will be reviewed in turn.

7 Budgeting and participation

There are basically two ways in which a budget can be set: from the top down (imposed budget) or from the bottom up (participatory budget).

Imposed style

An imposed/top-down budget is 'a budget allowance which is set without permitting the ultimate budget holder to have the opportunity to participate in the budgeting process'

Advantages of imposed style

There are a number of reasons why it might be preferable for managers not to be involved in setting their own budgets:

(1) Involving managers in the setting of budgets is more time consuming than if senior managers simply imposed the budgets.

(2) Managers may not have the skills or motivation to participate usefully in the budgeting process.

(3) Senior managers have the better overall view of the company and its resources and may be better-placed to create a budget which utilises those scarce resources to best effect.

(4) Senior managers also are aware of the longer term strategic objectives of the organisation and can prepare a budget which is in line with that strategy.

(5) Managers may build budgetary slack or bias into the budget in order to make the budget easy to achieve and themselves look good.

(6) Managers cannot use budgets to play games which disadvantage other budget holders.

(7) By having the budgets imposed by senior managers, i.e. someone outside the department, a more objective, fresher perspective may be gained.

(8) If the participation is only pseudo-participation and the budgets are frequently drastically changed by senior management, then this will cause dissatisfaction and the effect will be to demotivate staff.

Participative budgets

Participative/bottom up budgeting is 'A budgeting system in which all budget holders are given the opportunity to participate in setting their own budgets'

Advantages of participative budgets

(1) The morale of the management is improved. Managers feel like their opinion is listened to, that their opinion is valuable.

(2) Managers are more likely to accept the plans contained within the budget and strive to achieve the targets if they had some say in setting the budget, rather than if the budget was imposed upon them. Failure to achieve the target that they themselves set is seen as a personal failure as well as an organisational failure.

(3) The lower level managers will have a more detailed knowledge of their particular part of the business than senior managers and thus will be able to produce more realistic budgets.

Budgetary control – Behavioural aspects

Another very important aspect of budgetary control systems and this is its impact on the human beings who will operate and be judged by those systems.

It is only comparatively recently that the results of years of study of personal relationships in the workplace have percolated into the field of management accounting. It is now recognised that failure to consider the effect of control systems on the people affected could result in a lowering of morale and a reduction of motivation. Further, those people may be induced to do things that are not in the best interests of the organisation.

Specific behavioural issues encountered in budgeting include the following:

Motivation and co-operation

To be fully effective, any system of financial control must provide for motivation and incentive. If this requirement is not satisfied, managers will approach their responsibilities in a very cautious and conservative manner. It is often found that adverse variances attract investigation and censure but there is no incentive to achieve favourable variances. Failure to distinguish controllable from uncontrollable costs in budgetary control can alienate managers from the whole process.

Personal goals and ambitions are, in theory, strongly linked to organisational goals. These personal goals may include a desire for higher income and higher social standing. To simultaneously satisfy the goals of the organisation and the goals of the individual there must be 'goal congruence'. That is, the individual manager perceives that his or her own goals are achieved by his or her acting in a manner that allows the organisation to achieve its goals. The problem is that reliance on budgetary control systems does not always result in goal congruence.

The success of a budgetary control system depends on the people who operate and are affected by it. They must work within the system in an understanding and co-operative manner. This can only be achieved by individuals who have a total involvement at all stages in the budget process. However, it is often found that

(1) A budget is used simply as a pressure device. If the budget is perceived as 'a stick with which to beat people', then it will be sabotaged in all sorts of subtle ways.

(2) The budgeting process and subsequent budgetary control exercises induce competition between individual departments and executives. Managers may be induced to do things in order to 'meet budget' that are not in the best interests of the business as a whole.

Failure of goal congruence

It has been seen that an essential element in budgetary control is performance evaluation. Actual results are compared with budget or standard in order to determine whether performance is good or bad. What is being evaluated is not just the business operation but the managers responsible for it. The purpose of budgetary control is to induce managers to behave in a manner that is to the best advantage of the organisation. Compliance with budget is enforced by a variety of negative and positive sanctions.

When adverse variances are reported for operations then this implies poor performance by the managers of the operations. If they are unable to correct or explain away the adverse variances, then they may suffer negative sanctions. They may have forgo salary increases, or they may be demoted to a less prestigious post. Other more subtle negative sanctions are possible that anyone who has ever worked for a large organisation will be aware of.

Positive inducements may be offered to encourage managers to avoid adverse variances. A manager who meets budget may be granted a performance-related salary bonus, promotion, a new company car or use of the executive dining room.

Consequently, the manager has a considerable incentive to ensure that the department or operation he is responsible for achieves its budgeted level of performance. However, there are a variety of ways of doing this that might not be to the advantage of the organisation as a whole.

For example, the manager of a production line can cut costs and hence improve its reported performances by reducing quality controls. This may result in long-term problems concerning failure of products in service, loss of customer goodwill and rectification costs – but these are not the concern of the production line manager. This is a clear failure of goal congruence.

The control system is capable of distorting the process it is meant to serve – or 'the tail wags the dog'. The enforcement of a budgetary control system requires sensitivity if this is not to happen.

The budget as a pot of cash

In some environments managers may come to consider the budget as a sum of money that has to be spent. This arises particularly in service departments or public sector organisations, the performance of which is gauged mainly through comparison of actual and budget spending.

The manager of a local authority 'street cleaning' department may be given an annual budget of £120,000 to clean the streets. The manager knows that she will be punished if she spends more than £120,000 in the year. She also knows that if she spends less than £120,000 in the year then her budget will probably be reduced next year. Such a reduction will involve a personal loss of status in the organisation and will make her job more difficult in the next year.

In order to ensure that she does not overspend her annual budget in the current year the manager may spend at a rate of £9,000 per month for the first 11 months of the year. This can be achieved by reducing the frequency of street cleaning and using poor-quality materials. It allows a contingency fund to be accumulated in case of emergencies.

However, in the final month of the year the manager has to spend £21,000 if she wishes to ensure that her whole budget is fully used. She might achieve this by using extra labour and high-quality materials.

Does this behaviour make sense? Of course it does not. The whole pattern of behaviour is distorted by the control system. It means that local residents have a substandard service for 11 months of the year and money is wasted in the 12th month.

It is, however, a fact that suppliers to government departments and local councils often experience a surge in orders towards the end of the financial year. This surge is caused by managers placing orders at the last moment in order to ensure that their full budget for the year is committed.

Budget negotiation

Budgets are normally arrived at by a process of negotiation with the managers concerned. A budget may actually be initiated by departmental managers and then corrected as a result of negotiation with the budget officer.

Clearly, a manager has an incentive to negotiate a budget that is not difficult to achieve. This produces a phenomenon known as 'padding the budget' or 'budgetary slack'. A manager will exaggerate the costs required to achieve objectives. This has the following results:

(1) If the manager succeeds in padding his budget, then the whole control exercise is damaged. Comparison of actual with budget gives no meaningful measure of performance and the manager is able to include inefficiencies in his operation if he wishes.

(2) A successful manager becomes one who is a hard negotiator. The problem with this is that the negotiations in question are between colleagues and not with customers. 'Infighting' may become entrenched in the management process.

(3) A great deal of time and energy that could be directed to the actual management of the business is distracted by what are essentially administrative procedures.

These are all examples of a control system distorting the processes they are meant to serve.

Influence on accounting policies

Any management accountant who has been engaged in the preparation of financial control reports will be familiar with attempts by managers to influence the accounting policies that are used. For example, the apportionment of indirect costs between departments often contains subjective elements. Should security costs be apportioned on the basis of floor space or staff numbers?

The manner in which the indirect costs are apportioned can have a considerable impact on how the performance of individual departments is perceived. This position creates the scope and incentive for managers to argue over accounting policies.

If a manager perceives that her department's performance is falling below budget, then she may sift through the costs charged to her department and demand that some be reclassified and charged elsewhere. The time and energy that goes into this kind of exercise has to be diverted from that available for the regular management of the business.

Budget constrained management styles

When the performance of a manager is assessed by his ability to meet budget, then he is likely to adopt a conservative approach to new business opportunities that appear. The immediate impact of new business ventures is likely to be a rise in capital and operating costs – with an adverse impact on current period profit. The benefits of such ventures may only be felt in the long term. Hence, when a new opportunity appears, the manager evaluating it may only perceive that its acceptance will result in below-budget performance in the current period – and turn it down on this ground alone. Another consideration is that reliance on budgetary control is an approach to management that involves sitting in an office and reading financial reports. Such an approach (in conjunction with features such as executive dining rooms) may result in an unsatisfactory corporate culture based on hierarchies and social divisions. Large organisations that rely heavily on budgetary control systems often take on an 'ossified' character.

Yet another consideration is that a reliance on budgetary planning may induce managers to favour projects and developments that are most amenable to the construction of budgets. Projects that involve little uncertainty and few unknowns are easy to incorporate in budgets and hence managers may be more inclined to adopt such projects than the alternatives. Projects that involve significant uncertainties may be attractive if they incorporate some combination of high expected returns and low cost interim exit routes – but a budget constrained manager may be disinclined to adopt such projects simply because they are difficult to incorporate in budgets. Some writers (see Section 12.8.3, 'contingency theory') suggest that the budgetary approach may be particularly inappropriate in a dynamic and turbulent business environment.

The general conclusion concerning this and previous points is that good budgetary control can offer certain benefits. However, when budgetary control is enforced in a rigid or insensitive manner it may end up doing more harm than good.

Budgets and motivation

Much of the early academic work on budgets concerned the extent to which the 'tightness' or looseness' of a budget acted as an incentive or disincentive to management effort. This was the issue of 'budget stretch'. Seminal works in this general area included studies by A.C. Stedry (see his 1960 text 'Budget Control and Cost Behaviour') and G.H. Hofstede (see his 1968 text 'The Game of Budget Control').

The main thrust of the findings that emerged from these studies was:

(1) Loose budgets (i.e. ones easily attainable) are poor motivators

(2) As budgets are tightened, up to a point they become more motivational

(3) Beyond that point, a very tight budget ceases to be motivational.

The role of budget participation and the manner in which aspirations and objectives are stated was also explored in certain studies. It was suggested that the participation of managers in budget setting was a motivational factor – but see earlier discussion concerning budget padding and negotiation.

Test your understanding 4

Bottom up budgeting is generally seen as preferable because it leads to improved managerial motivation and performance. However, there are situations for which top down budgeting is preferable.

Describe three situations where top down budgeting would be more applicable.

Incremental budgets

An incremental budget starts with the previous period's budget or actual results and adds (or subtracts) an incremental amount to cover inflation and other known changes.

It is suitable for stable businesses, where costs are not expected to change significantly. There should be good cost control and limited discretionary costs.

Advantages of incremental budgets	Disadvantages of incremental budgets
(1) Quickest and easiest method.	(1) Builds in previous problems and inefficiencies.
(2) Suitable if the organisation is stable and historic figures are acceptable since only the increment needs to be justified.	(2) Uneconomic activities may be continued. E.g. the firm may continue to make a component in-house when it might be cheaper to outsource.
	(3) Managers may spend unnecessarily to use up their budgeted expenditure allowance this year, thus ensuring they get the same (or a larger) budget next year.

Test your understanding 5

AW Inc produces two products, A and C. In the last year (20X4) it produced 640 units of A and 350 units of C incurring costs of $672,000. Analysis of the costs has shown that 75% of the total costs are variable. 60% of these variable costs vary in line with the number of A produced and the remainder with the number of C.

The budget for the year 20X5 is now being prepared using an incremental budgeting approach. The following additional information is available for 20X5:

- All costs will be 4% higher than the average paid in 20X4.
- Efficiency levels will remain unchanged.
- Expected output of A is 750 units and of C is 340 units.

What is the budgeted total variable cost of products A and C for the full year 20X5?

Zero-based budgeting

A 'method of budgeting that requires each cost element to be specifically justified, as though the activities to which the budget relates were being undertaken for the first time. Without approval, the budget allowance is zero'.

It is suitable for:

- allocating resources in areas were spend is discretionary, i.e. non-essential. For example, research and development, advertising and training.
- public sector organisations such as local authorities.

There are four distinct stages in the implementation of ZBB:

(1) Managers should specify, for their responsibility centres, those activities that can be individually evaluated.

(2) Each of the individual activities is then described in a decision package. The decision package should state the costs and revenues expected from the given activity. It should be drawn up in such a way that the package can be evaluated and ranked against other packages.

(3) Each decision package is evaluated and ranked usually using cost/benefit analysis.

(4) The resources are then allocated to the various packages.

Advantages of ZBB	Disadvantages of ZBB
(1) Inefficient or obsolete operations can be identified and discontinued	(1) It emphasises short-term benefits to the detriment of long-term goals
(2) ZBB leads to increased staff involvement at all levels since a lot more information and work is required to complete the budget	(2) The budgeting process may become too rigid and the organisation may not be able to react to unforeseen opportunities or threats
(3) It responds to changes in the business environment	(3) The management skills required may not be present
(4) Knowledge and understanding of the cost behaviour patterns of the organisation will be enhanced	(4) Managers may feel demotivated due to the large amount of time spent on the budgeting process
(5) Resources should be allocated efficiently and economically	(5) Ranking can be difficult for different types of activities or where the benefits are qualitative in nature

Additional information on decision packages

A decision package was defined by **Peter Pyhrr** (who first formulated the ZBB approach at Texas Instruments) as:

A document that identifies and describes a specific activity in such a manner that senior management can:

(a) evaluate and rank it against other activities competing for limited resources, and
(b) decide whether to approve or disapprove it.'

A decision package is a document that:

- analyses the cost of the activity (costs may be built up from a zero base, but costing information can be obtained from historical records or last year's budget)
- states the purpose of the activity
- identifies alternative methods of achieving the same purpose
- assesses the consequence of not doing the activity at all, or performing the activity at a different level
- establishes measures of performance for the activity.

Pyhrr identifies two types of package.

(i) Mutually exclusive packages: these contain different methods of obtaining the same objective.
(ii) Incremental packages: these divide the activity into a number of different levels of activity. The base package describes the minimum effort and cost needed to carry out the activity. The other packages describe the incremental costs and benefits when added to the base.

For example, a company is conducting a ZBB exercise, and a decision package is being prepared for its materials handling operations.

- The manager responsible has identified a base package for the minimum resources needed to perform the materials handling function. This is to have a team of five workers and a supervisor, operating without any labour-saving machinery. The estimated annual cost of wages and salaries, with overtime, would be $375,000.

- In addition to the base package, the manager has identified an incremental package. The company could lease two fork lift trucks at a cost of $20,000 each year. This would provide a better system because materials could be stacked higher and moved more quickly. Health and safety risks for the workers would be reduced, and there would be savings of $5,000 each year in overtime payments.
- Another incremental package has been prepared, in which the company introduces new computer software to plan materials handling schedules. The cost of buying and implementing the system would be $60,000, but the benefits are expected to be improvements in efficiency that reduce production downtime and result in savings of $10,000 each year in overtime payments.

The base package would be considered essential, and so given a high priority. The two incremental packages should be evaluated and ranked. Here, the fork lift trucks option might be ranked more highly than the computer software.

In the budget that is eventually decided by senior management, the fork lift truck package might be approved, but the computer software package rejected on the grounds that there are other demands for resources with a higher priority.

Test your understanding 6

For a number of years, the research division of Z Inc has produced its annual budget (for new and continuing projects) using incremental budgeting techniques. The company is now under new management and the annual budget for 20X4 is to be prepared using ZBB techniques.

Explain how Z Inc could operate a ZBB system for its research projects.

ZBB and incremental budgeting in the public sector

The process of identifying decision packages and determining their purpose, costs and benefits is massively time consuming and costly.

One solution to this problem is to use incremental budgeting every year, and then use ZBB every three to five years, or when major change occurs. This means that an organisation can benefit from some of the advantages of ZBB without an annual time and cost implication.

Another option is to use ZBB for some departments but not for others. Certain costs are essential rather than discretionary and it could be argued that it is pointless to carry out ZBB in relation to these. For example, heating and lighting costs in a school or hospital are expenses that will have to be paid, irrespective of the budget amount allocated to them. Incremental budgeting would seem to be more suitable for costs like these, as with building repair costs.

Rolling budgets

A budget (usually annual) kept continuously up to date by adding another accounting period (e.g. month or quarter) when the earliest accounting period has expired.

Suitable if:

- accurate forecasts cannot be made. For example, in a fast moving environment.
- or for any area of business that needs tight control.

Illustration 1 – Rolling budgets

A typical rolling budget might be prepared as follows:

(1) A budget is prepared for the coming year (say January – December) broken down into suitable, say quarterly, control periods.

(2) At the end of the first control period (31 March) a comparison is made of that period's results against the budget. The conclusions drawn from this analysis are used to update the budgets for the remaining control periods and to add a budget for a further three months, so that the company once again has budgets available for the coming year (this time April – March).

(3) The planning process is repeated at the end of each three-month control period.

Advantages of rolling budgets	Disadvantages of rolling budgets
(1) Planning and control will be based on a more accurate budget	(1) Rolling budgets are more costly and time consuming than incremental budgets
(2) Rolling budgets reduce the element of uncertainty in budgeting since they concentrate on the short-term when the degree of uncertainty is much smaller	(2) May demotivate employees if they feel that they spend a large proportion of their time budgeting or if they feel that the budgetary targets are constantly changing
(3) There is always a budget that extends into the future (normally 12 months)	(3) There is a danger that the budget may become the last budget 'plus or minus a bit'
(4) It forces management to reassess the budget regularly and to produce budgets which are more up to date	(4) An increase in budgeting work may lead to less control of the actual results
	(5) Issues with version control, as each month the full year numbers will change
	(6) Confusion in meetings as to each numbers the business is working towards; this can distract from the key issues. as managers discuss which numbers to achieve

Test your understanding 7

A company uses rolling budgeting and has a sales budget as follows:

	Quarter 1	Quarter 2	Quarter 3	Quarter 4	Total
	$	$	$	$	$
Sales	125,750	132,038	138,640	145,572	542,000

Actual sales for Quarter 1 were $123,450. The adverse variance is fully explained by competition being more intense than expected and growth being lower than anticipated. The budget committee has proposed that the revised assumption for sales growth should be 3% per quarter.

Update the budget as appropriate.

Activity Based Budgeting

ABB is defined as: 'a method of budgeting based on an activity framework and utilising cost driver data in the budget-setting and variance feedback processes'.

Or, put more simply, preparing budgets using overhead costs from activity based costing methodology.

Test your understanding 8 – Preparing an ABB

The operating divisions of Z plc have in the past always used a traditional approach to analysing costs into their fixed and variable components. A single measure of activity was used which, for simplicity, was the number of units produced. The new management does not accept that such a simplistic approach is appropriate for budgeting in the modern environment and has requested that the managers adopt an activity-based approach in future.

Required:

Explain how ABB would be implemented by the operating divisions of Z plc.

The advantages of ABB are similar to those provided by activity-based costing (ABC).

- It draws attention to the costs of 'overhead activities' which can be a large proportion of total operating costs.
- It recognises that it is activities which drive costs. If we can control the causes (drivers) of costs, then costs should be better managed and understood.
- ABB can provide useful information in a total quality management (TQM) environment, by relating the cost of an activity to the level of service provided.

Disadvantages of ABB

- A considerable amount of time and effort might be needed to establish the key activities and their cost drivers.
- It may be difficult to identify clear individual responsibilities for activities.
- It could be argued that in the short-term many overhead costs are not controllable and do not vary directly with changes in the volume of activity for the cost driver. The only cost variances to report would be fixed overhead expenditure variances for each activity.

Activity matrix

An activity-based budget can be constructed by preparing an activity matrix. This identifies the activities in each column, and the resources required to carry out the activities in each row.

The following 'activity matrix' shows the resources used (rows) and major functions/activities (columns) of a stores department. In this example, all the identified activities occur within a single department.

- The total current annual costs of each resource consumed by the department are shown in the final column; they have then been spread back over the various activities to establish the cost pools. The allocation of resource costs between activities will, to some extent, be subjective.
- Each of the first four activities has an identifiable cost driver, and the total resource cost driver rates can be determined (cost per unit of activity).
- The last two activities that occur within the department are non-volume related, and are sometimes referred to as 'sustaining costs'. They are necessary functions and should not be ignored in the budgeting process; however, they should not be attributed to particular cost drivers, as this would not reflect their true cost behaviour and would result in inappropriate budgets being set.

Activity cost matrix for stores department

Activity:	**Receiving deliveries**	**Issuing from store**	**Stock ordering**	**Stock counting**	**Keeping records**	**Super-vision**	**Total**
Cost driver:	Deliveries	Store requisi-tions	Number of orders	Number of counts	–	–	
Number:	400	800	400	12			
	$000	$000	$000	$000	$000	$000	$000
Management salary	–	–	–	1	4	25	30
Basic wages	20	25	6	4	11	–	66
Overtime payments	5	–	–	5	5	–	15
Stationery, etc	1	2	2	1	3	–	9
Other	6	5	2	1	1	5	20
Total	**32**	**32**	**10**	**12**	**24**	**30**	**140**
Cost per activity unit	$80	$40	$25	$1,000			

Sustaining costs will effectively be treated as fixed costs. However, for control purposes, activity-based costs can be assumed to be variable, and actual costs can be compared with the expected costs for the given level of activity.

Test your understanding 9

Which statement is correct regarding the benefits to be gained from using ABB?

A If there is much inefficiency within the operations of a business then ABB will identify and remove these areas of inefficiency.

B In a highly direct labour intensive manufacturing process, an ABB approach will assist management in budgeting for the majority of the production costs.

C In an organisation currently operating efficiently, where the next period will be relatively unchanged from the current one, then ABB will make the budgeting process simpler and quicker.

D If an organisation produces many different types of output using different combinations of activities then ABB can provide more meaningful information for budgetary control.

8 Feedback control

Feedback control is defined as 'the measurement of differences between planned outputs and actual outputs achieved, and the modification of subsequent action and/or plans to achieve future required results'. This is the most common type of control system.

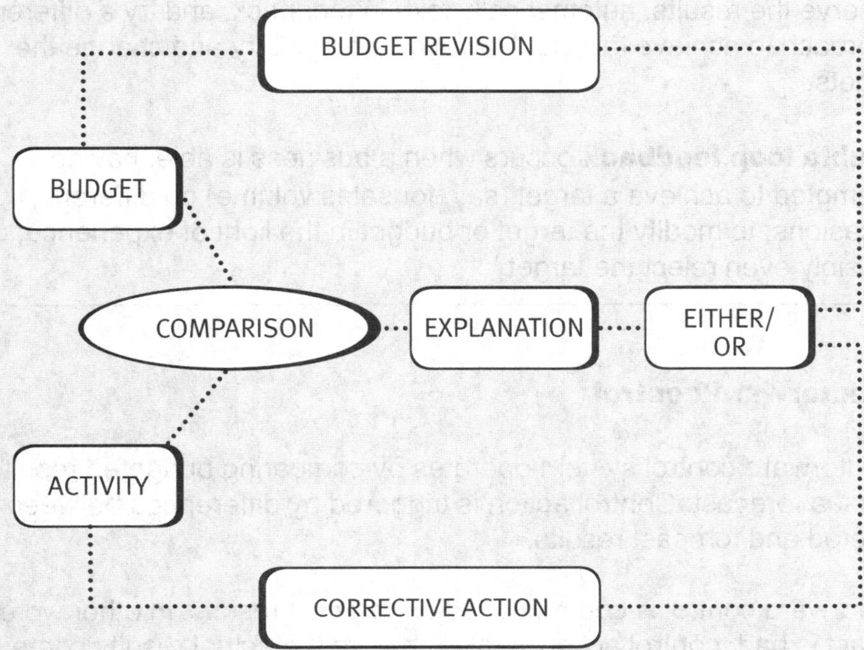

Positive feedback is feedback taken to reinforce a deviation from standard. The inputs or processes would not be altered.

Negative feedback is feedback taken to reverse a deviation from standard. This could be by amending the inputs or process, so that the system reverts to a steady state. For example, a machine may need to be reset over time to its original settings.

Single/Double loop feedback

Single loop feedback is control which regulates the output of a system. It involves connecting a strategy for action with a result. For example, if an action we take yields results that are different to what we expected ('target costs are not achieved'), through single-loop feedback, we will observe the results, automatically take in feedback, and try a different approach to achieve targets. However, we don't try and change the targets.

Double loop feedback occurs when a business is able, having attempted to achieve a target (say, for sales volume) on different occasions, to modify the target or budget in the light of experience, or possibly even reject the target.

9 Feedforward control

A feedforward control system operates by comparing budgeted results against a forecast. Control action is triggered by differences between budgeted and forecast results.

Feedforward control is control based on forecast results. In other words, if forecast is bad, control action is taken before the actual results come through. For example, the graph below shows the feedback and feedforward system for sales:

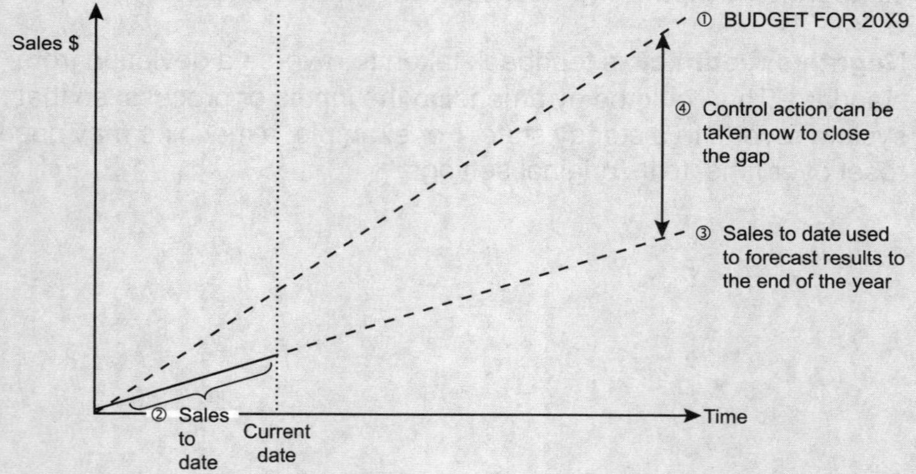

Illustration 2 – Feed-forward control

A sales manager receives monthly control reports about sales values. The budgeted sales for the year to 31 December are $600,000 in total. At the end of April the manager might receive the following **feedback control** report.

Sales report for April

	Month			**Cumulative**		
	Budget	**Actual**	**Variance**	**Budget**	**Actual**	**Variance**
Product	$000	$000	$000	$000	$000	$000
P1	35	38	3 (F)	90	94	4 (F)
P2	20	14	6 (A)	50	39	11 (A)
P3	25	23	2 (A)	50	45	5 (A)
Total	80	75	5 (A)	190	178	12 (A)

Alternatively, the sales manager might be presented with a **feed-forward control** report, as follows:

Sales report, April

	Budget	**Latest forecast for the year**	**Expected variance**
Product	$000	$000	$000
P1	240	250	10 (F)
P2	150	120	30 (A)
P3	210	194	16 (A)
Total	600	564	36 (A)

The use of a feed-forward control system means that corrective action can be taken to avoid expected adverse variances.

Test your understanding 10

Explain why feed-forward control may be particularly appropriate for the capital expenditure budget.

10 Selecting a suitable budgetary system

As seen, there are many approaches to budgeting and an organisation will wish to select a system which is most appropriate.

Factors, which will determine suitability include:

- type and size of organisation
- type of industry
- type of product and product range
- culture of the organisation.

Illustration 3 – Selecting a suitable budgetary system

A hospital operates in a relatively stable financial environment, has a very high proportion of fixed costs and a diverse range of activities. Factors to consider when selecting a suitable budgetary system may be:

- An incremental approach may be suitable for all routine activities. New ventures may use a zero-based approach.
- The fixed costs may need close control and therefore some form of ABB may be appropriate.
- The culture of the organisation may dictate whether a participative or imposed budgeting style is more effective. If there are managers who are trained in budgeting and costs are mainly controllable then it may be preferable to adopt a participative approach to empower and motivate staff. If costs are mainly uncontrollable it may be preferable to use a centrally controlled, imposed budget.

Test your understanding 11

Select and justify a suitable budgeting system for a company operating in the mobile phone market.

Information for budgeting

Budgeting requires a great deal of information that can be drawn from many sources.

The main sources of information for budgeting purposes are:

- previous year's actual results.

- other internal sources which may include manager's knowledge concerning the state of repair of fixed assets, training needs of staff, long-term requirements of individual customers, etc.
- estimates of costs of new products using methods such as work study techniques and technical estimates.
- statistical techniques may help to forecast sales.
- models, such as the EOQ model, may be used to forecast optimal inventory levels.
- external sources of information may include suppliers' price lists, estimates of inflation and exchange rate movements, strategic analysis of the economic environment.

Change factors impacting budgeting

The PESTEL model met in paper F1 is useful for identifying change factors:

Political change

A change in government policy, for example fiscal policy, may affect the demand for an organisation's products, and/or the costs incurred in providing them. Any such changes will affect both short-term and long-term planning. This is one reason why planning is a continuous process.

Social change

Changes in social responsibilities and people's attitude towards them affect every organisation. In recent years there has been much more concern about social responsibilities, some of which are now recognised by law. All of these factors may impinge on the plans of the organisation.

Economic change

When there is a change in the economic climate from boom through to recession, the demands upon people's income become more focused. Money tends to be spent on necessary goods with little left for 'luxury goods' and savings. The lack of savings deters investment, with the result that plans have to be modified if they are to be realistic targets. Economic factors could be local, national or international and include global factors such as the banking crisis and its ongoing impact on world economies.

Technological change

When plans are made, they are based upon the use of certain methods and equipment. As technology advances, the older methods are proven to be inefficient, with the result that decisions are taken to update the operation. As a consequence, the aspects of the budgets and plans which related to the old method are no longer relevant. Revised plans must now be drawn up on the basis of the new technology.

Legal change

When plans are made they are based on the current legal framework and known changes to this are also factored in over time. However, changes to the legal framework can cause information that is used when pulling budgets together to become redundant. An example of this might be the government introducing legislation that bans fast food from being advertised during the intervals between children's TV programmes.

Other factors

Note that while a PESTEL analysis can be very useful to identify drivers of change in the industry, it does not automatically detect all factors that cause uncertainty, such as

- Competitive factors, such as the activities of rivals
- Stakeholder factors, such as increased pressure from trade unions to initiate change.

Test your understanding 12

Describe the sources of information required for a company's cash budget.

Changing a budgetary system

A change in the budgetary system could bring about improved planning, control and decision making.

However, before a change is made the following issues should be considered:

- Are suitably trained staff available to implement the change successfully?

- Will changing the system take up management time which should be used to focus on strategy?
- All staff involved in the budgetary process will need to be trained in the new system and understand the procedure to be followed in changing to the new approach. A lack of participation and understanding builds resistance to change.
- All costs of the systems change, e.g. new system costs, training costs, should be evaluated against the perceived benefits. Benefits may be difficult to quantify and therefore a rigorous investment appraisal of the project may be difficult to prepare.

Test your understanding 13

A large holiday complex currently uses incremental budgeting but is concerned about its very high proportion of overhead costs and is considering changing to an activity based budgeting system. Demand follows a fairly predictable seasonal pattern.

Discuss the issues that should be considered before changing to a new budgetary system.

Dealing with uncertainty in budgeting

Budgets are open to uncertainty. For example, non-controllable factors such as a recession or a change in prices charged by suppliers will contribute to uncertainty in the budget setting process.

Uncertainty arises largely because of changes in the external environment, over which a company will have little control. Reasons include:

(1) Social or political unrest could affect productivity (e.g. through industrial action), as could natural disasters like earthquakes and storms.

(2) Machines may break down unexpectedly, and the business may fail to meet production schedules.

(3) Customers may decide to buy more or less goods or services than originally forecast. For example, if a major customer goes into liquidation, this has a huge effect on a company and could also cause them to go into liquidation.

(4) The workforce may not perform as well as expected because of a lack of motivation, illness, etc. On the other hand, they may perform better than thought.

(5) Competitors may strengthen or emerge, and take some business away from a company. On the other hand, a competitor's position may weaken, leading to increased business.

(6) Technological advances may take place which lead a company's products or services to become out-dated and therefore less desirable.

(7) Materials may increase in price because of global changes in commodity prices.

(8) Inflation, as well as movement in interest rates, can cause the price of all inputs to increase or decrease.

There are several **techniques** available to help deal with uncertainty. These have been discussed before and include:

- Flexible budgets: these are budgets which, by recognising different cost behaviour patterns, are designed to change as the volume of activity changes. Flexible budgets are prepared under marginal costing principles, and so mixed costs are split into their fixed and variable components. This is useful at the control stage : it is necessary to compare actual results to the actual level of activity achieved against the results that should have been expected at this level of activity – which are shown by the flexible budget (more on next chapter).
- Rolling budgets: the budget is updated regularly and, as a result, uncertainty is reduced.
- Sensitivity analysis: variables can be changed one at a time and a large number of budgets produced. For example, what would happen if the actual sales volume was only 75% of the budgeted amount?
- Simulation: similar to sensitivity analysis but it is possible to change more than one variable at a time.

Spreadsheets

A spreadsheet is a computer package which stores data in a matrix format where the intersection of each row and column is referred to as a cell. They are commonly used to assist in the budgeting process.

Advantages of spreadsheets

- Large enough to include a large volume of information.
- Formulae and look up tables can be used so that if any figure is amended, all the figures will be immediately recalculated. This is very useful for carrying out sensitivity analysis.
- The results can be printed out or distributed to other users electronically quickly and easily.
- Most programs can also represent the results graphically e.g. balances can be shown in a bar chart.

Closing cash balances

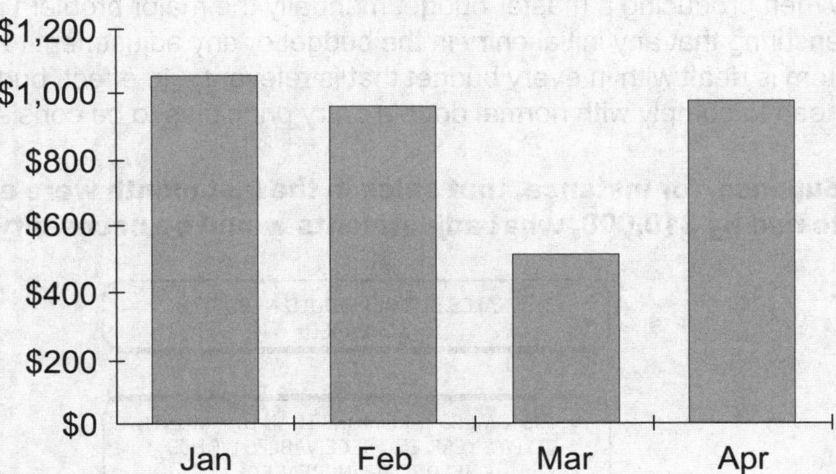

Disadvantages of spreadsheets:

- Spreadsheets for a particular budgeting application will take time to develop. The benefit of the spreadsheet must be greater than the cost of developing and maintaining it.
- Data can be accidentally changed (or deleted) without the user being aware of this occurring.
- Errors in design, particularly in the use of formulae, can produce invalid output. Due to the complexity of the model, these design errors may be difficult to locate.
- Data used will be subject to a high degree of uncertainty. This may be forgotten and the data used to produce, what is considered to be, an 'accurate' report.
- Security issues, such as the risk unauthorised access (e.g. hacking) or a loss of data (e.g. due to fire or theft).
- Version control issues can arise.
- Educating staff to use spreadsheets/models and which areas/cells to use as inputs can be time consuming.

Illustration 4 – Using spreadsheets in budgeting

When producing a master budget manually the major problem is ensuring that any initial entry in the budget or any adjustment to a budget item is dealt with in every budget that is relevant – in effect, budgets need to comply with normal double entry principles to be consistent.

Suppose, for instance, that sales in the last month were expected to rise by $10,000, what adjustments would be necessary?

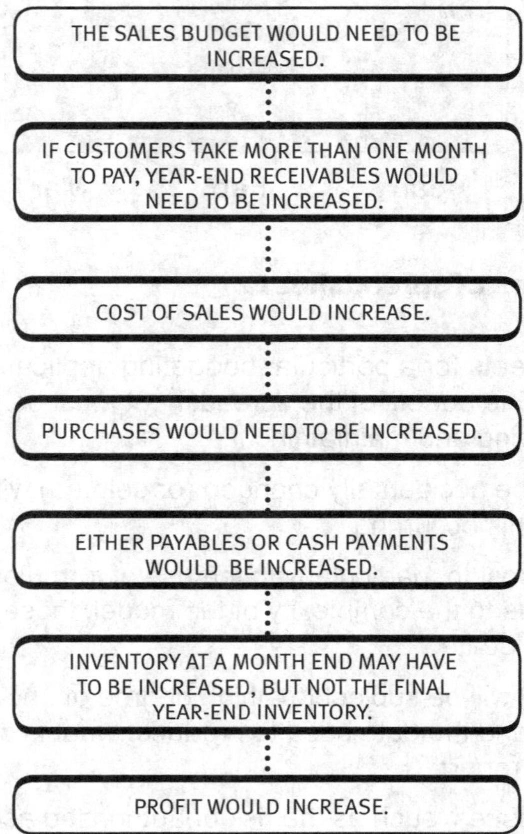

THE SALES BUDGET WOULD NEED TO BE INCREASED.
IF CUSTOMERS TAKE MORE THAN ONE MONTH TO PAY, YEAR-END RECEIVABLES WOULD NEED TO BE INCREASED.
COST OF SALES WOULD INCREASE.
PURCHASES WOULD NEED TO BE INCREASED.
EITHER PAYABLES OR CASH PAYMENTS WOULD BE INCREASED.
INVENTORY AT A MONTH END MAY HAVE TO BE INCREASED, BUT NOT THE FINAL YEAR-END INVENTORY.
PROFIT WOULD INCREASE.

Using spreadsheets all of the above adjustments could be processed automatically if the relevant formulae were set up properly. Receivables, cost of sales, purchases, payables, cash, inventory and profit could change instantly on adjusting sales of month 12.

11 Beyond Budgeting

The whole concept of budgeting turns around the idea that the operation of an organisation can be meaningfully planned for in some detail over an extended period into the future. Further, that this plan can be used to guide, control and co-ordinate the activities of numerous departments and individuals within the organisation.

The modern economic environment is associated with a **rapidly changing environment**, **flexible manufacturing, short product life-cycles and products/services which are highly customised**. The 'lean business' and the 'virtual business' are responses to this. Such businesses own limited assets of the traditional kind but assemble resources as and when needed to meet customer demand. The keys to their operation are flexibility and speed of response. They are able to move quickly to exploit opportunities as they arise and do not operate according to elaborate business plans.

In an age of discontinuous change, unpredictable competition, and fickle customers, few companies can plan ahead with any confidence – yet most organisations remain locked into a 'plan-make-and-sell' business model that involves a protracted annual budgeting process based on negotiated targets and that assumes that customers will buy what the company decides to make. Such assumptions are no longer valid in an age when customers can switch loyalties at the click of a mouse.

J Hope and R Fraser. *Beyond Budgeting* (Strategic Finance 10/2000)

'Beyond Budgeting' (BB) is the generic name given to a body of practices intended to replace budgeting as a management model. The core concept is the need to move from a business model based on centralised organisational hierarchies to one based on devolved networks.

Beyond Budgeting is defined in CIMA's *Official Terminology* as 'the idea that companies need to move *beyond budgeting* because of the inherent flaws in budgeting especially when used to set incentive contracts. It is argued that a range of techniques, such as rolling forecasts and market-related targets, can take the place of traditional budgets.'

12 Beyond Budgeting – 6 principles

A BB implementation should incorporate the following six main principles:

(1) An organisation structure with **clear principles and boundaries**; a manager should have no doubts over what he/she is responsible for and what he/she has authority over; the concept of the internal market for business units may be relevant here.

(2) Managers should be given goals and targets which are based on **relative success** and linked to shareholder value; such targets may be based on key performance indicators and benchmarks following the balanced scorecard principle.

(3) Managers should be given a **high degree of freedom** to make decisions; this freedom is consistent with the total quality management and business process reengineering concepts; a BB organisation chart should be 'flat'.

(4) Responsibility for decisions that generate value should be placed with **'front line teams'**; again, this is consistent with TQM and BPR concepts.

(5) Front line teams should be made responsible for **relationships** with customers, associate businesses and suppliers; direct communication between all the parties involved should be facilitated; this is consistent with the SCM concept.

(6) Information support systems should be transparent and ethical; an activity based accounting system which reports on the activities for which managers and teams are responsible is likely to be of use in this regard.

BB is essentially an approach that places modern management practices within a cultural framework.

'The process of management is not about administering fixed budgets, it is about the dynamic allocation of resources'

Lord Browne, former CEO of BP

13 Benefits of Beyond Budgeting

All the cases studied are different, but the following general benefits for BB are claimed:

(1) **Faster response time** – operating within a flexible organisational network and with strategy as an 'adaptive process' allows managers to respond quickly to customer requests.

(2) **Better innovation** – managers working within an environment wherein performance is judged on the basis of team and business unit results encourages the adoption of new innovations. Relations with customers and suppliers through SCM may facilitate the adoption of new working methods and technologies.

(3) **Lower costs** – in the context of BB managers are more likely to perceive costs as scarce resources which have to be used effectively than as a budget 'entitlement' that has to be used. BB is also likely to promote an awareness of the purposes for which costs are being incurred and thereby the potential for reductions.

(4) **Improved customer and supplier loyalty** – the leading role of front line teams in dealing with customers and suppliers is likely to deepen the relevant relationships.

As with many innovations in management practice, BB was a creature of its time. It appeared in the mid-1990s at a time when globalisation and advances in IT were tending to speed up the business environment. In particular, customers had greater choice and expected faster service. The key competitive constraint in most business situations is no longer land, labour or capital. For example, if labour is locally scarce then work can be outsourced to India or manufacturing can be relocated to China. In many practical business situations the key competitive factor is likely to be intellectual and knowledge based in character.

The BB model appeared as a set of information-age best practices which was attuned to the new situation. BB is intended to be an exercise in mobilising competent managers, skilled workers and loyal customers. However, traditional budgeting still has its defenders. Such defenders claim that while budgeting may be associated with a 'command and control' management style, it is the management style that is the problem and not budgeting.

Svenska Handelsbanken

Researchers have explored the history of BB implementations to determine whether or not these have delivered improved results. BBRT has reported several case studies, the best known of which is that of **Svenska Handelsbanken**.

This Swedish bank abandoned budgeting in 1972 and switched to delegation model (involving 600 autonomous work units) that avoids formal planning and target setting. Branch managers run their own businesses and are able to decide how many staff they need, where they obtain support services from and what products they market to which customers. Branch performance is assessed using measures such as customer profitability, customer retention and work productivity.

The Svenska Handelsbanken model might indicate a higher level of corporate risk with all that would imply for cost of money and market capitalisation. However, it is claimed that the model favours flexibility. In the absence of a fixed plan, products and projects are designed to allow easy modification and exit routes. This view suggests that the model invites a different approach to risk management rather than the acceptance of higher risk.

14 Chapter summary

BUDGETING

APPROACHES TO BUDGETING

- Top down/ bottom up budgeting
- Incremental budgets
- Zero-based budgets
- Rolling budgets
- Activity-based budgets
- Feed-forward budgets

SELECTING A SUITABLE SYSTEM

- Dealing with change
- Incorporating uncertainty
- Use of spreadsheets

Test your understanding answers

Test your understanding 1 – Evaluation of managers

The key point here is that the answer depends on who awarded the pay increase.

If this was the production manager's decision, then the cost would be controllable. Depending on the culture of the firm, the manager would then be under pressure to explain why they departed from the budget in this instance.

If awarded by, say, the board of directors, then the cost increase was not controllable by the manager and should not feature in their appraisal.

Note: The concept of controllability is important for the exam.

Test your understanding 2

The manager may try to:

- delay discretionary short-term expenditure, e.g. maintenance, at the expense of long-term performance to improve results.
- manipulate results to make sure the relevant targets are achieved.
- incorporate budgetary slack into the targets to make them easier to achieve.

The process can be improved by measuring performance against a variety of targets, including non-financial targets, and linking performance to long-term objectives.

Test your understanding 3

Sales are expected to be $550,000 ×110% × 103% = $623,150. The manager may accept this as a fair target for performance appraisal, planning and control purposes. To encourage the manager to improve further an aspirations target incorporating a further improvement, say to $650,000, could be used and linked to the reward system.

Test your understanding 4

(1) Operational managers may not have the knowledge and experience to set a budget. For example, in a small business only the owner may be involved in all aspects of the business and may therefore set the budget.

(2) In times of crisis there may be insufficient time to set a participative budget and targets may have to be imposed to ensure survival.

(3) Participation has to be genuine for it to result in improved motivation. Pseudo-participation, where senior managers seek the opinions of the ultimate budget holders but do not act on these views, may lead to demotivation.

Test your understanding 5

	Total variable cost	**Variable cost per unit**
20X4:		
Product A	$672,000 × 75% × 60% = $302,400	$302,000 ÷ 640 units = $472.50
Product C	$672,000 × 75% × 40% = $201,600	$201,600 ÷ 350 units = $576
20X5:		
Product A	$472.50 × 1.04 × 750 units = $368,550	n/a
Product C	$576 × 1.04 × 340 units = $203,674	n/a

Test your understanding 6

Stage 1: Managers should specify the activities that can be evaluated

The managers/researchers responsible for each project should decide which projects they wish to undertake in the forthcoming period. These projects will be a mixture of continued projects and new projects.

Stage 2: Each activity is described in a decision package

For the projects which have already been started and which the managers want to continue in the next period, we should ignore any cash flows already incurred (they are sunk costs), and we should only look at future costs and benefits. Similarly, for the new projects we should only look at the future costs and benefits.

Stage 3: Each decision package is evaluated and ranked

Different ways of achieving the same research goals should also be investigated and the projects should only go ahead if the benefit exceeds the cost.

Stage 4: Resources are allocated to the various packages

Once all the potential projects have been evaluated if there are insufficient funds to undertake all the worthwhile projects, then the funds should be allocated to the best projects on the basis of a cost-benefit analysis.

ZBB is usually of a highly subjective nature. (The costs are often reasonably certain, but usually a lot of uncertainty is attached to the estimated benefits.) This can be shown by the example of a research division where the researchers may have their own pet projects, which they are unable to view in an objective light.

Test your understanding 7

The revised budget should incorporate 3% growth starting from the actual sales figure of Quarter 1 and should include a figure for Quarter 1 of the following year.

	Quarter 2	Quarter 3	Quarter 4	Quarter 1	Total
	$	$	$	$	$
Sales	127,154	130,969	134,898	138,945	531,966

Test your understanding 8 – Preparing an ABB

Step 1	Identify cost pools and cost drivers.
Step 2	Calculate a budgeted cost driver rate based on budgeted cost and budgeted activity.
Step 3	Produce a budget for each department or product by multiplying the budgeted cost driver rate by the expected usage.

Test your understanding 9

D is the correct answer.

Situation A would be best suited by implementing Zero Base Budgeting. Situation B does not require ABB since it has relatively low overheads. Situation C would be suitable for incremental budgeting. ABB will certainly not be quicker.

Test your understanding 10

Capital expenditure is often long-term in nature. It is more useful to compare actual costs to forecast completion costs so that action can be taken when a project is in progress rather than waiting for completion.

Test your understanding 11

The mobile phone market is intensely competitive so a company will need sophisticated systems to gather information about the market and competitors. The market is also fast changing so a rolling budget approach may be suitable to keep budget targets up to date. It will be very important to incorporate the latest information into budgets and a participative approach will be important as production managers and sales managers may have local knowledge which would improve the budgeting process.

Test your understanding 12

Internal information will be required from the:

- sales department relating to volume and estimated collection periods
- the production manager will estimate material, labour and overhead usage
- the purchasing manager will estimate material prices and payment terms
- human resources will forecast pay rates, bonus payments and overtime requirements
- the finance office may forecast payments of interest, dividends and general office costs.

External information may be required relating to forecast interest rates, tax rates, payment terms for tax, exchange rates, inflation, etc.

Test your understanding 13

An analysis of overheads should be carried out to determine the proportion that have identifiable cost drivers which differ from the normal volume related cost drivers which may be used when carrying out incremental budgeting. If a substantial volume of overhead is non-volume related then implementing ABB may lead to more accurate planning and control.

Issues, which should then be considered include:

- the development or purchase of a suitable computer system to support an ABB process
- training of staff to operate and interpret the information produced
- development of an implementation plan and whether this should run in tandem with the existing process for a trial period.

chapter

9

Quantitative analysis

Chapter learning objectives

Upon completion of this chapter you will be able to:

- explain and evaluate the use of high/low analysis to separate the fixed and variable elements of total cost
- explain the use of judgement and experience in forecasting
- explain the learning curve effect
- estimate the learning effect and apply this to a budgetary problem
- calculate production times when the learning curve has reached a steady state
- explain the limitations of the learning curve model.

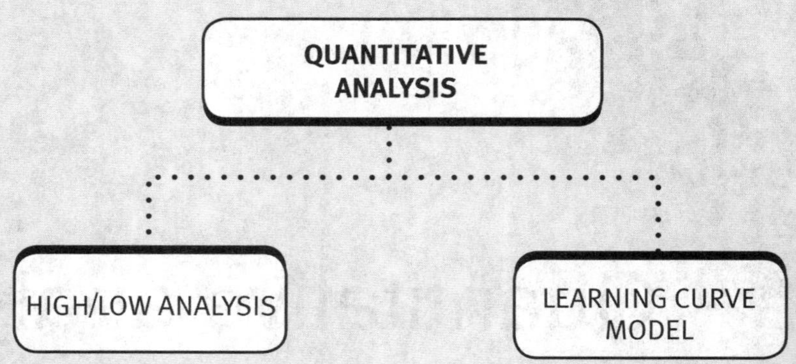

1 High/low analysis

A method of analysing a semi-variable cost into its fixed and variable elements based on an analysis of historical information about costs at different activity levels.

The fixed and variable costs can then be used to forecast the total cost at any level of activity.

The approach is as follows:

Step 1

Select the highest and lowest **activity** levels, and their costs.

Step 2

Find the variable cost/unit.

Variable cost/unit = (Cost at high level of activity – Cost at low level activity)/(High level activity – Low level activity)

Step 3

Find the fixed cost, using either the high or low activity level.

Fixed cost = Total cost at activity level – Total variable cost

Step 4

Use the variable and fixed cost to forecast the total cost for a specified level of activity.

Advantages of high/low analysis

- The high-low method has the enormous advantage of simplicity.
- It is easy to understand and easy to use.

Disadvantages of high/low analysis

- It assumes that activity is the only factor affecting costs.
- It assumes that historical costs reliably predict future costs.
- It uses only two values, the highest and the lowest, so the results may be distorted due to random variations in these values.

Test your understanding 1

Cost data for the six months to 31 December 20X8 is as follows:

Month	Units	Inspection costs
		$
July	340	2,240
August	300	2,160
September	380	2,320
October	420	2,400
November	400	2,360
December	360	2,280

Required:

Use high/low analysis to find the variable cost per unit and the total fixed cost. Forecast the total cost when 500 units are produced.

Additional example on high/low

Output (units)	Total cost ($)
200	7,000
300	8,000
400	9,000

(a) Find the variable cost per unit.

(b) Find the total fixed cost.

(c) Estimate the total cost if output is 350 units.

(d) Estimate the total cost if output is 600 units.

Solution

(a) Variable cost per unit = ($9,000 – $7,000) ÷ (400 – 200)

= $10 per unit

(b) Using high activity level:

Total cost	=		$9,000
Total variable cost	=	400 × $10	$4,000
Therefore Fixed cost	=		$5,000

(c) If output is 350 units:

Variable cost	=	350 × $10 =	$3,500
Fixed cost	=		$5,000
Total cost	=		$8,500

(d) If output is 600 units:

Variable cost	=	600 × $10	$6,000
Fixed cost	=		$5,000
Total cost	=		$11,000

2 Introduction to learning curves

Examiner's article: visit the ACCA website, www.accaglobal.com, to review the examiner's article written on this topic (September 2014).

It has been observed in some industries that there is a tendency for labour time per unit to reduce in time: as more of the units are produced, workers become more familiar with the task and get quicker.

From the experience of aircraft production during World War II, aircraft manufacturers found the rate of improvement was so regular that it could be reduced to a formula, and the labour hours required could be predicted with a high degree of accuracy from a **learning curve**.

The first time a new operation is performed, both the workers and the operating procedures are untried. As the operation is repeated, the workers become more familiar with the work, labour efficiency increases and the **labour cost per unit declines**.

Wright's Law

Wright's Law states that as cumulative output doubles, the cumulative average time per unit falls to a fixed percentage (the **'learning rate'**) of the previous average time.

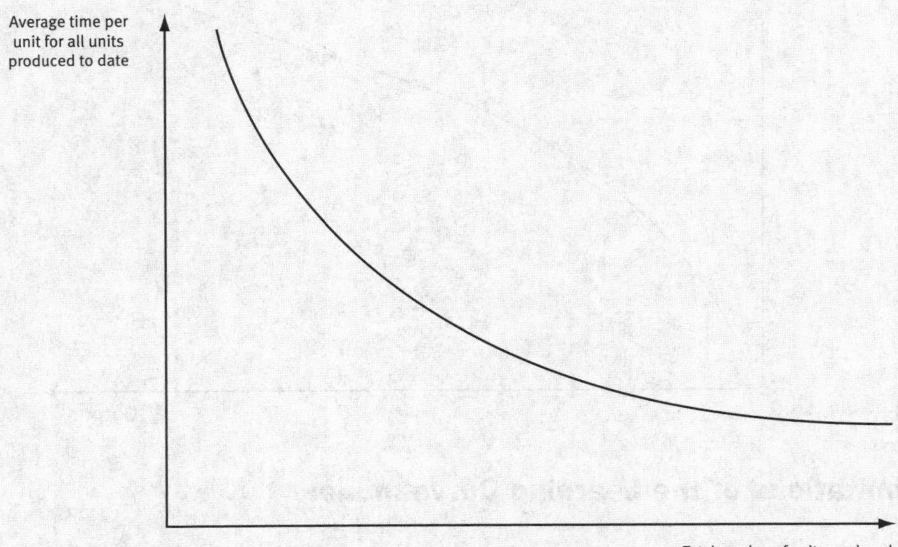

The learning curve is '*The mathematical expression of the commonly observed effect that, as complex and labour-intensive procedures are repeated, unit labour times tend to decrease.*'

The learning process starts from the point when the first unit comes off the production line. From then on, each time **cumulative** production is doubled, the **cumulative average time per unit** is a fixed percentage of its previous level.

For example, a 90% learning curve means that each time cumulative output doubles the cumulative average time per unit falls to 90% of its previous value.

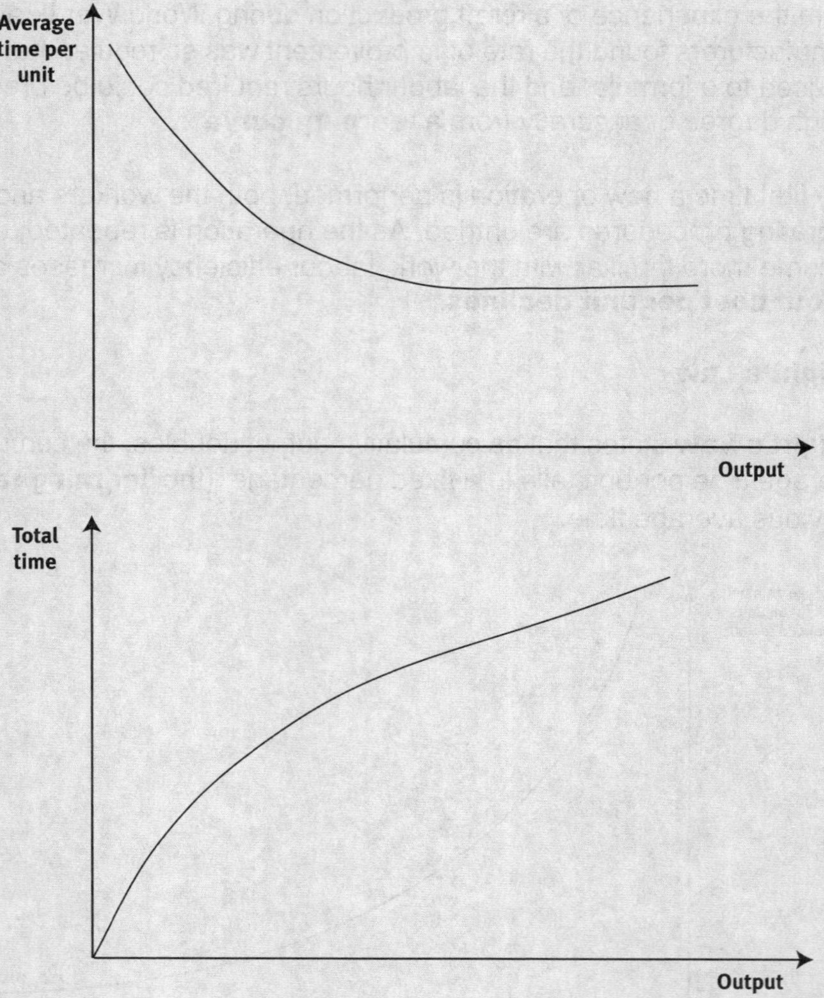

3 Limitations of the Learning Curve model

The learning curve model has its limitations. Learning effects are most likely to be seen if:

- **The process is labour intensive.**

  Modern manufacturing environments may be very capital intensive (i.e. machine intensive) and the labour effect cannot apply if machines limit the speed of labour.

- **The product is new.**

  This may be the case in the modern environment as products have short lives and therefore new products will be introduced on a regular basis. The introduction of a new product makes it more probable that there will be a learning effect.

- **The product is complex.**

  The more complex the product the more likely that the learning curve will be significant, and the longer it will take for the learning curve to reach a steady state or 'plateau' (beyond which no more learning can take place).

- **Production is repetitive and there are no breaks in production.**

  The learning effect requires that production is repetitive with no major breaks in which the learning effect may be lost. JIT production has moved towards multi-skilled and multi-tasked workers. It is possible that some of the benefits of the learning effect in a single tasking environment may be lost. The production of small batches of possible different products in response to customer demand may also lead to the loss of some of the learning effect.

4 The tabular approach

Consider the following example of the time taken to make the first four units of a new product:

Serial number of units	Time to make the unit concerned (hours)
01	10 hours
02	8 hours
03	7.386 hours
04	7.014 hours

While it is clear that we are getting quicker, it is not obvious how the times to make successive units are related. However, a pattern becomes apparent if we look at the cumulative average time per unit instead:

Serial number of unit	Time to make the unit concerned (hours)	Total cumulative time to make all units so far	Cumulative average time per unit	
01	10.000	10.000	10.000	× 90%
02	8.000	18.000	9.000	
03	7.386	25.386	8.462	× 90%
04	7.014	32.400	8.100	

In this example, Wright's Law is verified as the cumulative average decreases to 90% of the previous average every time we double the cumulative output, such as from 1 to 2 or from 2 to 4 units. We therefore say that the process demonstrates a **90% learning rate**.

All learning curve calculations use this idea of a cumulative average, so imagine all units having serial numbers so you can see how they fit into the cumulative picture.

For example, how long would it take to make a further 4 units, doubling the cumulative total to 8? The order of calculations is very important:

Step 1: Calculate the cumulative average time for the target production. Here, the cumulative average for the first 8 units = 8.100 × 90% = 7.290 hours per unit

Step 2: Calculate the total cumulative time. The total cumulative time for the first 8 units = 7.290 × 8 = 58.320 hours

Step 3: Time to make the next 4 units = the time to make 8 in total – the time to make the first 4

Time to make next 4 units = 58.320 – 32.400 = **25.920 hours**.

Or, shown as a table:

Serial number of unit	Total cumulative time	Cumulative average time	
04	32.400	8.100	× 90%
08	58.320 ⟸	7.290	

Test your understanding 2

A new product will take 100 hours for the first unit. An 80% learning curve applies.

Required:

Complete the table.

Cumulative			Incremental		
Units	**Average time per unit**	**Total time**	**Units**	**Total time**	**Average time per unit**

5 The algebraic approach

The problem with total doubling is that we cannot calculate averages for all levels of production. For example, how would we go about calculating how long the fifth unit should take to make?

The learning curve table in the tabular approach is useful if output keeps doubling, but for intermediate output levels we can obtain the information we need with the following formula:

$$Y = a * x^b$$

Where

- x = cumulative number of units
- Y = cumulative average time per unit to produce X units
- a = time required to produce the first unit of output
- b = index of learning = log r/log 2, where r = the learning rate expressed as a decimal.

Test your understanding 3

The first unit of a new product is expected to take 100 hours. An 80% learning curve is known to apply.

Calculate:

(a) the average time per unit for the first 16 units

(b) the average time per unit for the first 25 units

(c) the time it takes to make the 20th unit.

Test your understanding 4

The first batch of a new product took 20 hours to produce. The learning rate is 90%.

Required:

If the learning effect ceases after 72 batches (i.e. all subsequent batches take the same time as the 72nd), how long will it take to make a grand total of 100 batches?

Additional example on method 2

Assume that it takes 400 direct labour hours to produce the first unit of a new product and an 85% learning curve applies.

Required:

Calculate the total time to produce the third unit.

Solution

- b = log(0.85)/log 2

  b = –0.0706/0.3010 = –0.234

- The cumulative average time to produce the first two units is

  $y = 400 \times 2^{-0.234} = 340.1$.

  The total time to produce the first two units = 340.1 × 2 = 680.2 hours.

- The cumulative average time to produce the first three units is

  $y = 400 \times 3^{-0.234} = 309.3$.

  The total time to produce the first three units = 309.3 × 3 = 927.9 hours.

- The time to produce the third unit = 927.9 – 680.2 = 247.7 direct labour hours.

Test your understanding 5

Average unit times for product X have been tabulated as follows :

Unit number	Cumulative average time per unit Y_x
1	20 minutes
2	17.2 minutes
4	14.792 minutes
8	12.72 minutes

Required:

What is the Learning Curve rate?

Test your understanding 6

SCW plc has budgeted for a learning rate of 95% on the production of its new product Q, which is still at the development stage.

Actual results were as follows:

- Time to make the first unit of Q = 40 minutes
- Time to make the first 8 units = 233 minutes

Required:

(a) Calculate the actual learning rate, assuming a steady state has not been reached.

(b) Give TWO possible reasons why the rate is different from anticipated.

Test your understanding 7 – Calculate the learning rate

The times taken to produce each of the first four batches of a new product were as follows:

Batch number	Time taken
1	100 minutes
2	70 minutes
3	62 minutes
4	57 minutes

Based upon the above data, the rate of learning was closest to

A 70%

B 72.25%

C 82%

D 85%

Test your understanding 8

'The learning curve is a simple mathematical model but its application to management accounting problems requires careful thought.'

Required:

Having regard to the above statement:

(a) **explain** the 'cumulative average-time' model commonly used to represent learning curve effects.

(b) **explain** the use of learning curve theory in budgeting and budgetary control; explain the difficulties that the management accountant may encounter in such use.

(c) **explain** the circumstances in which the use of the learning curve may be most relevant.

Test your understanding 9

A Swiss watch making company wishes to determine the minimum price it should charge a customer for a special order of watches. The customer has requested a quotation for 10 watches (1 batch), but might subsequently place an order for a further 10. Material costs are $30 per watch. It is estimated that the first batch of 10 watches will take 100 hours to manufacture and an 80% learning curve is expected to apply. Labour plus variable overhead costs amount to $3 per hour. Setup costs are $1,000 regardless of the number of watches made.

Required:

(a) What is the minimum price the company should quote for the initial order if there is no guarantee of further orders?

(b) If the company was then to receive the follow-on order, what would the minimum price of this order be?

(c) What would be the minimum price if both orders were placed together?

(d) Having completed the initial orders for a total of 20 watches (price at the minimum levels recommended in (a) and (b)), the company thinks that there would be a ready market for this type of watch if it brought the unit selling price down to $45. At this price, what would be the profit on the first 140 'mass-production' watches (i.e. after the first 20 watches) assuming that marketing costs totalled $250?

Applications of the learning effect

- Pricing decisions: prices will be set too high if based on the costs of making the first few units.
- Work scheduling: less labour per unit will be required as more units are made. This may have management implications, e.g. workers may be laid off.
- Product viability: the viability of a product may change if a learning effect exists.
- Standard setting: if a product enjoys a learning effect but this effect is ignored, then the standard cost will be too high. The presence of a learning effect can also make standard setting difficult. Ignoring a learning effect could result in a need to calculate planning and operating variances.
- Budgeting: the presence of a learning effect should be taken into account when setting budgets. For example, the labour budget may be reduced by a learning effect but working capital may be required sooner than expected.

6 Learning curve and steady state

The learning effect will only apply for a certain range of production. (For example, in TYU 4, the learning effect ceases after 72 batches).

For example, machine efficiency may restrict further improvements or there may be go-slow arrangements in place.

Once the steady state is reached the direct labour hours will not reduce any further and this will become the basis on which the budget is produced.

The experience curve

It has been stressed that the learning curve was derived from observations of the reductions in direct labour time taken to complete successive repetitive but complex assembly tasks. However, learning rates have frequently been determined by fitting curves to total cost per unit data. For example, DePuy (1993) used this method to ascertain for the US government the learning rate achieved by defence contractors. The purpose in gathering this data was to help in price negotiations with the contractors.

The slope of the learning curves derived ranged from 0.718 to 1.021, with a mean of 0.858. These data suggest that defence contractors typically enjoy a reduction of 14 per cent of average unit cost on each doubling of output. The strict application of the learning curve phenomenon is seen in the area of direct labour, and it is arguable that, in using unit cost data, the result outlined above actually reflects the so-called 'experience curve; rather than the learning curve as strictly defined. The 'experience curve' extends the learning curve approach to areas other than direct labour. Rather than relating indirectly to cost via time, an experience curve relates directly to cost, and it is a function which shows how total cost per unit declines as output increases.

Total cost in experience curves includes all overhead types – production, marketing and distribution – and thus cost reduction arising from factors such as factory size, production technology, substitution of materials and design modifications are reflected in an experience curve.

Experience curves, like learning curves, can be regarded as statements of what will happen in practice. This could be considered to be a western approach. An alternative approach, adopted by the Japanese, is that these curves should be taken as expressions of what is desirable, and hence what should be striven for.

The improvement-oriented Japanese typically aim actively to foster a 67 per cent learning curve, as against the 80 per cent curve more usually found in the west.

Objective Test Case Question – Bike Racers Co

Bike Racers Co has designed a radically new concept in racing bikes, with the intention of selling them to professional racing teams. The estimated cost and selling price of the first bike to be manufactured and assembled is as follows:

Materials	$1,000
Assembly labour (50 hours at $10 per hour)	$500
Fixed overheads (200% of assembly labour)	$1,000
Profit (20% of total cost)	$500
Selling price	**$3,000**

Bike Racers Co plans to sell all bikes at total cost plus 20%, and the material cost per bike will remain constant, irrespective of the number sold. Bike Racers Co's management expects the assembly time to gradually improve with experience, and has estimated a 80% learning curve.

(1) Mr Wiggo, a racing team manager, approached Bike Racers Co in January 2015 and committed to buy the first bike, as well as the second bike produced.

What price should be charged by Bike Racers Co for the second bike produced?

A $2,280

B $2,400

C $2,640

D $2,750

(2) Mr Froome, the manager of another racing team, approaches Bike Racers Co after Mr Wiggo. He offers to wait until the first two bikes are sold to Mr Wiggo and to then order the third and fourth bikes to be produced.

What would be the average price per bike charged to Mr Froome?

A $2,064

B $2,280

C $2,640

D $4,128

(3) The manager of a third racing team, Mr Hoy, approaches Bike Racers Co shortly after Mr Froome. He offers to immediately equip his entire team of eight racers with the new bikes, before a sale is made to anyone else.

What would be the price per bike if Mr Hoy placed an order for the first eight bikes, to the nearest $?

A $2,048

B $2,122

C $3,000

D $4,128

(4) The first phase of production has now been completed for the new bike. The first bike actually took 45 hours to make, and the total time for the first eight bikes amounted to 151.875 hours, at which point the learning effect came to an end.

What was the actual rate of learning which occurred?

A 72.5%

B 75%

C 82%

D 85%

(5) **Which of the following statements on the presence of a learning curve are not correct?**

(1) A standard costing system would need to set standard labour times after the learning curve has reached a steady state.

(2) Identification of the learning curve will permit the company to better plan its marketing, work scheduling, recruitment and material acquisition activities.

(3) Careful and accurate budgeting will ensure the learning curve effects are favourably impacting on labour costs.

(4) Accurate and appropriate learning curve data are easy to estimate.

A Statements (1) and (2)

B Statements (2) and (3)

C Statements (1) and (4)

D Statements (3) and (4)

7 Chapter summary

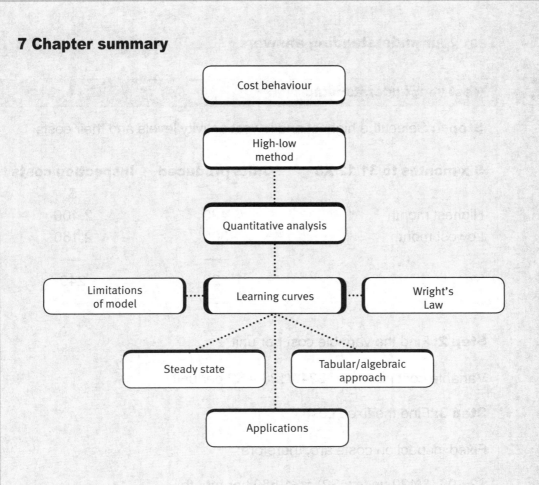

Cost behaviour

High-low method

Quantitative analysis

Limitations of model

Learning curves

Wright's Law

Steady state

Tabular/algebraic approach

Applications

Test your understanding answers

Test your understanding 1

Step 1: Select the highest and lowest activity levels and their costs

Six months to 31/12/X8	Units produced	Inspection costs
		$
Highest month	420	2,400
Lowest month	300	2,160
Range	120	240

Step 2: Find the variable cost per unit

Variable cost per unit = $240/120 = $2 per unit

Step 3: Find the fixed cost

Fixed inspection costs are, therefore:

$2,400 – (420 units × $2) = $1,560 per month

or $2,160 – (300 units × $2) = $1,560 per month

i.e. the relationship is of the form y = $1,560 + $2x.

Step 4: Use these costs to forecast the total costs for 500 units

Total cost = fixed cost + variable cost

Total cost = $1,560 + ($2 × 500)

Total cost = $2,560

Test your understanding 2

Cumulative			Incremental		
Units	**Average time p.u.**	**Total time**	**Units**	**Total time**	**Average time p.u.**
1	100	100	1	100	100
2	80	160	1	60	60
4	64	256	2	96	48
8	51.2	409.6	4	153.6	38.4
16	40.96	655.36	8	245.76	30.72

Test your understanding 3

(a) a = 100   b = –0.3219   x = 16

y = $100.16^{-0.3219}$

= 40.96 hours

(b) x = 25

y = $100.25^{-0.3219}$

= 35.48 hours

(c) x = 20

y = $100.20^{-0.3219}$

= 38.12 hours

Total time for 20 units = 38.12 × 20 = 762.42

x = 19

y = $100.19^{-0.3219}$

= 38.76 hours

Total time for 19 units = 38.76 × 19 = 736.35

= 762.42 – 736.35

= **26.07 hours**

Test your understanding 4

Step 1: Calculate the cumulative average time for the number of units/ batches at which the learning effect ceases.

$b = \log 0.9/\log 2 = -0.152003$

$y = ax^b$

Cumulative average time for 72 batches, y is:

$y = 20 \times 72^{-0.152003} = 10.44$ hrs/batch

Step 2: Calculate the cumulative average time for the number of units/ batches, at which the learning effect ceases, minus 1

x = 71 batches

$y = 20 \times 71^{-0.152003} = 10.46$ hrs/batch

Step 3: Calculate the time taken to make the unit/ batch at which the learning effect ceases.

Batches	1–71 will take 71 × 10.46 =	742.66 hrs
Batches	1–72 will take 72 × 10.44 =	751.68 hrs
Batch	72 will take	9.02 hrs

Step 4: Calculate the total time for the number of units/batches

Batches	1–72 will take	751.68 hrs
Batches	73–100 will take 28 × 9.02 =	252.56 hrs
Batches	1–100 will take	1,004.24 hrs

Test your understanding 5

Using Wright's Law, each time the cumulative output doubles, the cumulative average time per unit will go down by the learning rate.

To get from 1 to 8 the total has doubled 3 times, we need to apply a factor of × r^3 to the average time:

20 minutes × r^3 = 12.72 minutes

r^3 = (12.72)/20 = 0.636 so

r = $0.636^{1/3}$ = 0.86 or **86%**

Test your understanding 6

(a) Actual learning rate achieved

Given we have figures for cumulative output of 1 and 8 units, we can use total doubling (3 times) rather than the formula:

Cumulative average time to make 1 unit = 40 minutes

Cumulative average time to make 8 units = 233/8 = 29.125 minutes

The learning rate, r, can be calculate using 29.125 = 40 × r^3

r^3 = 29.125/40 = 0.728125

r = 0.8996, or 90%

(b) The reasons for the quicker learning could include the following:

The process for product Q was more familiar than expected, perhaps because the product was more like existing products than thought.

The workers used were more experienced or higher skilled than would be the case for normal production, so were able to resolve the complexities of the new task more quickly.

Test your understanding 7 – Calculate the learning rate

Answer D

Cumulative average time for 2 units = (100 + 70)/2 = 85 hours

Test your understanding 8

(a) The 'cumulative average time' model commonly used to represent the learning curve effects is demonstrated below for a 70 per cent learning curve:

Number of units produced	Cumulative average time required per unit	Total time required	Incremental time required for additional units
1	100	100	0
2	70	140	40
4	49	196	56
8	34.3	274.4	78.4

In this model, the cumulative average time required to produce a unit of production is reduced by a constant proportion of the previous cumulative average time, every time the cumulative output doubles.

In the above example, unit 1 requires 100 hours, but units 1 and 2 require only 140 hours, unit 2 being produced in 40 hours due to labour having learned how to perform more efficiently. Units 3 and 4 require only a further 56 hours' work, etc.

This may be modelled mathematically by the equation

$$\mathbf{Y = a\,x^n}$$

where Y = cumulative average hours per unit, x = cumulative demand, and *a* and *n* are constants. This is only one of the several models that may be used to predict the relationship between output and labour requirements.

(b) Budgeting, budgetary control and project evaluation all rely upon the preparation of accurate forecasts of production capacity and operating costs. Learning curve theory may be used in such forecasts.

In particular, the learning curve theory may be used when repetitive manual tasks are introduced into a production process. Under these circumstances, application of this theory may result in more accurate prediction of labour time, labour costs, variable overhead costs that are driven by labour usage, and possibly material usage savings. Furthermore, if absorption costing is used, then this theory will enable the relationship between fixed overhead recovery and production rate to be accurately included in the budgeting process.

For budgetary control to be effective, the variances calculated must be based on realistic targets. A constant standard for labour, materials and variable overhead variances is not appropriate when the learning curve effect is present. By incorporating the learning curve theory into the targets, meaningful variances may be calculated and used in budgetary control.

Problems may be experienced in obtaining data on the rate of the learning curve until significant production has taken place. High labour turnover and changes in motivation levels may have significant effects upon the learning process. If there are extensive periods of time between batches of a particular product then the learning effect may be lost. The learning curve does not model long-term behaviour when there are no further productivity gains due to the learning process.

(c) The learning curve models the speeding up of a relatively new production process that involves repetitive manual operations due to labour learning from the experience. It was first documented in the 1920s and 1930s in the aircraft industry in the United States.

It is unlikely to be noticeable in well-established organisations that operate in static markets (growth, technology, etc.) and use standardised production facilities and mainly promotional marketing strategies.

Test your understanding 9

(a) **Initial order**

	$
Material (10 × $30)	300
Labour and variable overhead (100 × $3)	300
Setting-up cost (see note)	1,000
Total	$1,600
Minimum price each ($1,600 ÷ 10)	$160

Note: If there is no guarantee of a follow-up order, the setup costs must be recovered on the initial order.

(b) **Follow-on order**

- b = log 0.8/log 2 = – 0.321928
- If production increases to 20 watches (2 batches) then the cumulative average time per batch is:

  $y = ax^b$

  $y = 100 \times 2^{-0.321928}$

  y = 80.00 hours

- i.e. cumulative time for 20 watches (2 batches) = 160 hours
- Therefore, the time taken for the second batch of ten watches = 160 – 100 = 60 hours.

Costs are therefore:

	$
Material (10 × $30)	300
Labour and variable overhead (60 × $3)	180
Total	480
Minimum price each	48

Note: The set up costs have been recovered on the initial order and can therefore be ignored.

(c) **Both orders together**

Total costs are:

	$
Material (20 × $30)	600
Labour (160 hours × $3)	480
Set-up cost	1,000
Total	2,080
Minimum price each	104

Note: This is the mean of the two previous prices.

(d) **Mass production**

- Total production = 20 watches for the special order + 140 watches for mass production = 160 watches or 16 batches.
- $y = ax^b$

  Average time/batch for first 2 batches (i.e. first 20 watches)

  $= 100 \times 2^{-0.3219} = 80$ hours

  Total time for first 2 batches = 80 × 2 = 160 hours (as before).

– Average time per batch for first 16 batches (i.e. first 160 watches) = $100 \times 16^{-0.321928}$ = 40.96 hours.

Total time for first 16 batches = 40.96 × 16 = 655.36 hours.

Hence total time for batches 3 to 16 (i.e. the 140 mass-produced units) = (655.36 — 160) hours = 495.36 hours.

Cost of first 140 mass-production models:

	$
Material (140 × $30)	4,200
Labour and variable overhead (495.36 × $3)	1,486
Marketing	250
Total cost	5,936
Revenue (140 × $45)	6,300
Profit	364

Objective Test Case Question – Bike Racers Co

(1) **A**

No of bikes		*Cumulative average time (hours)*	*Total time to date (hours)*	*Incremental time for additional bikes (hours)*
1		50		50
2	(×0.8)	40	80	80–50 = 30

Quotation:	
Materials	$1,000
Labour (30 × $10)	$300
Overheads	$600
Total cost	$1,900
Profit (20%)	$380
Selling price	**$2,280**

(2) **A**

No of bikes		Cumulative average time (hours)	Total time to date (hours)	Incremental time for additional bikes (hours)
1		50		50
2	(×0.8)	40	40 × 2 = 80	80–50 = 30
4	(×0.8)	32	32 × 4 = 128	128–80 = 48

Quotation:	
Materials	$2,000
Labour (48 × $10)	$480
Overheads	$960
Total cost	$3,440
Profit (20%)	$688
Selling price for bikes 3 and 4	**$4,128**

$4,128/2 = **$2,064 per bike**

(3) **B**

No of bikes		Cumulative average time (hours)	Total time to date (hours)	Incremental time for additional bikes (hours)
1		50		50
2	(×0.8)	40	40 × 2 = 80	80–50 = 30
4	(×0.8)	32	32 × 4 = 128	128–80 = 48
8	(×0.8)	25.6	25.6 × 8 = 204.8	204.8–128 = 76.8

Quotation:	
Materials	$8,000
Labour (204.8 × $10)	$2,048
Overheads	$4,096
Total cost	$14,144
Profit (20%)	$2,828.8
Selling price for 8 bikes	**$16,972.8**

$16,972.8/8 = **$2,122 per bike**

(4) **B**

Cumulative number of bikes	*Cumulative total hours*	*Cumulative average hours per unit*
1	45	45
2	?	$45 \times r$
4	?	$45 \times r^2$
8	151.875	$45 \times r^3$

Using algebra: $151.875 = 8 \times (45 \times r^3)$

$18.98 = (45 \times r^3)$

$0.421875 = r^3$

r = 0.75

(5) **D**

Statements 3 and 4 are not correct. Careful and accurate budgeting will not always ensure the learning curve effects are favourably impacting on labour costs. The stable conditions necessary for the learning curve to take place may not be present . Unplanned changes in production techniques or labour turnover will cause problems and affect the learning rate. The employees need to be motivated, agree to the plan and keep to the learning schedule; these assumptions may not hold.

Also, accurate and appropriate learning curve data may be difficult to estimate.

chapter

10

Advanced variances

Chapter learning objectives

Upon completion of this chapter you will be able to:

- define, for a manufacturing company, material mix and yield variances
- calculate, from information supplied, material mix and yield variances
- for given or calculated material mix and yield variances, interpret and explain possible causes, including possible interrelationships between them
- explain, using simple non-numerical examples, the wider issues involved in changing mix, e.g. cost, quality and performance measurement issues
- identify and explain the interrelationship between price, mix and yield, using a simple numerical example
- suggest and justify alternative methods of controlling production processes in manufacturing environments
- using revised standards supplied, calculate a revised budget
- calculate and explain sales mix and quantity variances
- from supplied data, calculate planning and operational variances for sales (including market size and market share)
- from supplied data, calculate planning and operational variances for materials
- from supplied data, calculate planning and operational variances for labour
- identify and explain those factors that, in general, should and should not be allowed to revise an original budget
- explain and resolve the typical manipulation issues in revising budgets

- describe the dysfunctional nature of some variances in the modern environment of Just-in-time (JIT) and total quality management (TQM)
- describe the major behavioural problems resulting from using standard costs in rapidly changing environments
- discuss the major effects that variances have on staff motivation and action.

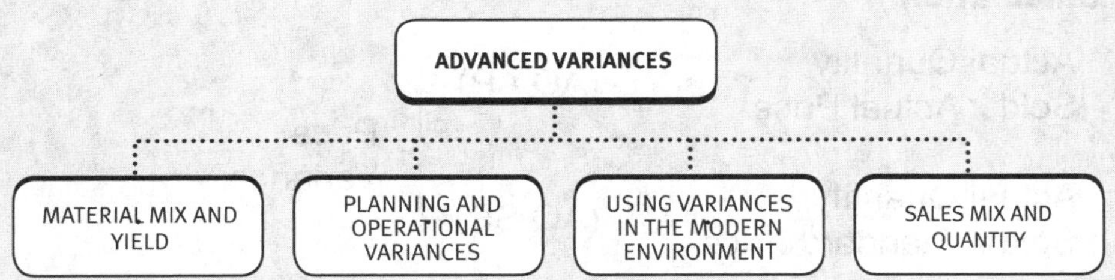

1 Revision of basic variance analysis

Variance analysis is the process by which the total difference between standard and actual results is analysed.

Standard costing was revised in chapter 1, so you might want to recap this before starting this chapter if you are feeling rusty on the basics.

A number of basic variances can be calculated. If the results are better than expected, the variance is favourable (F). If the results are worse than expected, the variance is adverse (A).

It is important to be able to:

- calculate the variance
- explain the meaning of the variance calculated
- identify possible causes for each variance.

Once the variances have been calculated, an operating statement can be prepared reconciling actual profit to budgeted profit, under marginal costing or under absorption costing principles.

Basic variances can be calculated for sales, material, labour, variable overheads and fixed overheads. Each of these will be reviewed in turn.

2 Sales variances

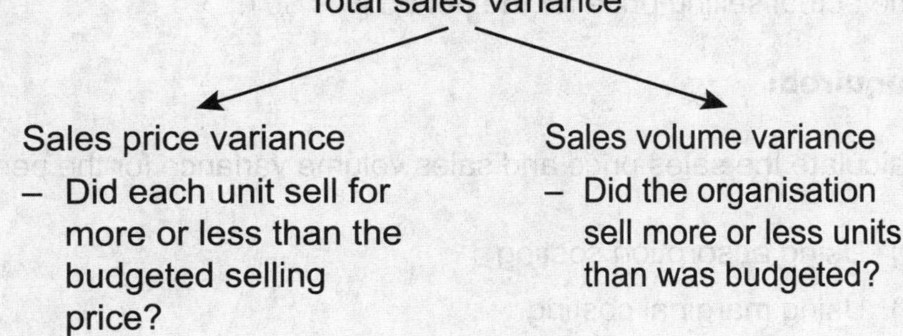

Calculation

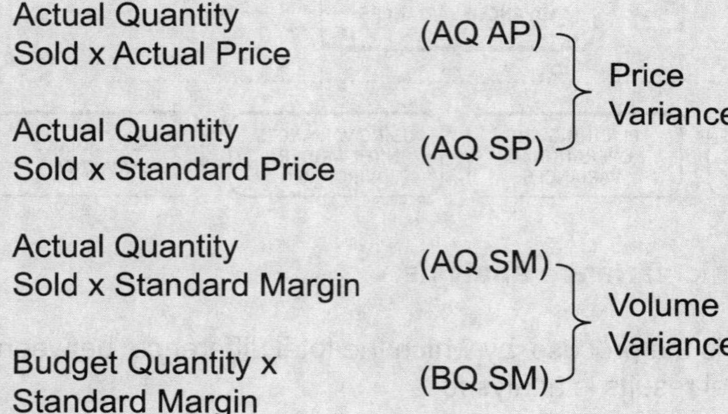

Note: 'Margin' = contribution per unit (marginal costing) or profit per unit (absorption costing).

Test your understanding 1 – Sales variances

W Ltd has budgeted sales of 6,500 units but actually sold only 6,000 units. Its standard cost card is as follows:

	$
Direct material	25
Direct wages	8
Variable overhead	4
Fixed overhead	18
Total standard cost	55
Standard gross profit	5
Standard selling price	60

The actual selling price for the period was $61.

Required:

Calculate the sales price and sales volume variance for the period:

(a) Using absorption costing

(b) Using marginal costing.

3 Causes of sales variances

Variance	Favourable	Adverse
Sales price	Unexpected price increase due to: • higher than anticipated customer demand • lower than anticipated demand for competitor's products • an improvement in quality or performance	Unexpected price decrease due to: • lower than anticipated customer demand • higher than anticipated demand for competitor's products • a reduction in quality or performance
Sales volume	Unexpected increase in demand due to: • a lower price • improved quality or performance • a fall in quality or performance of competitor's products • a successful marketing campaign	Unexpected fall in demand due to: • a higher price • lower quality or performance of the product • an increase in quality or performance of competitor's products • an unsuccessful marketing campaign

Note: The sales price and volume variance may be linked. For example, an increase in the price of a product will result in a favourable sales price variance but may also result in an adverse sales volume variance, due to a fall in demand.

Materials variances

Total materials variance

Materials price variance
– Did each unit of material cost more or less than expected?

Materials usage variance
– Did actual production use more or less units of material than expected?

Calculation

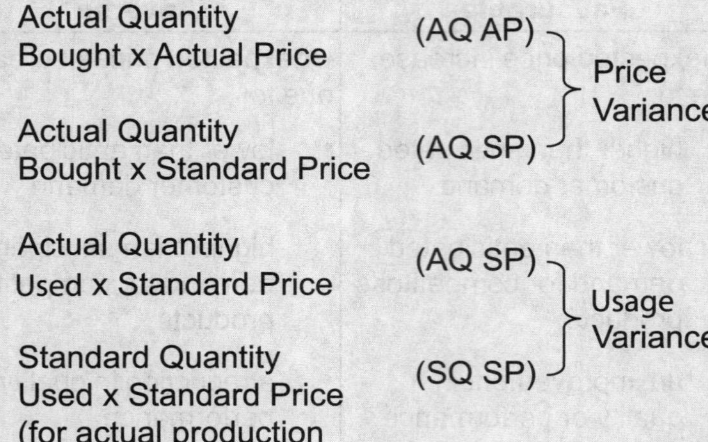

Test your understanding 2 – Materials variances

James Marshall Co makes a single product with the following budgeted material costs per unit:

2 kg of material A at $10/kg

Actual details:

Output 1,000 units

Material purchased and used 2,200 kg

Material cost $20,900

Calculate material price and usage variances.

Causes of material variances

Variance	Favourable	Adverse
Material price	• Poorer quality materials • Discounts given for buying in bulk • Change to a cheaper supplier • Incorrect budgeting	• Higher quality materials • Change to a more expensive supplier • Unexpected price increase encountered • Incorrect budgeting
Material usage	• Higher quality materials • More efficient use of material • Change is product specification • Incorrect budgeting	• Poorer quality materials • Less experienced staff using more materials • Change in product specification • Incorrect budgeting

Note: The material price variance and the material usage variance may be linked. For example, the purchase of poorer quality materials may result in a favourable price variance but an adverse usage variance.

Labour variances

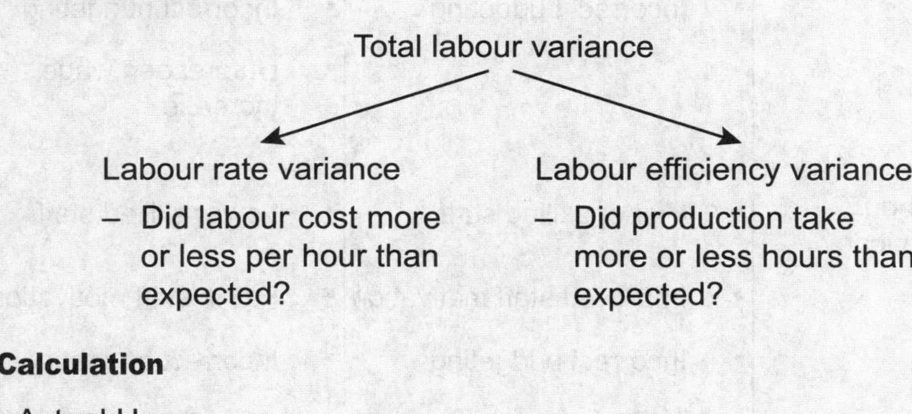
Total labour variance
Labour rate variance
– Did labour cost more or less per hour than expected?
Labour efficiency variance
– Did production take more or less hours than expected?

Calculation

Actual Hours x Actual Rate	(AH AR)	Rate Variance
Actual Hours x Standard Rate	(AH SR)	
Actual Hours x Standard Rate	(AH SR)	Efficiency Variance
Standard Hours x Standard Rate	(SH SR)	

Test your understanding 3 – Labour variances

Extract from the standard cost card for K Ltd

	$
Direct labour:	
(15 hours @ $4.80 per hour)	72

Actual direct wages for the period were:
15,500 hours costing $69,750 in total
Actual units produced 1,000

Calculate the labour rate and labour efficiency variances.

Causes of labour variances

Variance	Favourable	Adverse
Labour rate	• Lower skilled staff • Cut in overtime/ bonus • Incorrect budgeting	• Higher skilled staff • Increase in overtime/ bonus • Incorrect budgeting • Unforeseen wage increase
Labour efficiency	• Higher skilled staff • Improved staff motivation • Incorrect budgeting	• Lower skilled staff • Fall in staff motivation • Incorrect budgeting

Note: The labour rate variance and the labour efficiency variance may be linked. For example, employing more highly skilled labour may result in an adverse rate variance but a favourable efficiency variance.

Variable overhead variances

Total variable overhead variance

- **Variable overhead expenditure variance**
  – Did the variable overhead cost more or less per hour than expected?
- **Variable overhead efficiency variance**
  – Did production take more or less labour hours than expected?

Calculation

Actual Hours Worked x Actual Rate	(AH AR)	Expenditure Variance
Actual Hours Worked x Standard Rate	(AH SR)	
Actual Hours Worked x Standard Rate	(AH SR)	Efficiency Variance
Standard Hours Worked x Standard Rate (for actual production)	(SH SR)	

Test your understanding 4 – Variable overhead variances

Extract from the standard cost card for K Ltd

	$
Variable overhead:	
15 hours @ $1 per hour	15

Actual variable overheads for the period were:

15,500 hours — Total cost $14,900

Actual units produced 1,000

Calculate the variable overhead expenditure and variable overhead efficiency variances.

Causes of variable overhead variances

Variance	Favourable	Adverse
Var. o/h expenditure	• Unexpected saving in cost of services • More economic use of services • Incorrect budgeting	• Unexpected increase in the cost of services • Less economic use of services • Incorrect budgeting
Var. o/h efficiency	• As for labour efficiency	• As for labour efficiency

Fixed overhead variances

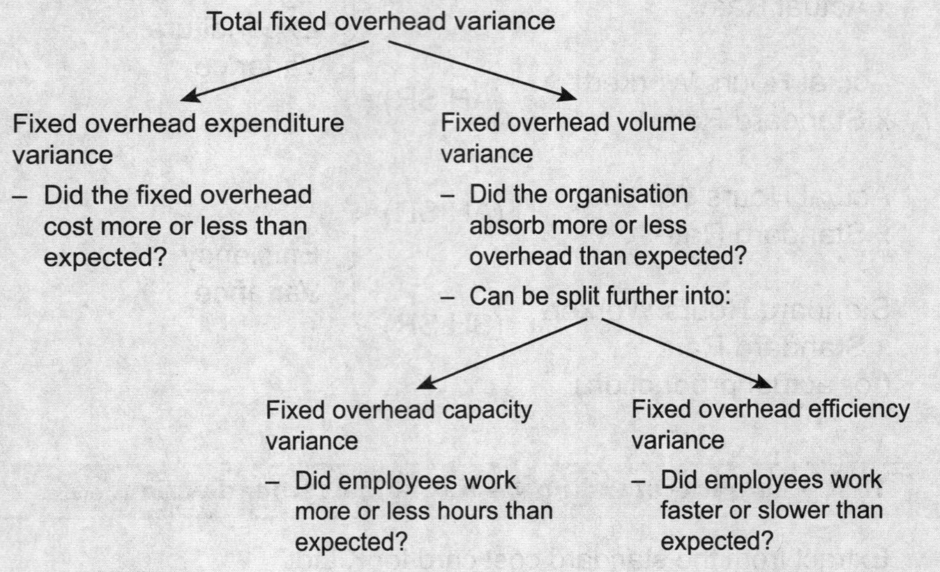
Total fixed overhead variance
Fixed overhead expenditure variance
– Did the fixed overhead cost more or less than expected?
Fixed overhead volume variance
– Did the organisation absorb more or less overhead than expected?
– Can be split further into:
Fixed overhead capacity variance
– Did employees work more or less hours than expected?
Fixed overhead efficiency variance
– Did employees work faster or slower than expected?

Marginal costing system

With a marginal costing profit and loss, no overheads are absorbed, the amount spent is simply written off to the income statement.

So with marginal costing the only fixed overhead variance is the difference between what was budgeted to be spent and what was actually spent, i.e. the fixed overhead expenditure variance.

Absorption costing system

Under absorption costing we use an overhead absorption rate to absorb overheads. Variances will occur if this absorption rate is incorrect (just as we will get over/under-absorption).

So with absorption costing we calculate the fixed overhead expenditure variance and the fixed overhead volume variance.

The fixed overhead volume variance can be further split into a capacity and efficiency variance:

Fixed OH volume variance = Fixed OH efficiency variance + Fixed OH capacity variance

Calculation

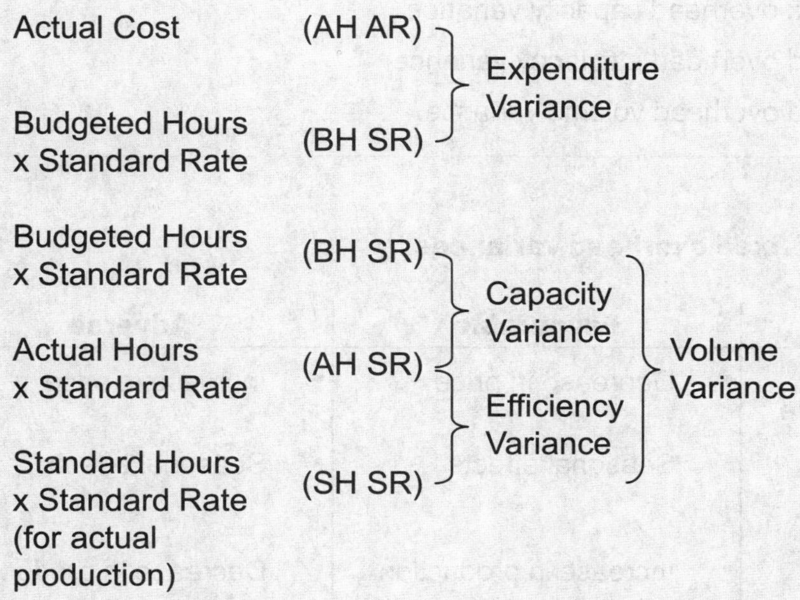

Test your understanding 5 – Fixed overhead variances

The following information is available for J Ltd for Period 4:

Budget	
Fixed production overheads	$22,960
Units	6,560
The standard time to produce each unit is 2 hours	
Actual	
Fixed production overheads	$24,200
Units	6,460
Labour hours	12,600 hrs

Required:

If J Ltd uses an absorption costing system, calculate the following:

(a) FOAR per labour hour

(b) Fixed overhead expenditure variance

(c) Fixed overhead capacity variance

(d) Fixed overhead efficiency variance

(e) Fixed overhead volume variance.

Causes of fixed overhead variances

Variance	Favourable	Adverse
Fixed o/h expenditure	• Decrease in price • Seasonal effects	• Increase in price • Seasonal effects
Fixed o/h volume	• Increase in production volume • Increase in demand • Change is productivity of labour	• Decrease in production volume • Decrease in demand • Production lost through strikes
Fixed o/h capacity	• Hours worked higher than budget	• Hours worked lower than budget
Fixed o/h efficiency	• As for labour efficiency	• As for labour efficiency

Operating statement under absorption costing

The purpose of calculating variances is to identify the different effects of each item of cost/income on profit compared to the expected profit. These variances are summarised in a reconciliation statement or operating statement.

Illustration 1 – Operating statement under absorption costing

Proforma operating statement under absorption costing (AC)

			$
Budgeted profit			X
Sales volume profit variance			X/ (X)
Standard profit on actual sales (= flexed budget profit)			X
Selling price variance			X/ (X)
			X
Cost variances:	**F**	**A**	
	$	$	
Material price	X	(X)	
Material usage	X	(X)	
Labour rate	X	(X)	
Labour efficiency	X	(X)	
Variable overhead expenditure	X	(X)	
Variable overhead efficiency	X	(X)	
Fixed production overhead expenditure variance	X	(X)	
Fixed production overhead capacity variance	X	(X)	
Fixed production overhead efficiency variance	X	(X)	
Total			X/ (X)
Actual profit			X

Test your understanding 6 – AC operating statement

Riki Ltd, produces and sells one product only. The standard cost and price for one unit being as follows:

	$
Direct material A – 10 kilograms at $12 per kg	120
Direct material B – 6 kilograms at $5 per kg	30
Direct wages – 5 hours at $8 per hour	40
Fixed production overhead	60
Total standard cost	250
Standard gross profit	50
Standard selling price	300

The fixed production overhead included in the standard cost is based on an expected monthly output of 750 units. Riki Ltd use an absorption costing system.

During April the actual results were as follows:

	$
Sales 700 units @ $320	224,000
Direct materials:	
A: 7,500 Kg	91,500
B: 3,500 Kg	20,300
Direct wages 3,400 hours	27,880
Fixed production overhead	37,000
	176,680
Gross profit	47,320

Note: Riki Ltd does not hold any inventories.

Required:

You are required to reconcile budgeted profit with actual profit for the period, calculating the following variances:

Selling price, sales volume, material price, material usage, labour rate, labour efficiency, fixed overhead expenditure and fixed overhead volume.

Operating statement under marginal costing

The operating statement under marginal costing is the same as that under absorption costing except:

- a sales volume contribution variance is included instead of a sales volume profit variance
- the only fixed overhead variance is the expenditure variances
- the reconciliation is from budgeted to actual contribution then fixed overheads are deducted to arrive at a profit.

Illustration 2 – Operating statement under marginal costing

Proforma operating statement under marginal costing (MC)

			$
Budgeted contribution			
(budgeted production × budgeted contn/unit)			X
Sales volume contribution variance			X/(X)
Standard contribution on actual sales			
(= flexed budget contribution)			X
Selling price variance			X/(X)
			X
Variable cost variances:			
	F	**A**	
	$	$	$
Material price	X	(X)	
Material usage	X	(X)	
Labour rate	X	(X)	
Labour efficiency	X	(X)	
Variable overhead expenditure	X	(X)	
Variable overhead efficiency	X	(X)	
Total	X	(X)	X/(X)
Actual contribution			X
Budgeted fixed production overhead			X
Fixed overhead expenditure variance			X/(X)
Actual profit			X

Test your understanding 7 – MC operating statement

Chapel Ltd manufactures a chemical protective called Rustnot. The following standard costs apply for the production of 100 cylinders:

		$
Materials	500 kgs @ $0.80 per kg	400
Labour	20 hours @ $1.50 per hour	30
Fixed overheads	20 hours @ $1.00 per hour	20
		450

The monthly production/sales budget is 10,000 cylinders.

Selling price = $6 per cylinder.

For the month of November the following production and sales information is available:

Produced/sold	10,600 cylinders
Sales value	$63,000
Materials purchased and used 53,200 kgs	$42,500
Labour 2,040 hours	$3,100
Fixed overheads	$2,200

Required:

You are required to prepare an operating statement in a marginal costing format for November detailing all the variances.

Labour idle time and material waste

Idle time

Idle time occurs when employees are paid for time when they are not working e.g. due to machine breakdown, low demand or stockouts.

If idle time exists an idle time labour variance should be calculated.

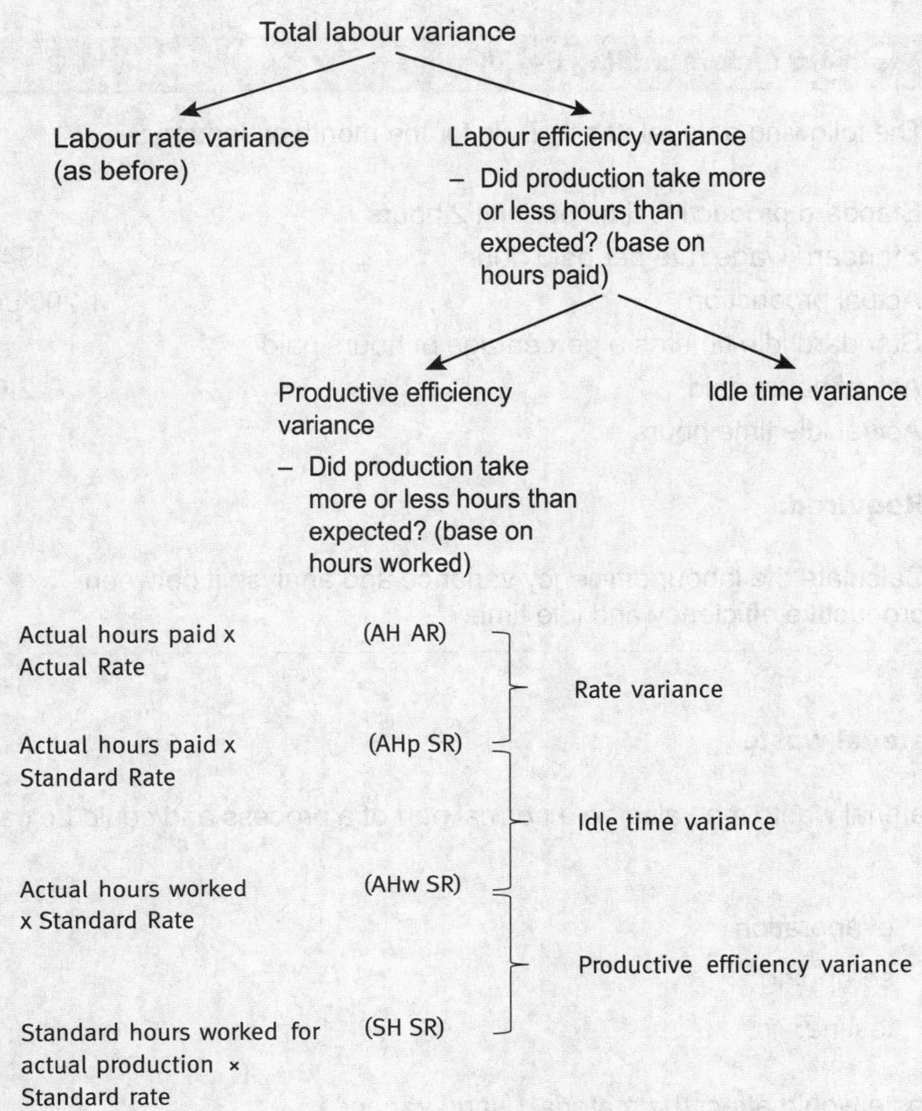

4 Controlling idle time

Idle time can be prevented or reduced considerably by:

(1) Proper maintenance of tools & machinery

(2) Advanced production planning

(3) Timely procurement of stores

(4) Assurance of supply of power

(5) Advance planning for machine utilisation.

Test your understanding 8 – Idle time

The following data relates to T plc for the month of January:

Standard productive time per unit 2 hours	
Standard wage rate per paid hour	$4.00
Actual production	1,200 units
Standard idle time as a percentage of hours paid	4%
Actual hours paid	2,600
Actual idle time hours	110

Required:

Calculate the labour efficiency variance and analyse it between productive efficiency and idle time.

Material waste

Material waste may also be a normal part of a process and could be caused by:

- evaporation
- scrapping
- testing.

Waste would affect the material usage variance.

The purchasing of materials is a highly specialised function, that can control waste by:

(1) Ordering the right quantity and quality of materials at the most favourable price

(2) Ensuring the material arrives at the right time in the production process

(3) Take active measures against theft, deterioration, breakage and additional storage costs.

When should a variance be investigated?

Factors to consider include:

Size

A standard is an average expected cost and therefore small variations between the actual and the standard are bound to occur. These are uncontrollable variances and should not be investigated.

In addition, a business may decide to only investigate variances above a certain amount. The following techniques could be used:

- Fixed size of variance, e.g. investigate all variances over $5,000
- Fixed percentage rule, e.g. investigate all variances over 10% of the budget
- Statistical decision rule, e.g. investigate all variances of which there is a likelihood of less than 5% that it could have arisen randomly.

Favourable or adverse

Firms often treat adverse variances as more important than favourable and therefore any investigation may concentrate on these adverse variances.

Cost

For investigation to be worthwhile, the cost of investigation must be less than the benefits of correcting the cause of the variance.

Past pattern

Variances should be monitored for a number of periods in order to identify any trends in the variances. A firm would focus its investigation on any steadily worsening trends.

The budget

The budget may be unreliable or unrealistic. Therefore, the variances would be uncontrollable and call for a change in the budget or an improvement in the budgeting process, not an investigation of the variance.

Reliability of figures

The system for measuring and recording the figures may be unreliable. If this is the case, the variances will be meaningless and should not be investigated.

Methods used when investigating variances

A process has a standard time of 50 minutes. Control limits may be set as a fixed amount, a fixed percentage or using a statistical model. Assume they are set at a fixed amount 30 and 70 minutes, and actual times recorded as follows:

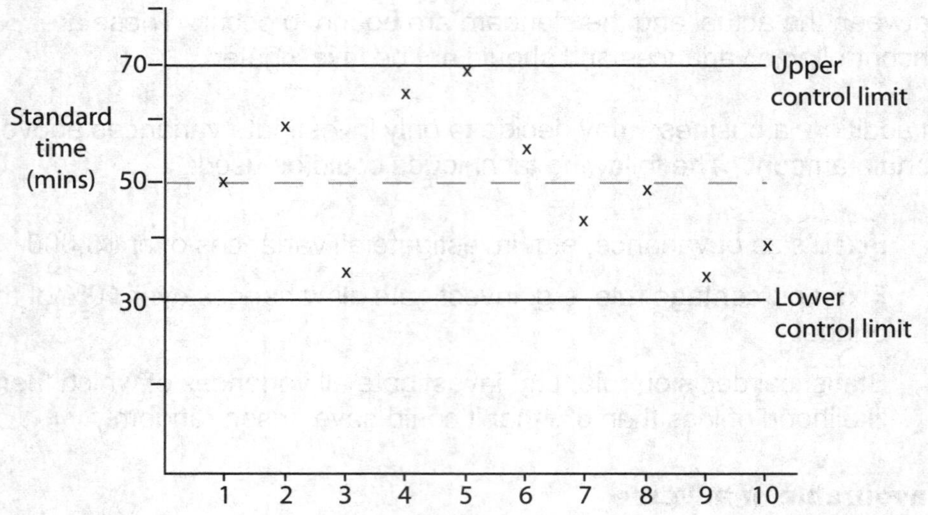

If the actual time taken falls within the bands, the variance is not significant.

Control limits should be set so that there is only a small chance of a random fluctuation falling outside them.

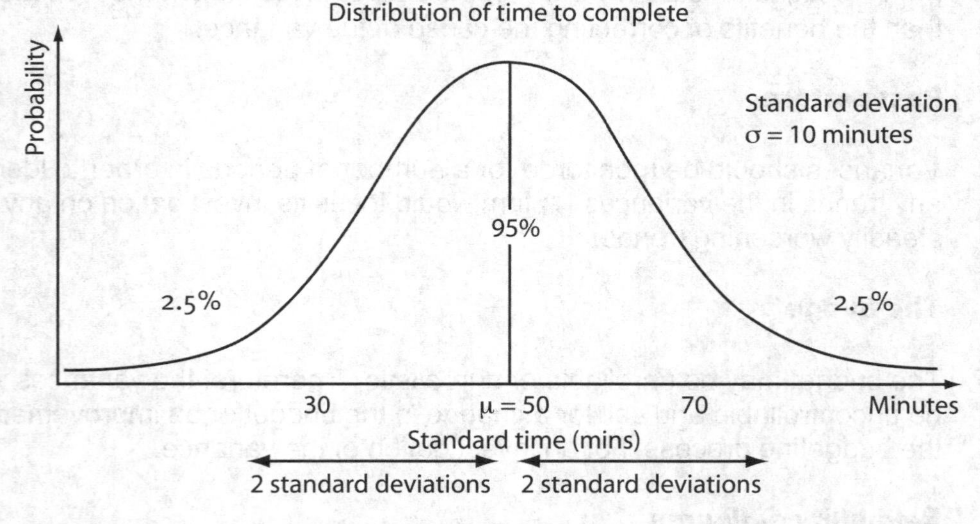

- In this example the control limits are set two standard deviations from the mean. This means that 95% of the recorded process times should lie within the control limits.
- The actual time is recorded on the chart after the completion of each process. It will soon be apparent if the mean time is shifting from 50 minutes, as the recorded times move outside the control limits.
- If more than 5% of the observed results do lie outside the control limits, then the system may be referred to as being statistically out of control. At this stage management must decide what further action to take.

5 Material mix and yield

Material mix and yield variances are calculated if:

- A product contains more than one type of material.
- These materials are interchangeable.

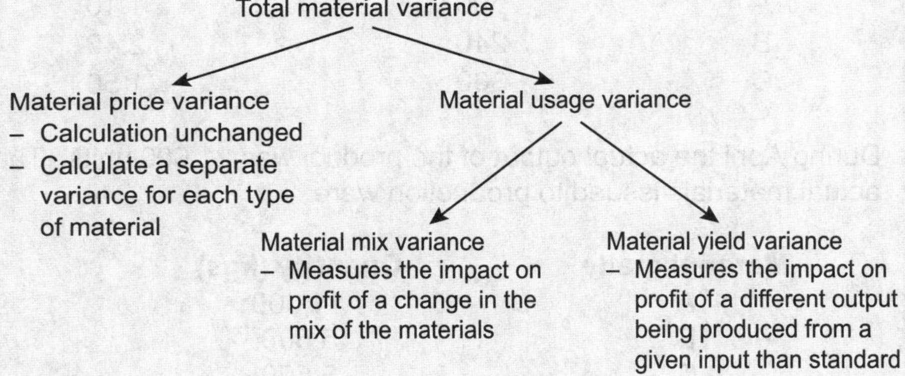

A **mix** variance is used to monitor the cost of material. For instance, if more of an expensive material has been used and less of a cheap material, then the cost will be higher – and the variance adverse.

Method:

Material	**Actual Quantity, Actual Mix (AQAM)**	**Actual Quantity, Standard Mix (AQSM)**	**Difference**	**@ standard price**	**Variance in $**
M_1	X kgs	A kgs	A – X	$x	$Var.(F/A)
M_2	Y kgs	B kgs	B – Y	$x	$Var (F/A)
M_3	Z kgs	C kgs	C – Z	$x	$Var (F/A)
	Sum (X+Y+Z)	**Sum (X+Y+Z)**	(Total = 0)		**$ Total mix (F/A)**

(1) Write down the actual input of each material in a column (this is the **actual total quantity split in the actual mix = AQAM**).

(2) Take the actual input in total and copy is across to another column. Then, work it back in the standard proportions (this is the **actual total quantity split in the standard mix = AQSM**).

(3) Calculate the difference between the standard mix (AQSM) and the actual mix (AQAM). This is the mix variance in terms of physical quantities, and must add up to zero in total. (If you use a higher than expected proportion of one material, you must use a lower than expected proportion of something else!)

(4) Multiply the difference by the standard price per kilogram.

(5) This gives the mix variance in financial terms.

Test your understanding 9 – Material mix

Hondru operates a standard costing system. The standard direct materials to produce 1,000 units of output is as follows:

Material grade	Input quantity (kgs)	Standard price per kg ($)
A	600	1.10
B	240	2.40
C	360	1.50

During April the actual output of the product was 21,000 units. The actual materials issued to production were:

Material grade	Quantity (kgs)
A	14,000
B	5,500
C	5,500

Required:

Calculate the material mix variance for each material, and in total. Comment on the figures calculated.

6 Material yield

A yield variance measures the efficiency of turning the inputs into outputs. If the yield variance is adverse, it suggests that actual output is lower than the expected output. This could be due to labour inefficiencies, higher waste, inferior materials, or using a cheaper mix with a lower yield.

Method 1: The 'total' method

Actual output (given)	X
Expected outputs from actual input	X
Difference	X
Multiplied by standard material cost per unit of output	$X
Variance	$X

Method 2: The 'individual' method

Material	**Actual Quantity, Standard Mix (AQSM)**	**Standard Quantity, Standard Mix (SQSM)**	**Difference**	**@ standard price**	**Variance in $**
M_1	A kgs	D kgs	D – A	$x/kg	$Var (F/A)
M_2	B kgs	E kgs	E – B	$x/kg	$Var (F/A)
M_3	C kgs	F kgs	F – C	$x/kg	$Var (F/A)
	Sum (A+B+C)	**Sum (D+E+F)**			**$ Total yield (F/A)**

'SQSM' is the standard quantity of material used for actual production, shared in the standard mix.

(1) Copy **Actual Quantity, Standard Mix (AQSM)** from the mix variance.

(2) Calculate **Standard Quantity, Standard Mix (SQSM)** for EACH material using the following formula:

Material quantity used from standard cost card × Total actual output produced/Material output quantity produced by the standard cost card.

Or

Calculate the total standard quantity of all materials used to produce the actual output then share this out between the different materials using the standard proportions calculated from the standard cost card.

(3) Calculate difference between the Standard Quantity, Standard Mix (SQSM) and Actual Quantity, Standard Mix (AQSM) for each material.

(4) Multiply by the difference by the standard price per kilogram.

(5) This gives the yield variance in financial terms.

Test your understanding 10 – Material yield

Hondru operates a standard costing system. The standard direct materials to produce 1,000 units of output is as follows:

Material grade	Input quantity (kgs)	Standard price per kg ($)
A	600	1.10
B	240	2.40
C	360	1.50

During April the actual output of the product was 21,000 units. The actual materials issued to production were:

Material grade	Quantity (kgs)
A	14,000
B	5,500
C	5,500

Required:

Calculate the material yield variance. Comment on the figures calculated.

Test your understanding 11 – Material mix and yield

A company manufactures a chemical using two components, A and B. The standard information for one unit of the chemical are as follows:

		$
Material A	10 kg at $4 per kg	40
Material B	20 kg at $6 per kg	120
		160

In a particular period, 160 units of the chemical were produced, using 1,000 kgs of material A and 1,460 kgs of material B.

Required:

Calculate the material usage, mix and yield variances for each material.

7 Interpretation of material mix and yield variances

Mix – a favourable total mix variance would suggest that a higher proportion of a cheaper material is being used hence reducing the overall average cost per unit.

Yield – an adverse total yield variance would suggest that less output has been achieved for a given input, i.e. that the total input in volume is more than expected for the output achieved.

- These variances may be interrelated. A favourable material mix variance may lead to an adverse material yield variance. This is due to differences in quality between the materials used.
- Any change in mix should be judged by the impact on the overall total materials variance.
- The operating statement would include a separate line for each variance.

Test your understanding 12 – Mix and yield with material waste

Pan-Ocean Chemicals has one product, which requires inputs from three types of material to produce batches of Synthon. Standard cost details for a single batch are shown below:

Material type	**Standard quantity (kgs)**	**Standard price per kg** ($)
S1	8	0.30
S2	5	0.50
S3	3	0.40

A standard loss of 10% of input is expected. Actual output was 15,408 kgs for the previous week. Details of the material used were:

Material type	**Quantity (kgs)**
S1	8,284
S2	7,535
S3	3,334

Required:

Calculate the individual material mix and yield and the total usage variance.

Changing the mix – the wider issues

It has already been shown that changing the mix of material input can affect the material yield of the process. It can impact on:

- cost
- quality
- performance measurement.

Illustration 3 – Mix and yield: wider issues

A company produces pre-cast concrete sections for the construction industry. The mix of materials used to produce the concrete can be varied and different mixes are suitable for different products. Discuss the issues that management should consider when setting standard material costs.

Solution

For each product management should consider the optimum mix of input materials that will maximise profits to the business. This may involve consideration of:

- the relationship between cost, quality and price. Reducing the cost of input materials by using a greater proportion of a cheaper material may reduce the quality of the product and lead to a reduction in the price that can be charged
- costs of reduced quality. Using a greater proportion of a cheaper input material may lead to higher quality failure costs
- impact on other variances. Increasing the proportion of a cheaper input material may result in increased labour costs or overhead costs if this leads to more time having to be spent producing a product. Increased rejects may lead to higher overhead costs.

It may be the case that, whilst changing a material mix could lead to an overall favourable material variance this could have an adverse impact on the profitability of the business if prices have to be reduced because of reduced quality or quality failure costs exceed material cost savings. Thus it is important to set the standard mix at the level which optimises profit taking all factors into consideration.

Test your understanding 13

Discuss how the performance measurement system should be designed when the mix of input materials can be varied in a process.

The control of production processes in manufacturing environments

As well as variances, organisations can also use other performance measures and targets for controlling production processes, e.g.:

- quality measures e.g. reject rate, time spent reworking goods, % waste, % yield
- average cost of inputs
- average cost of outputs
- average prices achieved for finished products
- average margins
- % on-time deliveries
- customer satisfaction ratings
- detailed timesheets
- % idle time.

8 Sales mix and quantity variances

Sales variances can be explained as follows:

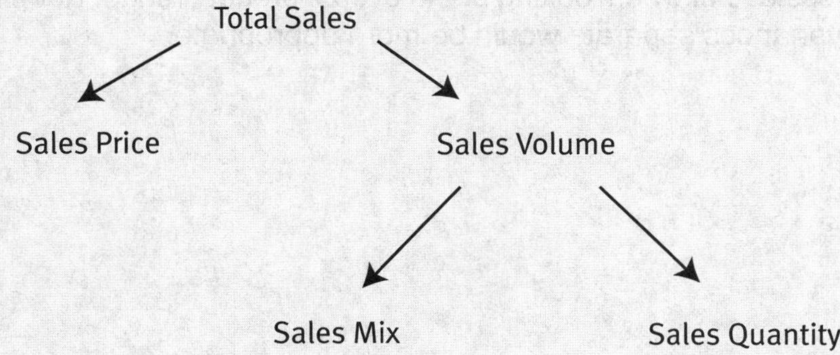

Context

Sales price and volume variances were first met in the F2 paper and recapped at the beginning of this chapter.

- Sales price variances are calculated for each product separately by comparing the actual selling price per unit and the budgeted selling price per unit; each price variance is multiplied by the number of units for each type of product.
- Similarly sales volume variances are calculated for each product separately by comparing the actual number of units sold, and the budgeted number. Each difference is multiplied by the budgeted profit per unit.

In F5 we introduce the idea that instead of **separate** sales volume variances, a firm may prefer to calculate **combined** sales mix and sales quantity variances.

This is only valid if the concept of sales mix is meaningful – would customer choose to buy product A instead of B – has **substitution** occurred? For example, considering car manufacturers:

- Based on differences in price a customer may choose to upgrade and buy a more expensive deluxe variant of a particular car model, so the concept of mix is a useful management tool when discussing sales of variants within a particular range – e.g. did we sell more DLX versions instead of SL versions?
- However, it is highly unlikely customers would choose to buy a lorry instead of a car based on price differences so the concept of mix is less useful when looking at the overall product range. Keeping the variances separate would be more appropriate.

Sales mix variances

A sales mix variance indicates the effect on profit of changing the mix of actual sales from the standard mix. A sales mix variance can be calculated in one of two ways:

Method 1:

The difference between the actual total quantity sold in the standard mix and the actual quantities sold, valued at the standard profit per unit:

Product	**Actual Sales Quantity, Actual Mix (AQAM)**	**Actual Sales Quantity, Standard Mix (AQSM)**	**Difference**	**@ standard margin**	**Variance in $**
P_1	X units	A units	X – A	$\$M_1$	$Var.(F/A)
P_2	Y units	B units	Y – B	$\$M_2$	$Var (F/A)
P_3	Z units	C units	Z – C	$\$M_3$	$Var (F/A)
	Sum (X+Y+Z)	**Sum (X+Y+Z)**	(Total = 0)		**$ Total sales mix**

(1) Write down the actual sales quantity for each product in a column (this is the **actual total sales quantity split in the actual mix = AQAM**).

(2) Take the actual sales quantity in total and copy is across to another column. Then, work it back in the standard proportions (this is the **actual total sales quantity split in the standard mix = AQSM**).

(3) Calculate the difference between the standard mix (AQSM) and the actual mix (AQAM). This is the mix variance in terms of physical quantities (units), and must add up to zero in total. (If you sell a higher than expected proportion of one product, you must sell a lower than expected proportion of something else!)

(4) Multiply the difference by the standard margin per unit.

(5) This gives the sales mix variance in financial terms.

Method 2:

The difference between the actual sales and budgeted sales, valued at the standard profit per unit less the budgeted weighted average profit per unit.

Product	Actual Sales Quantity, Actual Mix (AQAM)	Actual Sales Quantity, Standard Mix (AQSM)	Difference	Standard margin	Weighted average standard margin	Difference	Variance in $
P_1	X units	A units	X – A	$\$M_1$	$\$M_A$	$M_1 - M_A$	$Var.(F/A)
P_2	Y units	B units	Y – B	$\$M_2$	$\$M_A$	$M_2 - M_A$	$Var (F/A)
P_3	Z units	C units	Z – C	$\$M_3$	$\$M_A$	$M_3 - M_A$	$Var (F/A)
	Sum (X+Y+Z)	**Sum (X+Y+Z)**	(Total = 0)				**$ Total sales mix**

Sales quantity variances

A **sales quantity variance** indicates the effect on profit of selling a different total quantity from the budgeted total quantity. Like the mix variance, it can be calculated in one of two ways:

Method 1:

The difference between actual sales volume in the standard mix and budgeted sales valued at the standard profit per unit.

Product	Actual Sales Quantity, Standard Mix (AQSM)	Budget Sales Quantity, Standard Mix (BQSM)	Difference	@ standard margin	Variance in $
P_1	A units	D units	A – D	$\$M_1$	$Var.(F/A)
P_2	B units	E units	B – E	$\$M_2$	$Var (F/A)
P_3	C units	F units	C – F	$\$M_3$	$Var (F/A)
					$ Total sales quantity

(1) Copy Actual Quantity, Standard Mix (AQSM) from the mix variance method 1.

(2) Copy the budgeted sales units under the column Budget Sales Quantity, Standard Mix (BQSM).

(3) Calculate difference between the Actual Sales Quantity, Standard Mix (AQSM) and Budgeted Sales Quantity, Standard Mix (BQSM) for each product.

(4) Multiply by the difference by the standard margin per unit.

(5) This gives the sales quantity variance in financial terms.

Method 2:

The difference between actual sales volume and budgeted sales valued at the weighted average profit per unit.

Sales quantity variance = (Actual total sales quantity – budgeted total sales quantity) × Standard weighted average margin.

Test your understanding 14 – Sales mix and quantity variances

CABCo operates an absorption costing system and sells three products B, R and K which are substitutes for each other. The following standard selling price and cost data relate to these three products:

Product	Unit selling price	Direct material/unit	Direct labour/unit
B	$14.00	3 kgs @ $1.80/kg	0.5 hours @ $6.50/hour
R	$15.00	1.25 kgs @ $3.28/kg	0.8 hours @ $6.50/hour
K	$18.00	1.94 kgs @ $2.50/kg	0.7 hours @ $6.50/hour

Budgeted fixed production overhead for the last period was $81,000. This was absorbed on a machine hour basis. The standard machine hours for each product and the budgeted levels of production and sales for each product for the last period are as follows:

Product	B	R	K
Standard machine hours per unit	0.3 hours	0.6 hours	0.8 hours
Budgeted production and sales (units)	10,000	13,000	9,000

Actual volumes and selling prices for the three products in the last period were as follows:

Product	B	R	K
Actual selling price per unit	$14.50	$15.50	$19.00
Actual production and sales (units)	9,500	13,500	8,500

Required:

Calculate the following variances for overall sales for the last period:

(i) sales price variance

(ii) sales volume profit variance

(iii) sales mix profit variance

(iv) sales quantity profit variance.

9 Planning and operational variances

The standard is set as part of the budgeting process which occurs before the period to which it relates.

This means that the difference between standard and actual may arise partly due to an unrealistic budget and not solely due to operational factors. The budget may need to be **revised** to enable actual performance to be compared with a standard that reflects these changed conditions.

Traditional variance

– Compares actual results with the original (flexed) budget.

Planning variance

– Compares the revised (flexed) budget and the original (flexed) budget.

– Often deemed to be uncontrollable. Management should not be held accountable.

Operational variance

– Compares actual results with the revised (flexed) budget.

– Deemed controllable. Management held responsible for operational variances.

Planning and operational variances may be calculated for:

- Sales
- Materials
- Labour.

The operating statement would include a separate line for each variance calculated.

Each of the variances will be reviewed in turn.

Benefits and problems of planning and operating variances

Benefits of planning and operational variances

- In volatile and changing environments, standard costing and variance analysis are more useful using this approach.
- Operational variances provide up to date information about current levels of efficiency.
- Operational variances are likely to make the standard costing system more acceptable and to have a positive effect on motivation.
- It emphasises the importance of the planning function in the preparation of standards and helps to identify planning deficiencies.

Problems of planning and operational variances

- There is an element of subjectivity in determining the ex-post standards as to what is 'realistic'.
- There is a large amount of labour time involved in continually establishing up to date standards and calculating additional variances.
- There is a great temptation to put as much as possible of the total variances down to outside, uncontrollable factors, i.e. planning variances.
- There can then be a conflict between operating and planning staff, each laying the blame at each other's door.

On the face of it, the calculation of operational and planning variances is an improvement over the traditional analysis. However, you should not overlook the considerable problem of data collection for the revised analysis: where does this information come from, and how can we say with certainty what should have been known at a particular point in time?

Planning and operational variances for sales

The sales volume variance can be sub-divided into a planning and operational variance:

Actual sales quantity x standard margin	
	Market share variance (operational)
Revised budgeted sales x standard margin (to achieve target share of actual market)	
	Market size variance (planning)
Original budgeted sales x standard margin	

Test your understanding 15 – Market size and share

Hudson has a sales budget of 400,000 units for the coming year based on 20% of the total market. On each unit, Hudson makes a profit of $3. Actual sales for the year were 450,000, but industry reports showed that the total market volume had been 2.2 million.

(a) Find the traditional sales volume variance.

(b) Split this into planning and operational variances (market size and market share). Comment on your results.

Test your understanding 16 – Additional example

A company sets its sales budget based on an average price of $14 per unit and sales volume of 250,000 units. Competition was more intense than expected and the company only achieved sales of 220,000 and had to sell at a discounted price of $12.50 per unit. The company was unable to reduce costs so profit per unit fell from $4 per unit to $2.50 per unit. It was estimated that the total market volume grew by 10% from 1,000,000 units to 1,100,000 units.

Required:

(a) Calculate the sales price and volume variances.

(b) Analyse the volume variances into market share and market size.

(c) Discuss whether the price variance is a planning or operational variance.

Objective Test Case Question – The Alpha Company

The Alpha Company operates an absorption costing system and sells three products A, B and C. Each product line is managed by a divisional manager (Manager A, Manager B and Manager C) who is only responsible for his line of products. Sales budgets information on the three products is provided as follows:

Product	Sales units	Standard profit per unit	Budgeted profit
A	400 units	$8	$3,200
B	600 units	$6	$3,600
C	1,000 units	$4	$4,000

Actual sales are achieved at the standard selling price, as follows:

Product	Sales units	Standard profit per unit	Actual profit
A	300 units	$8	$2,400
B	700 units	$6	$4,200
C	1,200 units	$4	$4,800

(1) **What is the sales quantity variance?**

A $0

B $480 F

C $480 A

D $1,080 F

(2) **Which of the following statements regarding market size variances are true are true?**

(1) A fall or increase in market size in uncontrollable by management, and therefore results in a planning variance.

(2) The sales volume planning variance reveals the extent of which the original standard (estimation of market size) was at fault.

(3) Managers should be appraised on both the operational and planning variances for sales.

A Statements (1) and (2)

B Statements (2) and (3)

C Statements (1) and (3)

D Statements (1), (2) and (3)

(3) **Which of the following statements regarding the sales mix variance in the Alpha Company are true?**

(1) The overall mix variance is adverse because more products with a higher profit per unit are sold, in place of products with a lower profit per unit.

(2) The actual proportion of products B and C, which have a lower profit per unit, is more than the budgeted proportion whereas the actual proportion of product A, which yields a higher profit per unit, is lower than budgeted.

(3) Providing a manager with a sales mix variance when he can only control one product is meaningless.

A Statements (1) and (2)

B Statements (2) and (3)

C Statements (1) and (3)

D Statements (1), (2) and (3)

(4) A recession in 2014 meant that the market for all of the company's products declined by 10%.

What is the market size variance (planning variance) for product B in 2014?

A $200 A

B $360 F

C $360 A

D $960 F

(5) A recession in 2014 meant that the market for all of the company's products declined by 10%.

What is the market share variance (operational variance) for product B in 2014?

A $200 A

B $360 F

C $360 A

D $960 F

Planning and operational variances for materials

Planning and operational variances can be calculated for materials in the same way as above.

Test your understanding 17 – Price variances

The standard cost per unit of raw material was estimated to be $5.20 per unit. However, due to subsequent improvements in technology, the general market price at the time of purchase was $5.00 per unit. The actual price paid was $5.18 per unit. 10,000 units of the raw materials were purchased during the period.

Required:

Calculate the planning and operational materials price variances. Comment on the results.

Test your understanding 18 – Price and usage variances

Holmes Ltd uses one raw material for one of their products. The standard cost per unit at the beginning of the year was $28, made up as follows:

Standard material cost per unit = 7 kg per unit at $4 per kg = $28.

In the middle of the year the supplier had changed the specification of the material slightly due to problems experienced in the country of origin, so that the standard had to be revised as follows:

Standard material cost per unit = 8 kg per unit at $3.80 per kg = $30.40.

The actual output for November was 1,400 units. 11,000 kg of material was purchased and used at a cost of $41,500.

Calculate

(a) material price and usage variances using the traditional method

(b) all planning and operational material variances.

Planning and operational variances for labour

Planning and operational variances for labour can be calculated in the same way as for materials.

Test your understanding 19

The standard hours per unit of production for a product is 5 hours. Actual production for the period was 250 units and actual hours worked were 1,450 hours. The standard rate per hour was $10. Because of a shortage of skilled labour it has been necessary to use unskilled labour and it is estimated that this will increase the time taken by 20%.

Required:

Calculate the planning and operational efficiency variances.

Learning curves and variances

The direct labour efficiency variance in respect of a new product has been calculated as $14,700 Favourable. The variance was calculated using standard cost data which showed that each unit of the product was expected to take 8 hours to produce, at a cost of $15 per hour.

The actual output was 560 units, and the actual time worked in the manufacture of the product totalled 3,500 hours, at a cost of $57,750. However, the production manager now realises that the standard time of 8 hours per unit was the time taken to produce the first unit and that a learning curve rate of 90% should have been anticipated for the first 600 units.

Required:

Calculate the planning and operational efficiency variances for labour efficiency, following the recognition of the learning curve effect (b = –0.1520 for a 90% learning curve).

Revising the budget

When applying planning and operating principles to cost variances (material and labour), care must be taken over flexing the budgets. The accepted approach for use in the exam is to flex both the original and revised budgets to actual production levels:

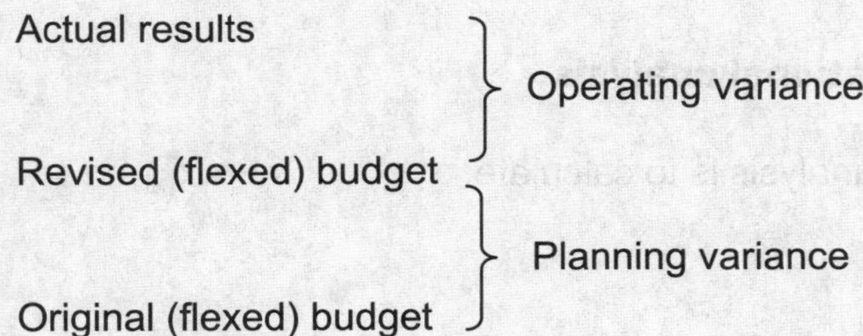

Note: If pushed for time in the exam, then calculate detailed operating variances but give a single total planning variance for each category.

When should a budget be revised?

There must be a good reason for deciding that the original standard cost is unrealistic. Deciding in retrospect that expected costs should be different from the standard should not be an arbitrary decision, aimed perhaps at shifting the blame for bad results due to poor operational management or poor cost estimation.

A good reason for a change in the standard might be:

- a change in one of the main materials used to make a product or provide a service
- an unexpected increase in the price of materials due to a rapid increase in world market prices (e.g. the price of oil or other commodities)
- a change in working methods and procedures that alters the expected direct labour time for a product or service
- an unexpected change in the rate of pay to the workforce.

These types of situations do not occur frequently. The need to report planning and operational variances should therefore be an occasional, rather than a regular, event.

If the budget is revised on a regular basis, the reasons for this should be investigated. It may be due to management attempting to shift the blame for poor results or due to a poor planning process.

Illustration 4 – Revising the budget

Rhodes Co manufactures Stops which it is estimated require 2 kg of material XYZ at $10/kg In week 21 only 250 Stops were produced although budgeted production was 300. 450 kg of XYZ were purchased and used in the week at a total cost of $5,100. Later it was found that the standard had failed to allow for a 10% price increase throughout the material supplier's industry. Rhodes Ltd carries no stocks.

Planning and operational analysis

The first step in the analysis is to calculate:

(1) Actual results

(2) Revised flexed budget(ex-post)

(3) Original flexed budget (ex-ante).

(W1)	Actual results			
	450kg for		$5,100	↑ Operational variance
(W2)	Revised flexed budget (ex post)			
	250 units at 2kg per unit for $11/kg	=	$5,500	↓↑ Planning variance
(W3)	Original flexed budget (ex-ante)			
	250 units at 2kg per unit for $10/kg	=	$5,000	↓

Additional example on revising the budget

A transport business makes a particular journey regularly, and has established that the standard fuel cost for each journey is 20 litres of fuel at $2 per litre. New legislation has forced a change in the vehicle used for the journey and an unexpected rise in fuel costs. It is decided retrospectively that the standard cost per journey should have been 18 litres at $2.50 per litre.

Required:

Calculate the original and revised flexed budgets if the journey is made 120 times in the period.

Solution

Original flexed budget:

120 × 20 × $2	$4,800

Revised flexed budget:

120 ×18 ×$2.50	$5,400

Pros and cons of revising the budget

A company is operating in a fast changing environment and is considering whether analysing existing variances into a planning and operational element would help to improve performance. Discuss the advantages and disadvantages of the approach.

Solution

Advantages may include:

- Variances are more relevant , especially in a turbulent environment.
- The operational variances give a 'fair' reflection of the actual results achieved in the actual conditions that existed.
- Managers are, theoretically, more likely to accept and be motivated by the variances reported which provide a better measure of their performance.
- The analysis helps in the standard-setting learning process, which will hopefully result in more useful standards in the future.

Disadvantages:

- The establishment of ex-post budgets is very difficult . Managers whose performance is reported to be poor using such a budget are unlikely to accept them as performance measures because of the subjectivity in setting such budgets.
- There is a considerable amount of administrative work involved first to analyse the traditional variances and then to decide on which are controllable and which are uncontrollable.
- The analysis tends to exaggerate the interrelationship of variances, providing managers with a 'pre-packed' list of excuses for below standard performance. Poor performance is often excused as being the fault of a badly set budget.
- Frequent demands for budget revisions may result in bias.

Variance analysis in the modern manufacturing environment

Variance analysis may not be appropriate because:

Non-standard products

Standard product costs apply to manufacturing environments in which quantities of an identical product are output from the production process. They are not suitable for manufacturing environments where products are non-standard or are customised to customer specifications.

Standard costs become outdated quickly

Shorter product life cycles in the modern business environment mean that standard costs will need to be reviewed and updated frequently.

This will increase the cost of operating a standard cost system but, if the standards are not updated regularly, they will be of limited use for planning and control purposes. The extra work involved in maintaining up-to-date standards might limit the usefulness and relevance of a standard costing system.

Production is highly automated

It is doubtful whether standard costing is of much value for performance setting and control in automated manufacturing environments. There is an underlying assumption in standard costing that control can be exercised by concentrating on the efficiency of the workforce. Direct labour efficiency standards are seen as a key to management control.

However, in practice, where manufacturing systems are highly automated, the rates of production output and materials consumption, are controlled by the machinery rather than the workforce.

Ideal standard used

Variances are the difference between actual performance and standard, measured in cost terms. The significance of variances for management control purposes depends on the type of standard cost used.

JIT and **TQM** businesses often implement an ideal standard due to the emphasis on continuous improvement and high quality. Therefore, adverse variances with an ideal standard have a different meaning from adverse variances calculated with a current standard.

Emphasis on continuous improvement

Standard costing and adherence to a preset standard is inconsistent with the concept of continuous improvement, which is applied within **TQM** and **JIT** environments.

Detailed information is required

Variance analysis is often carried out on an aggregate basis (total material usage variance, total labour efficiency variance and so on) but in a complex and constantly changing business environment more detailed information is required for effective management control.

Monitoring performance is important

Variance analysis control reports tend to be made available to managers at the end of a reporting period. In the modern business environment managers need more 'real time' information about events as they occur.

Dysfunctional variances in a JIT and TQM environments

Some variances are not useful in JIT or TQM environment, for example:

(1) **The material price variance:** in a JIT environment, the business is prepared to pay a higher price for materials, as suppliers will consistently deliver raw material with no defects. In a TQM environment, the company is prepared to pay a higher price to acquire better quality material, so that production will 'get it right first time'. Therefore, the material price variance may not be relevant for measuring performance.

(2) **The labour, variable overhead and fixed overhead efficiency variances:** in a TQM production environment, labour is working toward minimizing waste and improving quality. In a traditional standard costing environment, efficiency variance could be adverse, but would be 'allowed' in a TQM environment as long as the final product meets customers' expectations.

(3) **The material usage variance:** in a JIT environment, since the workforce needs to be fast in the production process, more wastage could occur. In a TQM environment, the final product sent to customer must be absolutely fault-free, and so more materials might be used as only good quality finished goods are acceptable. Material usage variance might not be useful to assess performance.

Test your understanding 20

Comment on whether standard costing applies in both manufacturing and service businesses and how it may be affected by modern initiatives of continuous performance improvement and cost reduction.

Standard costs and behavioural issues

Standard costs are set with a view to measuring actual performance against the standard, and reporting variances to the managers responsible. The aims of setting standards include:

- setting a target for performance
- motivating the managers responsible to achieve those targets
- holding these managers accountable for actual performance
- perhaps rewarding managers for good performance and criticising them for poor performance.

Managers and employees might respond in different ways to standard setting.

Factors to consider include:

The type of standard set

Individuals might respond to standards in different ways, according to the difficulty of achieving the standard level of performance.

- **Ideal standard:** When a standard level of performance is high, e.g. an ideal standard, employees and their managers will recognise that they cannot achieve it. Since the target is not achievable, they might not even try to get near it.
- **Current standard:** When the standard of performance is not challenging (e.g. a current standard), employees and their managers might be content simply to achieve the standard without trying to improve their performance.

- **Attainable standard:** An attainable standard might be set which challenges employees and their managers to improve their performance. If this attainable standard is realistic, it might provide a target that they try to achieve. Some employees will be motivated by this challenge and will work harder to achieve it. However, some employees may prefer standards to be set at a low level of performance, in order to avoid the need to work harder.
- **Basic standard:** This type of standard may motivate employees since it gives them a long-term target to aim for. However, the standard may become out of date quickly and, as result, may actually demotivate employees.

Standard costs in changing environments

Variance analysis can be unhelpful, and potentially misleading in the modern organisation; this is especially true of JIT and TQM environments. Standard costing is most appropriate in a stable, standardised and repetitive environment. However, modern business environment is rapidly changing, which highlights the following problems with standard costing:

(1) Standard costing focuses on reducing costs, and ignores quality and customer satisfaction. A high quality output is at the centre of a TQM environment. The cost of failing to achieve the required level of quality is not measured in standard costs and variances, but in terms of internal and external failure costs, neither of which would be identified by a traditional standard costing analysis.

(2) A standard costing system puts too much emphasis on direct labour costs. However, in the modern business environment, production is largely automated, so direct labour is only a small proportion of costs.

(3) A standard costing system puts too much emphasis on the control of short-term, variable costs. However, in the modern environment, most costs (including direct labour costs), are fixed costs – or fixed at least in the short term.

(4) Standard costing is most appropriate in a stable, standardised and repetitive environment; one of the main objectives of standard costing is to ensure that processes conform to standards, that they do not vary, and that variances are eliminated. The modern business environment is dynamic, unstable, more competitive, and operations are more complex – standard costing is not always suitable for it.

(5) Achieving standards is acceptable is standard costing, when the modern business environment insists more on **continuous improvement**.

(6) Standard costing systems produce control statements weekly or monthly, but in a dynamic business environment, managers need more prompt control information in order to deal with any changes.

Participation in standard setting

The level of participation in standard setting

Arguments in favour of participation	Arguments against participation
It could motivate employees to set higher standards for achievement.	Senior management might be reluctant to share responsibilities for budgeting.
Staff are more likely to accept standards that they have been involved in setting.	The standard-setting process could be time consuming.
Morale and actual performance levels might be improved.	Staff might want to set standards that they are likely to achieve, rather than more challenging targets. They might try to build some 'slack' into the budget.
Staff will understand more clearly what is expected of them.	The standard-setting process could result in conflicts rather than co-operation and collaboration.
	Staff might feel that their suggestions have been ignored.

Test your understanding 21

Which one of the following is not an advantage of participation in standard setting?

(a) The time taken to reach decisions will be quicker via assorted committee meetings.

(b) The quality of decisions should improve with collective decision making.

(c) There will be improved communication between staff.

(d) Staff are more likely to accept standards that they have helped set.

The use of pay as a motivator

If standards are used as a way of encouraging employees to improve their performance, motivation could be provided in the form of higher pay if targets are reached or exceeded.

However, if employees are offered a bonus for achieving standard costs, this could increase their incentive to set low standards of performance, i.e. include 'slack' in the standard cost. Lower standards will increase the probability that the standards will be achieved and a bonus will be earned.

10 Chapter summary

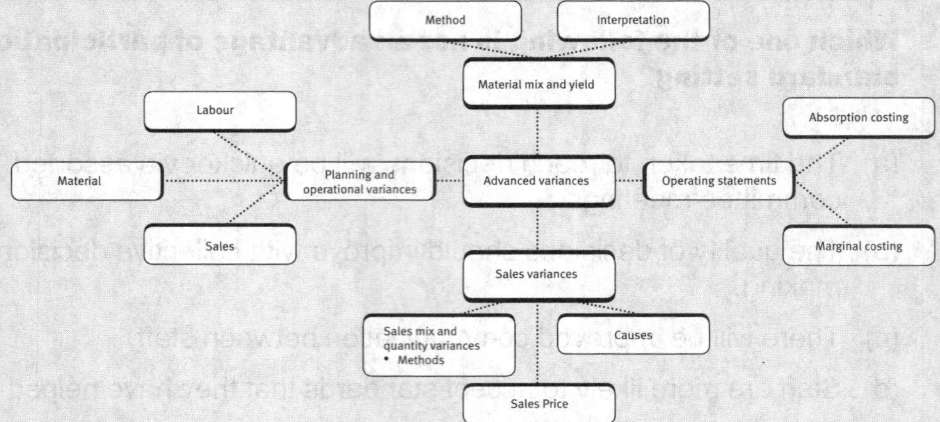

Test your understanding answers

Test your understanding 1 – Sales variances

(a) Under absorption costing, the variance is calculated using the standard profit per unit. $

Using the three line method:

Sales price variance

AQ AP = 6,000 × $61 = $366,000

Variance = **$6,000 F**

AQ SP = 6,000 × $60 = $360,000

Sales volume variance

AQ SM = 6,000 × $5 = $30,000

Variance = **$2,500 A**

BQ SM = 6,500 × $5 = $32,500

Alternative calculations:

6,000 units **should** have sold for 6,000 × $60 =	$360,000
6,000 units **did** sell for 6,000 × $61 =	$366,000
Sales price variance	**$6,000 F**
Budgeted sales	6,500 units
Actual sales	6,000 units
Variance in units	500 units A
@ standard profit $5	**$2,500 A**

(b) The sales price variance is the same under marginal costing, but the sales volume variance is calculated using the standard contribution per unit. Here, standard contribution = $60 – ($25 + $8 + $4) = $23.

Sales volume variance

AQ SM = 6,000 × $23= $138,000

Variance = **$11,500 A**

BQ SM = 6,500 × $23 = $149,500

Alternative calculation:

Budgeted sales =	6,500
Actual sales =	6,000
Variance	500 A

Variance = 500 A units × **standard contribution** of $23 per unit = $11,500 A

Test your understanding 2 – Materials variances

Using the three line method:

$

Material price variance

AQ AP = $20,900

Variance = **$1,100 F**

AQ SP = 2,200 kgs × $10 = $22,000

Material usage variance

AQ SP = 2,200 kgs × $10= $22,000

Variance = **$2,000 A**

SQ SP = 1,000 units × 2 kgs × $10 = $20,000

Alternative calculations:

2,200 kgs should have cost 2,200 × $10	$22,000
2,200 kgs **did** cost	$20,900
Materials price variance	**$1,100 F**

1,000 units of output should have used 1,000 × 2 kgs	2,000 kgs
1,000 units of output did use	2,200 kgs
Therefore variance is adverse by	200 kgs
@ standard cost per kg £10	**$2,000 A**

Test your understanding 3 – Labour variances

Labour rate variance	$
Actual hours paid, 15,500 hours, **should** cost $4.80 per hour	74,400
Actual hours paid, 15,500 hours, **did** cost	69,750
Variance	4,650 F

Labour efficiency variance	**Hours**
Actual production, 1,000 units, **should** take 15 hours per unit	15,000
Actual production, 1,000 units, **did** take	15,500
Variance	500 A

Variance = 500 A hours × **standard cost** of $4.80 per hour = $2,400 A

Labour rate variance – three line method

AH AR = $69,750

Variance = $4,650 F

AH SR = 15,500 × $4.80 = $74,400

Labour efficiency variance – three line method

AH SR = 15,500 × $4.80 = $74,400

Var. = $2,400 A

SH SR = (1,000 × 15 hours) × $4.80 = $72,000

Test your understanding 4 – Variable overhead variances

Variable overhead expenditure variance	$
Actual hours paid, 15,500 hours, **should** cost $1 per hour	15,500
Actual hours paid, 15,500 hours, **did** cost	14,900
Variance	600 F

Variable overhead efficiency variance	**Hours**
Actual production, 1,000 units, **should** take 15 hours per unit	15,000
Actual production, 1,000 units, **did** take	15,500
Variance	500 A

Variance = 500 A hours × **standard cost** of $1 per hour = $500 A

Variable overhead expenditure variance – three line method

AH AR = $14,900

Variance = $600 F

AH SR = 15,500 × $1 = $15,500

Variable overhead efficiency variance – three line method

AH SR = 15,500 × $1 = $15,500

Variance = $500 A

SH SR = (1,000 × 15 hours) × $1 = $15,000

Test your understanding 5 – Fixed overhead variances

(a) FOAR = $22,960 ÷ (6,560 units × 2 hours per unit) = $1.75 per hour

(b) **Fixed overhead expenditure variance**

	$
Budgeted fixed overhead	22,960
Actual fixed overhead	24,200
Variance	1,240 A

Fixed overhead expenditure variance – three line method

AH AR = $24,200

Var. = $1,240 A

BH SR = $22,960

(c) **Fixed overhead capacity variance**

	Hours
Budgeted hours worked = 2 hours × 6,560 units	13,120
Actual hours worked	12,600
Variance	520 A

Variance in $ = 520A hours × **standard FOAR** $1.75/hr = $910 A

Fixed overhead capacity variance – three line method

BH SR = $22,960

Variance = $910 A

AH SR = 12,600 × $1.75 = $22,050

(d) **Fixed overhead efficiency variance**

	Hours
Actual production, 6,460 units, **should** take 2 hours per unit	12,920
Actual production, 6,460 units, did take	12,600
Variance	320 F

Variance in \$ = 320F hours × **standard FOAR** per hour \$1.75 = \$560 F

Fixed overhead efficiency variance – alternative method

AH SR = 12,600 × \$1.75 = \$22,050

Variance = \$560 F

SH SR = (6,460 × 2) × \$1.75 = \$22,610

(e) **Fixed overhead volume variance**

	Units
Budgeted production	6,560
Actual production	6,460
Variance	100 A

Variance in \$ = 100 A units × **standard hours** of 2 × **standard FOAR** per hour \$1.75 = \$350 A

Fixed overhead volume variance – alternative method

BH SR = \$22,960

Variance = \$350 A

SH SR = (6,460 × 2) × \$1.75 = \$22,610

Note: The fixed overhead volume variance of \$350A is the total of the capacity and efficiency variances (\$910 A + \$560 F).

Test your understanding 6 – AC operating statement

	$	$
Material A variances:	$	$
AQ AP =	91,500	
Price variance		} 1,500 (A)
AQ SP = 7,500 kg × $12 =	90,000	
Usage variance		} 6,000 (A)
SQ SP = (700 units × 10 kg) × $12 =	84,000	
Material B variances:	$	$
AQ AP =	20,300	
Price variance		} 2,800 (A)
AQ SP = 3,500 kg × $5 =	17,500	
Usage variance		} 3,500 (F)
SQ SP = (700 units × 6 kg) × $5 =	21,000	
Labour variances:	$	$
AH AR =	27,880	
Rate variance		} 680 (A)
AH SR = 3,400 hours × $8 =	27,200	
Efficiency variance		} 800 (F)
SH SR = (700 units × 5 hours) × $8 =	28,000	
Fixed overhead variances:	$	$
AH AR =	37,000	
Expenditure variance		} 8,000 (F)
BH SR = 750 units × $60 per unit	45,000	
Volume variance		} 3,000 (A)
SH SR = 700 units × $60 per unit	42,000	
Sales variances:	$	$
AQ AP	224,000	
Price variance		} 14,000 (F)
AQ SP = 700 units × $300 per unit	210,000	
AQ SM = 700 units × $50 per unit	35,000	
Volume variance		} 2,500 (A)
BQ SM = 750 units × $50 per unit	37,500	

Operating statement

	F	A	$
Budgeted profit (750 × $50)			37,500
Sales volume variance			(2,500)
Standard profit on actual sales			35,000
Selling price variance			14,000
Cost variances:	**F**	**A**	
Material price (combined)		(4,300)	
Material usage (combined)		(2,500)	
Labour rate		(680)	
Labour efficiency	800		
Fixed overhead expenditure	8,000		
Fixed overhead volume		(3,000)	
Total	8,800	10,480	(1,680)
Actual profit			47,320

Test your understanding 7 – MC operating statement

Standard contribution = $6 – $4.30 = $1.70 per cylinder

Sales variances:	$	$
AQ AP	63,000	
Price variance	}	600 (A)
AQ SP = 10,600 units × $6 per unit	63,600	
AQ SM = 10,600 units × $1.70 per unit	18,020	
Volume variance	}	1,020 (F)
BQ SM = 10,000 units × $1.70 per unit	17,000	

Material variances:

	$	$
AQ AP =	42,500	
Price variance		} 60 (F)
AQ SP = 53,200 kg × $0.80 =	42,560	
Usage variance		} 160 (A)
SQ SP = (10,600 units × 5 kg) × $0.80 =	42,400	

Labour variances:

	$	$
AH AR =	3,100	
Rate variance		} 40 (A)
AH SR = 2,040 hours × $1.50 =	3,060	
Efficiency variance		} 120 (F)
SH SR = (10,600 units × 0.2 hours) × $1.50 =	3,180	

Operating statement

	$
Budgeted contribution (10,000 × $1.70)	17,000
Sales volume contribution variance	1,020 F
Standard contribution on actual sales (10,600 × 1.70)	18,020
Sales price variance	(600 A)
	17,420

Variable cost variances:

	F	A	
	$	$	$
Materials price	60		
Wages rate		40	
Materials usage		160	
Labour efficiency	120		
	180	200	(20 A)
Actual contribution			17,400
Budgeted fixed overhead			2,000
Fixed overhead expenditure variance			(200 A)
Actual profit			15,200

Test your understanding 8 – Idle time

Labour efficiency variance

AH SR = 2,600 × $4 = $10,400

Variance = $400 A

SH SR = (1,200 × 2 hours × 100/96) × $4 = $10,000

Productive efficiency variance

AH SGR = (2,600 – 110) × ($4 × 100/96) = $10,375

Variance = $375 A

SH SGR = (1,200 × 2) × ($4 × 100/96) = $10,000

Excess idle time variance

AIH SGR = 110 × ($4 × 100/96) = $458.33

Variance = $25 A

SIH SGR = (2,600 × 4%) × ($4 × 100/96) = $433.33

Test your understanding 9 – Material mix

Material mix variance

Material	Std mix	Actual material usage (kgs)	Actual usage @ std mix (kgs)	Mix variance (kgs)	Std cost per kg ($)	Mix variance ($)
A	600/1200	14,000	12,500	1,500 A	1.10	1,650 A
B	240/1200	5,500	5,000	500 A	2.40	1,200 A
C	360/1200	5,500	7,500	2,000 F	1.50	3,000 F
		25,000	25,000	0	–	150 F

Comment

The favourable mix variance is due to more of materials A and B being used in place of material C.

Test your understanding 10 – Material yield

(1)	Total input of 25,000 kgs should produce. (÷ 1.2 kgs per unit)	20,833 units of output
(2)	25,000 kgs did produce	21,000 units of output
(3)	Difference = yield variance in units	167 units F
(4)	Value at the standard cost of (Working)	$1.78 per unit
(5)	Yield variance	$297 F

Working

Standard cost per unit = ((600 × $1.10) + (240 × $2.40) + (360 × $1.50)) ÷ 1,000 units = $1.78 per unit

Comment

The favourable variance is due to more output being achieved than was expected from the materials input.

Test your understanding 11 – Material mix and yield

Material A usage variance

AQ SP = 1,000 × $4 = $4,000

Variance = $2,400 F

SQ SP = (160 units × 10 kg/unit) × $4 = $6,400

Material B usage variance

AQ SP = 1,460 × $6 = $8,760

Var. = $10,440 F

SQ SP = (160 units × 20 kg/unit) × $6 = $19,200

Total usage variance = $2,400 + $10,440 = $12,840

Material mix variance

Material	Std mix	Actual material usage (kgs)	Actual usage @ std mix (kgs)	Mix variance (kgs)	Std cost per kg ($)	Mix variance ($)
A	10/30	1,000	820	180 A	4	720 A
B	20/30	1,460	1,640	180 F	6	1,080 F
		2,460	2,460	0	–	360 F

Material yield variance

Material	Std usage for actual output (kgs)	Actual usage @ std mix (kgs)	Yield variance (kgs)	Std cost per kg ($)	Yield variance ($)
A	160 × 10 kg = 1,600	820	780 F	4	3,120 F
B	160 × 20 kg = 3,200	1,640	1,560 F	6	9,360 F
	4,800	2,460	2,340 F	–	12,480 F

Alternatively, the material yield variance can be calculated in total using the following method:

(1)	Total input = 1,000 kgs + 1,460 kgs = 2,460 kgs	
	This should produce (÷ 30 kgs)	82 units of output
(2)	2,460 kgs did produce	160 units of output
(3)	Difference = yield variance in units	78 units F
(4)	Value at the standard cost of	$160 per unit
(5)	Yield variance	$12,480 F

Total mix and yield variance = $12,480 F + $360 F = $12,840 F (as per the usage variance)

Test your understanding 12 – Mix and yield with material waste

Material mix variance

The material mix variance is not affected by the material wastage and should be calculated in the normal way:

Material	Std mix	Actual material usage (kgs)	Actual usage @ std mix (kgs)	Mix variance (kgs)	Std cost per kg ($)	Mix variance ($)
S1	8/16	8,284	9,576.5	1,292.5 F	0.30	387.75 F
S2	5/16	7,535	5,985.3	1,549.7 A	0.50	774.85 A
S3	3/16	3,334	3,591.2	257.2 F	0.40	102.88 F
		19,153	19,153	0	–	284.22 A

Material yield variance

The yield variance will take account of the material wastage of 10%:

Material	Std usage for actual output (kgs)	Actual usage @ std mix (kgs)	Yield variance (kgs)	Std cost per kg ($)	Yield variance ($)
S1	8/16 = 8,560	9,576.5	1,016.5 A	0.30	304.95 A
S2	5/16 = 5,350	5,985.3	635.3 A	0.50	317.65 A
S3	3/16 = 3,210	3,591.2	381.2 A	0.40	152.48 A
	15,408 × 100/90 = 17,120	19,153	2,033 A	–	775. 08 A

Material usage variance

Total usage variance = $775.08 A + $284.22 A = $1,059.3 A

Test your understanding 13

In a performance measurement system managers are often rewarded for improving the performance of cost and/or revenues under their control. The production manager may be responsible for the material mix decision and, if the reward system is based on achieving cost savings, then the cheapest mix may be used. This may have a detrimental effect on company profit if quality is reduced and this leads to a lower price or quality failure costs.

It may therefore be preferable to reward managers on the basis of total company profit so that the full impact of the mix decision is taken into account.

Test your understanding 14 – Sales mix and quantity variances

Working 1: OAR

$$\text{OAR} = \frac{\$81{,}000}{3{,}000 + 7{,}800 + 7{,}200}$$

so OAR = $4.50 per machine hour

Working 2: Standard profit

	B	R	K
Materials	$5.40	$4.10	$4.85
Labour	$3.25	$5.20	$4.55
Overheads	$1.35	$2.70	$3.60
Total cost	$10	$12.00	$13.00
Selling price	$14	$15.00	$18.00
Standard profit	$4.00	$3.00	$5.00

Working 3: Weighted average standard profit

	B	R	K
Standard profit	$4.00	$3.00	$5.00

$$\text{W.A. standard profit} = \frac{(\$4 \times 10{,}000 \text{ units}) + (\$3.00 \times 13{,}000 \text{ units}) + (\$5 \times 9{,}000 \text{ units})}{32{,}000 \text{ budgeted units}}$$

= **$3.875**

(i) **Sales price variance:**

	B	R	K
Actual selling price per unit	$14.50	$15.50	$19.00
Standard selling price per unit	$14.00	$15.00	$18.00
Variance	$1.50 F	$0.50 F	$1.00 F
	× 9,500 units	× 13,500 units	× 8,500 units
Total variance	**$4,750 F**	**$6,750 F**	**$8,500 F**

Therefore, total sales price variance = $4,750 F + $6,750 F + $8,500 F = **$20,000 F**

(ii) **Sales volume profit variance:**

	B	R	K
Expected volumes	10,000 units	13,000 units	9,000 units
Actual volumes	9,500 units	13,500 units	8,500 units
Variance	500 units A	500 units F	500 units A
× standard profit	$4.00	$3.00	$5.00
Total variance	**$2,000 A**	**$1,500F**	**$2,500 A**

Therefore, total sales volume profit variance = $2,000 A + $1,500 F + $2,500 A = **$3,000 A**

(iii) **Sales mix profit variance:**

	Standard Mix	**Standard Mix, Actual Quantity**	**Actual Mix, Actual Quantity**	**Difference**	**@ standard profit**	**Variance**
B	10,000 units	9,843.75	9,500 units	343.75 A	$4	$1,375 A
R	13,000 units	12,796.875	13,500 units	703.125 F	$3	$2,109.375 F
K	9,000 units	8,859.375	8,500 units A	359.375 A	$5	$1,796.875 A
	32,000	**31,500**	**31,500**			**$1,062.5 A**

Alternative method:

	Standard Profit per unit	**Weighted Average profit per unit**	**Difference**	**Difference actual sales/ budgeted sales**	**Difference**
B	$4	$3.875	$0.125	(500 units)	$62.50 A
R	$3	$3.875	$(0.875)	500 units	$437.50 A
K	$5	$3.875	$1.125	(500 units)	$562.50 A
					$1,062.5 A

(iv) **Sales quantity profit variance:**

	Standard Mix Actual Quantity	**Budgeted sales**	**Difference**	**Standard profit per unit**	**Variance**
B	9,843.75	10,000	156.25 A	$4	$625.00A
R	12,796.875	13,000	203.125 A	$3	$609.375A
K	8,859.375	9,000	140.625 A	$5	$703.125A
					$1,937.50A

Alternative method:

Budgeted total quantity		32,000 units
Actual total quantity	=	31,500 units
Variance		500 units Adverse

500 units adverse @ standard profit $3.875 = $1,937.5 Adverse

Test your understanding 15 – Market size and share

(a) Traditional sales volume variance

= (Actual units sold – Budgeted sales) × Standard profit per unit

= (450,000 – 400,000) × $3 = $150,000 F.

(b) Planning and operational variances The revised (ex-post) budget would show that Hudson Ltd should expect to sell 20% of 2.2 million units = 440,000 units.

Original sales × standard margin = 400,000 × $3 = $1,200,000

Market size = $120,000 F

Revised sales × standard margin = 440,000 × $3 = $1,320,000

Market share = $30,000 F

Actual sales × standard margin = 450,000 × $3 = $1,350,000

Total sales volume variance = $120,000 F + $30,000 F = $150,000 F

Comment:

Most of the favourable variance can be attributed to the increase in overall market size. However, some can be put down to effort by the sales force which has increased its share from 20% to 20.5% (450,000/ 2,200,000).

Managers should only be appraised on the operational variance, i.e. the market share variance.

Test your understanding 16 – Additional example

(a) Sales price variance

= 220,000 × ($14 – $12.50) = $330,000 A

Sales volume variance

= (250,000 – 220,000) × $4 = $120,000 A

(b) Budgeted market share = 250,000/1,000,000 = 25%

The company would have expected to achieve sales of 25% × 1,100,000 = 275,000 in the actual market conditions.

The market size variance

= (275,000 – 250,000) × $4 = $100,000 F

The market share variance

= (275,000 – 220,000) × $4 = $220,000 A

The increased market size is favourable as the company should sell more if market share can be maintained. The market share variance was adverse as market share fell from 25% to 220,000/1,100,000 = 20%.

(c) It could be argued that the increased competition in the market was not foreseen when the budget was set and the variance is thus a planning variance. However, this line of reasoning would suggest that any unforeseen issues give rise just to planning variances. Perhaps sales managers should have identified potential threats sooner? Also, once extra competition was experienced, managers had to decide how to respond. This could have involved additional advertising rather than price cuts, e.g. it could be argued that price cuts were made to try (unsuccessfully) to protect market share, in which case managers should be held (at least partly) responsible for such a decision.

Objective Test Case Question – The Alpha Company

(1) **D**

	AQSM	BQSM	Difference	Standard profit per unit	Variance ($)
A	440	400	40 A	$8	320 F
B	660	600	60 F	$6	360 F
C	1,100	1,000	100 F	$4	400 F
	2,200	2,000	200 F		1,080 F

(2) **A**

Statement (3) is not correct: managers can only be appraised on what they can control, i.e. on the operational variances for sales.

(3) **B**

Statement (1) is not correct; this would cause a favourable variance, not an adverse variance.

(4) **C**

Original budgeted sales 600 units × standard profit $6	$3,600
Revised budgeted sales 600 units × (1–10%) = 540 units, @ $6	$3,240
Planning variance (market size variance)	$360 A

(5) **D**

Revised budgeted sales 600 units × (1–10%) = 540 units, @ $6	$3,240
Actual sales quantity 700 units × standard profit $6	$4,200
Operational variance (market share variance)	$960 F

Test your understanding 17 – Price variances

AQ × AP: 10,000 × $5.18 = $51,800

> Operational variance $1,800 adverse

AQ × RSP: 10,000 × $5.00 = $50,000

> Planning variance $2,000 favourable

AQ × SP: 10,000 × $5.20 = $52,000

Operational variance: The cost per unit was higher than the revised budgeted cost resulting in the adverse variance. This variance is controllable by management and should be linked to their performance evaluation

Planning variance: The improvement in technology resulted in a lower price per unit and hence a favourable variance. This is a planning difference and is therefore uncontrollable by management.

A traditional variance calculation would present as follows:

AQ × AP : 10,000 × $5.18 = $51,800

> Price variance $200 Favourable

AQ × SP : 10,000 × $5.20 = $52,000

Test your understanding 18 – Price and usage variances

(a) **Traditional variances**

AQAP =		$41,500	
		Price variance	$2,500 F
AQSP =	11,000 × $4 =	$44,000	
		Usage variance	$4,800 A
SQSP =	1,400 × 7 × $4 =	$39,200	

(b) **Planning and operational variances**

Price

AQ × AP		= $41,500		
		Operational variance	**$300 F**	
AQ × RSP	11,000 × $3.80	= $41,800		
		Planning variance	**$2,200 F**	
AQ × SP	11,000 × $4	= $44,000		
			$2,500 F	

Usage

AQ × SP	11,000 × $4	= $44,000	
		Operational variance	**$800 F**
RSQ × SP	11,200 × $4	= $44,800	
		Planning variance	**$5,600 A**
SQ × SP	9,800 × $4	= $39,200	
			$4,800 A

Test your understanding 19

AH × SR	1,450 × $10	= $14,500	
		Operational variance	**$500 F**
RSH × SR	1,500 × $10	= $15,000	
		Planning variance	**$2,500 A**
SH × SR	1,250 × $10	= $12,500	
			$2,000 A

Learning curves and variances

The '8 hours' original standard does not take into account the presence of a learning curve effect, that affects the first 600 units. By the time we reach 560 units of production, we have an average time per unit of 3.0574 hours:

$$Y = 8 \text{ hours} \times 560 \text{ units}^{-0.1520}$$

Y = 3.0574 hours on average per unit (revised standard).

Therefore, the first 560 units should have taken:

8 hours per unit × 560 units = 4,480 hours using the original, old standard labour hours per unit, and

3.0574 hours per unit × 560 units = 1,712 hours, using the revised standard labour hours per unit.

This is a favourable difference of 2,768 hours and therefore the planning variance for labour efficiency may be calculated as 2,768 hours × $15 = $41,520 Favourable.

To calculate the operational variance, we compare the standard number of labour hours for actual production (1,712 hours, using the revised standard) and the actual time of 3,500 hours, giving 1,788 hours ADV × $15 = $26,820 ADV.

AH × SR	1,450 × $10	= $14,500	
		Operational variance	**$500 F**
RSH × SR	1,500 × $10	= $15,000	
		Planning variance	**$2,500 A**
SH × SR	1,250 × $10	= $12,500	
			$2,000 A

Test your understanding 20

Standard costing is most suited to organisations whose activities consist of a series of common or repetitive operations. Typically, mass production manufacturing operations are indicative of its area of application. It is also possible to envisage operations within the service sector to which standard costing may apply, though this may not be with the same degree of accuracy of standards which apply in manufacturing. For example, hotels and restaurants often use standard recipes for preparing food, so dealing with conference attendance can be like a mass production environment. Similarly, banks will have common processes for dealing with customer transactions, processing cheques, etc. It is possible therefore that the principles of standard costing may be extended to service industries.

In modern manufacturing and service businesses, continuous improvement and cost reduction are topical. In order to remain competitive it is essential that businesses address the cost levels of their various operations. To do this they have to deal with the costing of operations. But the drive to 'cost down' may mean in some cases that standards do not apply for long before a redesign or improvement renders them out of date. In such a setting an alternative to the use of standard costs is to compare actual costs with those of the previous operating period. We have seen above that a standard costing system has a variety of purposes. It is for management to judge their various reasons for employing standard costing and, consequently, whether their aims of continuous improvement and cost reduction render the system redundant.

Test your understanding 21

A is the correct answer.

Greater participation by staff in standard setting is likely to slow down the process of agreeing values.

[illegible]

Standard costing is most suited to organisations whose activities consist of a series of common or repetitive operations. Typically, mass production manufacturing [illegible] operations are [illegible] application. It is also possible to envisage operations within the service sector [illegible] though this may not be with the same degree of accuracy of standards which apply in manufacturing. For example, hotels and restaurants often use standard recipes for preparing food, so dealing with conference attendees can be like a mass production environment. [illegible] will have common processes for dealing with [illegible]. Here it is possible [illegible] standard costing may be extended to service industries.

In modern [illegible] and service businesses, continuous improvement and change [illegible] in order to remain competitive. It is essential that businesses address the cost levels of their various operations. [illegible] But the need to cost down may mean [illegible] standards do not [illegible] quality improvements [illegible] standard costs is to compare actual costs with those of the previous [illegible] period. [illegible] standard costing system [illegible] for management to judge their variance [illegible] consequently, whether that [illegible] continuous improvement [illegible] the system redundant.

[illegible]

A is the correct answer.

A greater participation by staff in standard setting is likely to slow down the process of agreeing values.

chapter

11

Performance measurement and control

Chapter learning objectives

Upon completion of this chapter you will be able to:

- describe, calculate from given data, and interpret financial performance indicators (FPIs) for profitability, in both manufacturing and service businesses, and suggest methods for improving these measures
- describe, calculate from given data, and interpret FPIs for liquidity in both manufacturing and service businesses, and suggest methods for improving these measures
- describe, calculate from given data, and interpret FPIs for risk in both manufacturing and service businesses, and suggest methods for improving these measures
- describe, calculate from given data and interpret non-financial performance indicators (NFPIs) in both manufacturing and service businesses, and suggest methods for improving the performance indicated
- explain, using non-numerical examples, the causes of, and problems created by, short-termism and financial manipulation of results, and suggest methods to encourage a long-term view
- describe the main behavioural aspects of performance management
- explain the need to allow for external considerations in performance management, in general, with particular reference to:
  - stakeholders
  - market conditions
  - allowance for competitors

- describe ways in which external considerations could be allowed for in performance management, in general, and interpret performance in the light of external considerations
- using simple non-numerical examples, explain and interpret the balanced scorecard and its elements
- using simple non-numerical examples, explain and interpret the building block model proposed by Fitzgerald and Moon
- describe, using simple non-numerical examples, the difficulties of target setting in qualitative areas.

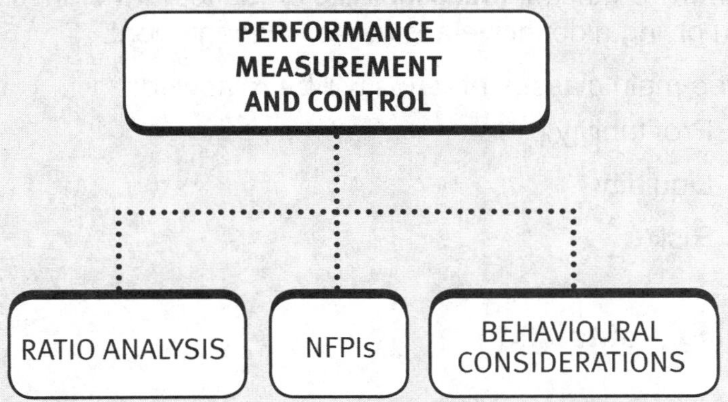

1 Introduction

The calculation of a particular indicator of performance will probably mean very little, unless it is set in some context. Establishing the value of a particular indicator will add little benefit until it is:

(1) compared with a budget

(2) set in a trend

(3) and/or set against a best practice benchmark.

2 Financial performance and ratio analysis

A key aspect of performance measurement is ratio analysis. Specific ratios are discussed below but some general considerations need to be taken into account with all ratio analysis:

- Many ratios use figures at a particular point in time and thus may not be representative of the position throughout a period. For example, seasonal trade or large one-off items may make year-end figures uncharacteristic.
- Ratios are of little use in isolation. Comparisons could be made to:
  - last year's figures to identify trends
  - competitors' results and/or industry averages to assess performance.
- Ratios can be manipulated by management. A well known example of 'window dressing' is to issue spurious invoices before the year end and then issue credit notes just after.

- As with variances, ratios indicate areas for further investigation, rather than giving a definitive answer for management.
- Three main classes of ratios will be reviewed:
  - Profitability
  - Liquidity
  - Risk.

Measuring profitability

The primary objective of a company is to maximise profitability. Profitability ratios can be used to monitor the achievement of this objective.

Gross profit margin

This is the gross profit as a percentage of turnover.

$$\text{Gross profit margin} = \frac{\text{Gross profit}}{\text{Turnover}} \times 100$$

A high gross profit margin is desirable. It indicates that either sales prices are high or that production costs are being kept well under control.

Net profit margin

This is the net profit (turnover less all expenses) as a percentage of turnover.

$$\text{Net profit margin} = \frac{\text{Net profit}}{\text{Turnover}} \times 100$$

A high net profit margin is desirable. It indicates that either sales prices are high or that all costs are being kept well under control.

Return of capital employed (ROCE)

This is a key measure of profitability. It is the net profit as a percentage of the capital employed. The ROCE shows the net profit that is generated from each $1 of assets employed.

$$\text{ROCE} = \frac{\text{Net profit}}{\text{Capital employed}} \times 100$$

Where capital employed = total assets less current liabilities **or** total equity plus long term debt.

ROCE is sometimes calculated using operating profit (profit before finance charges and tax) instead of net profit. If net profit is not given in the question, use operating profit instead.

A high ROCE is desirable. An increase in ROCE could be achieved by:

- Increasing net profit, e.g. through an increase in sales price or through better control of costs.
- Reducing capital employed, e.g. through the repayment of long term debt.

The ROCE can be understood further by calculating the net profit margin and the asset turnover:

ROCE = net profit margin × asset turnover

Asset turnover

This is the turnover divided by the capital employed. The asset turnover shows the turnover that is generated from each $1 of assets employed.

$$\text{Asset turnover} = \frac{\text{Turnover}}{\text{Capital employed}}$$

A high asset turnover is desirable. An increase in the asset turnover could be achieved by:

- Increasing turnover, e.g. through the launch of new products or a successful advertising campaign.
- Reducing capital employed, e.g. through the repayment of long term debt.

Test your understanding 1 – Profitability ratios

The following figures are extracted from the accounts of Super Soups, a company selling gourmet homemade soups.

	20X9	20X8
	$	$
Total production costs	6,538,000	5,082,000
Gross profit	3,006,000	2,582,000
Net profit	590,000	574,000
Total capital employed	6,011,000	5,722,000

Required:

Using appropriate ratios, comment on the profitability of Super Soups.

Additional example on profitability ratios

Companies X and Y are both involved in retailing. Relevant information for the year ended 30 September 20X5 was as follows:

	X	Y
	$000	$000
Sales revenue	50,000	200,000
Profit before tax	10,000	10,000
Capital employed	50,000	50,000

Required:

Prepare the following ratios for both companies and comment on the results:

(a) ROCE

(b) profit margin

(c) asset turnover.

Solution

	X		Y	
ROCE	$\frac{10{,}000}{50{,}000}$	× 100%	$\frac{10{,}000}{50{,}000}$	× 100%
	= 20%		= 20%	
Profit margin	$\frac{10{,}000}{50{,}000}$	× 100%	$\frac{10{,}000}{200{,}000}$	× 100%
	= 20%		= 5%	
Asset turnover	$\frac{50{,}000}{50{,}000}$		$\frac{200{,}000}{50{,}000}$	
	= 1		= 4	

The ROCE for both companies is the same. X has a higher profit margin, whilst Y shows a more efficient use of assets. This indicates that there may be a trade-off between profit margin and asset turnover.

Measuring liquidity

A company can be profitable but at the same time encounter cash flow problems. Liquidity and working capital ratios give some indication of the company's liquidity.

Current ratio

This is the current assets divided by the current liabilities.

$$\text{Current ratio} = \frac{\text{Current assets}}{\text{Current liabilities}}$$

The ratio measures the company's ability to meet its short term liabilities as they fall due.

A ratio in excess of 1 is desirable but the expected ratio varies between the type of industry.

A decrease in the ratio year on year or a figure that is below the industry average could indicate that the company has liquidity problems. The company should take steps to improve liquidity, e.g. by paying creditors as they fall due or by better management of receivables in order to reduce the level of bad debts.

Quick ratio (acid test)

This is a similar to the current ratio but inventory is removed from the current assets due to its poor liquidity in the short term.

$$\text{Current ratio} = \frac{\text{Current assets} - \text{Inventory}}{\text{Current liabilities}}$$

The comments are the same as for the current ratio.

Inventory holding period

$$\text{Inventory holding period} = \frac{\text{Inventory}}{\text{Cost of sales}} \times 365$$

This indicates the average number of days that inventory items are held for.

An increase in the inventory holding period could indicate that the company is having problems selling its products and could also indicate that there is an increased level of obsolete stock. The company should take steps to increase stock turnover, e.g. by removing any slow moving or unpopular items of stock and by getting rid of any obsolete stock.

A decrease in the inventory holding period could be desirable as the company's ability to turn over inventory has improved and the company does not have excess cash tied up in inventory. However, any reductions should be reviewed further as the company may be struggling to manage its liquidity and may not have the cash available to hold the optimum level of inventory.

Receivables (debtor) collection period

$$\text{Receivables collection period} = \frac{\text{Receivables}}{\text{Turnover}} \times 365$$

This is the average period it takes for a company's debtors to pay what they owe.

An increase in the receivables collection period could indicate that the company is struggling to manage its debts. Possible steps to reduce the ratio include:

- Credit checks on customers to ensure that they will pay on time
- Improved credit control, e.g. invoicing on time, chasing up bad debts.

A decrease in the receivables collection period may indicate that the company's has improved its management of receivables. However, a receivables collection period well below the industry average may make the company uncompetitive and profitability could be impacted as a result.

Payables (creditor) period

$$\text{Payables period} = \frac{\text{Payables}}{\text{Purchases}} \times 365$$

This is the average period it takes for a company to pay for its purchases.

An increase in the company's payables period could indicate that the company is struggling to pay its debts as they fall due. However, it could simply indicate that the company is taking better advantage of any credit period offered to them.

A decrease in the company's payables period could indicate that the company's ability to pay for its purchases on time is improving. However, the company should not pay for its purchases too early since supplier credit is a useful source of finance.

Test your understanding 2 – Liquidity ratios

Calculate the liquidity and working capital ratios for P for the year ended 31 December 20X9.

	$m
Sales revenue	1,867.5
Gross profit	489.3
Inventory	147.9
Trade receivables	393.4
Trade payables	275.1
Cash	53.8
Short-term investments	6.2
Other current liabilities	284.3

Measuring risk

In addition to managing profitability and liquidity it is also important for a company to manage its risk. The following ratios may be calculated:

Financial gearing

This is the long term debt as a percentage of equity.

$$\text{Gearing} = \frac{\text{Debt}}{\text{Equity}} \times 100$$

$$\textbf{or} = \frac{\text{Debt}}{\text{Debt + Equity}} \times 100$$

A high level of gearing indicates that the company relies heavily on debt to finance its long term needs. This increases the level of risk for the business since interest and capital repayments must be made on debt, where as there is no obligation to make payments to equity.

The ratio could be improved by reducing the level of long term debt and raising long term finance using equity.

Interest cover

This is the operating profit (profit before finance charges and tax) divided by the finance cost.

$$\text{Interest cover} = \frac{\text{Operating profit}}{\text{Finance cost}}$$

A decrease in the interest cover indicates that the company is facing an increased risk of not being able to meet its finance payments as they fall due.

The ratio could be improved by taking steps to increase the operating profit, e.g. through better management of costs, or by reducing finance costs through reducing the level of debt.

Dividend cover

This is the net profit divided by the dividend.

$$\text{Dividend cover} = \frac{\text{Net profit}}{\text{Dividend}}$$

A decrease in the dividend cover indicates that the company is facing an increased risk of not being able to make its dividend payments to shareholders.

Ratio analysis – Additional example

You are employed in the small business section of a medium-sized bank. Some time ago the bank provided a local manufacturing company, F, with an overdraft facility of $3,000,000. This limit was reached on 30 September 20X4 but was increased then to $5,000,000.

Your section head has just received the half-yearly financial statements of F for the period to 30 September 20X5. Having read these statements, your section head is extremely concerned as to the performance of the company over the last year and is considering recommending the termination of the overdraft facility. Before making any further decision, your section head wishes to have a second opinion. Accordingly, he leaves a file of information concerning F on your desk and requires a report recommending the best course of action.

Information contained in the file:

Item 1: Profit and Loss/Income statements:

	Six months to 30 September 20X5	Six months to 31 March 20X5
	$000	$000
Sales	10,000	11,000
Cost of sales	(5,000)	(5,500)
Gross profit	5,000	5,500
Other operating expenses	(5,000)	(4,500)
Operating profit	–	1,000
Interest payable	(1,000)	(900)
Profit/(loss) before tax	(1,000)	100
Tax estimate	–	–
Profit/(loss) after tax	(1,000)	100

Item 2: Statements of Financial Position at 30 September

	20X5		20X4	
	$000	$000	$000	$000
Non-current assets:				
Property	5,000		5,200	
Plant	3,500		3,000	
		8,500		8,200
Current assets:				
Inventories	3,000		2,600	
Receivables	5,000		4,600	
Cash in hand	80		80	
	8,080		7,280	

Current liabilities:		
Trade payables	2,600	2,600
Bank overdraft	5,000	3,000
	7,600	5,600
NCAs	480	1,680
12% loan notes		
(secured against the property)	(4,800)	(4,800)
	4,180	5,080
Share capital ($1 shares)	4,000	4,000
Retained earnings	180	1,080
	4,180	5,080

Item 3: Estimated realisable values of the assets of F at 30 September 20X5, based on a 'forced sale' scenario:

	$000
Property	5,000
Plant	1,000
Inventories	800
Receivables	2,500
	9,300

(a) Using the items contained in the file, write a report to your section head which contains an appraisal of the performance and financial position of F and considers the implications for the bank of calling in the overdraft.

(b) Produce a short appendix to the report you have compiled in (a). This should summarise the limitations of the information available to you as a basis for making a recommendation as to the wisdom or otherwise of calling in the overdraft.

(c) Discuss THREE key areas, with recommendations, that the management of F need to address to improve performance.

Solution

REPORT

To: Section head

From: Bank accountant

Subject: F

Date: 22 November 20X5

(a) The performance of F appears to have deteriorated in the six months to 30 September 20X5. Sales and cost of sales have both fallen by 9%, so that the gross profit percentage of 50% has been maintained. However, operating expenses have increased, so that total operating costs equal operating income. There is no longer any cover for interest payments. The interest charge has also increased, following the increase in the overdraft facility.

Despite this deterioration in performance, non-current assets and current assets have increased. The additional $2 million provided by the bank (an increase in overdraft of 66%) appears to have been used to finance the purchase of plant at a cost of approximately $500,000 (the figure represents the change shown by the balance sheet and is net of depreciation). The additional depreciation has probably contributed to the increase in operating expenses.

The retained loss for the year is $900,000 but the actual cash outflow from operating activities is much greater than this. A rough calculation is given below:

	$000
Loss	900
Less depreciation (buildings only)	(200)
Increase in inventories	400
Increase in receivables	400
	1,500

The company's financial position has deteriorated during the year. At 30 September 20X5 it had a current ratio of 1.06 :1 and a quick ratio of 0.67:1 (compared with 1.3:1 and 0.83:1 at 30 September 20X4). The company is likely to experience severe liquidity problems in the near future.

The company's gearing also gives cause for concern. The company is very dependent upon finance from outside the business. The most recent balance sheet shows a debt to equity ratio of (5,000 + 4,800)/4,180 = 2.34. Interest on the loan notes amounts to $576,000 annually. At current activity levels, this means that there is very little profit available for distribution or investment and very little interest cover. The loan notes are barely covered by the property on which they are secured.

The combination of adverse cash flow, increase in non-current assets and working capital and fall in profits seems to suggest bad management. However, it is impossible to reach a firm conclusion without further information.

The withdrawal of the overdraft facility would result in the liquidation of the company. It is estimated that the assets would realise $9,300,000. The loan note holders would be repaid their $4,800,000 in full, leaving a balance of $4,500,000 for the other creditors. This does not cover the $7,600,000 owed to the bank and the other creditors. Assuming that all unsecured creditors would rank equally, the bank would receive 59c in the dollar or $2,950,000. The bank would make a loss of $2,050,000.

These calculations show that the bank is facing considerable risk. If the overdraft facility is to be continued, the bank should consider renegotiating the terms in order to take account of this risk.

(b) **Appendix**

Only limited information is available as a basis for making this decision.

One major shortcoming of conventional financial statements is that they are based on historical information. They give a good indication of the financial position at 30 September 20X5, but some time has already elapsed since that date. During that time the position could have changed dramatically. For example, the company could have won substantial new business, or receivables could have been realised, or inventory could have been sold. Financial statements are only of limited use in predicting the future of a company.

To make an informed decision, the bank would need information about several other factors which are not reflected in the financial statements. The velocity of circulation of working capital, the quality of the company's management and its ability to attract new business will all be crucial in determining whether or not F survives. For example, the decision to invest in additional plant and to increase inventory levels might have been taken as a result of several new orders. The bank would also need to assess the willingness of the loan note holders and other creditors to continue to support the company. For example, there is no information as to how soon the loan notes will become repayable or as to the means by which the company intends to repay the loan.

(c) Key areas the management of F need to address include the following:

Sales performance

Management need to investigate why sales have fallen and the extent to which this is a volume fall or/and a price drop. Based on the competitive/strategic reasons for the fall, the management can then take appropriate action. For example, given margins have remained constant it looks like the issue is one of lost customers. If research reveals that this is due to rivals' price cuts, then F will have to consider whether to respond with similar cuts to remain competitive.

Liquidity

The pressure on the overdraft, together with worsening quick and current ratios indicate that urgent action is required to improve working capital management. Both inventory and receivables days are higher so this is a good place to start. The management of F should investigate why customers are taking longer to pay and rectify. If simply an issue of inefficiency, then this can be sorted by recruiting a new credit controller. If however, there have been customer complaints due to poor quality, then the issue of delayed payment can only be rectified by resolving customer concerns more quickly. Similarly, inventory days may be due to poor sales and the solution thus the same.

Financing

Using the overdraft to finance the purchase of non-current assets is not sustainable. The management of F need to reconsider their long term financing strategy, say through seeking new equity via a rights issue or raising additional long term loan finance.

3 Issues surrounding the use of financial performance indicators to monitor performance

All of the ratios reviewed so far have concentrated on the financial performance of the business. Many of these ratios, e.g. ROCE, gross profit margin, may be used to assess the performance of a division and of the manager's in charge of that division.

Achievement of these target ratios (financial performance indicators) may be linked to a reward system in order to motivate managers to improve performance.

However, there are a number of problems associated with the use of financial performance indicators to monitor performance:

Short-termism

Linking rewards to financial performance may tempt managers to make decisions that will improve short-term financial performance but may have a negative impact on long-term profitability. E.g. they may decide to cut investment or to purchase cheaper but poorer quality materials.

Manipulation of results

In order to achieve the target financial performance and hence their reward, managers may be tempted to manipulate results. For example:

Accelerating revenue – revenue included in one year may be wrongly included in the previous year in order to improve the financial performance for the earlier year.

Delaying costs – costs incurred in one year may be wrongly recorded in the next year's accounts in order to improve performance and meet targets for the earlier year.

Understating a provision or accrual – this would improve the financial performance and may result in the targets being achieved.

Manipulation of accounting policies – for example, closing inventory values may be overstated resulting in an increase in profits for the year.

Do not convey the full picture

The use of these short-term financial performance indicators has limited benefit to the company as it does not convey the full picture regarding the factors that will drive long-term profitability, e.g. customer satisfaction, quality.

Therefore, when monitoring performance, a broader range of measures should be used. This will be reviewed in the next section.

Illustration 1 – Problems of financial performance indicators

A company may measure the performance of managers on the basis of a target ROCE. This may lead to the following undesirable behaviour:

- Managers may focus on generating short-term profit at the expense of long-term profit. For example, managers may reduce expenditure on training, research and development and maintenance.
- The ROCE will improve if the capital employed figure falls. Managers may therefore be reluctant to invest in new assets.
- Year-end results may be manipulated to improve ROCE. For example, managers may delay payments to creditors or stock purchases.
- Managers may focus their attention on financial performance and neglect non-financial performance such as quality and customer service. This may improve profit in the short-term but lead to a long-term decline in profitability.

Test your understanding 3

Suggest methods of overcoming the problems of short-termism and manipulation of results and encouraging a long-term view.

4 Non-financial performance indicators (NFPIs)

Introduction

- The previous section reviewed the problems of using financial performance indicators as the sole indicator of performance.
- This section will review the use of non-financial performance indicators as an additional tool to monitor performance and maximise long-term profitability.
- As we will see, a company may choose to use a mixture of financial and non-financial performance indicators in order to achieve the optimum system for performance measurement and control.

- A firm's success usually involves focussing on a small number of critical areas that they must excel at. These factors vary from business to business but could include:
  - Having a wide range of products that people want.
  - Having a strong brand name or image.
  - Low prices.
  - Quick delivery.
  - Customer satisfaction, perhaps through high quality.
- Most of these are best assessed using non-financial performance indicators. Financial performance appraisal often reveals the ultimate effect of operational factors and decisions but non-financial indicators are needed to monitor causes.

Illustration 2 – Non-financial performance measurement

BAA (the former state-owned British Airports Authority) uses regular customer surveys for measuring customer perceptions of a wide variety of service quality attributes, including:

- the cleanliness of its facilities
- the helpfulness of its staff
- the ease of finding one's way around the airport.

Public correspondence is also analysed in detail, and comment cards are available in the terminals so that passengers can comment voluntarily on service levels received.

Duty terminal managers also sample the services and goods offered by outlets in the terminals, assessing them from a customer perspective. They check the cleanliness and condition of service facilities and complete detailed checklists, which are submitted daily to senior terminal managers.

The company has also a wealth of internal monitoring systems that record equipment faults and failures, and report equipment and staff availability.

These systems are supported by the terminal managers who circulate the terminals on a full-time basis, helping customers as necessary, reporting any equipment faults observed and making routine assessments of the level of service provided by BAA and its concessionaires.

Test your understanding 4

Better Nutrition Ltd provides advice to clients in medical, dietary and fitness matters by offering consultation with specialist staff. The budget information for the year ended 31 May 2010 is as follows:

	Budget	**Actual**
Total client enquiries		
– New Business	50,000	80,000
– Repeat business	30,000	20,000
Number of client consultations		
– New Business	15,000	20,000
– Repeat business	12,000	10,000
Mix of client consultations		
– Medical	6,000	5,500 (note)
– Dietary	12,000	10,000
– Fitness	9,000	14,500
Number of consultants employed		
– Medical	6	4 (note)
– Dietary	12	12
– Fitness	9	12
Number of client complaints	270	600

Note: Client consultations includes those carried out by outside specialists. There are now 4 full-time consultants carrying out the remainder of client consultations.

Other information:

(i) Clients are charged a fee per consultation at the rate of: medical $75; dietary $50 and fitness $50.

(ii) Health foods are recommended and provided only to dietary clients at an average cost to the company of $10 per consultation. Clients are charged for such health foods at cost plus 100% mark-up.

(iii) Each customer enquiry incurs a variable cost of $3, whether or not it is converted into a consultation.

(iv) Consultants are each paid a fixed annual salary as follows: medical $40,000; dietary $28,000; fitness $25,000.

(v) Sundry other fixed cost: $300,000.

Actual results for the year to 31 May 2010 incorporate the following additional information:

(i) A reduction of 10% in health food costs to the company per consultation was achieved through a rationalisation of the range of foods made available.

(ii) Medical salary costs were altered through dispensing with the services of two full-time consultants and sub-contracting outside specialists as required. A total of 1,900 consultations were sub-contracted to outside specialists who were paid $50 per consultation.

(iii) Fitness costs were increased by $80,000 through the hire of equipment to allow sophisticated cardio-vascular testing of clients.

(iv) New computer software has been installed to provide detailed records and scheduling of all client enquiries and consultations. This software has an annual operating cost (including depreciation) of $50,000.

Required:

(a) Prepare a statement showing the financial results for the year to 31 May 2010 in tabular format. This should show:

(i) the budget and actual gross margin for each type of consultation and for the company

(ii) the actual net profit for the company

(iii) the budget and actual margin ($) per consultation for each type of consultation
(Expenditure for each expense heading should be shown in (i) and (ii) as relevant.)

(b) Suggest ways in which each of the following performance measures could be used to supplement the financial results calculated in (a). You should include relevant quantitative analysis for each performance measure:

(1) Competitiveness

(2) Flexibility

(3) Resource utilisation

(4) Quality

(5) Innovation.

The balanced scorecard

The balanced scorecard approach to performance measurement and control emphasises the need to provide management with a set of information which covers all relevant areas of performance.

It focuses on four different perspectives and uses financial and non-financial indicators.

The four perspectives are:

Customer – what is it about us that new and existing customers value?

Internal – what processes must we excel at to achieve our financial and customer objectives?

Innovation and learning – how can we continue to improve and create future value?

Financial – how do we create value for our shareholders?

Within each of these perspectives a company should seek to identify a series of goals and measures.

Test your understanding 5

Faster Pasta is an Italian fast food restaurant that specialises in high quality, moderately priced authentic Italian pasta dishes and pizzas. The restaurant has recently decided to implement a balanced scorecard approach and has established the following relevant goals for each perspective:

Perspective	**Goal**
Customer perspective	• To increase the number of new and returning customers
	• To reduce the % of customer complaints
Internal	• To reduce the time taken between taking a customer's order and delivering the meal to the customer
	• To reduce staff turnover
Innovation and learning	• To increase the proportion of revenue from new dishes
	• To increase the % of staff time spent on training
Financial	• To increase spend per customer
	• To increase gross profit margin

The following information is also available for the year just ended and for the previous year.

	20X8	20X9
Total customers	11,600	12,000
– of which are new customers	4,400	4,750
– of which are existing customers	7,200	7,250
Customer complaints	464	840
Time between taking order and customer receiving meal	4 mins	13 mins
% staff turnover	12%	40%
% time staff spend training	5%	2%
Revenue	$110,000	$132,000
– revenue from new dishes	$22,000	$39,600
– revenue from existing dishes	$88,000	$92,400
Gross profit	$22,000	$30,360

Required:

Using appropriate measures, calculate and comment on whether or not Faster Pasta has achieved its goals.

Additional example on the balanced scorecard

One example reported in management literature of how the balanced scorecard might be applied is the US case of Analog Devices (a semi conductor manufacturer) in the preparation of its five-year strategic plan for 1988–1992.

Analog Devices had as its main corporate objective:

'Achieving our goals for growth, profits, market share and quality creates the environment and economic means to satisfy the needs of our employees, stockholders, customers and others associated with the firm. Our success depends on people who understand the interdependence and congruence of their personal goals with those of the company and who are thus motivated to contribute towards the achievement of those goals.'

Three basic strategic objectives identified by the company were market leadership, sales growth and profitability.

The company adopted targets as follows:

Customer perspective

- Percentage of orders delivered on time. A target was set for the five-year period to increase the percentage of on-time deliveries from 85% to at least 99.8%.
- Outgoing defect levels. The target was to reduce the number of defects in product items delivered to customers from 500, to fewer than 10, per month.
- Order lead time. A target was set to reduce the time between receiving a customer order to delivery from 10, to less than 3, weeks.

Internal perspective

- Manufacturing cycle time. To reduce this from 15 weeks to 4–5 weeks over the five-year planning period.
- Defective items in production. To reduce defects in production from 5,000, to fewer than 10, per month.

Learning and innovation perspective

- Having products rated 'number one' by at least 50% of customers, based on their attitudes to whether the company was making the right products, performance, price, reliability, quality, delivery, lead time, customer support, responsiveness, willingness to co-operate and willingness to form partnerships.
- The number of new products introduced to the market.
- Sales revenue from new products.
- The new product sales ratio. This was the percentage of total sales achieved by products introduced to the market within the previous six quarters.
- Average annual revenues for new products in their third year.
- Reducing the average time to bring new product ideas to the market.

Financial targets were set for revenue, revenue growth, profit and return on assets. But the idea was that the financial targets would flow from achieving the other targets stated above.

Analog Devices sought to adopt financial and non-financial performance measures within a single system, in which the various targets were consistent with each other and were in no way incompatible.

Benefits of the balanced scorecard:

- It focuses on factors, including non-financial ones, which will enable a company to succeed in the long-term.
- It provides external as well as internal information.

Problems with the balanced scorecard:

- The selection of measures can be difficult. For example, how should the company measure innovation?
- Obtaining information can be difficult. For example, obtaining feedback from customers can prove difficult.
- Information overload due to the large number of measures that may be chosen.
- Conflict between measures. For example, profitability may increase in the short-term through a reduction in expenditure on staff training.

The building block model

Fitzgerald and Moon developed a framework for the design and analysis of performance management systems, particularly within the context of service industries.

They based their analysis on three building blocks:

Dimensions

Dimensions are the goals for the business and suitable measures must be developed to measure each performance dimension. Dimensions are the areas that yield specific performance metrics for a company.

The six dimensions in the building block model can be split into two categories:

- downstream results (competitive and financial performance) and
- upstream determinants (quality of service, flexibility, resource utilisation and innovation) of those results.

The last four are the drivers of the top two.

Standards

Standards are the targets set for the metrics chosen from the dimensions.

To ensure success it is vital that employees view standards as achievable, fair and take ownership of them.

Rewards

Rewards are the motivators for the employees to work towards the standards set.

The reward system should be clearly understood by the staff and ensure their motivation. The rewards should be related to areas of responsibility that the staff member controls in order to achieve that motivation.

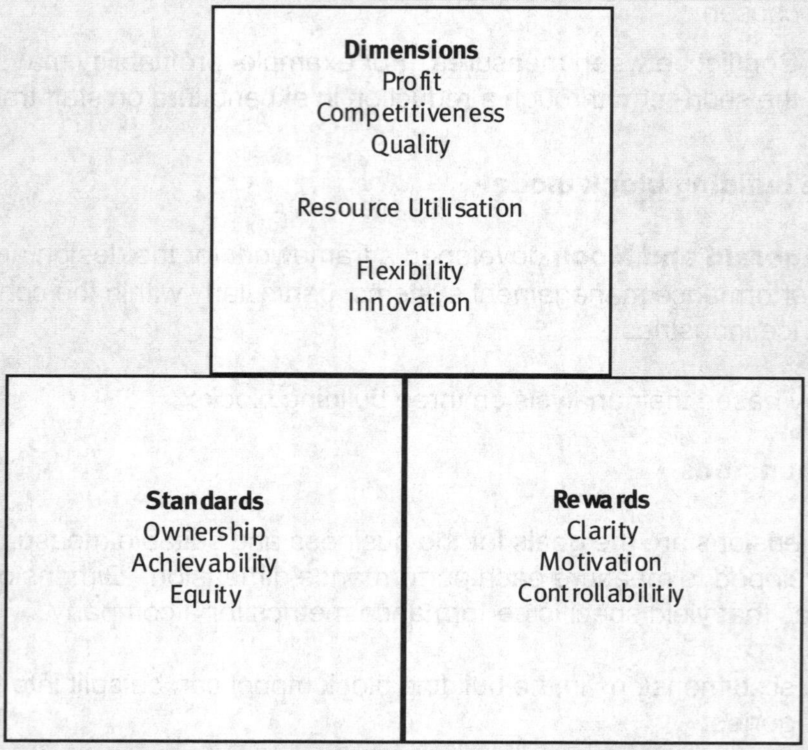

Dimensions
Profit
Competitiveness
Quality

Resource Utilisation

Flexibility
Innovation

Standards
Ownership
Achievability
Equity

Rewards
Clarity
Motivation
Controllabilitiy

Performance Dimension (goal)	Examples of standards (measures)
Competitive performance.	Market share. Sales growth. Customer base.
Financial performance.	Profitability. Liquidity. Risk.
Quality of service.	Reliability. Responsiveness. Competence.
Flexibility.	Volume flexibility. Delivery speed.
Resource utilisation.	Productivity. Efficiency.
Innovation.	Ability to innovate. Performance of the innovations.

Test your understanding 6 – Standards and rewards

Explain why it is important to:

(i) consider ownership, achievability and equity when setting standards

(ii) consider clarity, motivation and controllability when setting rewards.

Additional example on the building block model

Required:

Using the six dimensions of Fitzgerald and Moon suggest some measures (standards) for a national car dealership network.

Solution

Dimension	**Measures**
Financial performance.	• Profit per dealer. • Average margins. • Average discount agreed as a % of displayed list price.
Competitive performance.	• Local market share (e.g. look at new car registrations by postcode). • National market share (e.g. from published market research data).
Quality of service.	• 'Mystery shopper data', i.e. outside consultants visit or ring dealerships posing as customers. • Post-sale satisfaction surveys of customers.
Flexibility.	• Post-sale satisfaction surveys of customers to highlight whether they felt sales staff were flexible in getting different vehicle specifications, etc.
Resource utilisation.	• Sales per employee. • Sales per square metre of available floor space. • Average length of time a second hand car (e.g. taken as part-exchange) remains unsold.
Innovation.	• Central inspection by senior staff could enable a subjective assessment of local innovation to be made.

5 External considerations

Performance measures provide useful information to management which aid in the control of the business.

However, they need to be considered in the context of the environment external to the business to gain a full understanding of how the business has performed and to develop actions which should be taken to improve performance. External considerations which are particularly important are:

- **Stakeholders** – a stakeholder is any individual or group that has an interest in the business and may include:
  - shareholders
  - employees
  - loan providers
  - government
  - community
  - customers
  - environmental groups.

  Stakeholders will have different objectives and companies may deal with this by having a range of performance measures to assess the achievement of these objectives.

- **Market conditions** – these will impact business performance. For example, a downturn in the industry or in the economy as a whole could have a negative impact on performance.
- **Competitors** – the actions of competitors must also be considered. For example, company demand may decrease if a competitor reduces its prices or launches a successful advertising campaign.

Test your understanding 7 – Stakeholder considerations

NW is an electricity and gas provider for residential and business properties.

The business was nationalised in the past (State owned) but has more recently become a privatised company.

Annual data from NW's accounts are provided below relating to its first three years of operation as a private sector concern.

Also shown, for comparison, is the proforma data as included in the privatisation documents. The proforma accounts are notional accounts prepared to show the performance of the company in its last year under public ownership as if it had applied private sector accounting conventions. They also incorporate a dividend payment based on the dividend policy declared in the prospectus.

The activities of privatised utilities are scrutinised by a regulatory body, which restricts the extent to which prices can be increased.

The demand for gas and electricity in the area served by NW has risen over time at a steady 2% pa , largely reflecting demographic trends.

Key financial and operating data for year ending 31 December ($m)

	20X1 (proforma)	**20X2 (actual)**	**20X3 (actual)**	**20X4 (actual)**
Turnover	450	480	540	620
Met profit	26	35	55	75
Taxation	5	6	8	10
Profit after tax	21	29	47	65
Dividends	7	10	15	20
Total assets	100	119	151	191
Capital expenditure	20	30	60	75
Wage bill	100	98	90	86
Directors' emoluments	0.8	2.0	2.3	3.0
Employees (number)	12,000	11,800	10,500	10,000
Retail price index (RPI)	100	102	105	109

Required:

Using the data provided, assess the extent to which NW has met the interests of the following groups of stakeholders in its first three years as a privatised enterprise. If relevant, suggest what other data would be helpful in forming a more balanced view.

(i) Shareholders

(ii) Consumers

(iii) Workforce

(iv) Government, through NW's contribution to the achievement of the government's objectives of price stability and economic growth.

6 Chapter summary

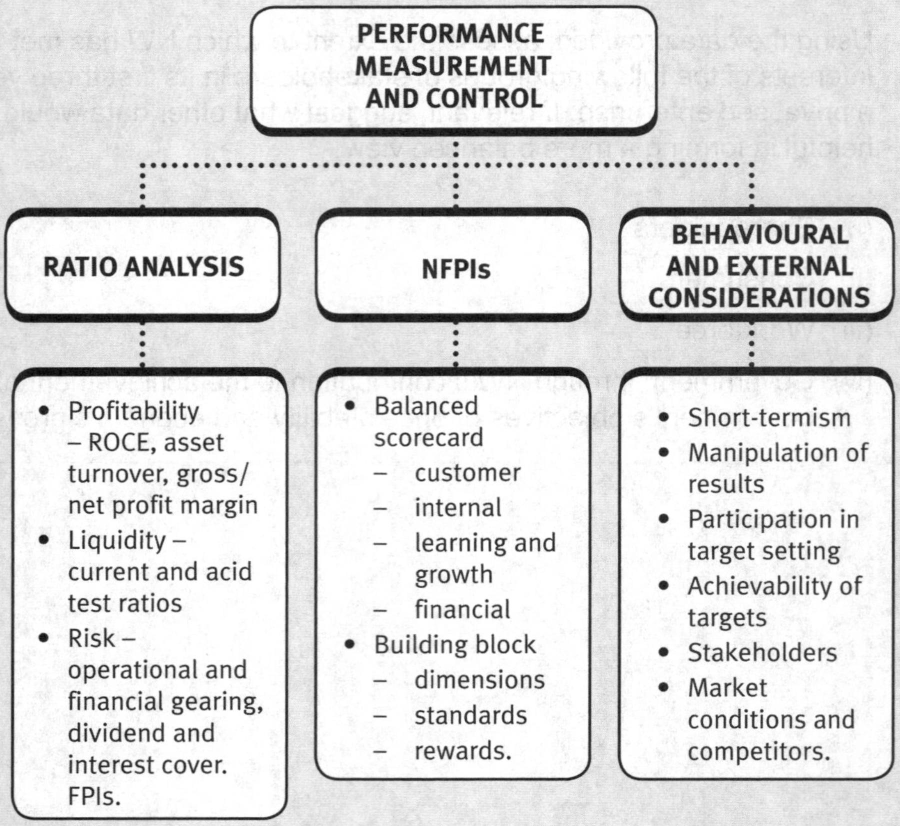

PERFORMANCE MEASUREMENT AND CONTROL

RATIO ANALYSIS

- Profitability – ROCE, asset turnover, gross/net profit margin
- Liquidity – current and acid test ratios
- Risk – operational and financial gearing, dividend and interest cover. FPIs.

NFPIs

- Balanced scorecard
  - customer
  - internal
  - learning and growth
  - financial
- Building block
  - dimensions
  - standards
  - rewards.

BEHAVIOURAL AND EXTERNAL CONSIDERATIONS

- Short-termism
- Manipulation of results
- Participation in target setting
- Achievability of targets
- Stakeholders
- Market conditions and competitors.

Test your understanding answers

Test your understanding 1 – Profitability ratios

Profitability ratios

	20X9	20X8
Gross profit margin = gross profit/turnover (%)	31.50%	33.69%
Net profit margin = net profit/turnover (%)	6.18%	7.49%
ROCE = net profit/cap. emp. (%)	9.82%	10.03%
Asset turnover = turnover/cap. emp.	1.59	1.34
Note: Turnover = total production cost + gross profit	9,544,000	7,664,000

Comment

Overall, profitability has deteriorated slightly year on year.

Gross profit margin – Despite an increase in turnover of 24.6%, the gross profit margin has fallen by over 2% to 31.5%. Although turnover has shown a significant increase, the production costs have increased at a faster rate of 28.7% year on year. The falling gross profit margin may indicate that the company is unable to achieve the same level of sales prices as it was in 20X8 or is not as efficient at controlling its production costs.

Net profit margin – Again, despite an increase in turnover of 24.6%, the net profit margin has fallen from 7.49% to 6.18%. The falling net profit margin may indicate that the company is unable to achieve the same level of sales prices as it was in 20X8 or is not as efficient at controlling all of its costs.

Asset turnover – this has actually shown a small improvement year on year from 1.34 in 20X8 to 1.59 in 20X9. This shows that the company is getting better at generating turnover from the capital employed within the business.

ROCE – Despite the improvement in asset turnover, the ROCE has actually fallen slightly from 10.03% in 20X8 to 9.83% in 20X9. This means that the company is not as good at generating net profit from its capital employed. The decrease in the ROCE is due to the fall in the net profit margin.

It would be useful to obtain a further breakdown of turnover and costs, in order to fully understand the reasons for the changes and to prevent any further decline in the ratios discussed. It would also be useful to obtain the average ratios for the industry in order to gauge Super Soups performance against that of its competitors.

Test your understanding 2 – Liquidity ratios

Current ratio	(147.9 + 393.4 + 53.8 + 6.2)/ = 601.3/559.4 (275.1 + 284.3)	
	=	1.07
Quick ratio	(601.3 – 147.9)/559.4 =	0.81
Receivables payment period	393.4/1,867.5 × 365 =	77 days
Inventory turnover period	147.9/(1,867.5 – 489.3) × 365 =	39 days
Payables payment period	275.1/(1,867.5 – 489.3) × 365 =	73 days

Test your understanding 3

- Rewards may be linked to a wider variety of performance measures including some non-financial measures.
- Capital investment decisions may be reviewed centrally and judged on the basis of net present value (NPV).
- Managers may be rewarded according to the overall performance of the company rather than their own responsibility centre. This may help goal congruence but may not be motivating if poorly-performing managers are rewarded in the same way as managers who are performing well.

Test your understanding 4

(a) **Operating statement for the year ended 31 May 2010**

	Medical	Dietary	Fitness	Total
	$000	$000	$000	$000
Budget				
Client fees	450.0	600.0	450.0	1,500.0
Healthfood mark-up (cost × 100%)		120.0		120.0
Salaries	(240.0)	(336.0)	(225.0)	(801.0)
Budget gross margin	210.0	384.0	225.0	819.0
Variances				
Fee income gain/(loss)	(37.5)	(100.0)	275.0	137.5
Health food mark-up loss		(30.0)		(30.0)
Salaries increase	(15.0)		(75.0)	(90)
Extra fitness equipment			(80)	(80)
Actual gross margin				
Less: Company costs				
Enquiry costs – budget				(240)
Enquiry costs – variance				(60)
General fixed costs				(300.0)
Software systems cost				(50.0)
Actual net profit				106.5
Budget margin per consultation ($)	35.00	32.00	25.00	
Actual margin per consultation ($)	28.64	25.40	23.79	

(b) Competitiveness may be measured in terms of the relative success/failure in obtaining business from enquiries from customers. The percentages are as follows.

	Budget	Actual
Uptake from enquiries		
New business	30%	25%
Repeat business	40%	50%

Repeat business suggests customer loyalty. The new business figures are disappointing, being below the budgeted level of uptake. In absolute terms, however, new business is 5,000 consultations above budget whereas repeat business is 2,000 consultations below budget.

There are variations within the types of consultation. Medical and dietary are down on budget by approximately 8% and 16% respectively. Fitness is up on budget by approximately 60%.

Flexibility may relate to the company being able to cope with flexibility of volume, delivery speed and job specification. Examples of each may be taken from the information in the management accounts. Additional fitness staff have been employed to cope with the extra volume of clients in this area of business.

Medical staff levels have been reorganised to include the use of external specialists. This provides flexibility where the type of advice required (the job specification) is wider than expected and may improve delivery speed in arranging a consultation more quickly for a client.

Dietary staff numbers are unchanged even though the number of consultations has fallen by 16% from budget. This may indicate a lack of flexibility. It may be argued that the fall in consultations would warrant a reduction in consultant numbers from 12 to 11. This could cause future flexibility problems, however, if there was an upturn in this aspect of the business.

Resource utilisation measures the ratio of output achieved from input resources. In this case the average consultations per consultant may be used as a guide:

	Average consultations per consultant		
	Budget	Actual	Rise (+) or fall (–) %
Medical (full-time only)	1,000	900	–10%
Dietary	1,000	833	–16.7%
Fitness	1,000	1,208	+20.8%

These figures show that:

(1) Medical consultants are being under-utilised. Could this be due to a lack of administrative control? Are too many cases being referred to the outside specialists? This may, however, be viewed as a consequence of flexibility – in the use of specialists as required.

(2) Dietary consultants are being under-utilised. Perhaps there should be a reduction in the number of consultants from 12 to 11 as suggested above.

(3) Fitness consultants are carrying out considerably more consultations (+20.8%) than budgeted. There are potential problems if their quality is decreasing. Overall complaints from clients are up by 120%. How many relate to fitness clients?

It may be, however, that the new cardio-vascular testing equipment is helping both throughput rates and the overall level of business from fitness clients.

Quality of service is the totality of features and characteristics of the service package that bear upon its ability to satisfy client needs. Flexibility and innovation in service provision may be key quality factors.

The high level of complaints from clients (up from 1% to 2% of all clients) indicates quality problems which should be investigated.

Quality of service may be improving. For example the new cardio-vascular testing equipment may be attracting extra clients because of the quality of information which it provides. Quality may also be aided through better management of client appointments and records following the introduction of the new software systems.

Innovation may be viewed in terms of the performance of a specific innovation. For example, whether the new computer software improved the quality of appointment scheduling and hence resource utilisation; improved competitiveness in following up enquiries and hence financial performance; improved flexibility in allowing better forward planning of consultant/client matching.

Innovation may also be viewed in terms of the effectiveness of the process itself. Are staff adequately trained in its use? Does the new software provide the data analysis which is required?

Test your understanding 5

Customer perspective

Goal: To increase the number of new and returning customers.

Measure: The number of new customers has increased year on year from 4,400 to 4,750. This is an 8.0% increase. The number of returning customers has also increased slightly from 7,200 to 7,250, i.e. a 1.0% increase.

Comment: The company has achieved its goal of increasing the number of new and existing customers. It is worth noting that the proportion of customers who are returning customers has fallen slightly from 62.1% to 60.4% of the total customers. This could indicate a small drop in the level of customer satisfaction.

Goal: To decrease the % customer complaints.

Measure: The percentage of customer complaints has increased from 4% (464 ÷ 11,600) to 7% (840 ÷ 12,000).

Comment: Faster Pasta should investigate the reasons for the increase in customer complaints and take the required action immediately in order to ensure that it can meet this goal in the future.

Internal perspective

Goal: To reduce the time taken between taking the customer's order and delivering the meal to the customer.

Measure: The time taken has more than tripled from an average of 4 minutes in 20X8 to an average of 13 minutes in 20X9.

Comment: Customers may place a high value on the fast delivery of their food. The increase in time may be linked to the increased number of customer complaints. If this continues customer satisfaction, and therefore profitability, will suffer in the long-term. The restaurant should take steps now in order to ensure that this goal is achieved going forward.

Goal: To reduce staff turnover.

Measure: This has risen significantly from 12% to 40% and hence the business has not achieved its goal.

Comment: The reasons for the high staff turnover should be investigated immediately. This may be contributing to longer waiting times and the increase in customer complaints. This will impact long-term profitability.

Innovation and learning perspective

Goal: To increase the proportion of revenue from new dishes.

Measure: This has increased year on year from 20% ($22,000 ÷ $110,000) in 20X8 to 30% ($39,600 ÷ $132,000) in 20X9. Therefore, the restaurant has achieved its goal.

Comment: This is a favourable increase and may have a positive impact on long-term profitability if the new products meet the needs of the customers.

Goal: To increase the % of staff time spent on training.

Measure: This has fallen significantly from 5% to only 2% and hence the company is not achieving its goal.

Comment: Staff may be unsatisfied if they feel that their training needs are not being met. This may contribute to a high staff turnover. In addition, staff may not have the skills to do the job well and this would impact the level of customer satisfaction.

Financial perspective

Goal: to increase spend per customer.

Measure: Spend per customer has increased from $9.48 ($110,000 ÷ 11,600) to $11.00 ($132,000 ÷ 12,000), i.e. a 16.0% increase.

Comment: This is a favourable increase. However, the issues discussed above must be addressed in order to ensure that this trend continues.

Goal: To increase gross profit margin.

Measure: The gross profit margin has increased year on year from 20% ($22,000 ÷ $110,000) to 23% ($30,360 ÷ $132,000).

Comment: This is a favourable increase. However, the issues discussed above must be addressed in order to ensure that this trend continues.

Test your understanding 6 – Standards and rewards

(i) Managers who participate in the setting of standards are more likely to accept and be motivated by the standards than managers on whom standards are imposed. An achievable standard is a better motivator than an unachievable one – although research has been undertaken into how much 'stretch' ought to be built into budgets. When setting standards across an organisation, care should be undertaken to ensure that all managers have equally-challenging standards. Achieving equity in this last regard may be difficult when measures used for different managers and business sectors within an organisation may be very different in character to one another.

(ii) Consideration of rewards involves use of concepts including 'clarity', 'motivation' and 'controllability'. Goal clarity contributes to motivation. For example, a standard of 'achieving 4 product innovations per year' might be a more effective motivator than 'giving a high profile to product innovation'. The actual means of motivation may involve performance-related salary bonuses, an assessment scheme point score or access to promotion channels. Managers will be better motivated if they actually control the factors contributing to achievement of the measures and standards on which their rewards are based.

Test your understanding 7 – Stakeholder considerations

Shareholders

Shareholders will want returns in the form of dividends and share price growth. By following policies to promote these requirements NW will maximise shareholder wealth.

The dividend has risen from a proforma 7c in 20X1 to 20c in 20X4. This represents growth of approximately 186% over the period. PAT has increased from 21 in 20X1 to 65 in 20X4, an increase of 210%. Since inflation is only 9% for the period, it would suggest that the needs of the shareholders have been met.

Consumers

Consumers will be interested in prices. The regulator restricts the extent by which prices can be increased.

We have information about the volume of the market (growing at 2% pa) and can therefore measure the price rises by removing the volume growth from turnover.

	20X1	20X2	20X3	20X4
Turnover	$450m	$480m	$540m	$620m
		× 1/1.02	× $1/1.02^2$	× $1/1.02^3$
Turnover in 20X1 volume	450	471	519	584

We can see that after taking out the growth, prices have risen at approximately 9.1% pa, which is well above the rate of inflation for the period (3%).

Whether or not this is justified depends on factors such as where the money has been spent. Has it gone into capital expenditure (improving the supplies or preventing leaks) or has it been used to increase dividends?

Workforce

The workforce has fallen by 2,000 from its 12,000 level in 20X1. Whilst it is possible that NW was overstaffed, shedding over 15% of the workforce will have affected morale.

Average wages have risen from $8,333 to $8,600 over the period, a rise of just over 3% for the period. Had the workforce enjoyed pay rises in line with inflation they could have expected to earn $9,083 in 20X4. This means they are actually worse off in real terms.

Without more information (e.g. skills mix of labour force, full/part-time employees) it is hard to comment, but the increased profitability of NW does not appear to have been passed on to them.

At the same time, the directors' emoluments have nearly quadrupled. We could again do with more information such as the number of directors involved. Part of the increase will be to bring fees in line with the private sector and part of it could be linked in with the share price. However, their fees as a percentage of the whole wage bill have risen from 0.8% to 3.4% over the period.

The figures probably will not include other perks such as share options.

The directors may increasingly find themselves having to justify 'fat cat' salaries.

Government

Price stability

Prices have risen by 38% in absolute, and 30% in real, terms which will not be in line with price stability.

Wages have been held down to less than the headline RPI, but at the same time directors' emoluments have risen sharply.

Economic growth

This is difficult to measure without more details, but we could calculate various ratios such as ROCE or net margin to measure the situation. Both have shown improvement over the period.

	20X1	20X2	20X3	20X4
Net margin	5.8%	7.2%	10.2%	12.1%

Capital expenditure has risen by 275% over the period. This would be expected to generate a knock-on growth elsewhere in the economy.

chapter

12

Divisional performance measurement and transfer pricing

Chapter learning objectives

Upon completion of this chapter you will be able to:

- explain the meaning of, and calculate from supplied data, return on investment (ROI) in the context of divisional performance appraisal
- discuss the shortcomings and benefits of using ROI for divisional performance appraisal
- explain the meaning of, and calculate from supplied data, residual income (RI) in the context of divisional performance appraisal
- discuss the shortcomings and benefits of using RI for divisional performance appraisal
- compare divisional performance using supplied data and recognise the problems that can arise from the comparison
- explain, using simple numerical examples, the basis for setting a transfer price using variable cost
- explain, using simple numerical examples, the basis for setting a transfer price using full cost
- explain, using simple numerical examples, how transfer prices can distort the performance assessment of divisions and decisions made, including dysfunctional decision making
- explain, using simple numerical examples, the principles behind allowing for intermediate markets.

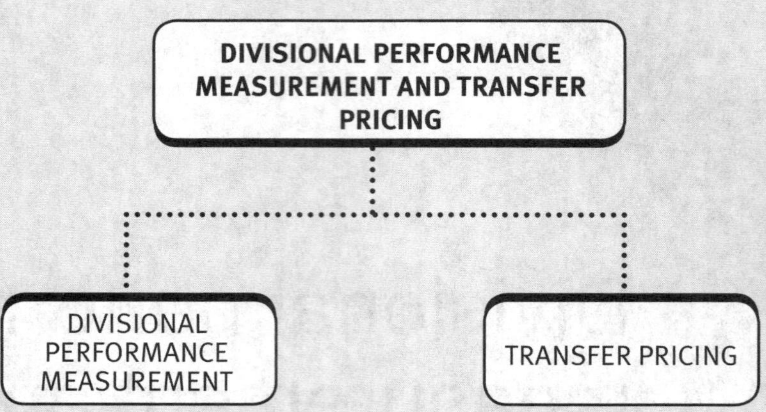

1 Divisional performance measurement

Type of division	Description	Typical measures used to assess performance
Cost centre.	• Division incurs costs but has no revenue stream, e.g. the IT support department of an organisation.	• Total cost and cost per unit • Cost variances. • NFPIs related to quality, productivity & efficiency.
Profit centre.	• Division has both costs and revenue. • Manager does not have the authority to alter the level of investment in the division.	All of the above PLUS: • Total sales and market share. • Profit. • Sales variances. • Working capital ratios (depending on the division concerned). • NFPIs e.g. related to productivity, quality and customer satisfaction.
Investment centre.	• Division has both costs and revenue. • Manager does have the authority to invest in new assets or dispose of existing ones.	All of the above PLUS: • ROI. • RI. These measures are used to assess the investment decisions made by managers and are discussed in more detail below.

Important point: For each of these care must be taken to assess managers on controllable factors only. So for example, the manager of a cost centre should only be assessed on controllable costs.

Return on investment (ROI)

This is a similar measure to ROCE but is used to appraise the investment decisions of an individual department.

$$ROI = \frac{\text{Controllable profit}}{\text{Capital employed}} \times 100$$

- Controllable profit is usually taken after depreciation but before tax. However, in the exam you may not be given this profit figure and so you should use the profit figure that is closest to this. Assume the profit is controllable, unless told otherwise.
- Capital employed is total assets less current liabilities **or** total equity plus long term debt. Use net assets if capital employed is not given in the question.
- Non-current assets might be valued at cost, net replacement cost or net book value (NBV). The value of assets employed could be either an average value for the period as a whole or a value as at the end of the period. An average value for the period is preferable. However, in the exam you should use whatever figure is given to you.

Test your understanding 1 – ROI calculation

An investment centre has reported a profit of $28,000. It has the following assets and liabilities:

	$	$
Non-current assets (at NBV)		100,000
Inventory	20,000	
Trade receivables	30,000	
		50,000
Trade payables	8,000	
		42,000
		142,000

Required:

Calculate the ROI for the division. State any additional information that would be useful when calculating the ROI.

Additional example on ROI

Division A of Babbage Group had investments at the year end of $56 million. These include the cost of a new equipment item costing $3 million that was acquired two weeks before the end of the year. This equipment was paid for by the central treasury department of Babbage, and is recorded in the accounts as an inter-company loan.

The profit of division A for the year was $7 million before deducting head office recharges of $800,000.

Required:

What is the most appropriate measure of ROI for Division A for the year?

Solution

Since the new equipment was bought just two weeks before the year end, the most appropriate figure for capital employed is $53 million, not $56 million.

The figure for profit should be the controllable profit of $7 million.

ROI = $7 million/$53 million = 13.2%

Evaluation of ROI as a performance measure

ROI is a popular measure for divisional performance but has some serious failings which must be considered when interpreting results.

Advantages

- It is widely used and accepted since it is line with ROCE which is frequently used to assess overall business performance.
- As a relative measure it enables comparisons to be made with divisions or companies of different sizes.
- It can be broken down into secondary ratios for more detailed analysis, i.e. profit margin and asset turnover.

Disadvantages

- It may lead to dysfunctional decision making, e.g. a division with a current ROI of 30% would not wish to accept a project offering a ROI of 25%, as this would dilute its current figure. However, the 25% ROI may meet or exceed the company's target.
- ROI increases with the age of the asset if NBVs are used, thus giving managers an incentive to hang on to possibly inefficient, obsolescent machines.
- It may encourage the manipulation of profit and capital employed figures to improve results, e.g. in order to obtain a bonus payment.
- Different accounting policies can confuse comparisons (e.g. depreciation policy).

Test your understanding 2 – Disadvantages of ROI

Nielsen Ltd has two divisions with the following information:

	Division A	**Division B**
	$	$
Profit	90,000	10,000
Capital employed	300,000	100,000
ROI	30%	10%

Division A has been offered a project costing $100,000 and giving annual returns of $20,000. Division B has been offered a project costing $100,000 and giving annual returns of $12,000. The company's cost of capital is 15%. Divisional performance is judged on ROI and the ROI-related bonus is sufficiently high to influence the managers' behaviour.

Required:

(a) What decisions will be made by management if they act in the best interests of their division (and in the best interests of their bonus)?

(b) What should the managers do if they act in the best interests of the company as a whole?

Residual income (RI)

RI = Controllable profit – Notional interest on capital

- Controllable profit is calculated in the same way as for ROI.
- Notional interest on capital = the capital employed in the division multiplied by a notional cost of capital or interest rate.
  - Capital employed is calculated in the same way as for ROI.
  - The selected cost of capital could be the company's average cost of funds (cost of capital). However, other interest rates might be selected, such as the current cost of borrowing, or a target ROI. (You should use whatever rate is given in the exam).

Test your understanding 3 – RI calculation

An investment centre has net assets of $800,000, and made profits before interest and tax of $160,000. The notional cost of capital is 12%.

Required:

Calculate and comment on the RI for the period.

Evaluation of RI as a performance measure

Compared to using ROI as a measure of performance, RI has several advantages and disadvantages:

Advantages

- It encourages investment centre managers to make new investments if they add to RI. A new investment might add to RI but reduce ROI. In such a situation, measuring performance by RI would not result in dysfunctional behaviour, i.e. the best decision will be made for the business as a whole.
- Making a specific charge for interest helps to make investment centre managers more aware of the cost of the assets under their control.
- Risk can be incorporated by the choice of interest rate used.

Disadvantages

- It does not facilitate comparisons between divisions since the RI is driven by the size of divisions and of their investments.
- It is based on accounting measures of profit and capital employed which may be subject to manipulation, e.g. in order to obtain a bonus payment.

Test your understanding 4 – ROI vs RI

An investment centre has net assets of $800,000, and made profits before interest of $160,000. The notional cost of capital is 12%. This is the company's target return.

An opportunity has arisen to invest in a new project costing $100,000. The project would have a four-year life, and would make profits of $15,000 each year.

Required:

(a) What would be the ROI with and without the investment? (Base your calculations on opening book values). Would the investment centre manager wish to undertake the investment if performance is judged on ROI?

(b) What would be the average annual RI with and without the investment? (Base your calculations on opening book values).Would the investment centre manager wish to undertake the investment if performance is judged on RI?

Additional example on ROI and RI

Two divisions of a company are considering new investments.

	Division X	**Division Y**
Net assets	$1,000,000	$1,000,000
Current divisional profit	$250,000	$120,000
Investment in project	$100,000	$100,000
Projected project profit	$20,000	$15,000

Company's required ROI = 18%

Required:

Assess the projects using both ROI and RI.

Solution

Consider divisional performance:

Without project	**Division X**	**Division Y**
Divisional ROI	25%	12%
Divisional RI ($)	+ 70,000	– 60,000
With project		
Investment ($)	1,100,000	1,100,000
Profit ($)	270,000	135,000
ROI	24.5%	12.3%
RI ($)	72,000	– 63,000
Project in isolation		
ROI	20%	15%
RI ($)	+ 2,000	– 3,000

Based on ROI, Division X will reject its project as it dilutes its existing ROI of 25%. This is the wrong decision from the company perspective as the project ROI of 20% beats the company hurdle of 18%.

Likewise Division Y will accept its project, which should be rejected as it fails to hit the company target.

In each case there is a conflict between the company and divisional viewpoints.

RI does not have this problem as we simply add the project RI to the divisional figures.

Comparing divisional performance

Divisional performance can be compared in many ways. ROI and RI are common methods but other methods could be used.

- Variance analysis – is a standard means of monitoring and controlling performance. Care must be taken in identifying the controllability of, and responsibility for, each variance.
- Ratio analysis – there are several profitability and liquidity measures that can be applied to divisional performance reports.

- Other management ratios – this could include measures such as sales per employee or square foot as well as industry specific ratios such as transport costs per mile, brewing costs per barrel, overheads per chargeable hour.
- Other information – such as staff turnover, market share, new customers gained, innovative products or services developed.

Test your understanding 5

Comment on the problems that may be involved in comparing divisional performance.

2 Transfer pricing

Introduction

A transfer price is the price at which goods or services are transferred from one division to another within the same organisation.

Objectives of a transfer pricing system

- Goal congruence

The decisions made by each profit centre manager should be consistent with the objectives of the organisation as a whole, i.e. the transfer price should assist in maximising overall company profits. A common feature of exam questions is that a transfer price is set that results in sub-optimal behaviour.

- Performance measurement

The buying and selling divisions will be treated as profit centres. The transfer price should allow the performance of each division to be assessed fairly. Divisional managers will be demotivated if this is not achieved.

- Autonomy

The system used to set transfer prices should seek to maintain the autonomy of profit centre managers. If autonomy is maintained, managers tend to be more highly motivated but sub-optimal decisions may be made.

- Recording the movement of goods and services

In practice, an extremely important function of the transfer pricing system is simply to assist in recording the movement of goods and services.

Setting the transfer price

There are two main methods available:

Method 1: Market based approach

If an external market exists for the transferred goods then the transfer price could be set at the external market price.

Advantages of this method:

- The transfer price should be deemed to be fair by the managers of the buying and selling divisions. The selling division will receive the same amount for any internal or external sales. The buying division will pay the same for goods if they buy them internally or externally.
- The company's performance will not be impacted negatively by the transfer price because the transfer price is the same as the external market price.

Disadvantages of this method:

- There may not be an external market price.
- The external market price may not be stable. For example, discounts may be offered to certain customers or for bulk orders.
- Savings may be made from transferring the goods internally. For example, delivery costs will be saved. These savings should ideally be deducted from the external market price before a transfer price is set, giving an "adjusted market price".

Method 2: Cost based approach

The transferring division would supply the goods at **cost plus a % profit**.

A standard cost should be used rather than the actual cost since:

- Actual costs do not encourage the selling division to control costs.
- If a standard cost is used, the buying division will know the cost in advance and can therefore put plans in place.

There are a number of different standard costs that could be used:

- Full cost
- Marginal (variable) cost
- Opportunity cost.

Each of these will be reviewed.

Test your understanding 6 – Full cost and marginal cost

A company has two profit centres, Centre A and Centre B. Centre A supplies Centre B with a part-finished product. Centre B completes the production and sells the finished units in the market at $35 per unit. There is no external market for Centre A's part-finished product.

Budgeted data for the year:

	Division A	Division B
Number of units transferred/sold	10,000	10,000
Material cost per unit	$8	$2
Other variable costs per unit	$2	$3
Annual fixed costs	$60,000	$30,000

Required:

Calculated the budgeted annual profit for each division and for the company as a whole of the transfer price for the components supplied by division A to division B is:

(a) Full cost plus 10%

(b) Marginal cost plus 10%

(c) Evaluate both transfer prices from the perspective of each individual division and from the perspective of the company as a whole.

Test your understanding 7 – Opportunity cost approach

A company operates two divisions, Able and Baker. Able manufactures two products, X and Y. Product X is sold to external customers for $42 per unit. The only outlet for product Y is Baker.

Baker supplies an external market and can obtain its semi-finished supplies (product Y) from either Able or an external source. Baker currently has the opportunity to purchase product Y from an external supplier for $38 per unit. The capacity of division Able is measured in units of output, irrespective of whether product X, Y or a combination of both are being manufactured.

The associated product costs are as follows:

	X	Y
	$	$
Variable costs per unit	32	35
Fixed overheads per unit	5	5
Total unit costs	37	40

Required:

Using the above information, advise on the determination of an appropriate transfer price for the sale of product Y from division Able to division Baker under the following conditions:

(i) when division Able has spare capacity and limited external demand for product X

(ii) when division Able is operating at full capacity with unsatisfied external demand for product X.

Additional example on transfer pricing

Archer Group has two divisions, Division X and Division Y. Division X manufactures a component X8 which is transferred to Division Y. Division Y uses component X8 to make a finished product Y14, which it sells for $20. There is no external market for component X8.

Costs are as follows:

	Division X	Division Y
	Component X8	Product Y14
Variable production cost	$5 per unit	$3 per unit*
Annual fixed costs	$40,000	$80,000

*Excluding the cost of transferred units of X8.

The budgeted output and sales for Product Y14 is 20,000 units. One unit of component X8 goes into the manufacture of one unit of Y14.

The profit of the company as a whole will be maximised if Divisions X and Y produce up to their capacity, or to the maximum volume of sales demand. For each extra unit sold, the marginal revenue is $20 and the marginal cost is $8 ($5 + $3); therefore the additional contribution is $12 for each extra unit of Y14 made and sold.

Since there is no external market for component X8, the transfer price will be cost-based. 'Cost' might be marginal cost or full cost. The transfer price might also include a mark-up on cost to allow a profit to Division X.

The maximum transfer price that the buying division will pay

Division Y has a marginal cost of $3 per unit, and earns revenue of $20 for each unit sold. In theory, Division Y should therefore be prepared to pay up to $17 ($20 – $3) for each unit of X8.

It could be argued, however, that Division Y would not want to sell Product Y14 at all if it made a loss. Division Y might therefore want to cover its fixed costs as well as its variable costs. Fixed costs in Division Y, given a budget of 20,000 units, are $4 per unit. The total cost in Division Y is $7 ($3 + $4). On this basis, the maximum transfer price that Division Y should be willing to pay is $13 ($20 – $7).

Transfer price = marginal cost

The short-term opportunity cost to Division X of transferring units of X8 to Division Y is the marginal cost of production, $5.

At a transfer price of $5, Division X would be expected to sell as many units of X8 to Division Y as Division Y would like to buy.

However, although marginal cost represents the opportunity cost to Division X of transferring units of X8, it is not an ideal transfer price.

- At a transfer price of $5, Division X would make $0 contribution from each unit transferred. The Division would therefore make a loss of $40,000 (its fixed costs).
- This transfer price would not motivate the manager of Division X to maximise output.
- It is unlikely that the manager of Division X would be prepared to negotiate this price with Division Y, and a decision to set the transfer price at $5 would probably have to be made by head office.
- If Division X is set up as a profit centre, a transfer price at marginal cost would not provide a fair way of measuring and assessing the division's performance.

Transfer price = marginal cost plus

If the transfer price is set at marginal cost plus a mark-up for contribution, the manager of Division X would be motivated to maximise output, because this would maximise contribution and profit (or minimise the loss).

As indicated earlier, Division Y would want to buy as much as possible from Division X provided that the transfer price is no higher than $17, or possibly $13.

If a transfer price is set at marginal cost plus a mark-up for contribution, the 'ideal' range of prices lies anywhere between $5 and $17. The size of the mark-up would be a matter for negotiation. Presumably, the transfer price that is eventually agreed would be either:

- imposed by head office, or
- agreed by negotiation between the divisional managers, with the more powerful or skilful negotiator getting the better deal on the price.

Additional requirement:

Discuss the implications of setting the transfer cost at full cost plus.

Solution

There is an argument that the opportunity cost of transfer, in the absence of an intermediate market, is full cost.

This assumes that, if the selling division decided against making any transfers at all, it would save all costs, both marginal and fixed costs, by shutting down.

In the above example, the full cost for Division X of making component X8 is $7 ($5 variable plus $2 fixed).

At this price, Division X would want to sell as many units as possible to Division Y, and Division Y would buy as many units as it could, subject to the limit on capacity or sales demand.

However, although full cost represents the long-term opportunity cost to Division X of transferring units of X8, it is not an ideal transfer price.

- At a transfer price of $7, Division X would make $0 profit from each unit transferred. If output and sales are less than the budget of 20,000, Division X would make a loss due to the under-absorbed fixed overhead. If output and sales are more than the budget of 20,000, Division X would make a profit due to the over-absorbed fixed overhead. The only ways in which Division X could make a profit are therefore:
  - to hope that sales demand exceeds the budgeted volume, and/or
  - reduce its variable costs and fixed cost expenditures.
- It is unlikely that the manager of Division X would be prepared to negotiate this price with Division Y, and a decision to set the transfer price at $7 would probably have to be made by head office.
- If Division X is set up as a profit centre, a transfer price at full cost would not provide a fair way of measuring and assessing the division's performance.

Test your understanding 8 – Additional example

Manuco company has been offered supplies of special ingredient Z at a transfer price of $15 per kg by Helpco company, which is part of the same group of companies. Helpco processes and sells special ingredient Z to customers external to the group at $15 per kg. Helpco bases its transfer price on full cost plus 25% profit mark-up. The full cost has been estimated as 75% variable and 25% fixed. Internal transfers to Manuco would enable $1.50 per kg of variable packing cost to be avoided.

Required:

Discuss the transfer prices at which Helpco should offer to transfer special ingredient Z to Manuco in order that group profit maximising decisions are taken in each of the following situations:

(i) Helpco has an external market for all its production of special ingredient Z at a selling price of $15 per kg.

(ii) Helpco has production capacity for 9,000 kg of special ingredient Z. An external market is available for 6,000 kgs of material Z.

(iii) Helpco has production capacity for 3,000 kg of special material Z. An alternative use for some of its spare production capacity exists. This alternative use is equivalent to 2,000 kg of special ingredient Z and would earn a contribution of $6,000. There is no external demand.

Objective Test Case Questions – Transfer Pricing

(1) Frankie co has two divisions, A and B. Division A makes a component at a marginal cost of $30, which it can only sell to Division B. Division A has no other outlet for sales. Division B takes A's component and turns it into a finished good, incurring its own cost of $55 per unit and selling it externally at $120.

Which ONE of the following statements is true?

A The minimum TP that Division A will accept from Division B is $ 30, the maximum TP that Division B will pay is $60 and the company makes a negative contribution.

B The minimum TP that Division A will accept from B is $ 30, the maximum TP that B will pay is $65 and the company makes a negative contribution.

C The minimum TP that Division A will accept from B is $ 30, the maximum TP that B will pay is $65 and the company makes a positive contribution.

D The minimum TP that Division A will accept from B is $ 30, the maximum TP that B will pay is $55 and the company makes a positive contribution.

(2) Division A has decided it wants to maximise its own profits by selling externally at a price of $45 to Customer Co, after incurring distribution costs on external sales of $3 per unit. As before, Division A can also sell internally to Division B.

Which of the following statements are correct?

(1) The net sales price per unit Division A gets externally is $42.

(2) $65 is the maximum transfer price B will pay.

(3) If working at full capacity, $42 is the lowest transfer price Division A will accept.

(4) If there is spare capacity in Division A, $30 is the lowest transfer price Division A will accept.

A Statements (1) and (2) only

B Statements (1), (2) and (4) only

C Statements (1), (3) and (4) only

D Statements (1), (2), (3) and (4).

(3) Division A operates at full capacity and sells all its components for $45 to Customer Co, after incurring distribution costs on external sales of $3 per unit. An external supplier, Third Co, has offered to supply Division B for $40 per unit.

What should each division do to maximise company profitability?

A Division A should not produce the component for Division B and keep all its units for external sales.

B Division A should redirect some of its external sales towards Division B and sell to Division B at price between $30 and $40.

C Division A should not produce at all and all supplies to Division B should be externally sourced from Third Co.

D Division A should try and sell all its components to Division B for $42.

(4) Division A operates at full capacity and sells all its components for $45 to Customer Co, after incurring distribution costs on external sales of $3 per unit. Third Co, the original external supplier to Division B, has now gone out of business but Fourth Co, another external supplier, has offered to supply Division B for $29 per unit.

What should Frankie Co do to maximise company profitability?

A Division A should not produce the component for Division B and keep all its units for external sales.

B Division A should redirect some of its external sales towards Division B and sell to Division B at price between $30 and $40.

C Division A should not produce at all and all supplies should be externally sourced from Fourth Co.

D Division A should try and sell all its components to Division B for $42.

(5) **Which of the following statements regarding the objectives of a transfer pricing system are correct?**

(1) A transfer pricing system should encourage output at an organisation-wide profit-maximising level.

(2) A transfer pricing system should encourage divisions to make autonomous decisions.

(3) A transfer pricing system should encourage dysfunctional decision making.

(4) A transfer pricing system should enable the realistic measurement of divisional profits.

A Statements (1) and (4) only

B Statements (1), (3) and (4) only

C Statements (1), (2) and (4) only

D Statements (1), (2), (3) and (4)

3 Chapter summary

DIVISIONAL PERFORMANCE MEASUREMENT AND TRANSFER PRICING

DIVISIONAL PERFORMANCE MEASUREMENT

- ROI = EBIT/CE x 100%
- RI = EBIT – notional interest
- Notional interest = CE x cost of capital
- Dysfunctional behaviour
  - conflict with NPV in the short-term
  - manipulation of profit/CE
- Alternative performance measures: variances, ratios, non-quantitative measures.

TRANSFER PRICING

- Objectives
- General rule = variable cost + opportunity cost
- Market prices
- Cost based
  - variable cost
  - full cost
- Dysfunctional behaviour.

Test your understanding answers

Test your understanding 1 – ROI calculation

- ROI might be measured as: $28,000/$142,000 = 19.7%.
- However, suppose that the centre manager has no responsibility for debt collection. In this situation, it could be argued that the centre manager is not responsible for trade receivables, and the centre's CE should be $112,000. If this assumption is used, ROI would be $28,000/$112,000 = 25.0%.

Test your understanding 2 – Disadvantages of ROI

(a)	**Division A**	**Division B**
	$000	$000
Old ROI	90/300	10/100
	= 30%	= 10%
New ROI	(90 + 20)/(300 + 100)	(10 + 12)/(100 + 100)
	= 27.5%	= 11%
Will manager want to accept project?	No	Yes

The manager of Division A will not want to accept the project as it lowers her ROI from 30% to 27.5%. The manager of Division B will like the new project as it will increase their ROI from 10% to 11%. Although the 11% is bad, it is better than before.

(b) Looking at the whole situation from the group point of view, we are in the ridiculous position that the group has been offered two projects, both costing $100,000. One project gives a profit of $20,000 and the other $12,000. Left to their own devices then the managers would end up accepting the project giving only $12,000. This is because ROI is a defective decision-making method and does not guarantee that the correct decision will be made.

Test your understanding 3 – RI calculation

If performance is measured by RI, the RI for the period is:

	$
Profit before interest and tax	160,000
Notional interest (12% × $800,000)	96,000
RI	64,000

(**Note:** Capital employed is not available in this question and therefore net assets should be used as a substitute value).

Investment centre managers who make investment decisions on the basis of short-term performance will want to undertake any investments that add to RI, i.e. if the RI is positive.

Test your understanding 4 – ROI vs RI

(a) ROI

	Without the investment	**With the investment**
Profit	$160,000	$175,000
Capital employed	$800,000	$900,000
ROI	20.0%	19.4%

ROI would be lower; therefore the centre manager will not want to make the investment. since his performance will be judged as having deteriorated. However, this results in dysfunctional behaviour since the company's target is only 12%.

(b) RI

		Without the investment		**With the investment**
		$		$
Profit		160,000		175,000
Notional interest	($800,000 × 12%)	(96,000)	($900,000 × 12%)	(108,000)
RI		64,000		67,000

The investment centre manager will want to undertake the investment because it will increase RI. This is the correct decision for the company since RI increases by $3,000 as a result of the investment.

Test your understanding 5

Problems may include:

- Divisions may operate in different environments. A division earning a ROI of 10% when the industry average is 7% may be considered to be performing better than a division earning a ROI of 12% when the industry average is 15%.
- The transfer pricing policy may distort divisional performance.
- Divisions may have assets of different ages. A division earning a high ROI may do so because assets are old and fully depreciated. This may give a poor indication of future potential performance.
- There may be difficulties comparing divisions with different accounting policies (e.g. depreciation).
- Evaluating performance on the basis of a few indicators may lead to manipulation of data. A wider range of indicators may be preferable which include non-financial measures. It may be difficult to find non-financial indicators which can easily be compared if divisions operate in different environments.

Test your understanding 6 – Full cost and marginal cost

(a)

	Division A ($)	**Division B** ($)	**Total** ($)
Sales:			
– internal	10,000 × $17.60 (W1) = 176,000	n/a	176,000
– external	n/a	10,000 × $35 = 350,000	350,000
Costs:			
– transfer costs	n/a	(176,000) (as above)	(176,000)
– variable costs	10,000 × $10 = (100,000)	10,000 × $5 = (50,000)	(150,000)
– fixed costs	(60,000)	(30,000)	(90,000)
Profit	16,000	94,000	110,000

(b)

	Division A ($)	Division B ($)	Total ($)
Sales:			
– internal	10,000 × $11 (W2) = 110,000	n/a	110,000
– external	n/a	10,000 × $35 = 350,000	350,000
Costs:			
– transfer costs	n/a	(110,000) (as above)	(110,000)
– variable costs	10,000 × $10 = (100,000)	10,000 × $5 = (50,000)	(150,000)
– fixed costs	(60,000)	(30,000)	(90,000)
Profit/(loss)	(50,000)	160,000	110,000

Working 1

	$
Material cost per unit	8
Other variable costs per unit	2
Fixed cost per unit ($60,000 ÷ 10,000)	6
Full cost	16
Plus 10% profit	1.60
Transfer price = full cost + 10%	17.60

Working 2

	$
Material cost per unit	8
Other variable costs per unit	2
Total variable cost	10
Plus 10% profit	1
Transfer price = marginal cost + 10%	11

(c)

- Division A would prefer the transfer price to be set at full cost plus 10%. This would give them a budgeted profit of $16,000, compared to a loss of $50,000 when the marginal cost transfer price is used.
- Division B would prefer the transfer price to be set at variable cost + 10%. This gives them a profit of $160,000 compared with a profit of $94,000 if the full cost transfer price is used.
- There is a natural conflict between the divisions and the transfer price would have to be negotiated to ensure that each division views it as being fair.
- The company as a whole will be indifferent to the transfer price. There is no external market for Division A's goods and the profit will be $110,000 regardless of the transfer price set.

Test your understanding 7 – Opportunity cost approach

(i) The transfer price should be set between $35 and $38. Able has spare capacity, therefore the marginal costs to the group of Able making a unit is $35. If the price is set above $38, Baker will be encouraged to buy outside the group, decreasing group profit by $3 per unit.

(ii) If Able supplies Baker with a unit of Y, it will cost $35 and they (both Able and the group) will lose $10 contribution from X ($42 sales – $32 variable cost). So long as the bought-in external price of Y to Baker is less than $45, Baker should buy from that external source. The transfer price should therefore be set at $45.

Test your understanding 8 – Additional example

(i) Since Helpco has an external market, which is the opportunity foregone, the relevant transfer price would be the external selling price of $15 per kg. This will be adjusted to allow for the $1.50 per kg avoided on internal transfers due to packing costs not required.

The transfer price offered by Helpco should be $15 – $1.50 = $13.50 per kg.

(ii) In this situation Helpco has no alternative opportunity for 3,000 kg of its special ingredient Z. It should, therefore, offer to transfer this quantity at marginal cost. This is variable cost less packing costs avoided = $9 (W1) – $1.50 = $7.50 per kg.

Working 1: Total cost = $15 × 80% = $12, Variable cost = $12 × 75% = $9.

If Manuco require more than 3,000 kgs the transfer price should be set at the adjusted selling price of $13.50 per kg as in (i) above.

(iii) Helpco Ltd has an alternative use for some of its production capacity, which will yield a contribution equivalent to $3 per kg of special ingredient Z ($6,000/2,000 kg). The balance of its square capacity (1,000 kg) has no opportunity cost and should still be offered at marginal cost.

Helpco should offer to transfer:

2,000 kg at $7.50 + $3 = $10.50 per kg; 1,000 kg at $7.50 per kg (= MC).

Objective Test Case Questions – Transfer Pricing

(1) **C**

Contribution = B's sales price – MC_a – MC_b

Contribution = 120 – 30 – 55

Contribution = 35

The minimum TP that A will accept is MC_a = $30

The maximum TP that B will pay is B's sales price – MC_b = $120 – $55 = $65

(2) **D**

A's net sales price is sales price $45 – selling costs $3 = $42

The maximum transfer price B will pay is B's sales price – MC_b = $120 – $55 = $65.

If A is at full capacity, every unit A has to supply to B causes a loss of external net revenue. Therefore, the TP must be at least $42 to compensate A and the company for its lost net revenue. If A has spare capacity, it is already selling all it can to the outside market and can make extra goods for B without losing external sales. Therefore, any TP must therefore cover MC_a = $30.

(3) **A**

Division A sells externally for net $42. Division B buys externally for $40, and no internal transfers should take place.

(4) **C**

From a purely financial perspective, Division A should not produce the product as the external supplier can undercut MCa. All supplies should be externally sourced for $29 per unit and sold by Frankie Co for a net $42, or incur MC_b and then be sold for $120.

(5) **C**

chapter

13

Performance measurement in not-for-profit organisations

Chapter learning objectives

Upon completion of this chapter you will be able to:

- comment on the problems, with particular reference to not-for-profit organisations and the public sector, of having non-quantifiable objectives in performance management
- describe how performance could be measured in not-for-profit organisations
- comment on the problems, using simple examples, of having multiple objectives in not-for-profit organisations and the public sector
- describe, in outline, value for money (VFM) as a public sector objective.

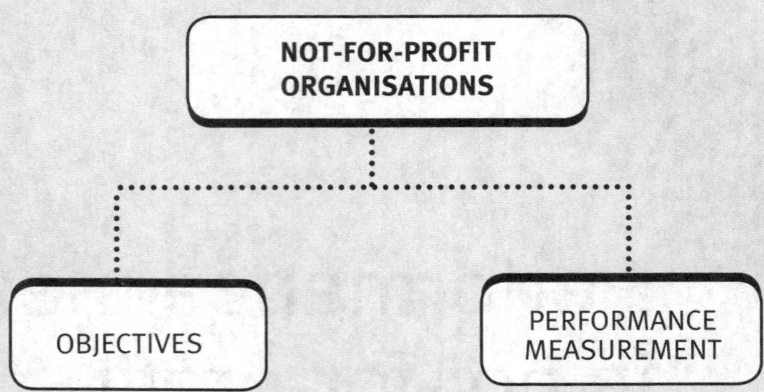

1 The problem of non-quantifiable objectives

The not-for-profit sector incorporates a diverse range of operations including national government, local government, charities, executive agencies, trusts and so on. The critical thing about such operations is that they are **not** motivated by a desire to maximise profit.

Many, if not all, of the benefits arising from expenditure by these bodies are non-quantifiable (certainly not in monetary terms, e.g. social welfare). The same can be true of costs. So any cost/benefit analysis is necessarily quite judgemental, i.e. social benefits versus social costs as well as financial benefits versus financial costs. The danger is that if benefits cannot be quantified, then they might be ignored.

Another problem is that these organisations often do not generate revenue but simply have a fixed budget for spending within which they have to keep (i.e. a capital rationing problem). Value for money ('VFM') is often quoted as an objective here but it does not get round the problem of measuring 'value'.

Illustration 1 – The problem of non-quantifiable objectives

A hospital might use a cheaper cleaning firm because of difficulties evaluating how well the cleaning is being done. This may create problems in many areas:

- It may indirectly lead to the spread of infection which is costly to eliminate.
- Nursing staff may become demotivated as they are unable to carry out their own work effectively.
- The general public may lose confidence in the quality of the service.

Test your understanding 1

Discuss how a hospital should determine whether to allocate limited surgical resources to expensive organ transplants or to more routine hip/knee joint replacements.

2 Performance measurement in not-for-profit organisations

Not-for-profit organisations may have some non-quantifiable objectives but that fact does not exempt them from the need to plan and control their activities.

Illustration 2 – Performance measurement in not-for-profit

A university is an example of a non-profit making organisation. The performance of this not-for-profit organisation must be assessed. Measures include:

University overall:

- overall costs compared with budget
- numbers of students
- amount of research funding received
- proportion of successful students (by grade)
- quality of teaching – as measured by student and inspector assessments
- number of publications by staff.

Individual department or faculty:

- cost per student
- cost per examination pass
- staff/student ratios
- students per class
- number of teaching hours per member of staff
- availability of learning resources, e.g. personal computer (PC) per student ratio
- number of library books per student
- average age of library books.

Test your understanding 2

St Alice's Hospice is a charity which collects funds and donations and utilises these in the care of terminally ill patients. The governing body has set the manager three performance objectives for the three months to 30 June 20X7:

- to achieve a level of donations of $150,000
- to keep administration costs to no more than 8% of donations
- to achieve 80% of respite care requested from the community.

Actual results were as follows:

	April	**May**	**June**
Donations($)	35,000	65,000	55,000
Administration costs ($)	2,450	5,850	4,400
Respite care requests (days)	560	570	600
Respite care provided (days)	392	430	510

Prepare a statement to assist the manager in evaluating performance against objectives and comment on performance.

3 The problem of multiple objectives

Multiple stakeholders in not-for-profit organisations give rise to multiple objectives. As a result, there is a need to prioritise objectives or to make compromises between objectives.

Illustration 3 – The problem of multiple objectives

A hospital will have a number of different groups of stakeholders, each with their own objectives. For example:

- Employees will seek a high level of job satisfaction. They will also aim to achieve a good work-life balance and this may result in a desire to work more regular daytime hours.
- Patients will want to be seen quickly and will demand a high level of care.

There is potential conflict between the objectives of the two stakeholder groups. For example, if hospital staff only work regular daytime hours then patients may have to wait a long time if they come to the hospital outside of these hours and the standard of patient care will fall dramatically at certain times of the day, if most staff only work regular hours.

The hospital must prioritise the needs of the different stakeholder groups. In this case, the standard of patient care would be prioritised above giving staff the regular daytime working hours that they would prefer. However, in order to maintain staff morale an element of compromise should also be used. For example, staff may have to work shifts but may be given generous holidays allowances or other rewards instead.

Test your understanding 3

Describe the different groups of stakeholders in an international famine relief charity. Explain how the charity may have conflicting objectives and the impact this may have on the effective operation of the organisation.

4 Value for money (VFM)

A common method of assessing public sector performance is to assess value for money (VFM). This comprises three elements:

Economy – an input measure. Are the resources used the cheapest possible for the quality required?

Efficiency – here we link inputs with outputs. Is the maximum output being achieved from the resources used?

Effectiveness – an output measure looking at whether objectives are being met.

Illustration 4 – Value for money

Value for money in a university would comprise the three element of:

Economy – this is about balancing the cost with the quality of the resources. Therefore, it will review areas such as the cost of books, computers and teaching compared with the quality of these resources. It recognises that the organisation must consider its expenditure but should not simply aim to minimise costs. e.g. low cost but poor quality teaching or books will hinder student performance and will damage the reputation of the university.

Efficiency – this focuses on the efficient use of any resources acquired. For example:

- How often are the library books that are bought by the university taken out on loan by students?
- What is the utilisation of IT resources?
- What % of their working time do lecturers spend teaching or researching?

Effectiveness – this measures the achievement of the organisation's objectives. For example:

- The % of students achieving a target grade.
- The % of graduates who find full time employment within 6 months of graduating.

Test your understanding 4

A local authority may have 'maintaining an acceptable quality of life for elderly residents' as one of its objectives. It has several means by which it may achieve this objective, including:

- providing 'meals on wheels' (Social Services Department)
- providing a mobile library (Libraries Department)
- maintaining access to and facilities in local parks (Parks Department)
- providing police support to the elderly at home (Police Department)
- providing nursing homes (Housing Department).

Required:

Explain how the local authority would determine whether the service was effective in providing VFM.

5 Chapter summary

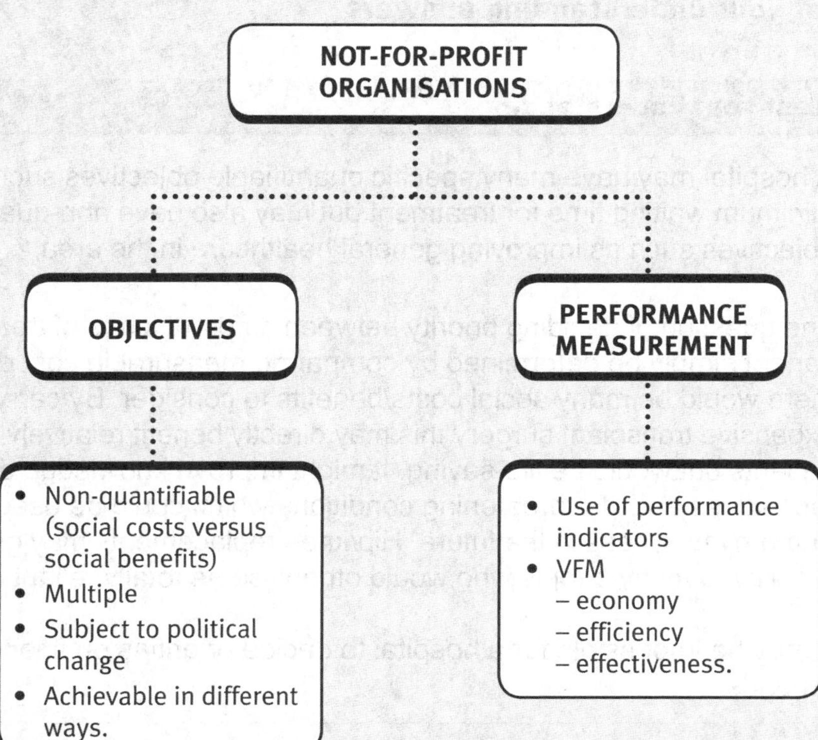
NOT-FOR-PROFIT ORGANISATIONS
OBJECTIVES
PERFORMANCE MEASUREMENT
• Non-quantifiable (social costs versus social benefits)
• Multiple
• Subject to political change
• Achievable in different ways.
• Use of performance indicators
• VFM
– economy
– efficiency
– effectiveness.

Test your understanding answers

Test your understanding 1

A hospital may have many specific quantifiable objectives such as a minimum waiting time for treatment but may also have non-quantifiable objectives such as improving general healthcare in the area.

The question of deciding priority between different kinds of treatment cannot simply be determined by comparing measurable cost data as there would be many social costs/benefits to consider. By carrying out expensive transplant surgery this may directly benefit relatively few patients but would be life-saving. It might improve knowledge of surgical techniques and life-threatening conditions which could be used to detect and prevent illness in the future. Hip/knee replacements may give mobility to many people who would otherwise be totally reliant on carers.

It may be impossible for a hospital to decide priorities on financial grounds.

Test your understanding 2

	April	**May**	**June**
Administration costs as a % of donations	7%	9%	8%
Target	8%	8%	8%
Respite care provided	70%	75.4%	85%

Total donations received have exceeded the target for the period. There is no discernable trend and it is possible that there were special fund-raising activities in May which generated greater income. Administration costs have been within the target of 8% in April and June but exceeded the target in May. More information is needed to establish why this occurred. There has been a steady improvement in the level of respite care provided and in June the target was exceeded.

Test your understanding 3

The stakeholders will include donors, people needing aid, voluntary staff, paid staff, the governments of the countries granting and receiving aid.

There may be conflicting objectives. Donors and people needing aid will want all of the funds to be spent on famine relief. Management staff may require a percentage of the funds to be spent on administration and promotion in order to safeguard the long-term future of the charity.

Donors may have their own views on how donations should be spent which conflict with management staff.

The charity may wish to distribute aid according to perceived need. Governments in receiving countries may have political reasons for distorting information relating to need.

These conflicts may make it difficult to set clear objectives on which all stakeholders agree.

Test your understanding 4

All of these departmental activities contribute to achievement of the objective. The problem is to find the optimum combination of spending for each of the departments.

- Many elderly people continue to live in their own homes, but are just on the threshold of requiring accommodation in a nursing home. A small cutback in spending in one area (e.g. the withdrawal of a mobile library) may push a lot of elderly people over that threshold. There is then an enormous demand for extra spending by the Housing Department. Nursing home accommodation is an expensive last resort in caring for the elderly.
- An occasional visit by a care worker or a police officer may enable many elderly people to stay in their own homes for much longer than would otherwise be the case.

The key to effectiveness is in finding an optimum pattern of spending to achieve a given objective.

[illegible]

The stakeholders will include donors, volunteers, paid staff, the governments of the countries granting and receiving aid.

There may be conflicting objectives. Donors and people receiving aid will want the funds to be spent on front-line activities. Management staff may require a percentage of the funds to be spent on administration and promotion in order to safeguard the long-term future of the charity.

Donors may have their own views on how donations should be spent, which conflict with management staff.

The charity may wish to distribute aid according to perceived need. Governments in receiving countries may have political reasons for directing aid to particular regions.

These conflicts may make it difficult to set clear objectives, or which all stakeholders can agree.

[illegible]

All of these departmental activities contribute to achievement of the objective. The problem is to find the optimum combination of spending for each of the departments.

- Many elderly people continue to live in their own homes but are just on the threshold of requiring accommodation in a nursing home. A small reduction in spending in one area (e.g. the withdrawal of a mobile library) may put a number of elderly people over that threshold. There is then an enormous demand for extra spending by the social services department. Nursing home accommodation is an expensive last resort in caring for the elderly.
- An increase in spending by a particular department (e.g. the police) may enable many elderly people to stay in their own homes for much longer than would otherwise be the case.

The key to effectiveness is in finding an optimum pattern of spending to achieve a given objective.

chapter

14

Performance management information systems

Chapter learning objectives

Upon completion of this chapter you will be able to:

- Identify the accounting information requirements and describe the different types of information systems used for strategic planning, management control and operational control and decision making
- Define and identify the main characteristics of transaction processing systems; management information systems; executive information systems; and enterprise resource planning systems
- Define and discuss the merits of, and potential problems with, open and closed systems with regard to the needs of performance management
- Identify the principal internal and external sources of management accounting information
- Demonstrate how these principal sources of management information might be used for control purposes
- Identify and discuss the direct data capture and process costs of management accounting information
- Identify and discuss the indirect cost of producing information
- Discuss the limitations of using externally generated information
- Discuss the principal controls required in generating and distributing internal information
- Discuss the procedures that may be necessary to ensure security of highly confidential information that is not for external consumption.

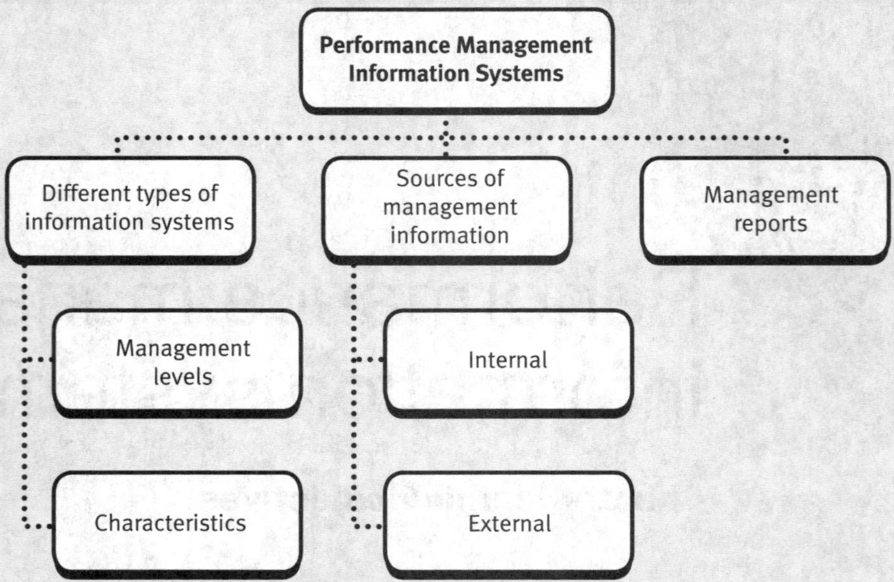

1 Data and information

Information and data are two different things.

Data consists of numbers, letters, symbols, raw facts, events and transactions, which have been recorded but not yet processed into a form that is suitable for making decisions.

Information is data that has been processed in such a way that it has meaning to the person that receives it, who may then use it to improve the quality of their decision-making.

It is a vital requirement within any business and is required both internally and externally. Management requires information:

- To provide records, both current and historical
- To analyse what is happening within the business
- To provide the basis of decision making in the short term and long term
- To monitor the performance of the business by comparing actual results with plans and forecasts.

Various third parties require information about the business, including:

- The owners, e.g. shareholders
- Customers and suppliers
- The employees
- Government agencies such as tax authorities.

Data processing is the conversion of data into information, perhaps by classifying, sorting or producing total figures. The conversion process may be manual or automated. In general, data may be transformed into information by:

- bringing related pieces of data together
- summarising data
- basic processing of data
- tabulation and diagrammatic techniques
- statistical analysis
- financial analysis.

Information Technology (IT) describes any equipment concerned with the capture, storage, transmission or presentation of information. The IT is the supporting hardward that provides the infrastructure to run the information systems.

Information Systems (IS) refer to the provision and management of information to support the running of the organisation.

Information systems are also seen as a valuable strategic source which can help an organisation gain competitive advantage, e.g. those instances where the information system:

- links the organisation to customers or suppliers
- creates effective integration of the use of information in a value-adding process
- enables the organisation to develop, produce, market and deliver new products and/or services based on information
- gives senior management information to help develop and implement strategy.

Information technology and information systems

For example, strong links with suppliers can be forged by the use of computerised Just-In-Time stock systems. Customers can be 'tied-in' to a company's products or services by being given an IT link for after-sales service. Computerised systems can also help not only by mechanising production systems but also by making the planning of production more efficient.

2 Performance management information systems

There are three levels of planning and control within an organisation:

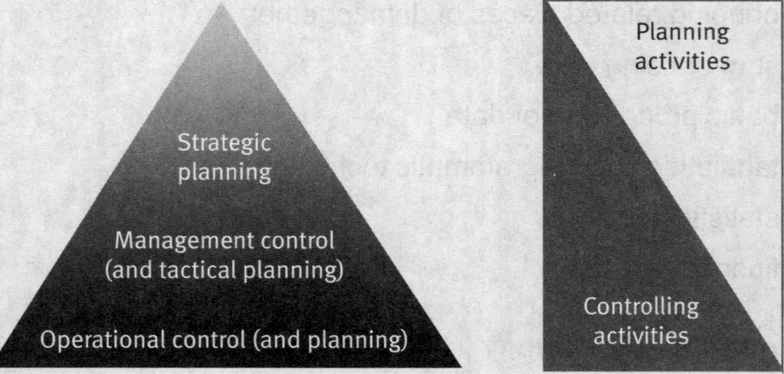

Level of control	**Key characteristics**	**Example of accounting information requirements**
Strategic planning	• Takes place at the top of the organisation. • Concerned with setting a future course of action for the organisation.	• Long-term forecasts
Management control	• Concerned with the effective use of resources to achieve targets set at strategic planning.	• Budgetary measures • Productivity measures • Labour statistics, e.g. hours, turnover • Capacity utilisation
Operational control	• Concerned with the day-to-day implementation of the plans of the organisation.	• Detailed, short-term transactional data

For example, at the operational level, sales ledger staff will be posting the sales ledger accounts, sending out statements and dealing with accounts queries. Credit approval for new orders will be given at this level also.

At the managerial level, credit control managers will be concerned to follow up slow paying customers to ensure that bad debts are minimised and that cash flow is kept healthy.

At the strategic level, the board might decide that more capital is needed and that factoring debts or invoice discounting might offer useful ways of raising cash balances.

3 Types of information systems

There are three levels of management – **strategic**, **tactical** and **operational**.

Each level creates different types of strategy within the organisation and therefore needs different types of information, as outlined by the following chart:

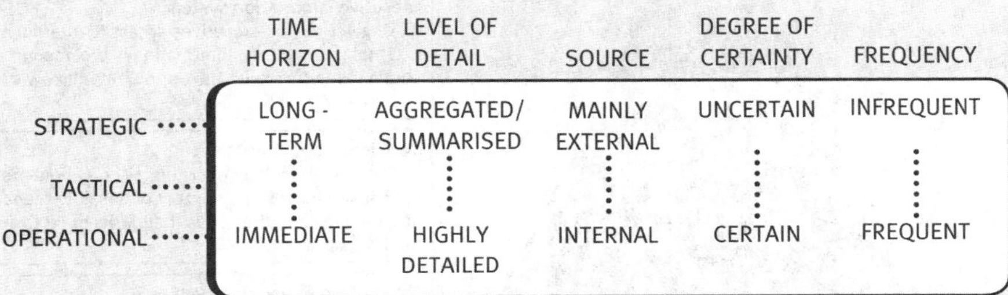

TIME HORIZON
LEVEL OF DETAIL
SOURCE
DEGREE OF CERTAINTY
FREQUENCY
STRATEGIC
TACTICAL
OPERATIONAL
LONG - TERM
AGGREGATED/ SUMMARISED
MAINLY EXTERNAL
UNCERTAIN
INFREQUENT
IMMEDIATE
HIGHLY DETAILED
INTERNAL
CERTAIN
FREQUENT

- The **strategic** level of management requires information from internal and external sources in order to plan the long-term strategies of the organisation. Internal information – both quantitative and qualitative – is usually supplied in a summarised form, often on an ad-hoc basis. **Strategic information** would relate to the longer-term strategy on the company's market share, which in turn informs the production plan. This plan would be used to pre-determine the level of investment required in capital equipment in the longer term. This process would also lead to investigating new methods and technology.
- The **tactical** level of management requires information and instructions from the strategic level of management, together with routine and regular quantitative information from the operational level of management. The information would be in a summarised form, but detailed enough to allow tactical planning of resources and manpower. **Tactical information** could include, for example, the short-term budget for 12 months and would show the budgeted machine use in terms of machine hours for each item of plant. The total machine hours being predetermined from the production budget for the period.

- The **operational** level of management requires information and instructions from the tactical level of management. The operational level is primarily concerned with the day-to-day performance of tasks and most of the information is obtained from internal sources. The information must be detailed and precise. For example, operational information would include a current week's report for a cost centre on the percentage capacity of the plant used in the period.

4 Information systems at different business levels

A modern organisation needs a wide range of systems to process, analyse and hold information. The different management decision-making levels within an organisation need different types of information:

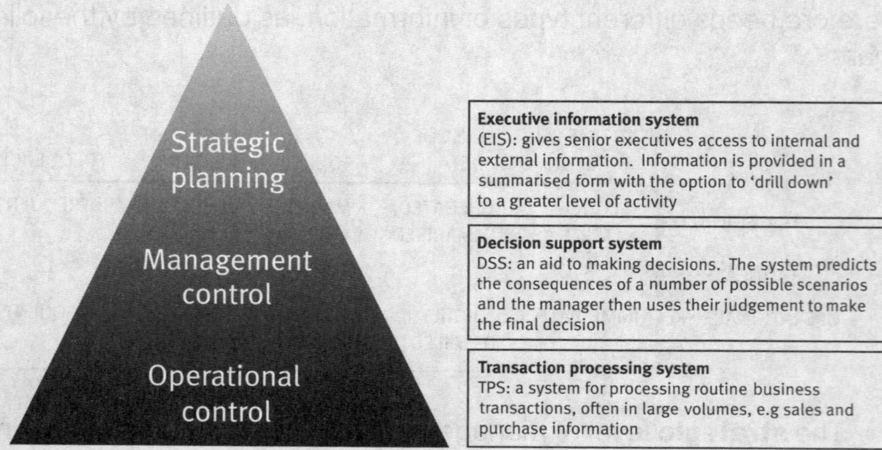

Strategic planning
Management control
Operational control
Executive information system
(EIS): gives senior executives access to internal and external information. Information is provided in a summarised form with the option to 'drill down' to a greater level of activity
Decision support system
DSS: an aid to making decisions. The system predicts the consequences of a number of possible scenarios and the manager then uses their judgement to make the final decision
Transaction processing system
TPS: a system for processing routine business transactions, often in large volumes, e.g sales and purchase information

As a basic idea, the systems towards the top of the tree will support the strategic decisions and they will use data from systems in the levels below.

5 Transaction Processing Systems (TPS)

A TPS records historic information and represents the simple automation of manual systems.

The TPS routinely captures, processes, stores and output the low level transaction data. This system is very important – data input incorrectly will affect every report produced using it, giving management mis-information and hence they will make poor decisions.

More on TPS

A TPS records all the daily transactions of the organisation and summarises them so they can be reported on a routine basis.

Transaction processing systems are used mainly by operational managers to make basic decisions.

Examples include:

- Sales/marketing systems – recording sales transactions and providing details on marketing and promotional activities
- Manufacturing production systems – recording details of purchases, production and shipping of goods
- Finance and accounting systems – maintenance of financial data in an organisation. The purchase ledger, sales ledger and payroll systems are all examples of a TPS system.

Additional systems that can be used at all levels of management are:

- **Management information systems** (MIS): provide information to all levels of management to enable them to make timely and effective decisions for planning and controlling the activities for which they are responsible. Middle managers will find these systems particularly useful:
  - A MIS will collate information from individual transactions recorded in the accounting system to allow middle managers to control the business.
  - Customer purchases are summarised into reports to identify the products and customers providing the most revenue.
  - The level of repeat business can be viewed giving an indication of customer satisfaction.
  - Management accounts can be produced by the system showing margins for individual products and customers. This will assist in setting individual/ team rewards.

More on MIS

Types of MIS

There are four broad types of MIS:

- **Database systems**. These systems process and store information, which becomes the organisation's memory.
- **Direct control systems**. Systems to monitor and report on activities such as output levels, sales ledger and credit accounts in arrears.
- **Enquiry systems**. Which are based on databases, which provide specific information such as the performance of a department or an employee.
- **Support systems**. Systems that provide computer-based methods and procedures for conducting analyses, forecasts and simulations.

Features of a management information system

Management information systems can be distinguished from other information systems within an organisation:

- They provide support for structured decision making at all management levels.
- They provide on-line access to the transaction processing systems of the organisation, to give summary information on the performance of the organisation.
- They provide an internal rather than external focus, with detail being provided internally about the organisation itself, rather than externally-generated information about competitors or the overall economic environment.
- If required, they can provide more detailed information about the organisation's operations, or individual transactions, through a 'drill down' facility.
- An MIS produces relatively simple summary reports and comparisons, and does not contain the more detailed mathematical models or statistical techniques found in a DSS, for example.

Management information systems can be found in almost any organisation above a small size. A few examples are given below:

- **Car manufacturing**. Systems to summarise sales of motor vehicles to assist in trend analysis and hiring of new workers.
- **Firm of accountants**. Summarising work performed on different audit engagements to assist in fee negotiation.
- **Training company**. Provision of details of students booked on to different courses to indicate the size of lecture rooms required and number of lecturers for each subject.
- **Manufacturing company**. Provision of stock ageing analysis to determine the amount of stock provision in the financial statements.

- **Decision Support Systems (DSS):** these are computer based systems which enable managers to confront ill-structured problems by direct interaction with data and problem-solving programs.

More on DSS

'A decision support system ... provides access to (mostly) summary performance data, using graphics to display and visualise the data in a very easy to use fashion (frequently with a touch screen interface), and with a minimum of analysis for modelling beyond the capability to 'drill down' in summary data to examine components' (Wallis).

The DSS does not make the decision, it merely assists in going through the phases of decision making:

- Gathering information and identification of situations requiring decisions.
- Design of possible solutions.
- Choice of solution.

The system sets up various scenarios and the computer predicts the result for each scenario by using a process of 'what if' analysis.

A decision support system will have the following characteristics:

- To provide support for decision making, especially for semi-structured or unstructured decision making.
- To provide support for all stages within the decision-making process.
- To provide support for decisions that are inter-dependent as well as for those that are independent.
- To support a variety of decision-making processes.
- To be user friendly.

A decision support system will include the following tools:

- Spreadsheets.
- Expert systems.
- 4GLs. (4th generation languages – a form of query language).
- Databases.
- Statistical programs.

There are three basic elements to the DSS:

- Language sub-system which is likely to be non-procedural (does not require significant programming ability to use).
- Problem processing sub-system which includes spreadsheet, graphics, statistical analysis.
- Knowledge sub-system which includes a database function.

- **Expert systems:** hold specialist knowledge, e.g. on law or taxation, and allow non-experts to interrogate them for information, advice and recommended decisions. Can be used at all levels of management.

More on ES

An expert system is a software system with two basic components: a knowledge base and an inference engine. The knowledge base is a structured database which stores the knowledge and experience of a number of experts. The inference engine makes it possible to draw on the knowledge base in an organised way. The system mimics an expert's reasoning process within a limited context.

The user accesses the system through a user-friendly graphical user interface (GUI) and asks questions of the system, or is prompted with questions by the system. The operating software or 'inference engine' then uses a mixture of rule-based logic and 'fuzzy logic' to infer a solution from the knowledge base.

There are many examples of expert systems in such areas as:

- law (e.g. how complex legislation applies to a specific firm?)
- taxation (e.g. how does a particular tax planning technique apply to a particular set of facts?)
- banking (e.g. should credit be granted to a new applicant?)
- medicine (e.g. what diagnosis best fits a set of symptoms?).

Non-experts can use this type of software to draw 'expert' conclusions from information input into the system. Experts can also use the software in order to confirm (or at least test) their own opinions against those offered by the system. This might speed up the decision-making process by giving less qualified managers the tools to draw conclusions or it might enhance the consistency of decision making across the organisation (e.g. reducing the scope for personal subjectivity in the decisions made by senior bank lending officers).

- **Enterprise resource planning system (ERPS):** this is a way of integrating the data from all operations within the organisation, e.g. operations, sales and marketing, human resources and purchasing, into one single system. It ensures that everyone is working off the same system and includes decision support features to assist management with decision making. Software companies like SAP and Oracle have specialised in the provision of ERP systems across many different industries.

More on ERPS

ERP systems offer:

- on-line/real-time information throughout all the functional areas of an organisation
- standardisation of data across the entire organisation
- common data files for all functions, thereby saving duplication.

ERP software providers offer ERP packages for areas of the business such as human resources, finance and accounting, customer data, supplier data, manufacturing, sales and distribution. Each ERP software provider may also offer different functions for different industries.

ERP Systems are installed on a Database Management System. Once installed, the user only enters data at one point, and the information is transferred automatically to other modules in the system. In effect, ERP systems integrate the different processes or functions in a business (manufacturing, inventory control, sales, distribution, accounting, human resources, etc) into a common, centralised data pool that facilitates data sharing and eliminates information redundancy.

Because they are enterprise-wide, ERP systems can be useful for extracting performance data relating to cross-functional or multi-functional activities, such as:

- supply chain management
- activity-based costing
- balanced scorecard performance reporting.

Test your understanding 1 – ERPS and the management

Explain how the introduction of an ERPS could impact on the role of management accountants.

6 Closed and open systems

An **open** system interacts with its environment.

Illustration 1 – Open systems

A supermarket may operate an inventory system which:

- is updated automatically as customers purchase different items of inventory
- sends an automatic order to the supplier when inventory reaches the re-order level
- is linked to the management accounting information system.

Internal and external (contingent) factors will be taken into account when designing the management accounting system. For example:

- If the external environment is stable it will be possible for the system to produce budgets and targets that provide meaningful measures of performance.
- The internal business strategy may be one of introducing new products or entering new markets. As a result, a comprehensive management information/performance evaluation system will be required.

7 The merits of open systems

The merits of open systems can be listed as follows:

(1) Open systems promote **better communication** by encouraging ongoing feedback among all the parts of the business.

(2) Open systems are **more adaptable** to the changing business environment, integrate external factors and provide clear understanding of the 'big picture', rather than a narrow focus on behaviours and events associated with problems in the workplace.

(3) Open systems **support leadership**: A systems view helps management to really understand the overall structures and dynamics of the business, and what must be done to guide the organisation towards its strategic vision and goals.

(4) Open systems help with **planning** by identifying desired results (targets and outcomes), what measures or outputs (tangible results) will indicate that those results have been achieved, what processes will produce those outputs, and what inputs are required to conduct those processes in the system. An open system often makes the planning process much clearer and orderly to planners.

A **closed system** has no contact with its environment. Information is not received from or provided to the environment.

Closed systems are rare because interaction with the environment is necessary for business survival. These systems will not provide adequate information for performance management.

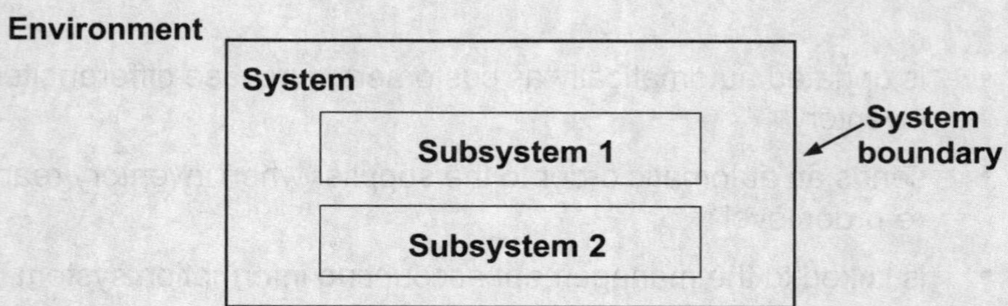

- Systems sit in their environments and are separated from their environment by the systems boundary.
- Examples are: accounting systems, manufacturing systems, quality control systems, IT systems.

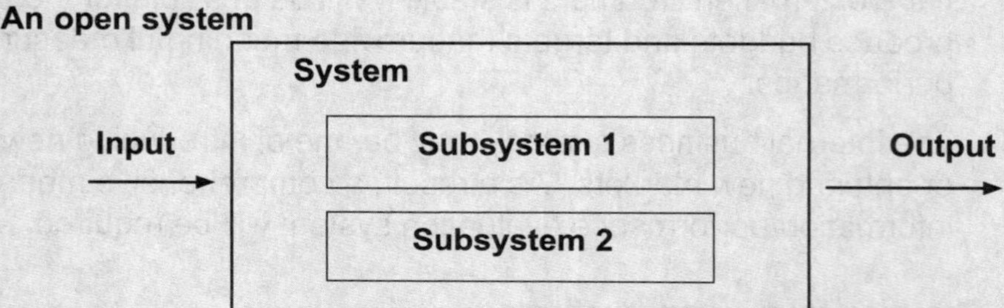

Management accounting systems should be **open,** for the following reasons.

- Closed systems can have only short lives. Without input, closed systems will usually run out of energy, material, information or some other resource needed to function.
- Closed systems, even if they can be self-sufficient, normally become increasingly irrelevant as environmental changes are not reflected in the system so the system becomes out of date. For example, a company might attempt to make the same products year after year whilst ignoring advances in technology and changes in customer taste.
- Internal information is relatively easy for organisations to capture, but that is not enough to ensure success. It is much more difficult to know what external information is going to be relevant and to capture that reliably. But it has to be done or the organisation will be operating in its own, isolated, short-lived world.

8 Sources of management information

Internal sources

Internal sources of information may be taken from a variety of areas such as the sales ledger (e.g. volume of sales), payroll system (e.g. number of employees) or the fixed asset system (e.g. depreciation method and rate).

Examples of internal data:

Source	Information
Sales ledger system	Number and value of invoices Volume of sales Value of sales, analysed by customer Value of sales, analysed by product
Purchase ledger system	Number and value of invoices Value of purchases, analysed by supplier
Payroll system	Number of employees Hours worked Output achieved Wages earned Tax deducted
Fixed asset system	Date of purchase Initial cost Location Depreciation method and rate Service history Production capacity
Production	Machine breakdown times Number of rejected units
Sales and marketing	Types of customer Market research results

External sources

In addition to internal information sources, there is much information to be obtained from external sources such as suppliers (e.g. product prices), customers (e.g. price sensitivity) and the government (e.g. inflation rate).

External source	Information
Suppliers	Product prices Product specifications
Newspapers, journals	Share price Information on competitors Technological developments National and market surveys
Government	Industry statistics Taxation policy Inflation rates Demographic statistics Forecasts for economic growth
Customers	Product requirements Price sensitivity
Employees	Wage demands Working conditions
Banks	Information on potential customers Information on national markets
Business enquiry agents	Information on competitors Information on customers
Internet	Almost everything via databases (public and private), discussion groups and mailing lists

9 Limitations of externally generated information

- External information may not be accurate, and the source of the data must always be checked.
- External information may be old, and out of date.
- The sample used to generate the secondary data may be too small.
- The company publishing the data may not be reputable.
- External information may not meet the exact needs of the business.
- It may be difficult to gather external information, e.g. from customers or competitors.

The internal and external information may be used in **planning** and **controlling** activities. For example:

- Newspapers, the Internet and business enquiry agents (such as Dun and Bradstreet) may be used to obtain external competitor information for benchmarking purposes.
- Internal sales volumes may be obtained for variance analysis purposes.

Test your understanding 2

Briefly explain the use of customer data for control purposes.

10 The costs of information

The benefit of management information must exceed the cost (**benefit > cost**) of obtaining the information.

The design of management information systems should involve a cost/benefit analysis. A very refined system offers many benefits, but at a cost. The advent of modern IT systems has reduced that cost significantly. However, skilled staff have to be involved in the operation of information systems, and they can be very expensive to hire.

Illustration

Let us illustrate this with a simple example. Production costs in a factory can be reported with varying levels of frequency ranging from daily (365 times per year) to annually (1 time per year). Costs of benefits of reporting tend to move as follows in response to increasing frequency of reporting.

- Information has to be gathered, collated and reported in proportion to frequency and costs will move in line with this. Experience suggests that some element of diseconomy of scale may set in at high levels of frequency.
- Initially, benefits increase sharply, but this increase starts to tail off. A point may come where 'information overload' sets in and benefits actually start to decline and even become negative. If managers are overwhelmed with information, then this actually starts to get in the way of the job.

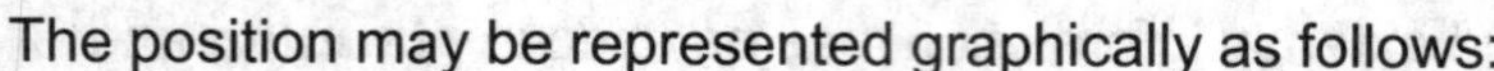

The position may be represented graphically as follows:

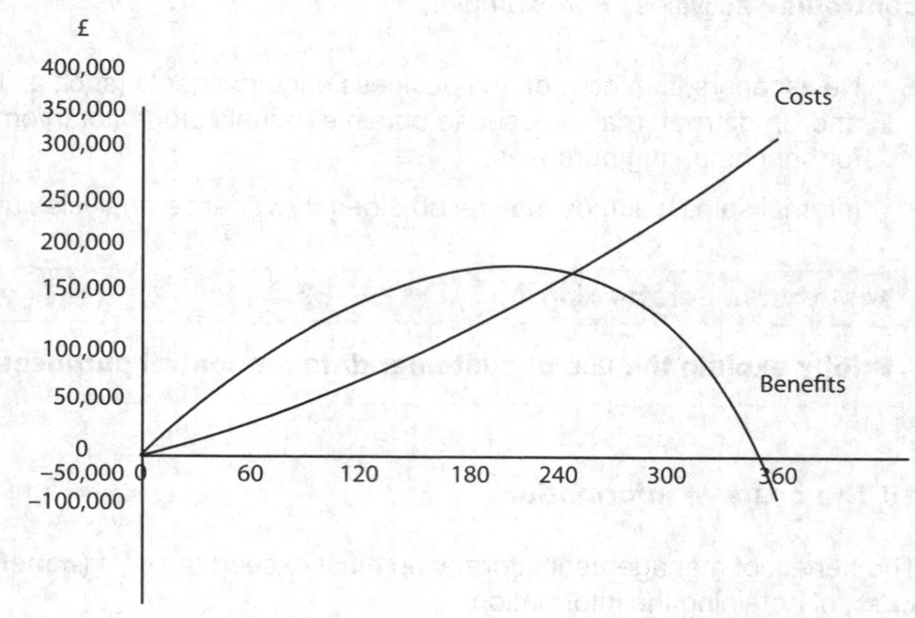

An information system is just like any part of a business operation. It incurs costs and it offers benefits. In designing an information system, the accountant has to find some means of comparing the two for different options and determining which option is optimal. In this sense, system design follows the same practices for investment appraisal and decision making which are explored later in this text.

In the above case it can be seen that net benefits (benefits less costs) are maximised at around 120 reports per year – suggesting an optimal information cycle of about 3 days. The system should be designed to gather, collate and report information at three-day intervals. This is an over-simplified example but it serves to illustrate a general logic which can be applied to all aspects of information system design.

Test your understanding 3

Discuss the factors that need to be considered when determining the capacity and development potential of a system.

11 Cost classification

The costs of information can be classified as follows:

Costs of internal information	Costs of external information
Direct data capture costs, e.g. the cost of barcode scanners in a supermarket.	Direct costs, e.g. newspaper subscriptions.
Processing costs, e.g. salaries paid to payroll processing staff.	Indirect costs, e.g. wasted time finding useful information.
Indirect costs, e.g. information collected which is not needed or is duplicated.	Management costs, e.g. the cost of processing information.
	Infrastructure costs, e.g. of systems enabling internet searches.

12 Direct data capture

Design of the data collection methods is an important part of designing a computer system. The organisation needs to consider its strategic plans in order to assess the future uses of its systems. If it is thought likely that it will be networking with other systems, then it will need to ensure that any new equipment purchased will be compatible with the network it wishes to join. When choosing input methods and media, most users are concerned with the following:

- How to economise on the use of manpower
- How to prevent or detect errors in the source data
- How to achieve data capture at the lowest possible cost
- How to achieve input sufficiently quickly
- How data gets into the system.

Input devices can be divided into two main categories:

- Those using a keyboard
- Those using **direct** input of the data.

Direct data capture means data is input into the computer through a reader. It is the collection of data for a particular purpose (e.g. barcodes being read at a supermarket so that the product can be identified, or account details being read directly from the chip embedded in the credit card.)

Some methods of data capture are:

- **Optical Character Recognition (OCR).** Some applications of OCR (sometimes called 'image-to-text' applications) are to insert financial data into a spreadsheet, or to scan articles into a word processor. If a business wants to go paperless by transferring all its printed documents to PDF files, using OCR makes the job much easier by eliminating manual input. The advantages of OCR are that it scans volumes of data fast and it is cheap to use. The disadvantages are that it doesn't always recognise handwriting properly and that dirt, fold and scratch marks will affect scanning results.
- **Optical Mark Recognition (OMR).** Some applications of OMR are to mark multiple-choice questions, to process student enrolment forms or to process questionnaires. The advantages of OMR are that it processes volumes of data fast and it is cheap, since data entry clerks are not needed. The disadvantages are that the OMR forms must be filled carefully using a suitable type of pencils and that dirt, fold and scratch marks will affect the accuracy of reading.
- **Magnetic Ink Character Recognition (MICR).** these applications are used mainly to clear bank cheques. Its advantages are that data is input fast and human errors are avoided; the main disadvantage is that the equipment is expensive.
- **Bar codes** are used to check out items at supermarket tills, to track stocks in a warehouse, to process the borrowing and returning of books in a library or to track passenger luggage of an airline. Bar codes enable data to be input fast, human errors are avoided and so are long queues; however, barcodes will be mis-read if dirty, and the equipment is expensive.
- **Magnetic strip cards** are used to withdraw money at ATMs and to pay goods by credit cards.
- **Voice recogniser** is the software that understands spoken commands.

13 The indirect costs of producing information

The most expensive cost of producing information is probably the cost of labour. People are needed to collect data, input data into the system, process the data and then output the resulting information. Throughout this process, the company needs to pay their wages and thus labour becomes part of the cost of producing information. When **new people are hired**, **a process is changed** or **software is upgraded**, then staff will require training.

Training, or re-training, is expensive in terms of:

(1) Paying for the trainer
(2) Paying wages for people being trained
(3) Paying the wages for someone to do the normal work for the person being trained
(4) Paying for the costs of the training venue
(5) Lost productivity whilst people are being trained
(6) Slower productivity whilst people 'learn on the job'.

Other indirect costs of providing information are those that are impossible to predict and quantify, and they may include:

- Loss of staff morale
- Delays caused in other projects of the business
- General dislocation caused by system change
- Upsetting customers from system change
- Incompatibility with other systems
- Unexpected costs of software amendments, tailoring and maintenance
- Cost of failure due to inappropriate systems or faulty implementation.

Further, more 'intangible' indirect costs of producing information include:

- Reduced quality of information, due to information overload
- Poor decision making, due to information overload
- Too many areas to focus on – so issues are not followed up
- Focus on the wrong things – i.e. only on those business areas and targets that are easy to measure and report on.

14 Management reports

Business data will often consist of information that is confidential and/or commercially sensitive.

Controls will be required when generating and distributing this information.

Type of control	Explanation	Example
Input	Inputs should be complete, accurate and authorised.	Passwords
Processing	Processing should be initiated by appropriate personnel and logs should be kept of any processing.	Audit trails
Output	The output should be available to authorised persons and third parties only.	Distribution lists

Controls over input

Method	Use
Passwords	Help to ensure data is authorised and they provide a software audit trail.
Range tests	Help to ensure data is accurate. For example, month fields to be in the range 1–12.
Format checks	Help to ensure data is accurate. For example, all account numbers must be in the format A123.
Check digits	Help to ensure data is accurate. Specially constructed numbers which comply with a mathematical test.
Sequence checks	Help to ensure data is compete. For example, ensuring all cheques are accounted for.
Matching	Primarily addresses completeness. For example, a system checking that each employee has input a time sheet for the month.
Control totals	Can help to ensure accuracy, completeness and authorisation as batches of input can be authorised manually.

Controls over processing

- Passwords and software audit trails are important to track what processing was carried out.
- Programmes should not be altered without authorisation and testing, otherwise incorrect or fraudulent processing could be carried out.

Controls over output

- Password systems can be very powerful controls – each password being allocated suitable access rights.
- Sensitive printed output could have a distribution list and should be physically safeguarded.

15 Security of confidential information

To protect highly confidential information that is not for external consumption, businesses may use a number of procedures:

- Personnel controls

  Recruitment, training and supervision needs to be in place to ensure the competence of those responsible for programming and data entry.

- Logical access control, including passwords

  Security over access is often based on a logical access system. Passwords and user names are a way of identifying who is authorised to access the system, and granting access to the system, or to specific programs or files, only if an authorised password is entered. There may be several levels of password, with particularly sensitive applications protected by multiple passwords.

- Firewalls

  A firewall will consist of a combination of hardware and software located between the company's intranet (private network) and the public network (Internet). A set of control procedures will be established to allow public access to some parts of the organisation's computer system (outside the firewall) whilst restricting access to other parts (inside the firewall).

- Data encryption

  Encryption is a technique of disguising information to preserve its confidentiality. It is disguised during processing/storage. In essence it is a method of scrambling the data in a message or file so that it is unintelligible unless it is unscrambled (or decrypted).

- Virus protection

  It is extremely difficult to protect systems against the introduction of computer viruses. Preventative steps may include:

  – control on the use of external software (e.g. checked for viruses before using new software)

  – using antivirus software, regularly updated, to detect and deal with viruses

  – educating employees to be watchful for viruses being imported as attachment files to email messages.

Test your understanding 4

Tel Insure is a major insurance company, specialising in insuring office and business premises. Last year they implemented a workflow software package for handling claims. Unfortunately the workflow package has not been well received by users in the insurance company who feel that it is a poor fit to their requirements. As a result, the processing of insurance claims is taking longer than before and is causing a large number of complaints from customers.

The senior management team of the insurance company is very concerned about this and so commissioned a management consultant to investigate the suitability of the workflow software and to investigate a possible upgrade and link to an extranet.

Required:

How could Tel Insure control the access to data (input, processing and output)?

Modern information systems illustration

One feature of modern information system design is that database material can be readily accessed from remote locations connected to the office network. This ease and immediacy of access offers many advantages to a business operation. For example, a salesman may be able to determine product costs, job resource requirements, resource availability and delivery times using his laptop computer from the premises of a potential customer. A salesman in this position can offer immediate firm quotes and delivery times to his customer. Such a salesman will always have an advantage over a competitor using inferior information systems who takes seven days to offer quotes and delivery times.

However, ease and flexibility of information access carry risks. Cost and price information are usually commercially sensitive. If a competitor is able to access this information then the competitor may be able to use this information to marginally undercut prices quoted on the most attractive jobs. In some sectors (e.g. banking and financial services), customer account information may also be very sensitive.

It is therefore normal to incorporate security features in the design of systems. Certain parts of a database or a website may have access restricted to certain users with passwords.

However, one should be aware that any information system, however sophisticated, is just as secure as the people who operate it. In most organisations there are mildly corrupt people who will provide information to outsiders in exchange for some consideration. The consideration offered may not always be monetary. An individual who has been passed over for promotion may derive some satisfaction from harming his employer. Many people do not perceive the theft of information to be as immoral as the theft of property – and indeed the law tends to follow this perception.

It is believed that there are firms of investigation agents who can readily access almost any information from police records, bank records and company records. Such agents maintain a list of contacts in relevant organisations. These contacts have authorised access to information and will pass on that information upon request from the agent. In the era of the cellphone, it is very easy to communicate with a contact in an organisation. It is often surprising how much access certain junior employees may have to sensitive information.

The management of a business should not therefore rely solely on electronic means of restricting access to information. Traditional methods of security (including locked doors, monitoring telephone calls and the use of open-plan offices) should not be overlooked. A random audit of information requests from staff may also be productive.

Traditional methods of securing information against the possibility of fire or equipment failure should also not be overlooked. An external back-up copy of each database might be made at intervals or after each update. This back-up copy should be retained at a different physical location from the main computer.

16 Output reports

The output reports produced for management should contain good information.

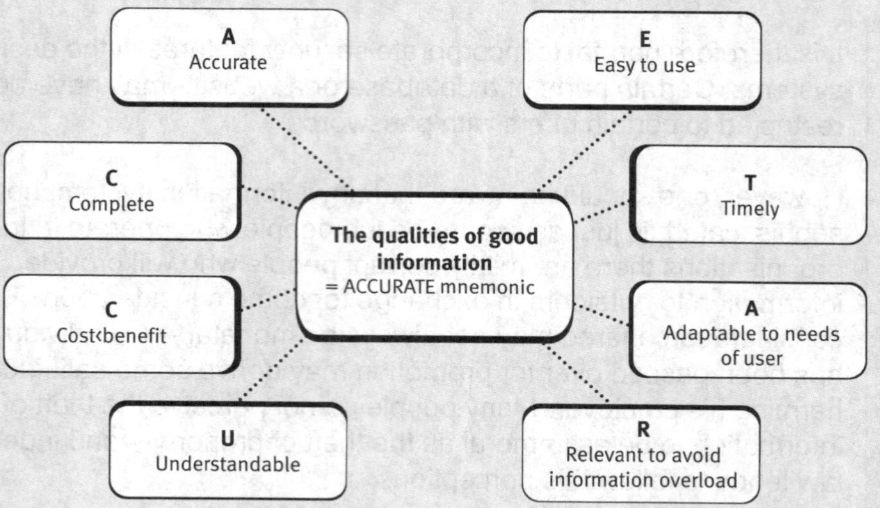

Test your understanding 5

Discuss the weaknesses in an information system that could result in poor output reports.

17 Chapter summary

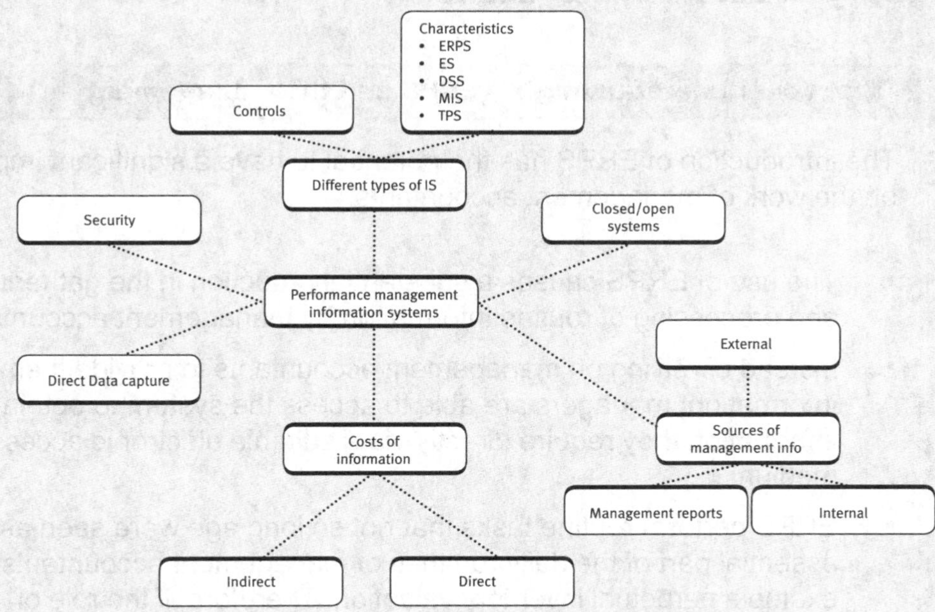

Test your understanding answers

Test your understanding 1 – ERPS and the management

The introduction of ERPS has the potential to have a significant impact on the work of management accountants.

- The use of ERPS causes a substantial reduction in the gathering and processing of routine information by management accountants.
- Instead of relying on management accountants to provide them with information, managers are able to access the system to obtain the information they require directly via a suitable electronic access medium.
- ERPS perform routine tasks that not so long ago were seen as an essential part of the daily routines of management accountants, for example perpetual inventory valuation. Therefore, if the role of management accountants is not to be diminished, then it is of necessity that management accountants should seek to expand their roles within their organisations.
- Management accountants may be involved in interpreting the information generated from the ERPS and to provide business support for all levels of management within an organisation.

Test your understanding 2

Historical customer data will give information about:

- product purchases and preferences
- price sensitivity
- where customers shop
- who customers are (customer profiling).

For a business that prioritises customer satisfaction this will give important control information. Actual customer data can be compared with plans and control action can be taken as necessary, e.g. prices may be changed or the product mix may be changed.

Test your understanding 3

An information system can be developed to varying levels of refinement. Specifically:

- **Reporting frequency** – information can be collected and reported with varying levels of frequency, e.g. for example, the management accounting system of a manufacturer can report actual production costs on a daily, weekly, monthly or even annual basis
- **Reporting quantity and level of detail** – information can be collected and reported at varying levels of detail e.g. in absorbing overheads into product costs one can use a single factory overhead absorption rate (OAR) or one can operate a complex ABC system. The information requirements of the latter are far more elaborate than those of the former
- **Reporting accuracy and back-up** – subtle qualitative factors can be incorporated into information systems at varying levels, e.g. information can be rigorously checked for accuracy or a more relaxed approach can be adopted.

Broadly, the more refined the system is, then the more expensive it is to establish and operate. The organisation has to decide if the increased benefits outweigh the increased costs.

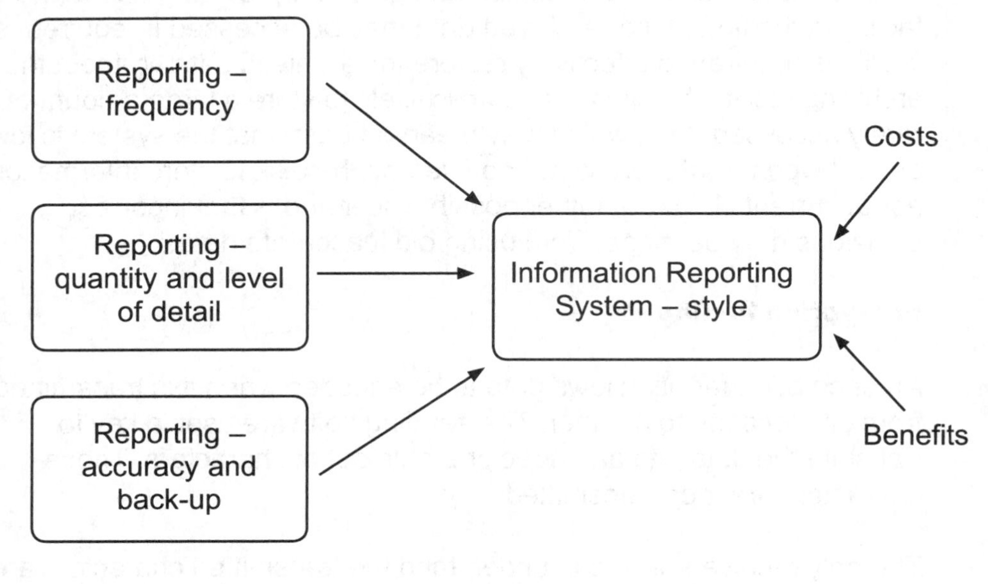

Test your understanding 4

Software audit trail

A software audit trail records selected transactions so that they can be subsequently verified. Typically, financial information is audited so that possible fraud can be detected. The claims information will be audited to ensure that claims are not paid without going through the normal procedure. The software audit trail usually records the type of transaction made (for example, make payment), the value of the transaction, who made the payment (the user identifier), where they made the payment from (terminal identifier) and the date and time of the transaction. The audit trail is usually inspected by internal auditors. Without this information they are unlikely to quickly identify potentially fraudulent activity and to monitor and eventually apprehend the culprit.

Archiving facility

An archiving facility is needed so that infrequently accessed data held on the system can be transferred to off-line storage, typically a disk, CD or DVD. This frees up space on the operational system. This not only means that there is more room for storing current data but also that infrequently accessed data that potentially slows the system down is also removed. This results in the system being quicker after archiving and indeed this is one of the reasons often given for providing an archiving facility in the first place. Archived data may be accessed if required, so a facility is required to effectively restore the archived data. Without the archiving facility the claims system is likely to store a large amount of rarely accessed data, which may mean (at best) that the system is low and (at worst) that there is no room left on the disk to store information about current claims. Another possible scenario is that incorrect decisions may be made, from using old inaccurate data.

Encryption facility

An encryption facility allows data to be encoded when it is transmitted from one location to another. The sending software uses a key to translate the data into an undecipherable set of characters. These characters are then transmitted.

The only receivers who can understand the transmitted characters are those with access to the key to turn the data back into its original state. Without encryption the insurance company is restricted in its use of the data. Unscrambled data transmitted across networks is open to unauthorized interception and to users who receive the data by mistake. In the example, this data will include both financial and customer information, valuable to both thieves and competitors. Hence encryption is necessary for multi-site use.

Password maintenance facility

Most software requires a password (or series of passwords) to restrict user access to certain defined areas of the computer system. A password maintenance facility is required to establish and maintain passwords which allow either read only or read and write access to certain specified parts of the system. Such a facility should also detect the currency of passwords, so that passwords which have not been changed for a defined period are detected and the user is prompted to change the password. Without a password facility the system (or more realistically parts of the system) cannot be protected from unauthorized access. Similarly, without checks on the currency of passwords, a password may be used for too long and hence make the software prone to unauthorized access by people who essentially 'steal' a user's identity.

Test your understanding 5

- **Unreliable information:** Information must be sufficiently reliable (e.g. accurate and complete) so that managers trust it to make judgements and decisions.
- **Timeliness:** Information must be available in time for managers to use it to make decisions.
- **Responsibility and controllability:** Information systems might fail to identify controllable costs, or indicate management responsibility properly. Information should be directed to the person who has the authority and the ability to act on it.
- **Information overload:** In some cases, managers might be provided with too much information, and the key information might be lost in the middle of large amounts of relatively unimportant figures.
- **Cost and value:** The cost of providing the information should not exceed the benefits obtained.

Index

Index